THE MESSAGE OF THE CITY

THE
MESSAGE OF THE CITY

Dawn Powell's New York Novels, 1925–1962

Patricia E. Palermo

SWALLOW PRESS

Athens, Ohio

Swallow Press
An imprint of Ohio University Press, Athens, Ohio 45701
ohioswallow.com

Printed in the United States of America
Swallow Press / Ohio University Press books are printed on acid-free paper ∞ ™

26 25 24 23 22 21 20 19 18 17 16   5 4 3 2 1

Library of Congress Cataloging-in-Publication Data

Names: Palermo, Patricia E., author.
Title: The message of the city : Dawn Powell's New York novels, 1925-1962 /
  Patricia E. Palermo.
Other titles: Dawn Powell's New York novels, 1925-1962
Description: Athens, Ohio : Swallow Press, 2016. | Includes bibliographical
  references and index.
Identifiers: LCCN 2016004246| ISBN 9780804011679 (hardback) | ISBN
  9780804011686 (pb) | ISBN 9780804040686 (pdf)
Subjects: LCSH: Powell, Dawn—Criticism and interpretation. | Women and
  literature—United States—History—20th century. | Satire,
  American—History and criticism. | New York (N.Y.)—In literature. |
  Powell, Dawn. | Authors, American—20th century—Biography. | BISAC:
  BIOGRAPHY & AUTOBIOGRAPHY / General. | LITERARY COLLECTIONS
  / American /
  General. | LITERARY COLLECTIONS / General.
Classification: LCC PS3531.O936 Z85 2016 | DDC 813/.52—dc23
LC record available at http://lccn.loc.gov/2016004246

For Tim Page

CONTENTS

ILLUSTRATIONS

Following page 74

Young Dawn Powell, with hand on heart
Young Dawn Powell in profile, ca. 1920s
Lobby card for *Footlights and Shadows,* 1920
Ernest Truex and Spring Byington onstage in *Jig Saw,* 1934
Powell friend and portraitist Peggy Bacon, ca. 1920
Peggy Bacon charcoal drawing of Powell, 1934, with inscription
Peggy Bacon charcoal drawing of Powell, 1934
Peggy Bacon charcoal drawing of Coburn "Coby" Gilman, 1934
Peggy Bacon drawing of cats Perkins vs. Calhoun
Powell drawing of cat in bed
Flier for *Walking down Broadway,* 2005
Playbill featuring *Big Night,* January 1933
Flier for *Big Night,* December 2012
Whither, Powell's first novel (1925), in dust jacket

Following page 212

Powell, elegant in pearls, ca. 1930s
Powell in publicity photo eating pineapple, 1933
Coburn "Coby" Gilman with Jackson Pollock and Rita Benton
Clare Booth Luce
Members of the Council on Books in Wartime, ca. 1943
A coy-looking Powell
Powell in her beloved Café Lafayette, 1946
Powell in her Greenwich Village apartment, ca. 1950
Powell and husband, Joseph Gousha, 1952
"The Lost Generation" from a 1963 *Esquire* article by Malcolm Cowley
Powell caricature by David Johnson
Powell's close friend Hannah Green, 1974
Author with Tim Page, 2014

ACKNOWLEDGMENTS

Many people helped make this project happen, most especially Tim Page, Powell biographer and editor extraordinaire, without whom it would not even have begun. I thank him first of all for writing her biography; for bringing out his edition of her letters, four of her plays, and a volume of her diaries; for being a tireless champion of Dawn Powell's works; and for seeing to it that so many of her long-out-of-print novels, plays, and short stories were reissued. I thank Mr. Page for his unfailing generosity, for being not only a tireless correspondent but also a most supportive champion of me and my work; for his sharp and quick editorial eye; for allowing me access to the Powell papers at Columbia University; for sharing with me the two known recordings of Powell's voice; and for giving me permission to reproduce photographs of Dawn Powell, Joseph Gousha, and other people or locations to which he or the friendly estate of Dawn Powell, represented by the generous and considerate Peter Skolnik, owns the rights. I also thank Mr. Page for kindly providing contact information for Carol Warstler, daughter of Dawn Powell's younger sister, Phyllis Powell Cook. The very kind Carol Warstler, with whom I have been in touch, sent me a copy of her daughter-in-law Debra Warstler's thesis on Powell. Indeed, Page has been so selfless and steadfast a friend that I cannot effectively describe all that he has done not only for me but also for Dawn, as he fondly refers to her and as I am sure she would insist he call her. I thank also Vicki Johnson, Carol Warstler's daughter, for sharing with me a copy of their family tree and also for sending me reproductions of the beautiful artwork done by Powell's elder sistern, Mabel Powell Pocock.

I am indebted to renowned Broadway lyricists and composers Lee Adams and Charles Strouse for their communications with me, their always considerate assistance, their interest in my work, and their willingness to share with me their warm memories of Dawn Powell. A special thanks to Charles

Strouse for having me up to his place in New York and for taking me to lunch that snowy spring day in April 2007.

A warm thank-you to Christopher Purdy, Executive Producer of Columbus, Ohio, radio station WOSU, for generously sending me a tape of his "Dawn Powell" radio program; and to Christopher Bennett, director of the Lincoln Library at Lake Erie College in Painesville, Ohio, for a lovely and lengthy telephone conversation and for kindly sending me the *Lake Erie Bulletin* and several copies of the school literary magazine, the *Lake Erie Record*, on which Powell had acted both as editor and contributor. Kind thanks to Debra Blanchard Remington, director of development and alumni relations at Lake Erie College, for providing me a copy of the very useful May 1940 alumna issue of the *Bulletin of Lake Erie College*.

I owe a debt of gratitude to Dr. Merrill Skaggs and Dr. Robert Ready, both of Drew University, for their suggestions and unfailing support. I wish also to thank Dr. Kathleen Hunter of the College of St. Elizabeth for her unwavering belief in me and for her inspiring words, "The enemy of 'done' is 'perfect.'" Thanks to Lynne McKinery, also of the College of St. Elizabeth, for her tireless support and assistance, and to Art "Vandelay" Layenberger, because he wanted me to.

I am grateful to Bruce Lancaster, Drew University reference librarian, for taking it upon himself to conduct some additional research that led me, with Tim Page's help, to Powell's family; to Kathleen Brennan, for pointing out a *New York Times* article I otherwise may not have known about; to Kim Macagnone, customer service representative at the *Village Voice*, for providing me a copy of Michael Feingold's important piece, "Dawn Powell's Acid Texts," which for some reason I could get no other way; to Barbara Meister, librarian at the Ohioana Library Association, for photocopying the rare Powell novel *A Man's Affair* for me at no charge; to Jeanine Krattiger, for generously printing out so many copies of this manuscript; to Mary Pradilla, graduate student at the College of St. Elizabeth and alumna of Lake Erie College, who located some information on Cleveland history for me; to Carl Thomas Engle, research librarian at Morley Library in Painesville, Ohio, for tracking down and sending me some elusive information on the Shore Club, where Powell worked as a teenager; to Kathleen Conry, theater actress and director who resided at New York's Rehearsal Club in 1966, for much vital information; to Muriel Keyes, assistant editor of the *Antioch Review*, for tracking down Gore Vidal's first published mention of Dawn Powell in an editorial by Robert S. Fogarty; and to Peter L. Skolnik, lawyer for the Powell estate, for all estate permissions and for letting me know about the rights to Powell's final novel, *The Golden Spur,* which Lee Adams and Charles Strouse said back in 2008 they may yet one day turn into a musical, though time is passing and the project at this date seems unlikely (an unfinished version of it, from 1962–64, is held at Columbia University Library); to Author's Guild attorney Michael Gross, for his tireless correspondence, astute eye, and indispensable lawyerly advice; to Arthur Vanderbilt, for putting me in touch with the Author's Guild in the first place; to Jeffrey Edmond Lawson, son of John Howard Lawson and his second wife, Sue Edmond Lawson, for generously recounting for me his fond and vivid memories of Powell; to Peter Reznikoff, actor and very young friend of Powell's—his parents were the photographer Genevieve Naylor and the artist Misha Reznikoff—for granting me permission to reproduce a rarely seen portrait of Powell taken at her beloved Café Lafayette by his mother; to Tricia Gesner of AP Images for her invaluable, prompt, reliable, cheerful, and tireless help, even on weekends; to brilliant and hardworking photographer William "Bill" Wittkop, without whom I could not have provided illustrations for this book; to David Johnson, for allowing me to reproduce his outstanding caricature of Dawn; to Jonathan Bank of the Mint Theater, New York, for giving me a digital image and permission to reproduce the theater's flier for their production of *Walking down Broadway;* to John Dos Passos Coggin, John Dos Passos's only grandson, for sharing information his mother, Lucy Dos Passos Coggin, remembers about Dawn; and especially to Allie Mulholland, founder and director of the ReGroup Theatre, which puts on plays that the Group Theatre first staged many decades ago, for his endless generosity in sharing so much with me and for being not only a Dawn Powell scholar and fan but also a dear friend.

Another delighted thank-you goes to David Earle, associate professor of the University of West Florida, who has located many if not all of Powell's early stories from the pulp magazines of the 1920s and '30s and who most graciously shared two of them with me, even giving me permission "to quote away" from them.

Thanks also go to Christine A. Lutz, staff member of the Seeley G. Mudd Manuscript Library at Princeton University, for her unflagging work on my behalf in trying to identify a rare wartime photograph of Dawn Powell, Bennett Cerf, Ludwig Bemelmans, and others. I must also thank my departed feline friend Mr. "Buncie" Benchley (namesake of the more famous Mr. Robert Benchley, friend and admirer of Powell's) for sitting on this keyboard and rarely leaving my side throughout the many years I have spent on this project.

I owe much gratitude to Dr. Nina Rulon-Miller for her unfailing support, advice, and invaluable editorial and pictorial assistance; to Dr. Gerry Smith Wright and Kathie Brown for their unflinching belief in me over these many years; to Dr. Sloane Drayson Knigge for her considerable encouragement and assistance in procuring interlibrary-loan and other materials; to Joyce Ann Goldberg and Jeana Taylor Schorr for their never-tiring corresponding with me and for becoming true Dawn Powell aficionados in their own right; to valued friend and champion Dr. Bob Thayer; and to Jessica Levee and Rebecca Mull for their unflagging friendship.

I would of course be remiss not to mention the fine folks at Ohio University Press, among them the first there to encourage me in this work: the attentive and thoughtful David Sanders, formerly of the Press; Director Gillian Berchowitz, for her empathy, understanding, patience, and encouragement; Rick Huard, also of the Press, who gently, tirelessly, and always promptly guided me through the daunting maze of attaining copyrights and permissions; Beth Pratt, cheerful director of production there; and Nancy Basmajian, for her prompt and reliable editorial assistance.

I owe much also to M. George Stevenson, former literary agent and beneficent legal adviser, for generously giving me so much time and attention; to Elsa Dorfman, for granting me permission to include her photograph of Hannah Green; and to the intelligent and always kind Katherine Degn of New York's Kraushaar Galleries for her friendship, for reliably prompt responses to my queries, and for granting me permission to reproduce drawings by Peggy Bacon of Powell, their cats, and Powell's close friend, Coburn Gilman.

Finally I wish to thank my dear friend, the late Regina Crimmins, one of two persons who upon our first meeting had already read Powell, for her inspired and inspiring idea that we celebrate the completion of this project in Greenwich Village, Dawn Powell's favorite home. It was a grand affair, one that even Tim Page attended.

ABBREVIATIONS

Bio   *Dawn Powell: A Biography,* by Tim Page (New York: Henry Holt, 1998)

Diaries   *The Diaries of Dawn Powell, 1931–1965,* edited by Tim Page (South Royalton, VT: Steerforth Press, 1995)

Letters   *Selected Letters of Dawn Powell, 1913–1965,* edited by Tim Page (New York: Henry Holt, 1999)

CHAPTER ONE

"Allow Me to Introduce You"

If you are asking yourself, "Who is Dawn Powell?" allow me to introduce you to one of the great American novelists of [the twentieth] century.

—Carleen M. Loper, "Discovering Dawn Powell," 2

Ohio-born writer Dawn Powell, who lived from 1896[1] to 1965, was always prolific, writing fifteen novels;[2] more than a hundred short stories; a dozen or so plays; countless book reviews; several radio, television, and film scripts; volumes of letters and diary entries; even poetry.[3] So productive was she that, following one spate of housecleaning, she wrote to her editor at Scribner's, Max Perkins, "I was appalled by the mountains of writing I had piled up in closets and file cases and trunks. . . . It struck me with terrific force that I just wrote too goddam much. Worse, I couldn't seem to stop" (*Letters*, 134). Weighing her literary output against that of some of her contemporaries, Powell joked to her close friend, writer and literary critic Edmund Wilson, "If I don't write for five years I may make quite a name for myself and if I can stop for ten I may give Katherine Anne [Porter] and Dorothy Parker a run for their money" (129). If in her lifetime Powell never did make either the name for herself or the money she had hoped, she did enjoy certain successes. In the year before her death, she was awarded the American Institute of Arts and Letters' Marjorie Peabody Waite Award for lifetime achievement; a few years before that, she was granted an honorary doctorate from her alma mater, Lake Erie College for Women. In 1963 her last novel, *The Golden Spur,* was nominated for the National Book Award; she appeared in a television interview with Harry Reasoner to discuss the novel, though it did not win. So far as I know, that interview is unavailable.

After she moved from Ohio to Manhattan in 1918 and began writing the many works that today are divided into the Ohio and the New York novels (with the exceptions of *Angels on Toast,* sometimes called a Chicago novel, and *A Cage for Lovers,* set in Paris), Malcolm Cowley hailed her as "the cleverest and wittiest writer in New York"; Diana Trilling called her "one of the wittiest women around"; and J. B. Priestley openly supported her work, as we shall see below. Other friends and admirers included Ernest Hemingway, John Dos Passos, Matthew Josephson, the afore-mentioned Edmund Wilson, and many more. Some of her books sold adequately, many less than adequately; none were blockbusters by any means, and virtually all were out of print by the time of her death in 1965.

Thanks to the late Gore Vidal and Tim Page—her biographer, the Pulitzer prize–winning former *Washington Post* music critic and professor in both the Annenberg School of Journalism and the Thornton School of Music at the University of Southern California—twelve of her novels, a volume of her letters, a collection of her diaries, and some of her plays and short stories have in recent decades been reissued to critical acclaim. Several of her plays have been either restaged or produced for the first time, and a 1933 film, *Hello Sister,* loosely based on Powell's play *Walking down Broadway,* was in the 1990s released on VHS, if only out of interest in its famous director, Erich von Stroheim; it was shown in a Greenwich Village cinema in 2012.

Of course, more important than quantity of writing is quality. Powell's novels are filled with astute observations, wry commentaries, spot-on characterizations. Despite her reputation as a tough and unflinching satirist, she is capable of moving tenderness and pathos, particularly in the Ohio novels. In an article originally published in the *New York Times Book Review,* Terry Teachout called *My Home Is Far Away,* one of the Ohio novels, a "permanent masterpiece of childhood" ("Far from Ohio," 6). Few novelists are better at depicting young children than is Powell; one need read but the first several chapters of *My Home Is Far Away* to see that. Edmund Wilson found her books "at once sympathetic and cynical" ("Dawn Powell," rpt., 236); Powell can make a reader weep in a brief portrait, as she does when describing old Mrs. Fox in *She Walks in Beauty,*[4] or when in the same early Ohio novel she conveys the humiliation young Dorrie endures at the hands of her classmates. But most remarkable perhaps is her sense of humor. Few writers are wittier, more scathing, more insightful than Powell. Not only Gore Vidal, Terry Teachout, and Diana Trilling, but Margo Jefferson, John Updike, Michael Feingold, and many other distinguished authors and critics have found much to like in the novelist. As Jefferson writes:

> So, we say to ourselves, another nearly forgotten writer exhumed, cleaned up, reissued and put on display with endorsements from Edmund Wilson, Diana Trilling, and Gore Vidal. Then a friend says no, she's terrific, read her, and we do, and here it is, that infinitely distinguished thing,[5] a dead writer so full of charm and derring-do that literature's canon makers should sit back, smile and say, Dawn Powell, where have you been all our lives? (1)

In this project I examine Powell's New York novels as separate from her haunting books of Ohio, because including all of Powell's novels is beyond the scope of this project.[6] Also because the Ohio publications are generally considered very different from the New York, both in theme and in tone, they should be considered separately: for one commentator, they are so dissimilar that "it is not surprising that many of Powell's greatest admirers have resorted to writing off one group or the other of her novels and basing their admiration on only half her work" (Hensher, "Country," 1). The New York books, overall, are more satiric, more comic, than the lyrical Ohio novels are, and it is in the New York works that Powell writes about "the Midnight People," who, like the characters in Sinclair Lewis's *Babbitt*, "drink and dance and rattle and are ever afraid to be silent" (Lewis, 327). Still, the Ohio series has much to say for itself. As one critic writes, "While the Manhattan novels are unquestionably wittier—urban pretensions and disputes seem to offer readier targets than rural—the Ohio novels are far from being simple accounts of grim life on the late Middle Border. The human comedy is no less comical" in Ohio than in New York (R. Miller, "Reintroducing," E8). Vidal, like many other Powell fans, preferred the New York novels: he said that it is with them that Powell "comes into her own, dragging our drab literature screaming behind her" ("Dawn Powell: American," xiii). Both cycles have much to recommend them, and a lengthy study of the Ohio novels still needs to be written.

As readers see in the *Diaries,* the *Selected Letters,* and Page's *Biography,* Powell's New York is largely the Village, a location that, Ross Wetzsteon reminds us, "has held such a mythic place in the American imagination that it has often served as a kind of iconographic shorthand. A novelist need only to write 'then she moved to the Village' to evoke an entire set of assumptions— she's a bit rebellious, artistically inclined, sexually emancipated, and eager to be on her own" (x). All of these characteristics prove true not only of the novelist's Village characters but of Powell and many of her friends themselves. Wetzsteon adds that "the mythology of the place has been created in large part by those who moved there from elsewhere," as Powell did and as nearly all of her principal characters do. Powell's love of the city she had known since her arrival there in 1918 never diminished; in novels from the 1930s to the 1960s she expresses her heartache about her once-vibrant but speedily deteriorating Manhattan.

I also look at the characters, including those based on the "real" people who populated the city, placing them beside the biographical facts of the author's life and using not only Page's biography but also Powell's own diaries and letters and other available sources. All of the players by now having long since departed, I discuss the real-life "victims" on whom she at least partly based some of her characters, among them Clare Boothe Luce, Ernest Hemingway, John Chapin Mosher, Dwight Fiske, Peggy Guggenheim, and others. Further, I place the works alongside the writings of some of her contemporaries, including Djuna Barnes, Edna Ferber, George S. Kaufman, William Carlos Williams, Virginia Woolf, Ruth McKenney, F. Scott Fitzgerald, and Dorothy Parker, to whom Powell is most often compared—a Dos Passos biographer even calls Powell "the poor man's Dorothy Parker" (Carr, 283)—though many commentators agree that the Round Tabler "had a comparatively modest talent" (Begley, 7). Parker's witty lines have come down to us largely because she voiced them in earshot of her newspaper chums, who took note of them and reported them posthaste.[7] Powell, however, as friend, writer, and critic Matthew Josephson remembers, uttered many of her best lines "before a bibulous company whose powers of recall became clogged" (25). Which is not to say that Parker's companions were sober—far from it. Instead, the Algonquin crowd had to hasten from their lunch table to their typewriters, if they were to remain employed, Parker's witticisms fresh in mind, rapidly jotting them down to flesh out a column. Powell and her friends, on the other hand, returned to their garrets or typewriters to finish the paintings and novels on which they had been working. Once pressed during a 1999 NPR interview to compare Powell to Parker, Tim Page said, "What [writings] do we really remember of Dorothy Parker's? . . . In my own opinion, there's no comparison whatsoever. . . . I don't think Parker was fit to carry Powell's typewriter." Despite the differences in their literary output and creative talent, Powell always "lived under the burden of being known as the second Dorothy Parker"; the comparison was so unsavory to her that, according to friend Jacqueline Miller Rice, "If someone called her another Dorothy Parker, she'd hit them" (Guare, x). To Powell the comparison may have seemed even more belittling because, as Wetzsteon writes, this "stress on her wit reduced her carefully crafted comedies of manners to glib collections of one-liners" (510); further, it exasperated her to think that anyone would believe that there could be but one female at a time writing satire in New York. And the playing field is hardly even for the two women writers who shared the same initials: Parker wrote very little, Powell wrote volumes; one critic says that Powell "out-Parkers Queen Dorothy" at every turn (Salter). And though it may seem that Powell disliked her more famous contemporary, the two were actually quite friendly, often going out together. If Powell objected to being compared to Parker, it was because of the latter's negligible writing production, not because she disliked the woman; in fact, she admired Parker's generosity. In a 1963 letter to her sister Phyllis, Powell wrote, "I used to have some good times with Dorothy Parker who gets too much credit for witty bitchery and not enough for completely reckless philanthropy—saving many people, really without a thought" (*Letters*, 316). Parker, who would die two years after Powell, left her estate to the Dr. Martin Luther King, Jr., Foundation; the funds went to the NAACP following King's assassination in 1968.

~~~~~~~~~~~~~~~~~~~~~

Even though Powell on occasion maintained that what she wrote was not satire but the truth, often with a capital T, she more often did call it satire, as do many of her readers. Attempting to explain why the novelist never achieved the readership or the recognition she should have achieved, Fran Lebowitz, quoted in Ann T. Keene's introduction to Mark Carnes's edition of *Invisible Giants*, says that "satire as meticulous, as adroit, as downright prosecutorial as that of Powell's stands little chance of popularity in any era, regardless of its tastes, so long as its author, and more importantly its victims, draw breath" (230).

Although I have long been a voracious reader, student of literature, and a film and theatre buff, I had never heard of Dawn Powell until a snowy Sunday morning in 2002 when I turned to the Arts section of the *New York Times*. The black-and-white photograph of the interesting-looking woman I saw there, under the headline "More Than a Witty Novelist, She Wrote Plays, Too," caught my eye.[8] The headline made it clear that the writer, Jonathan Mandell, presupposed that readers already knew Dawn Powell as a novelist. How was it, then, that I had never heard of her? The article provoked me to dig further, to order a collection of the novels, the biography, the letters. Reading her, I knew at once that I had encountered a most remarkable writer—a buried treasure, in fact.

Among Powell fans, an essay widely recognized as responsible for first reviving relatively recent interest in her appeared years before that 2002 *Times* article. In 1987 Gore Vidal's piece, "Dawn Powell, the American Writer," was published in the *New York Review of Books*.[9] In it he called Powell "our best comic novelist," adding that, as he spoke the words, he could almost hear Powell "snarling" that "the field is not exactly overcrowded" (1). It is noteworthy that he called her not our best *woman* comic novelist, but our best comic novelist, period. Vidal, who had known Powell in New York in the 1950s, had admired both the author and her books.[10] On the strength of Vidal's recommendation, a few of Powell's fifteen novels—*The Locusts Have No King, A Time to Be Born,* and her last, *The Golden Spur*—were reissued in 1989 under the title *Three by Dawn Powell*. The book, though, "quickly slid into remainderdom" (Lingeman 39). In the *Nation,* George Scialabba had this to say of Vidal's "find":

> Dawn Powell's novels were all out of print in 1987 when
> Vidal's long appreciation in *The New York Review of Books*
> pronounced her "our best comic novelist." Her studies of
> genuine Midwestern dullness and ersatz Manhattan gaiety,
> rendered with fearless, pungent wit and entirely without
> sentimentality or euphemism, may have been, as Vidal
> claimed, "Balzacian" and as good a portrait as we have of
> mid-twentieth-century America. But in this they were fatally
> unlike the top ten bestsellers of 1973 or any other year. She
> died more or less obscure in 1965, and Vidal's influential
> revaluation doubtless brought a smile to her long-suffering
> shade. (n.p.)

Not long afterward, in the early 1990s, Tim Page discovered Powell after reading in Edmund Wilson's 1965 essay collection, *The Bit between My Teeth*, an article called "Dawn Powell: Greenwich Village in the Fifties." Like Page, *Vanity Fair* contributor James Wolcott attributes his initial interest in Powell to that same piece in the same volume, which he had read a short time before the Vidal article appeared. Wilson's essay had originally been published, during Powell's lifetime, in a November 1962 edition of the *New Yorker*, a magazine to which Powell herself had contributed at least seven pieces of short fiction.[11]

"Dawn Powell: Greenwich Village in the Fifties" opened with a question that is still asked today: "Why is it that the novels of Miss Dawn Powell are so much less well known than they deserve to be?" (233). Because most of her works were out of print by the time of Page's discovery of her, it was difficult for him—and for Wolcott—to find copies of them, even though the afore-mentioned handful of paperback reissues had appeared. But still, where were the other thirteen? *Dawn Powell at Her Best*, a hardcover collection of two of her novels, several short stories, and an essay appeared in 1994, introduced and edited by Page; and the following year, a well-received volume of Powell's diaries, also edited by Page, was issued. By 1996 three of her novels—*Angels on Toast, A Time to Be Born*, and *The Wicked Pavilion*—had been published by Vermont's Steerforth Press at Page's urging. Though Page says that *Angels on Toast* is "a weird hybrid of a novel; not really an Ohio novel, not really a New York," (telephone call, March 7, 2013) and though I do agree with him, I place it here with the New York novels because I believe it merits examination alongside the others Powell sets in Manhattan and because scenes in it do take place in New York, characters travel to the city on trains, and the acerbic, satirical wit here is more akin to that of the New York series than the Ohio.

Thanks to Page, other novels followed from Steerforth throughout 2001 until all but three had been reissued: *Whither*, Powell's first novel, which she disclaimed almost immediately upon its 1925 release; *She Walks in Beauty*, published in 1928; and *A Cage for Lovers*, first issued in 1957 (it was reissued in paperback several times). In 1998, Page's biography of Powell—called simply *Dawn Powell: A Biography*—was published, generating much critical acclaim. Gore Vidal, whose words appear on the book's jacket, had this to say: "Tim Page's biography of Dawn Powell is not only a distinguished work in itself but illuminates one of our most brilliant—certainly most witty—novelists, whose literary reputation continues to grow long after her death: we are catching up to her." *Publishers Weekly* called it "a meticulously researched, well-written and sympathetic portrayal of Powell's life." Following the release of the biography came a volume of diaries and a book of her letters, both edited by Page; a collection of four of her plays soon followed, edited by Page and Michael Sexton. Notably, in 2001 the Library of America published nine of Powell's novels, selected by Page, in two volumes. Today interest in Powell seems to be climbing again (see "The Dawn Powell Revivals" section of chapter 2, below).

CHAPTER TWO

"Hidden in Plain View"

An Overview of Her Life and Career

"Ten years from now I will still be Dawn Sherman Powell—but girls, that name will be famous then. Ten years from now, I will have arrived."

—*Diaries, 2*[1]

BIOGRAPHICAL ACCOUNT

Dawn Powell was born on November 28, 1896, in Mt. Gilead, Ohio, to Elroy "Roy" King Powell, a charming rogue of a traveling salesman, and his young wife, Hattie Blanche Sherman Powell, by all accounts a doting mother to her three daughters. The first six years of Dawn's life seem to have been serene and generally uneventful, except that the clever little girl started reading at four and writing "from the time she was big enough to hold a pencil" (Farnham, 3).[2] But tragedy struck the tranquil household when her twenty-nine-year-old mother died on December 6, 1903, just eight days after Dawn's seventh birthday. From that moment forward, Dawn's childhood would be difficult; indeed, the next several years would be so brutal as to be almost unbearable. Through it all, she developed a determination and self-reliance that would serve her well for the rest of her life. She learned never to take anything too seriously, finding comedy in even the most tragic situations.[3] Good friend Jacqueline Miller Rice[4] remembers that the adult Powell always "hid her fear and despair. She showed her best face to the world. And what a glorious face it was" (Guare, x). Powell would consign her fear and despair to her diaries, which she kept faithfully most of her life.

Her mother's death, evidently of a botched abortion, left Dawn's irresponsible but generally well-meaning father alone to care for Dawn and her sisters: Mabel, who was older than Dawn by sixteen months, and Phyllis, who was three years younger. Because Roy Powell traveled for a living, the three young girls were frequently shuttled from one relation to another, among them Aunt Dawn Sherman Gates, whom the young girls adored and for whom Dawn had been named. But tragedy would soon strike again: Aunt Dawn died, presumably also as the result of an abortion, when she was just twenty and young Dawn merely ten years old. Page writes that a slip of paper found among Powell's papers upon her death read, "When I was 10 and Aunt Dawn died, I swore I at least would always remember. I did" (*Bio*, 16).[5]

The novelist would later would recall "liv[ing] around with other relatives in various villages and factory towns all over central Ohio" and staying "in grandmother's rooming house in Shelby and often called in by transient theatrical troupes to take part in plays" (*Letters*, 81). Still later, in an autobiographical entry for *Twentieth-Century Authors,* she wrote of "a year of farm life with this or that aunt, life in small-town boarding houses, life with very prim strict relatives, to rougher life in the middle of little factory towns" (1123). Those nomadic years would prove to be happier than the ones that would follow, however, when, in August 1907, Dawn's father married the wealthy but miserly and coldhearted Sabra Stearns. The family moved about ten miles southwest of Cleveland to Sabra's large farmhouse in North Olmsted, then a small farming community.

An observant child who did well in school, young Dawn loved to read, especially the novels of Dickens, Dumas, and Hugo.[6] From an early age, she developed a clear eye for the pretensions and airs of the adults she saw around her, filling notebook after notebook with sketches, poems, and stories of her observations. Dawn kept these books carefully hidden under the porch of the North Olmsted house, fearing her stepmother's rage if she found out about her writing. When Dawn was thirteen, her stepmother did discover the notebooks and immediately burned them[7]—calling them

Dawn's "trash"—in an act so cruel that it prompted the girl to leave home a short time later, immediately following her graduation from the eighth grade (*Diaries*, 186). Later, in her most autobiographical novel, 1944's *My Home Is Far Away*, Powell painted a harrowing picture of Sabra Stearns Powell, renamed Idah Hawkins Willard for the fictionalized portrait, although, according to biographer Page, Powell "seems actually to have *understated* Sabra's cruelty" (*Bio*, 197). "Although I set out to do a complete job on my family, I . . . diluted it through a fear of embarrassing my fonder relatives" (*Diaries*, 222), Powell admitted.

The fictional stepmother's way of bringing up the girls was to take a "stand," yet

> [her] "stand" was so elaborate, and involved so many
> contingencies, that her new family despaired of ever getting
> it straight. First, they were to stay out of the house except
> for sleeping and eating. Second, they were not to sit out on
> the lawn mooning where everybody could see them, nor
> were they to go visiting relatives or school friends or have
> them call. They were not to use their school paper for games,
> because it cost money, nor were they to keep reading in their
> school readers for fun after their lesson was learned. . . .
> They were not to go places where townspeople would talk
> about their ragged clothes, but they were not allowed to use
> their sewing boxes either, because needles and thread cost
> money. (*My Home*, 221)

Powell's diary recounts almost word for word many of the same incidents that the novel relates, including Sabra's "stand." In the diary Powell wrote, "Stepmother's greatest joy was in making us go downtown on errands with no hems in our ragged calico skirts (and forbidden needle and thread to sew them as Waste) so our schoolmates would sneer" (187). While such frugality might be understandable in a poor family, to begrudge shabby young children needle and thread makes no sense at all for a wealthy one; Sabra owned one of the most impressive houses in town. At any rate, the comments Powell wrote in her diary seem tame compared to what Page turned up in his research for the biography: he says that the "unbelievably vicious and sadistic" stepmother, who seemed to take an evil delight in her cruelty, would "beat the three girls regularly, almost, it seems, as a form of physical exercise" (*Bio*, 9). Powell reported both in her diaries and in her novel that She, as the girls referred to Sabra, would indeed keep her and her sisters locked out of the house until dark, prohibit them from entering the parlor, and forbid them to touch the books or the piano or anything else in the house not specifically theirs, but at the same time take from them any small item they might own. Once young Dawn with a quarter she had earned bought a silver-tasseled whip at a county fair; when the stepmother found it, she hung it in clear view in the kitchen and would regularly thrash the girls with it (*Diaries*, 187).[8]

In the same novel and in her diaries Powell painted a vivid portrait of her father as well, a man whom the girls adored but who had little practical sense. Debra Warstler, daughter-in-law of Powell's niece, Carol Warstler, says, "While [other] family members refer to him as a 'jerk,' they also recall that his daughters loved him" (14).[9] Painting a less forgiving portrait of the "selfish" Roy Powell, Debra Warstler writes that Phyllis Powell Cook (Powell's younger sister) told her that Roy Powell had opened an ice cream parlor in 1905 but that it was not until he sold it a year later that the girls were ever treated to a cone there, and that the treat came not from their father but from the new owner (6).

Powell told of her father's returning home from sales trips with such frills as a birdcage or a music box for his daughters while they remained ragged and shoeless, hungry and dirty. Even when he was not on the road he was ineffective in protecting his children from the harsh treatment of his new wife and generally seemed, at least to Dawn, almost as miserable in Sabra's presence as she and her sisters were. In 1941, looking back on her childhood, Powell remembered that her stepmother had ultimately "made my father give up the road" he so loved to "work in the mill. . . . Papa sat at table over burnt oatmeal, scorched potatoes, soggy bread, lifeless chicken with lumpy gravy. He discoursed on this spoon which he had picked up at the Palmer House in Chicago" in happier days (*Diaries*, 187). The proud but unfortunate Roy Powell seemed rarely to get things right. He had thought that marrying Sabra would bring some stability and social position to his daughters, but in fact the marriage did just the opposite.

On discovering that her notebooks had been burned, an event that would anger her for the rest of her life, young Dawn boarded a train for her aunt Orpha May Sherman Steinbrueck's home in small-town Shelby, Ohio, about an hour's ride from North Olmsted[10] and halfway between Cleveland and Columbus in Richland County."[11] Here she found refuge from the "psychopathic cruelty" (*Letters*, 132) she had faced in Sabra's house and the neglect she had met with since her mother's death. Clearly, the strong-minded Powell was never one to give up or to give in, and she was never one to lose her sense of humor. Despite the psychological injury that fleeing at such a young age the only home she knew must have caused, Powell would later write lightly of running away. In *My Home Is Far Away*, the portrait the author painted of young Marcia's escaping her stepmother's house resonates. Once safely on the train, Marcia is "still scared, but she felt light-headed and gay, the way Papa did when he was going away from home. She thought she must be like Papa, the kind of person who was always glad going away instead of coming home. She looked out the window, feeling the other self inside her, the self that had no feelings and could never be hurt, coming out stronger and stronger" (318). Much like Marcia, Powell learned to separate her inner being from her outer, almost always presenting a gay face to friends and strangers alike. Very few others knew of her demons, her nightmares, her troubles.

Just two years before her death, in an essay entitled "What Are You Doing in My Dreams?" a determined-sounding Powell would again write of leaving home: "There's something about farm life that gives you the strength to run anywhere in the world," she reflected (221). "What you have to do is walk right on down the street, keeping your eyes straight ahead, pretending you're on your way someplace a lot better. And that's the way it turns out, too; wherever you land is sure to be better than the place you left" (219). After first landing in the "better place" that was Auntie May's home in Shelby, Powell ultimately landed in the better place of her dreams, New York City.

Page writes that this successful flight from Sabra's house was actually Dawn's second attempt; after her first effort to leave she had been caught and forced to return (*Bio,* 13). One can only imagine the abuse she must have endured once she was brought back. This time she took better care to plan her escape so well that she would never have to return. Powell herself reported that she left home with thirty cents in her pocket (or ninety cents, as she later remembered in "What Are You Doing in My Dreams?") that she had earned picking berries, but Page writes that she received financial assistance from her older sister, Mabel, who had already run away from home and settled in Shelby at her grandmother Sherman's boardinghouse (*Bio,* 16). Powell's unconventional maternal aunt, who was always called Auntie May,[12] lived at 121 North Broadway—this heartland Broadway possibly helping fuel Powell's longing for the "real" one—which was located directly opposite a busy railroad station: Shelby was a transfer point for the New York Central, Baltimore & Ohio, and Pennsylvania railroads. Seeing the travelers come and go, hearing the whistles blow as the trains pulled into the station and then departed, piqued Powell's imagination and stirred her longing to escape small-town Ohio for more glamorous regions, just as characters do in her 1930 Ohio novel *Dance Night*. Young Dawn realized that she was much more like her restless father than, for example, her maternal grandmother, Julia Sherman, who "got her excitements on remote farms from traveling hucksters, cousins or distant relatives who wandered up the cow lane" (*Diaries*, 470). Such "excitement" would never do for Dawn; she was always anxious to experience the *real* excitement of the big cities, and what bigger and more glamorous city was there than New York?

Some time later, remembering her days living near the train station, Powell would quip that she had been brought up in Shelby, "not on the wrong side of the railroad tracks as is generally supposed, but right *on* the railroad tracks" (Farnham, 3; my emphasis). The travelers who would come and go from the train station, buying meals from accomplished cook Auntie May, or staying nearby at Dawn's grandmother's boardinghouse,[13] offered Powell abundant material for observation. Again the girl kept notebooks, but although this second collection of writings and drawings,[14] begun while Dawn was living with Auntie May, "survived into the late 1960s," according to Page, it now seems to have vanished (*Diaries*, 1).

The burned writings were not the only reason that Powell left home: she had learned that her stepmother was going to keep her from attending high school. Being forbidden to read the books in Sabra's house was bad enough for the bookish girl, but being kept out of school would have proved intolerable. Living now with Auntie May, in 1910 Dawn enrolled in Shelby High School, where she earned high marks and worked on the school paper, and, in her senior year, acted as editor of the yearbook. From the age of sixteen she worked as a reporter on the *Shelby Globe* (Gross, 112). Fellow reporter Eleanor Farnham remembers that an enthusiastic Powell "always got to the fires first" (Farnham, 3), determined to do her job well and eager, as always, for any fresh excitement the town might offer.

Powell was happy to be allowed to attend high school and grateful to be living with Auntie May. The two would "talk about all things all day, never bored with each other" (*Diaries*, 72). The eccentric older woman, Dawn recalled, "gave me music lessons and thought I had genius, and when I wrote crude little poems and stories, she cherished them" (Page, "Chronology," 1045). Her aunt, who not only loved her, cared for her, and supported her, proved a fine example for the girl. According to Page, "the emancipated, self-reliant Orpha May, who did as she pleased, followed her own moral code, and insisted on being treated as an equal among men, provided Dawn with her greatest role model" (*Bio*, 14). Auntie May's influence on Dawn was far reaching: without her, Powell may never have been able to attend even high school, let alone college; it is likely that she also would never have had the opportunity to flee small-town Ohio for New York City.

Some years later, after Powell had settled in New York, she would invite her aunt for a visit in a letter that reveals the free-spirited sense of humor of both women: "Unless we take another girl you can sleep in our living room," Dawn wrote, "or if Helen's father comes to see us you can sleep with him. He is a widower—a doctor—and has oil wells in Texas so you could do worse" (*Letters*, 43). Not only was her aunt unconventional and open minded, but she so believed in Dawn that she encouraged her to pursue her ambitions as no one else had done before. When Dawn was about to graduate from high school, Auntie May encouraged the girl to follow her dreams and go on to college, a luxury they could ill afford.[15] She suggested that her young charge write a letter seeking admittance to Lake Erie College for Women, founded in 1856, in Painesville, Ohio. And so Dawn wrote to Vivian Small, president of the college, promising to work hard in exchange for any tuition remission she might receive.[16] Though the letter no longer survives, early friend and college roommate Eleanor Farnham recalls that Powell had written something along the lines of "I'll do anything to work my way through, from scrubbing back stairs to understudying your job" (Gross, 111).[17] President Small, who believed that rich and poor alike were entitled to an education, saw to it that Dawn was admitted to Lake Erie College. The college, just five years before Powell's death, would award her an honorary Doctor of Literature degree.

Auntie May paid for some of Dawn's college expenses,[18] a lawyer friend of Dawn's aunt also contributed, and, according to Powell, "everybody in town helped me gather proper equipment for this mighty project, so that my borrowed trunk would scarcely close over the made-over dresses, sheets and towels blotted with my signature, tennis racket with limp strings, and a blue serge bathing suit in four sections, 1900 model, contributed by a fat neighbor on the assumption that going to 'Lake Erie' meant I would be spending most of my time in the water" (*Letters*, 249). The college assisted its new student financially: President Vivian Small herself made a personal loan to Powell; in a 1919 note to her friend and former Lake Erie College classmate Charlotte Johnson, Powell mentioned still owing President Smith $55.00 (38). Despite the financial assistance she received, still Dawn had to help pay her way, always putting in "five hours a day to earn her expenses," as she wrote in her entry for *Twentieth-Century Authors* (1123). She worked in the school's general office, where her duties included "answering doorbell [and] telephone, putting out mail, ringing bells for class and running a rotten, rheumatic old hydraulic elevator," which requires "some muscle" to operate and which "nearly kills my back" (*Letters*, 15).[19] She also found employment in the college library, and in the summer of 1915, between her freshman and sophomore years, she served as maid and waitress at the Shore Club in Painesville,[20] where she began keeping a diary addressed to Mr. Woggs, an imaginary confidant; those early journals are a precursor to the diaries Powell would keep until her death.

Resolved as she was to succeed academically, Dawn earned unremarkable marks at Lake Erie, partly because she kept herself involved in nearly everything the campus had to offer. She not only worked part time, but she also wrote for both the college yearbook and the school literary magazine, the *Lake Erie Record,* serving as literary editor from her sophomore year and as editor in chief in her final year.[21] She also put out an "anonymous, dissenting newspaper called *The Sheet* that competed with the [school] magazine" (Gross, 111); the paper offers glimpses of the wittily irreverent writer Dawn Powell would later become. Active with the school's theatrical group, she portrayed Puck in *A Midsummer Night's Dream* (*Letters*, 21); an unnamed role in *Mice and Men*[22] (9–10); and Miss Prism in *The Importance of Being Earnest* (15). She even wrote of masquerading as a performing dog with "a whisk-broom tail" one Halloween (15). As busy as she was, she still found time to write and perform skits for her classmates (17), donating the extra money she earned from them to the war effort or funding excursions into Cleveland to see such plays as *The Little Minister* with Maude Adams (15). Classmate Eleanor Farnham later said she felt sorry for anyone who had not attended Lake Erie while Dawn was enrolled there, for the lively Powell "turned everything upside down" (Gross, 111). Familiar with stories passed down about the famous alumna, today's Lake Erie College Lincoln Library director, Christopher Bennett, wrote to me in a personal letter (August 31, 2006) that "Dawn really did shake up things on this campus for those four years." Dawn herself, in a diary entry from the time of her sophomore year, insisted that a humdrum existence was not for her. "I must have days of rushing excitement," she wrote (2).

One yearns to go someplace where the band plays all the time and life is not so simple.

—*Letters,* 26

In September 1918, following her graduation from college, Dawn Powell did precisely what she had always firmly believed "the gods" had "written" for her (*Letters,* 26): she moved to New York, and the city did not disappoint. Powell contemporary E. B. White would write decades later of three New Yorks: the one of the native, the one of the commuter, and finally the one of the person who moves to Manhattan from somewhere else. "Of these three trembling cities," he said, "the greatest is the last—the city of final destination, the city that is a goal" (17–18). Having achieved her goal of moving to New York, she immediately felt that she had finally landed in the place she was meant to be. She delighted in New York from the moment she arrived, eager to "jump right in" (*Letters,* 26) and to savor all it had to offer, though she had brought with her little more than her determination, her talent, and fourteen dollars (26). The "slight, impoverished, and wide-eyed woman of twenty-one," as Tim Page describes her (*Bio,* 35),[23] first settled in a woman's boardinghouse on West Eighty-Fifth Street, a slightly fictionalized version of which is depicted in both her 1925 novel, *Whither,* and her 1931 play, *Walking down Broadway.* "Promptly and somewhat improbably," Page writes, "she found work as an 'assistant efficiency manager' with the Butterick Company" (36), which published then as now dress patterns[24] and in Powell's days an array of ladies' magazines, including *Women's* and the *Delineator.* A young Theodore Dreiser had served in managerial positions at Butterick and the *Delineator* before Powell spent time there. In 1930, long after she had left the Butterick Company's employ, the *Delineator* published a short piece of hers called "Discord in Eden," paying her $1,000; Powell says she had seen it "rejected 13 times" before (*Diaries,* 15).

After only five weeks she left Butterick for the better-paying job of "second-class yeomanette" (Lake Erie College, "Early 1900s," 1) with the United States Navy, offices at 44 Whitehall Street (B. H. Clark). When World War I ended, her "navy work [having] lost its urgency" (*Bio,* 38),

she found a position in the promotion department of the Red Cross; a
short time later she landed a publicity job with the Interchurch World
Movement, a group founded after the war, with aspirations to create a
better world.[25] It was in this position that she met Joseph Roebuck Gousha, a young blond-haired and blue-eyed writer, born in 1890, who had
lived in Pottstown, Norristown, Oil Town, and Pittsburgh, Pennsylvania,
where he worked as "a drama and music critic on the *Sun*" (*Bio*, 42). The
two were immediately attracted to one another; in fact, Powell in the last
months of her life would write in an article for *Esquire* that she had decided before their first date that he was the man she was going to marry
("Staten Island," 121). Gousha, who like Powell had recently moved to
New York, seemed to take as much pleasure in Manhattan as Dawn did.
Enjoying a conventionally romantic courtship, the pair frequently dined
out together, went to the theater, took carriage rides in Central Park, and
"drank at some of the embryonic speakeasies that were springing up in
Greenwich Village" (*Bio*, 42). So taken with him was she that she began
keeping a little booklet that she named "The Book of Joe" (*Diaries*, 3–4),
an undated sample from which reads

> I went to Joe's house for dinner and we walked to the Bay. . . . I
> made a peach pie—the very first and my Adorable said it was
> good. I love him so much and I will be so happy when we are
> together for always . . . My Dearest took me to the Bretton
> Hall[26] for lunch and then we rode in a hansom lined with plum
> color through the park. (*Diaries*, 3)

Later, in letters and diaries, she regularly referred to Joe as "Adorable," "Most
Adorable" (*Letters*, passim), and "that loving golden Leo lad" (*Bio*, 278). The
two were heavy drinkers even then, and their drinking would only escalate
over the years. Of their first date, a walking tour of Staten Island, Powell
wrote: "It was a Prohibition year, so naturally part of the hiking equipment
was a hip flask of some exquisite blend of lemonade and henbane with a zest
of metal rust" ("Staten Island," 121).

If her New York novels are filled with images of drinking and bars—
James Wolcott says of them, "Squeeze their pages and you can almost hear
them squish" (46)—her life story is full of boozy nights at home and out
on the town. In *The Thirties*, Edmund Wilson related the events of a party
at Bill Brown's[27] Village apartment, during which an inebriated Powell

"pour[ed] her drink down the back of a girl who was sitting on the stairs" (304); he later famously mentioned one of many "knock-down and drag-out" parties at Powell's place (405). In the next decade, when Powell was hospitalized awaiting the removal of a large tumor in her lungs, Wilson was surprised to see her looking "fresher and younger" than he had ever seen her, without "rings or pouches around her eyes," a fact he attributed to her being unable to drink there (*Forties*, 304). Her own diaries are full of references to drunken parties and nasty hangovers: she tells of one evening that began "at the Café Royale" (the actual spelling was Royal),[28] where she had been "drinking ferociously"; the evening ended hours later with Powell "spilling [her] drinks all over Peggy's[29] sofa, occasionally roused into consciousness by being very wet" (*Diaries*, 87). Gore Vidal remarked on the gin-filled aquarium he saw in Powell's apartment at 35 East Ninth Street in the summer of 1950 (*Golden Spur*, xi), though Page believes that the story is probably untrue: Powell, a cat owner, never once mentioned having owned either fish or aquarium, and that she would have gone to the expense of an aquarium is unlikely (phone call, March 7, 2013). But imbibe she did: Matthew Josephson writes that she "drank copiously for the joy of living" (21).[30] Still, Powell was not to be likened to the uptown Algonquin lunch set who drank away their afternoons and wrote comparatively little: she would in fact become angry if an acquaintance asked her to lunch. "Did they think she was the Village playgirl? she'd shout. Didn't they know she had some writing to do?" (Page, "Resurrection," 3).[31] Like Willa Cather, who believed that "the business of an artist's life" is "ceaseless, unremitting labor" (Benfey, 4), Powell had no tolerance for those artists who would squander their talent or waste their time, an intolerance she demonstrated in novels from 1925's *Whither* on. In her *Diaries* she complained of friends who "like to pester people who *are* working" and of those who are "happy to gnaw away at the bones of your energy and talent" (229). One simply could not write while entertaining or being entertained; in fact, from the time she was a child, she relished the sanctity of isolation. For writers, she said, "there is nothing to equal the elation of escaping into solitude" (228). Looking back, she would fondly recall the "sheer exhilaration" she had felt as a child when she had "got up into the attic or in the treetop or under a tree way off by the road where I was alone with a sharp pencil and notebook" (228–29). The serious artist always required seclusion, sobriety, and silence to produce.

At night ... I waken and see his dear yellow head on the pillow.

—*Diaries,* 4

Some nine months after their first date, on November 20, 1920, Dawn Powell and Joseph Gousha were married at the Little Church around the Corner,[32] located on Twenty-Ninth Street between Fifth and Madison. To Powell's delight, her beloved Auntie May traveled to New York from Ohio to attend the wedding (*Letters,* 51), after which the young couple honeymooned at the brand-new Hotel Pennsylvania[33] on Seventh Avenue (*Bio,* 43), then the world's largest hotel (Hirsh, *Manhattan,* 80). Both the church and the hotel stand today.

Powell's new husband, who like Dawn had been left to fend for himself from an early age, gave up his ambitions of becoming a critic, a poet, or a playwright, deciding that Dawn was the more talented of the two. Poet and friend Charles Norman remembers Joe's saying, "I married a girl with more talent than I have, and I think she should have the chance to develop it" (*Poets,* 51). It may be that this portrait of Gousha is overly kind: he was already deep in the throes of alcoholism by that time and was unable to produce what work he might otherwise have done. Whatever the reason, the couple agreed that Powell should quit her job and write, and that Joe, whom Norman describes as possessed of "charming old world manners" (51), would support the family with his work at a New York advertising agency, later as an executive with the firm.[34]

After first deciding to live apart in what was considered the "new Bohemian fashion," they ultimately changed their minds and rented their first apartment together at 31 Riverside Drive. An article without a byline that made the third page of the *Evening World* of January 3, 1921—this article, in which Powell received top billing, might have been so well placed because of the pair's work in publicity—had the following to say of the couple:

> When two nice young poets, Miss Dawn Powell and Joseph Gousha, were married ... they thought, the bride said later, they would "vindicate [Ohio-born novelist] Fannie Hurst," who had been married in 1915 but who kept her marriage a secret for five years.
>
> Accordingly Mr. Gousha returned to the home of his mother, brother and two sisters at number 540 81st Street Brooklyn, while the twenty-four-year-old Mrs. Gousha, pretty and brunette, continued living with a girl friend at number 549 West End Avenue.

> But—
> It took them only two weeks to find out that their . . .
> minds are quite elastic on the subject.
> This was said by Mrs. Gousha at a "New York Night"
> before going to Pelham, where the two were "enchanted" to
> pass the New Year holiday with friends. ("Wed to Vindicate")

The article continues in this same upbeat vein, ending with a flighty poem Powell had written, called "Inspiration," and the couple's earnest pronouncement that "they are not at all Greenwich Villagers" but that what they enjoyed most thus far about married life was "going on walks and seeing what we can't own." As it happens, they never would be able to afford much, though they would become stalwart Villagers.

In fact, it was only a short time later that they moved to their first Greenwich Village residence at 9 East Tenth Street (a plaque commemorating Powell's living there was erected at Page's urging and then later stolen); the couple subsequently moved to West Ninth, a street on which countless "wordsmiths" could be seen "shuffling up and down . . . like a pack of cards in pursuit of Lady Luck" (Loschiavo, 2). It was here, primarily, that Powell wrote her first novel, *Whither.* Later, in the summer of 1926, the young family moved to 106 Perry Street, also in the West Village, where they would remain for over a decade. The building, which still stands, is something of a literary landmark for those in the know, as it is here for the most part that Powell wrote "*Dance Night,* completed most of *The Tenth Moon* . . . and began *Turn, Magic Wheel*" (*Bio,* 100). Delighted to be living in the Village, where all the *real* artists lived and the place she would always consider her "creative oxygen" (*Diaries,* 391), Powell wrote, in 1934,

> This little room is [the] loveliest thing I ever had. Upstairs
> here at night you see the towers of lower Manhattan lit up,
> the Woolworth, etc., and the voices of extra-news in the
> street, bouncing from wall to wall: "Russia—oom-pah chah!
> Russia—oom pah chah!" These sounds mingle with the far-off
> skyscraper lights, distant boat whistles and clock chimes and
> across the street in the attic of the Pen and Brush Club[35] I see
> girls hanging out their meager laundry. (94–95)

In the early years the couple seems to have been very happy. But the marriage would be unconventional, Dawn having deep relationships with two other men, among them screenwriter/playwright John Howard Lawson, later one of the Hollywood Ten.[36] Lawson's son Jeffrey, in a telephone conversation with me in August 2012, recalled that in the 1930s Powell had been a frequent visitor to the Lawsons' Long Island home, where heavy drinking continued long into the evenings. Jeffrey, maybe seven or eight years old, would be given "a glass of ginger ale to join them." His beautiful mother, Sue Edmond Lawson, would occasionally get into physical fights with Powell. "After all the heavy drinking," he said, "inhibitions would slip away and they'd start in on each other's shortcomings. My mother more than once punched Dawn in the face. I always thought that Dawn wished my father had married her instead of my mother." In a diary entry of December 5, 1933, Powell wrote that she "didn't want to go anywhere with the Lawsons now that I see they are really dangerously insane so far as I am concerned" (*Diaries*, 78), though she did not explain further. But she would recall violent altercations with Sue Lawson even into the 1950s; one letter to Wilson tells of a surprise visit from an understandably upset Sue, her husband having been imprisoned for failing to cooperate with the House Un-American Activities Committee. "Suddenly she hauled off and started beating up Canby,"[37] then choking Margaret De Silver.[38] As Powell tried to pull Sue off Margaret, she "got a sock in the face." She added, parenthetically, "I gave [Sue] a good kick personally and pushed her into a chair where she sat with insane blazing eyes, face distorted with hate" (169–70). The younger Lawson concurs that his mother was "probably an alcoholic, flighty and temperamental, though very different and sort of sad in the afternoons when she was sober." Though Powell and Sue Lawson had a stormy relationship, Lawson recalls that his mother "seemed to be fascinated by her: I remember her standing outside of Scribner's whenever we were in New York, looking at the Dawn Powell books stacked in pyramids in the windows," despite the fact that he also remembers Powell referring more than once to his mother as "a Southern bimbo, or something like that" (personal e-mail, July 24, 2012).

Powell also likely had an affair with travel writer, translator, and editor Coburn "Coby" Gilman, born on September 3, 1893, in Denver, Colorado.[39] But Joe, too, was known to indulge in the occasional fling; as Page puts it, both of them "enjoyed a succession of lovers on the side" (*Bio*, 44). The marriage was a rocky one, after time, yet despite serious financial difficulties and painful misunderstandings, Powell's drinking and persistent health problems,[40] Gousha's alcoholism, the above-mentioned infidelities on both sides, and sometimes lengthy separations, Dawn Powell and Joseph Gousha would remain married until his death. Following a long battle with cancer during which she dutifully cared for him, Joe died in St. Vincent's Hospital on Valentine's Day, 1962. The marriage had lasted forty-two years. After his death Powell would fondly reflect, "He was the only person in the world I found it always a kick to run into on the street" (*Diaries,* 436). Never fully recovering from his death, she often meditated on the loss in her diaries and would follow him in death just three years later.

A beloved, astonishingly smart little boy

—*Bio,* 50

On August 22, 1921, when Powell was twenty-four years old, her only child, a boy, was born. From her bed at St. Luke's Hospital on Amsterdam Avenue, Dawn wrote a letter to her sisters, Mabel and Phyllis, about the difficult birth: "I had a terrible time and it was just as hard on the baby. He is awfully husky but being born was a tough business for him and just before he came out his heart went bad." Further, Powell said that she "didn't dilate at all" (*Letters,* 46). The infant would suffer a blood clot on his brain and bruising caused by the doctor's forceps, she wrote. Even while having to deliver such terrible news, Powell's trademark humor surfaced in the next lines: "Doctors said I should have had my babies five or six years ago. That would have been awkward, as I would have had some difficulty in explaining them" (46).

Despite the difficult birth, the young mother went on lovingly to describe her child: "He has coal-black hair and big blue eyes and a tiny little nose and a beautiful mouth and one ear flat and the other sticks out. He is unusually tall. Got that from me.[41] He has a fat little face—looks just like a Chinese mandarin but very very beautiful" (47). Obviously, Dawn Powell was a proud new mother.

Sadly, Joseph Jr., who would always be called Jojo, suffered from a disability perhaps caused, at least in part, by his difficult birth. From about the time he turned three years old, it became apparent that something was terribly wrong. Though there was never any clear diagnosis, he was sometimes thought to be suffering from schizophrenia, sometimes mental retardation, sometimes cerebral palsy, often a combination of the three (*Bio,* 49). Edmund Wilson in *The Fifties* referred to the "defective" (435) boy as Powell's "spastic son" (637); a cousin, Phyllis Poccia, remembers him as something of "an idiot savant" (*Bio*, 49); even Gore Vidal, as late as 1996, described him as "retarded" ("Queen," 18). Today one might refer to the boy's condition as autism, though the disease was not understood then and not even named until the 1940s. Powell friend Matthew Josephson described Jojo's case effectively. Soon enough after the boy's birth, he wrote, Dawn and Joe "discovered that their child was 'retarded,' had weak motor impulses, moved awkwardly, spoke with difficulty, and would need attention and help all his life. He was a borderline case, not feebleminded, but giving evidence of having been brain-damaged at birth" (35). Josephson went on to say, quite movingly, "After having suffered tragedy in childhood and then having won a modicum of happiness and security, Dawn Powell suffered new sorrows over her Jojo, whom, in spite of everything, she greatly loved" (36).

Jeffrey Lawson was five years younger than Jojo. He remembers the older boy as "strange; I was afraid of him. He never spoke to me or paid me any attention. He would walk with his arms held out, mumbling to himself. But it was clear that Dawn loved him very much." During our first telephone call, Lawson remembered Dawn as maternal, even to him, saying, "She would always look at me with a certain kind of love, I think, probably because she was in love with my father. She would talk to me and treat me as if I mattered to her. I recall her, in the early 1930s, as zaftig, feminine, soft, and kind, very serious and intellectual, but witty and often laughing" (August 25, 2012).

Jojo was in many ways brilliant but antisocial, stubborn yet loving, serene one moment and fierce the next. Throughout his life he would almost always require medical attention and often institutionalization; as a child he would often stay up "howling" all night long, in "inconsolable tantrums" (*Bio*, 49), to the chagrin and mystification of his parents. Difficult always and sometimes violent, throughout his youth he was in and out of mental hospitals, treatment clinics, psychiatrists' offices, and given one therapy after another, including shock treatments.[42] Unfortunately, nothing worked. The cost of his care was enormous, and Powell wrote madly, trying to keep up with the doctor bills that kept her and Gousha in a perpetual state of anxiety and often, especially in later years, almost homeless and very near poverty.

As much as the young family needed money, however, Dawn Powell was a proud young artist with standards that she refused to compromise. Although Hollywood often came calling, she at first wanted nothing to do with it, refusing offer after offer. Many of her friends, acquaintances, and contemporaries, including John Howard Lawson, Dorothy Parker, F. Scott

Fitzgerald,[43] Robert Benchley, Ernest Hemingway, William Faulkner, and others famously did time there, but Powell found the idea less than appealing and in fact found Hollywood and the huge sums of money it offered poisonous to the creative spirit.[44] In March 1930, in the midst of the Great Depression, she was offered $500 a week to go West for three months but declined, writing in her diary, "We need money but that stuff is not in my direction and life is too short to go on unpleasant byroads" (14). A year later she sold her play *Walking down Broadway* to the films for $7,500.00, a huge sum in 1931, though she was disappointed to find that the resulting movie, retitled *Hello Sister,* had almost nothing at all to do with her play. In the early months of 1932, Powell did do some screenwriting in Hollywood but found the work distasteful. Later still she turned down both Paramount's offer to pay her $1,500 a week in the summer of 1934 and United Artists' invitation to work on a screenplay of *The Wonderful Wizard of Oz* (*Bio,* 142). Finally, in 1936, her resolve having weakened, she agreed to go out and work with Samuel Goldwyn Studios for one month. Once there, she was offered a three-year contract and hefty paychecks, but, she wrote, "This quick money ruins every writer in the business" (*Letters,* 94). Further, she said, "I quaver at signing away years like that" (92), for if ever she were to do so, "New York [would] become only an interlude between jobs." She knew too that churning out the melodramas that Hollywood wanted from her would keep her too busy to write her novels. Once finally back in Manhattan, she refused all further offers to return to Hollywood. As attractive as the money always was, writing film scripts, Powell said, "makes you hate yourself" (Josephson, 40). Instead she would stay home and continue working on what she considered her first *real* New York novel, the book that would become *Turn, Magic Wheel.*[45]

She also loathed the celebrity book promotion circuit, believing that what made one a writer was *writing* rather than all the posturing that, in her view, too frequently accompanied it. As Suzanne Keen says, "Powell has little patience with those who believe in their myths of self-presentation" (24). Her first novel, *Whither,* focuses on the idea; *Turn, Magic Wheel* explores it fully, lampooning a celebrated writer based on Ernest Hemingway; *A Time to Be Born* rips it apart, lambasting a character inspired by Clare Boothe Luce.

Powell's father had been a traveling salesman, her Auntie May a department store buyer, her husband an advertising man, and she herself had worked in publicity. Given this background, it should come as no surprise that the fostering of consumer desire emerges in nearly all of her writings. But, for Powell, the marketing of merchandise was one thing; the peddling of one's art was another. Close friend Edmund Wilson wrote of her "complete indifference to self-promotion," noting that "she rarely goes to publishers' lunches or has publishers' parties given her; she declines to play the great lady of letters, and she does not encourage interviews" ("Dawn Powell," 233). Vidal, similarly, recalled that Powell was "not about to ingratiate herself with book reviewers like the *New York Herald Tribune*'s Lewis Gannett," whom Vidal considered "as serenely outside literature as his confrere in the daily *New York Times,* Orville Prescott, currently divided into two halves of equal density" ("Queen," 23). Despite Vidal's vitriol, Gannett was quite a fine critic. Still, Powell was more apt to tell critics what she thought of their reviews than to attempt to curry favor with them, even though she knew that their favor might have resulted in more positive commentaries. As Sanford Pinsker says, with "a bit of horn-tooting she might well have unseated Dorothy Parker as the wickedest wit in town" (67), adding, "When the literati might have done her some good, she held their feet to the fire rather than sucking up" (68). Although in her diary she would comically lament that "all my life has been spent killing geese that lay golden eggs, and it's a fine decent sport," she still refused to seek out the spotlight or to do anything she would label "false" to achieve it. In fact, she so disliked being "the observed instead of the observer" (*Diaries,* 453) that she would paint in *Turn, Magic Wheel* a portrait of a female character terribly uneasy under observation, while fictional author Dennis Orphen, based on Powell herself, observes her unremittingly. For Powell, as for Stephen Dedalus, James Joyce's literary alter ego, the artist remains a "tranquil watcher of the scenes before him"; it is the novelist's job to watch and to study rather to be watched and studied. As Powell noted in a diary entry of March 8, 1963, "I realize I have no yen for any experience (even a triumph) that blocks observation, when I am the observed instead of the observer" (453). Writing to Gerald Murphy, purportedly about his sister and her good friend, Esther Murphy, Powell wrote, "Some people don't want to be the action—they really want to be spectator" (L. Cohen, 135), revealing more about herself, perhaps, than about her friend.

Instead of putting on airs or lusting after fame, Powell quite simply, as Page says, "lived to write" (*Diaries,* 1). It was true: she rarely felt comfortable without at least one, or more often several, sizable writing projects underway at a time. In a letter of August 4, 1940, in the space of one small paragraph, she wrote of the many genres in which she was working simultaneously: "I have been frantically finishing and reading proofs on my novel *Angels on Toast* which is coming out next month so my theatrical itch has been under control. I do have a half-idea for a new play but am trying to hold its head under water until I get some short stories done" (*Letters*, 109).

To attempt to understand these fevered undertakings, one should note that Powell found solace and sanity in writing and felt especially lost whenever working on anything but a novel, the genre that would calm her "hysterics" and give them a place to exist "instead of rioting all over my person" (*Diaries*, 90). For Powell, "the novel is my normal breath . . . my lawful married mate" (69). If writing was her sanity and her solace, she found it also a grueling task: one diary entry says simply, "Wonderful day—murderous hard work but results" (427). Writing was the only activity she knew of that would help keep her demons at bay. Frances Keene,[46] who had met the novelist in the 1950s, understood that writing for Powell "was the bulwark against the chaos and tragedy of her life" (*Bio*, 266). Powell's diary entry of February 3, 1936, for example, records the following account of trying to write in the presence of her fourteen-year-old son:

> This is the longest period of Jojo being completely hopeless.
> I can scarcely remember any time since fall that he has put
> through a calm normal day. He requires the most intense
> control, for from morning to night he bursts in, plants himself
> before me and shouts meaningless sentences over and over. (113)

Free time was a precious commodity, even though Powell and her husband, about three years after Jojo's birth, had hired a day nurse, Louise Lee, to come in to tend to the boy. Lee would remain with the family for thirty-three years, until a stroke prevented her from continuing. The arrangement worked out well for all concerned: Jojo was relatively content in her care, Gousha felt less burdened, and Powell gained a few hours of freedom each day that enabled her to go elsewhere to write. Before she was married, the young author had often escaped the noise of the boardinghouse in which she lived to write in comparative solitude in Central Park; now she chose the children's room of the New York Public Library at Forty-Second Street, because "they have those low tables in there that are just the right height for me. And it is always quiet in the children's room. Children aren't allowed there, so far as I know" she quipped (Van Gelder, "Some Difficulties," 102).[47] Writer Hope Hale Davis,[48] who like Powell had published short pieces in *Snappy Stories*[49]

(Davis, 70), recalled in an essay requested by Steerforth shortly before her death often seeing the young author crouched over the small tables hard at work, but rarely interrupting her, knowing that for Powell "every undisturbed moment" had to count (*Bio*, 52).

Later, when she and her family had moved to an apartment near University Place, Powell would often escape to the relative peace of the rooftop to write. Fleur Cowles, associate editor at *Look* and, later, founder and editor of *Flair* magazine,[50] remembers the author sitting up there writing all day, coming out only at night "to take a quizzical look at what's going on" (5).

Dedicated to her work, Powell took in nightlife as much for observation and camaraderie as for entertainment, though surely she enjoyed her evenings on the town. Matthew Josephson wrote that in the café of the Hotel Lafayette, formerly located at University Place and Ninth Street, Powell "set up a little café society of her own . . . where she had people laughing with her for more than thirty years" (19) until the hotel was razed to make way for apartment buildings. Dos Passos biographer Virginia Spencer Carr writes similarly that Powell's "ear was privy to almost every literary and theatrical grapevine" holding "forth at a corner table" there (283). Another favorite haunt was the nearby Hotel Brevoort, owned, like the Lafayette, by Raymond Orteig;[51] the Brevoort, at Fifth Avenue and Eighth Street, had been in existence since 1854, the Lafayette since the 1870s. The little society who would meet at the stylish Lafayette café consisted not only of Powell's many literary friends, but also of "theatre people and some notable artists of the American school, such as Niles Spencer,[52] Stuart Davis,[53] and Reginald Marsh,[54] as well as assorted Bohemians and tipplers" (Josephson, 20)—and it did far more than keep people laughing: it provided Powell a never-ending supply of material for her writings and a convenient place to meet and consult with other artists. But after the gaiety of her evenings at the Lafayette, the equally well-loved Brevoort, or elsewhere in the city, Powell would always return home to the troubles awaiting her there.

She rarely longed to escape from New York, however. From the time she arrived in Manhattan until her death, she would almost always hate to leave her adopted home. When her father suffered a stroke in July 1926, Powell returned to Ohio but wrote, "I was just sick as we pulled away from NY. I don't see how I could be happy anyplace else" (*Letters*, 64).[55] Her husband would later report that Dawn was never happy away from the city "until she smells the sidewalks of New York once again" (*Bio*, 275). In her last novel, *The Golden Spur*, an artist character "was always so glad to get back to Manhattan . . . that he started walking as soon as he hit the beloved pavements so as to get the empty, clean smell of the country sunshine out of his system and let God's own dirt back in" (83). Like the character, Powell always "hated going to the country, she used to say, and could not breathe well until she had returned to the polluted air of New York" (Josephson, 48). She did return to Ohio a few more times after her father's death, once in the spring of 1940, having accepted an invitation from her alma mater to speak at a college assembly. Of her doings in New York since her graduation, she said with characteristic wit and modesty, "I did publicity work and book reviewing, I married and now have a son and a player piano" (Farnham, 3). Of course by then she had done much more than some "publicity work and book reviewing": by 1940 she had written and published nine novels, to say nothing of the many other pieces she had produced.

Other trips from Manhattan served to make her miss it all the more; a jacket blurb on the first edition of her *Sunday, Monday and Always* quotes her as saying, "The past winter spent in Paris has only increased my passion for New York. I explore it endlessly. The fact that it is getting more and more bedlamish, dirtier, more dangerous, and more impossible seems to heighten my foolish infatuation with it." She answered friends who questioned her distaste for traveling away from the city, "There was no place on earth I wouldn't go if I lived anyplace but New York" (*Diaries*, 302). Why should she leave New York? she would ask. Though she would always consider herself a "permanent visitor" to Manhattan, she genuinely believed she belonged nowhere else. As Richard Lingeman writes, "She was the classic New Yorker from somewhere else . . . a self-styled 'permanent visitor' who observed the natives with the sophistication of an insider and the wide-eyed innocence of an eternal small-towner" (40). Or as Wilson said of Powell in a letter to Alfred Kazin, who had written a piece about New York transplants from the Midwest for *Harper's*, she "is the perfect example of the Westerner coming to New York and becoming a New Yorker, but observing it with the eye of someone who has come to it from outside" (*Letters on Literature*, 699).[56]

And nowhere else could she write as skillfully, though it was a difficult balancing act to shift from the small and large tragedies of her daily life to the comic sensibility of the satire she wrote. The balancing act became particularly difficult in later decades: on Christmas Day 1957, Powell wrote of Gousha's imminent "retirement" from the advertising agency, to occur in January of the next year, and bemoaned the fact that he would no longer be drawing a salary (*Diaries*, 378). By then nurse Louise Lee had died, and their finances were now far too depressed for them to afford help anyway. Soon enough, Powell would begin spending several years tending to Joe as he lay dying of cancer.

Her last novel, the almost universally lauded *The Golden Spur*, was published in 1962, the same year that her husband died, despite her having been "so harassed with a dozen piddling things" (*Letters*, 295). While caring for Joe, she complained in a petulant letter to her sister Phyllis: "I have to do EVERYTHING. Get up, cook, wash dishes, make beds, rush to get chapter ready and then take off for two o'clock appointment uptown, rush back and do book review for *Post*, rush to deliver THAT myself downtown, back to pick up stuff for supper, swig a drink and fall asleep" (295).

Even when she herself was suffering from cancer, she continued reading and reviewing the latest publications. In her last year she contributed a "jacket valentine" to the newest novel of fellow writer and editor friend Morris Philipson (Poore, "Young," 29),[57] provided commentary for the *Washington Post* on Joseph Mitchell's new publication, *Joe Gould's Secret*,[58] and reviewed novels for the *New York Post*. At the same time she continued working on an unfinished play, *The Brooklyn Widow;* a fragmentary novel, *Summer Rose;* and even an incomplete children's book about cats, called *Yow* (*Bio*, 223, 307). In the same year she published her essay about her first date with Joe, "Staten Island, I Love You," and gave what is the only surviving taped interview we know of to a young reporter who had no idea that she was dying. "She offered me whisky," he wrote, "but would herself drink only ice water: later I learned that she was dying of stomach cancer, a fact no word, no inflection revealed" (Hethmon, "Memories," 40). Friends hovered about to comfort her in her last weeks. Matthew Josephson reported that "whereas she had been made terribly insecure by the want of love in her childhood, she did not lack for it at the end" (50). Hannah Green and Jacqueline Miller Rice cared for her daily, and even "the very aged Coburn Gilman now made heroic efforts to curb his drinking habits and attended her at her bedside every night like a nurse" (50).[59]

The final entry in her *Diaries* appeared on September 30 (477); the last letter she is known to have written is dated October 22 (*Letters*, 350–51). That final letter, written to her beloved cousin John Franklin "Jack" Sherman, to whom Page almost always refers as "one of the world's great gentlemen," expresses Powell's wonder at not being able to "even dodder to the living room without difficulty—let alone nip out into the gay world" of Manhattan (350).

As painful as that realization must have been to her, she nevertheless did not let on, refusing to sound morose in this last letter she would write.[60]

On November 14, 1965, just two weeks shy of her sixty-ninth birthday, Dawn Powell died at St. Luke's,[61] the same hospital where she had given birth to her only child so many years before. She left her eyes to New York's Eye Bank and the rest of her body to Cornell Medical Center. Her final remains were later taken to Potter's Field on Hart Island, where they were interred in a mass pauper's grave bearing no name.[62]

CRITICAL RECEPTION

*Matthew Josephson said I was the wittiest
woman in New York. Impossible!*

—*Diaries*, 34

Powell certainly enjoyed some successes; she was also admired by many of the top writers, artists, and critics of the day and knew many notables who resided in or visited New York while she lived there. Although she never made the bestseller lists, "her books weren't exactly neglected in her lifetime; par for her was a sale of around 5000 copies" (Lingeman, 38). To some the very "personification of Manhattan" (Vidal, "Queen," 25), Powell enjoyed close friendships, as we have seen, not only with Edmund Wilson, John Dos Passos, and Matthew Josephson but also with Malcolm Cowley, John Latouche,[63] Sara and Gerald Murphy, Malcolm Lowry, Dwight Fiske,[64] and her editor, Max Perkins, widely considered "the most distinguished editor in the book business" (Cowley, "Unshaken" II, 30). She was acquainted with many other noteworthies, among them Robert Benchley, Djuna Barnes,[65] e. e. cummings, Rex Stout, Sherwood Anderson, Dylan Thomas, John Cheever, and Theodore Dreiser. Edmund Wilson, who had met Powell in 1933 and referred to her as "one of his only real friends" (*Sixties*, 64),[66] wrote in a *New Yorker* article of her "gift of comic invention and individual accent that make her books unlike all others" ("Dawn Powell," 233). Ernest Hemingway, who called Powell his "favorite living writer" (*Diaries*, 226), told Lillian Ross that Powell "has everything that Dotty Parker is

supposed to have [but] is not tear-stained" (Ross, 69–70). Malcolm Cowley
in a 1963 *Esquire* piece spoke of his "lasting gratitude" for Powell's works and
for those of "one or two other women of the generation" but added rather
presciently that those same women writers "have been less widely read than
male contemporaries of no greater talent" (78). John Dos Passos, who always
admired Powell's work, admired the writer as well: in his autobiography, he
named her "one of the wittiest and most dashingly courageous women I
ever knew" (154). "Dos," as she and all his other friends always called him,
was proud that his friendship with Powell had lasted from their meeting in
the 1920s until her death. A publisher friend said Powell had a "New York
following that considered her in the class of Madame Recamier,[67] Lady
Mary Wortley Montagu, and Dorothy Parker" (Crichton, 84). She was famous enough that her name sometimes appeared in gossip columns and in
such places as the *New York Times*' "Books and Authors" feature, which on
September 28, 1930, offered readers this curious tidbit:

> Dawn Powell, whose novel of an Ohio boomtown, *Dance
> Night,* is to be published October 10 by Farrar and Rinehart,
> is becoming known in literary circles as a clever entertainer.
> One of her best stunts is to give an imitation of Mr. and Mrs.
> Martin Johnson,[68] a cannibal, a cannibal's wife, a wounded lion,
> three dead elephants, and a movie camera. The elephants, we
> presume, are silent, as in rigor mortis. (BR8)

Evidently her antics at some party or other had drawn sufficient attention to find their way into the *Times*. Her name also appeared in such columns as Frank Sullivan's annual *New Yorker* Christmas poem, "Greetings,
Friends!" in which he would mention various celebrities of the days whose
names were recognizable to his readers (Sullivan, 27),[69] and in a silly poem
attributed to one Walgrove Snood in reviewer Charles Poore's "Books of
the Times" column of December 4, 1932 (39). Clearly, Dawn Powell had
before long achieved more than a little renown in her adopted city.

As we have noted, she was uncomfortable playing up to reviewers and
preferred the role of observer; she was similarly uncomfortable with the adu-
lation of fans, when she did come upon them. Charles Norman recounted
one memorable encounter Powell had with an admirer: "At a party I gave on
Perry Street," he wrote, "there was a woman who sat on the floor. Dawn was
in a chair yards away from her, but little by little the woman came closer,
crawling with a glass in her hand, and looking up admiringly at Dawn.

Soon she was beside Dawn, who jumped up. 'I didn't want a lapful of ears,' she told me" (*Poets*, 53). As always, Powell remained uneasy in the spotlight.

~~~~~~~~~~~~~~~~~~~~~~~~~~~~~~

If critics today almost uniformly sing Powell's praises, many well-known commentators of her day did so as well. J. B. Priestley, who said he "never misses anything Dawn Powell writes" (*Bio*, 246), saw in her work "an admirable mixture, not often found, of humour, genuine sentiment (born of compassion), and very shrewd and sharp satire" ("Dawn Powell"). Diana Trilling famously wrote that "Miss Powell, one of the wittiest women around, suggests the answer to the old question, 'Who really makes the jokes that Dorothy Parker gets the credit for?'" ("Four Recent Novels," 243). Powell may have approved of Trilling's comment, even though her carefully constructed novels and Parker's slick one-liners had little in common.

~~~~~~~~~~~~~~~~~~~~~~~~~~~~~~
The Second Novel as First . . .
~~~~~~~~~~~~~~~~~~~~~~~~~~~~~~

Despite Powell's distaste for her first novel, *Whither,* the book earned some fairly positive notices on its release. The author herself so firmly disliked it that she thereafter always disavowed it, saying, in the entry she wrote for *Twentieth-Century Authors,* that she "preferred to let the error be forgotten" (1123). Thirty-five years after the publication of *Whither,* when Hannah Green[70] found a copy in a secondhand bookstore, Powell was not at all pleased (*Diaries,* 4). Still, four noteworthy publications—the *New York Times,* the *Literary Review,* the *Saturday Review of Literature,* and the *Boston Evening Transcript*—considered it important enough to merit reviews in their pages. Friend and the *New York Evening Post*'s Charles Norman wrote that "*Whither* is a much finer conception of the jazz age than even [John Howard Lawson's] *Processional* is.[71] There is an ironic, tender mockery in Miss Powell's book, and a delicate, refreshingly humorous satire. I laughed aloud over many paragraphs. For escape from the heavy, all-observing (and all-recording) popular novels, I recommend *Whither*" ("Jazz," 5).[72] Two days after Norman's piece appeared, Powell recorded in her diary, "Macy's, Brentano's, and Womrath begin to move *Whither* as a result of Charles' review. Things look brighter" (5).

For a time Powell held out hope for the novel, though she was disappointed to find that a commentary soon to follow in the *Saturday Review of Literature* was less positive:

... While the author writes with earnestness, and evident
sincerity and produces a thoroughly readable story, the book is
neither searching in its insight into character, nor conspicuous
as a study of life. The plot is thoroughly conventional in texture
and the ending departs not at all from the usual, and if there be
anything to distinguish the book it is a certain freshness with
which the author writes and a certain engaging air of being
deeply and seriously concerned about her characters and their
lives. (694)

Though by no means a rave, the review did capture one of the hallmarks of
Powell's writings that critics would thereafter comment upon, for better or
worse: her empathy for her characters, no matter how difficult, unlikable, or
troubled they were.

Another contemporary reviewer, one S.L.R. writing in the *Boston
Evening Transcript,* found much to like about the novel:

Sophistication and good humor are not usually associated, yet
Mrs. [sic] Powell has managed to make them boon companions
for three-hundred pages. *Whither* is a satire upon New York's
great army of Discontent—these thousands of girls who go
to the city from Great Harrington, or Moline, or Hoosack
Corners for their "great opportunity" which, because they are
never willing to work up to it, never arrives. And so the years
pass, waiting for Ethel Barrymore to die or the idea for the
greatest novel of the decade to happen along. (5)

The *New York Times* review was partially positive as well, maintaining that
the book had "real value" in its depiction of the struggle writers too often
face between security and artistry, and in its "deft and lively characterizations" ("New York Adventures," 19). But light sales and her own evaluation
of the novel convinced her that the book was a failure.

Powell's hometown Ohio paper, the *Cleveland Plain Dealer,* also spilled
a few lines of ink on *Whither,*[73] though reviewer Ted Robinson was not
impressed:

For the romantically inclined sweet young things who will "do"
their two weeks at the sundry seasides and shadynooks this
summer and who demand "snappy"[74] fiction in which young or
youngish heroines, "living their own lives," brusquely choose

their mates without consulting the brutes, or who feverishly carve out careers—letting the chips fall where they may—here is some new fiction of that sort. (9)

The first novel he mentions "of that sort" is *Whither*, which he calls simply "The romance of a small-town girl in New York's Bohemia" (9). Books he includes alongside Powell's are the rather undistinguished-sounding titles *Last Year's Nest*[75] and *Singing Waters*,[76] among others. *Whither*, too, is a none-too-impressive title; in fact, many of Powell's titles are less than intriguing.

For years the novelist would claim that her second publication, the Ohio novel *She Walks in Beauty*, was her first (*Diaries*, 12), much like Willa Cather before her, who admitted in "My First Novels (There Were Two)" having done the same thing. In 1943, eighteen years after the publication of *Whither*, in a brief autobiography to be included with the short story "You Should Have Brought Your Mink" in *Story Magazine*, Powell still refused to acknowledge *Whither* as her first novel:

> My mother's people, the Shermans, have lived [in Ohio] for five generations around Morrow County. This makes every person north of Columbus my cousin. Graduated from Lake Erie College. Did publicity and magazine writing in New York. First novel, *She Walks in Beauty*, appeared in 1938, and after that came The *Bride's House, Dance Night, Tenth Moon, Story of a Country Boy*, all stories of a changing Ohio . . . and the last one published last August *A Time To Be Born*. Have contributed to various magazines, *New Yorker*, etc., and have done some work for the theatre. Have one husband, Joseph Gousha, and one son, Joseph, Jr., age 18. (103)

The author was so harsh in her assessment of *Whither* that many of today's reviewers follow her lead and rarely mention it.[77] Anne T. Keene, however, did scare up a copy and included it in her essay in *Invisible Giants: Fifty Americans Who Shaped the Nation but Missed the History Books*. She wrote that "what became the classic elements of Dawn Powell's work were in evidence from the outset" (232). The book is now available on a print-on-demand basis on Amazon.com, a fact that would surely horrify Powell.

Many of Powell's next publications would be fairly well received; in fact, as Page says, the critical "neglect of Powell during her own lifetime has been overstated" (*At Her Best*, xvi). The Ohio works were often praised for their lyricism, realism, and believability: *She Walks in Beauty*, the first Ohio novel, was called, on its 1928 release, "very well written" by the *Saturday*

Review, its characters "striking and complete" (869). *The Bride's House*, published in 1929, "a strong, direct, and seemingly very intimate book about a woman torn between affection for her husband and passion for a dashing and mysterious stranger" (*Bio*, 66), received some positive critical attention, including this line from the *New York Times:* "A striking story, macabre in its intensity, [the author] painting her characters with a remarkable sureness and precision" (*Bio*, 90). Her fourth novel, 1930's *Dance Night*, always one of Powell's favorites of the Ohio books, received some encouraging commentary, though for such a fine piece not nearly as much as it should have.[78] In one of the few positive notices it received, an unnamed *New York Times* commentator appreciated its "unforgettably real people drawn with an unerring instinct for characterization" (*Bio*, 115), but others faulted what they considered her unsavory characters and contrived ending. The next work, 1932's *Tenth Moon* (which Powell had titled *Come Back to Sorrento*) was lauded by Harold Stearns in the Sunday *Tribune* for its "fusing of the new stream-of-consciousness school and the directly realistic" (*Diaries*, 53); another reviewer of the same novel, Powell happily recorded, likened it to "the sound of a flute heard across water at twilight, like a lark at sunrise" (*Diaries*, 54).[79]

A handful of her short stories received some recognition: "Such a Pretty Day" was included in the *New Yorker*'s "pretty swell garland of reading" (Poore, "Books: Short Stories"), the 1940 anthology of sixty-eight of the best short stories it had published in its first fifteen years, placing Powell in the company of John Cheever and Irwin Shaw, Sherwood Anderson (to whom John Updike likened her) and Erskine Caldwell, John O'Hara and James Thurber. The story would become so well known that Powell more than a decade later would complain that "somebody is always saying, 'Miss Powell, did you write anything besides that *New Yorker* short story "Such a Pretty Day"?'" (*Letters*, 204). On the 1952 appearance of her collection of short fiction, *Sunday, Monday and Always*, one reviewer said that Powell's "observation is merciless, her style a marvel of economy, her pen double-edged" (Nerber, 5); another reviewer, William Peden, called it "a welcome rarity in today's book world, a volume of humorous short stories" that are "deftly and expertly put together" (10).[80]

~~~~~~~~~~~~~~~~

When more than a decade after *Whither* was published and Powell again began setting her novels in New York, critics sometimes found her a skilled portraitist and a gifted satirist. Charles Poore, in 1940 reviewing the newly released *Angels on Toast,* found it not only "hilarious" and "blistering" but "warmhearted and yet singularly penetrating" ("Diversity," 19). Similarly, Alice Morris, a contemporary of the author's, said of another Powell novel written in that decade,

> If the art of satire at Miss Powell's hands is less baleful, less knife-edged and glittering than when Mr. Evelyn Waugh puts his hand to it, it is equally relevant, and more humane. In *The Locusts Have No King,* Miss Powell pins down her locusts— some New York barflies, bigwigs and gadabouts—with drastic precision, but never without pity. She laughs at them, but never laughs against them. . . . The combination of a waspish sense of satire with a human sense of pathos results in a novel that is highly entertaining and curiously touching. (1)

Comparisons with Waugh would surface again; Edmund Wilson in the *New Yorker* wrote that "Dawn Powell's novels are among the most amusing being written, and in this respect quite on a level with those of Anthony Powell, Evelyn Waugh, and Muriel Spark. . . . Miss Powell's books are more than merely funny; they are full of psychological insights that are at once sympathetic and cynical" ("Dawn Powell," 236).

Another contemporary of the author's, also reviewing *The Locusts Have No King,* spoke of "the justice of Miss Powell's satire . . . the human honesty of her insights, [and] her wit . . ." all of which make for "an accomplished and engaging novel" (A. Morris, 2). Such praise met many others of her books as well. *The Wicked Pavilion,* when released in 1954, was even "given pride of place on the front page of the *New York Herald Tribune* Sunday Book Review" (Page, Intro *At Her Best,* xvi).

Yet Powell suffered many bitter professional disappointments; as Vidal says, she endured a "lifetime of near misses" ("Queen," 23). In her own day, as in this, she was never as well known or as widely read as many believe she deserved to be. Often critics contemporary to Powell wrote mixed reviews of her novels and plays, praising her wit, intelligence, and skill while railing at her so-called cynicism. In her diary Powell responded to the charge: "The artist who really loves people loves them so well the way they are he sees no need to disguise their characteristics—he loves them whole, without retouching. Yet the word always used for this unqualifying affection is 'cynicism'" (*Diaries,* 273). Reviewers too often faulted not her characterizations but, curiously, her characters, calling them unsavory, objectionable, hardly worthy of the reader's notice. It was the complaint that most exasperated Powell; one sees her over and over again in her diaries wrestling with it, at one time trying to understand the charge, at another to respond to it.

I have always been fond of drama critics . . . I think it is so
frightfully clever of them to go night after night to the theatre
and know nothing about it.

—Noel Coward

The same sort of unfavorable commentary that greeted her novels met her first produced play, *Big Night,* which she had originally called *The Party.* It was a satire of the advertising industry that Powell wrote in response to her husband's having been fired from his position in the late 1920s. Produced by the Group Theatre in 1933, the play, Group Theatre cofounder Harold Clurman remembered, had seemed "very funny" to the actors when first they read it (81); Wendy Smith, too, says that before the Group got hold of it, it was "a tough, bitingly funny drama" (81). A terrible disappointment, it closed after only nine performances. Director Robert "Bobby" Lewis recalled that of all those working at the Group Theatre, "nobody understood Dawn's characters, her sophisticated dialogue, her wit" (*Bio,* 128). Sitting in on a rehearsal one afternoon, Powell quipped, "Isn't that remarkable? . . . That was a funny line when I wrote it" (W. Smith, 115).

Clifford Odets, who recalled landing the bit part of a doorman in the play, spoke of Clurman's plodding take on Powell's piece:

> It was astonishing how he could take this little comedy with
> its bitter undertone and relate it to all of American life. In fact,
> sometimes in rehearsal it became necessary to say, "Don't try
> to act all of this solemn stuff, because this is after all a light
> comedy. Don't load it all down with these significances. To the
> contrary, this has to be played as if it's a series of cartoons in
> *The New Yorker.*" (Hethmon, "Days," 190)

Clurman admitted that the Group had not known what they were doing when they staged the play (100), after which, he recalled, the press "ran screaming" from the performance, "like so many maiden aunts" (100).[81]

Richard Schickel, in his biography of Elia Kazan, wrote of the play that "Powell thought it was a comedy. The Group thought it was a waste of its idealism" (19). The biographer goes on to say that Group cofounder Cheryl Crawford, "who started directing it, and Clurman, who finished it, kept sobering it up, thus betraying what merits the play had. As Powell, a merry and shrewd social observer, put it, 'The Group has put on a careful production with no knowledge whatever of the characters—as they might put on a picture of Siberian home life—made up bit by bit of exact details but [with] the actual realism of the whole missing'" (20).

Even though she recognized that the produced play had little to do with what she had written, Powell believed that the critics had roundly censured *Big Night* for being "too brutal, too real," her characters faulted for being too seedy, too sordid (*Letters,* 285).[82] Answering the critical complaints, Robert Benchley, "who adored Powell" (Guare, x), wrote in his *New Yorker* review of the comedy that other contemporary plays such as "*Dinner at Eight*[83] and *Dangerous Corner*[84] are about unpleasant people for the most part, but they wear evening clothes. Are we only to have high-class cads on our stage?" (26).[85] A drama critic for the *New York Evening Post* went so far as to call the play's cast of characters a "tiresome" band of "odious little microbes" (Sexton, 3–4). Powell responded to the criticism in typically undaunted if defensive fashion:

> At first I was dashed, then the accumulation of stupidity challenged me and even flattered me—to be attacked as a menace to the theater was the first real sign that I had a contribution to make there. It was like finding out you could hurt the elephant— the only defeat or failure is in being ignored or being told you have appeased it. In either case you are lost—just so much hay for the elephant. I was not hay; I was the barbed wire in it, and so I made far more impression. (*Diaries,* 62–63)

Not all the reviews were negative: Brooks Atkinson, reviewing for the *New York Times,* found a small thing or two to like in it, writing that the play possessed a "good theme for a drama of modern customs and amenities. Although Miss Powell has given at least two-thirds of her attention to the befuddled squalors of apartment dissipation, she is not unmindful of the tragic implications; and in one good scene in the third act she shapes them into concrete drama." In the end, however, the critic found that "the wildness of the party runs away with the play" (n.p.).

Richard Lockbridge, theater reviewer for the *New York Sun,* was less fond of *Big Night,* calling it "a really venomous comedy" that "provides food for thought—and, on the part of all males, for wincing. Miss Powell does not care much for men, particularly for men employed as salesmen by advertising agencies, particularly for men who exploit their wives in an effort to promote business" (16). A curious statement, that last: why would any woman "care much" for men who would exploit their wives for business? The reviewer adds, "But the venom of the author's distaste for all these singularly distasteful persons makes it interesting; gives it a bite and a refreshing air of being about something" (16). That "being about something" may have had more to do with the Group than with Powell.

A recently unearthed copy of the playbill for Powell's first produced play quoted a review by well-respected theater critic and editor Barrett H. Clark: "The cruelty of what Dawn Powell writes is not an author's cruelty, it is the facts as she sees and feels them. Perceiving accurately what goes on about her, she dramatizes it without sentimentality, and with something of the brutality of Restoration comedy" (14). These lines must have pleased Powell, who admired Barrett and had heard him lecture at Lake Erie while she was enrolled there. It was Barrett who assisted Powell in getting the Group Theatre to take on the play (*Bio,* 127).

A final word appeared in the *New York World-Telegram.* More a summary than a review, the unsigned piece was likely the work of Heywood Broun, that paper's drama critic at the time. Powell recounts his having joined her dinner party at Tony's restaurant when *Big Night* closed (*Diaries,* 63).

Despite the few kind and even noncommittal words the play received, it was an abject failure, and Powell knew it. She would write in her diary that "I learned out of the attacks on my play more of what I could do, what I was prepared to fight for in my plays, and what I must improve, than in any classroom acceptance of fairly good stuff" (82). Never one to accept defeat, within four months of its pillorying in the press she would complete her second play, 1934's *Jig Saw,* the only one of her plays to be published in her lifetime. One commentator notes that in it Powell's "wit and observation [remained] intact, her topsy-turvy sense of truth and falsehood sparkling from every page. The acute, piercing observations that make her New York novels such madcap wonders are prefigured brilliantly in *Jig Saw*" (Sexton, 7). The play concerns, among other things, empty-headed materialistic women and, as usual, a sprightly cast of ne'er-do-wells.

In 2001, the Yale Repertory Theatre produced the comedy for the first time in nearly seventy years and for the first time in its original rendering. In November and December 2012, the ReGroup also restaged the play as closely as possible to the way Powell had wanted it: they even scared up her notes from the original production, a copy of which Allie Mulholland generously provided me.

Jig Saw, produced by the Theatre Guild,[86] was more favorably received than its predecessor *Big Night* had been, but then what play wasn't? Roy S. Waldau judges that the play, which starred Spring Byington, Earnest Truex, and Cora Witherspoon, "was barely distinguishable from the majority of commercial entertainments that Broadway provides yearly" (187), but that lukewarm appraisal is a far cry from the lambasting that *Big Night* had received. Waldau goes on to cite a somewhat favorable Brooks Atkinson review that appeared in the *New York Times* immediately after the play opened:

> Miss Powell has learned her craft by close attention to the
> accepted patterns. She knows when to be daring, when to be
> perverse, what foibles are most risible and how to twist lines
> into laughs. . . . *Jig Saw* may be dull under the surface, but
> it is bright on top, where facile humors are displayed to best
> advantage. (187)

Though the review is by no means a rave, neither is it a pan. Powell may have come to learn stagecraft better than she had known it previously, or she had succumbed to convention more thoroughly by that time, and she was fortunate to have left the Group Theatre. Closing after forty-nine performances, this second stage effort was a "modest" little achievement (Sheehy, 126). *Jig Saw*, in all its "extra-dry urbanity," was "nearly *Big Night*'s counterpoint in every way," quite different in "tone . . . temperament, [and] tactics" from "the scrappy, urgent comedy of *Big Night*" (Sheehy, 126).

Years after that production of *Jig Saw*, sounding frustrated with her failure at writing for the stage, Powell had a thing or two to say, whether fairly or no, about theater critics: "The fault it not that they know little about drama, it's that they know so little else. 'Life-like' is a word they use for a form of life they have seen sufficiently on the stage for it to seem normal to them" (*Diaries*, 191). Soon enough, however, the author realized that the novel was her forte.

~~~~~~~~~~~~~~~~~~~~~~~~~~~~~

By 1936 she had become accustomed to hearing the same line of criticism of her novels that she had heard about her first play. For example, awaiting the publication of that year's *Turn, Magic Wheel*, she feared that the book would "probably . . . annoy people as 'Big Night' did, according to the way Carol[87] and Halliday[88] react. . . . 'Unpleasant, dreadful people'—what they always say when I have congratulated myself on capturing people who need no dressing up or prettifying to be real" (*Diaries*, 112). Although the novel earned many glowing notices, it received its share of complaints, too. Edith H. Walton, in an otherwise positive review, wrote that "Amusing and witty as it is, this tale of publishers and writers, of night-club addicts and the padded rich, is not precisely comfortable to read" ("Ironic," 7).

Worse criticism awaited her second (or third, if we count *Whither*) New York novel, *The Happy Island*, published in 1938. In the *New Yorker's* "Briefly Noted" column, an unsigned review chided the author for choosing to write about the "doings of a pretty worthless and ornery lot of people," even though she "serves it all up with a dash of wit" (94). Still another complained of the "dimwitted" "playboys and playgirls who cavort through its pages" (Walton, "Café," 7). In a final insult, William Soskin, of the *New York Herald Tribune*, wrote that Powell seemed to dislike people so much that "the smell of men and women is a stench in her nostrils" (3).[89] Soskin clearly had missed Powell's response, in the very novel he was reviewing, to this exact sort of criticism: *The Happy Island's* playwright character, Jefferson Abbott, newly transplanted to New York from a small town in Ohio, has been savagely attacked by the critics as full of "brutality and bitterness," a despiser of humankind, to which he replies, "I never set out to be a literary Elsa Schiaparelli, dressing up human nature to hide its humps" (118). These words echo Powell's own response to the familiar charge, but they somehow missed the reviewer.

A less favorable commentary on *Angels on Toast* than Charles Poore's, above, found the Chicago/New York novel "cleverly surprising" and Powell a writer with an "exceptionally keen ear for dialogue," but ultimately faulted the writer for creating "characters who are pretty hopeless because nothing much worth hoping for ever caught their attention" (Van Gelder, "Business," 6).

A few years later, Powell's next novel, *A Time to Be Born,* was called "another of her very enjoyable books about very disagreeable people" (Sherman, 6). Why this line of criticism, one wonders? Clearly O'Neill[90] was writing much more sordid characters than Powell was, as were Faulkner, Steinbeck, Dreiser, and other contemporary American playwrights and novelists. It was almost becoming a mantra, as if each reviewer were repeating what each had said before and echoing what each was saying now. As Heather Joslyn says, Powell "was criticized in her time (and still is by some '90s readers) for her propensity for 'unpleasant' characters, but they're not so much unpleasant as unvarnished. Her small-town portraits owe more to Edward Hopper than Norman Rockwell. Her big-city swells don't just utter precious witticisms between sips of martini; they exploit each other, bed-hop, and social-climb" ("Bright").

Even Diana Trilling, who usually championed Powell's novels, criticized the writer of *The Locusts Have No King* for "the insignificance of the human beings upon which she directs her excellent intelligence" ("Fiction in Review," 611). Powell responded in her diary to the familiar complaint: "Gist of criticisms (Diana Trilling, etc.) of my novel is if they had my automobile they wouldn't visit my folks, they'd visit *theirs*" (271). Teachout said of the comment, "Trilling is nobody's fool, but she went to see the wrong family" ("Far," 6).

Forty years after Trilling's review first appeared, it annoyed Gore Vidal, who wrote,

> Trilling does acknowledge the formidable intelligence, but
> because Powell does not deal with morally complex people
> (full professors at Columbia in mid-journey?),[91] "the novel as
> a whole fails to sustain the excitement promised by its best
> moments." Apparently to be serious a novel must be about very
> serious—even solemn—people rendered in a very solemn—
> even serious—manner. ("American," 2)

Always considering herself a "serious novelist," Powell wrote in her diary that her habit was simply "telling the truth. It's very odd that [critics] should say you hate people because you don't prettify them. But I like them the way they are, not gussied up for company" (213). If what she did was satire, as her reviewers often said, then why fault her for telling the truth? One of her favorite works, which she read over and over again, was Frances Trollope's 1832 travel memoir *Domestic Manners of the Americans.*[92] She defended Mrs.

Trollope's initially controversial book largely on the grounds that it told the truth of the new country rather than sugar-coat it, precisely what Powell always aimed to do.

As for her own works being labeled satires, she famously wrote, "Satire is people as they are; romanticism, people as they would be; realism, people as they seem with their insides left out" (*Diaries,* 119). Though she wrote again and again of her unhappiness with the critical indictment that too often was leveled at her, she did not answer the charges publicly, preferring to confine her feelings to her diaries, just as she confined her personal troubles there.

By the 1940s the author had begun to believe that she was writing in "an age that Can't Take It"; it seemed to her that readers and critics alike were always crying "Where's our Story Book? . . . Where are our Story Book people?" (*Diaries,* 188). For Powell, the public was uncomfortable with her clear eye and sharp wit; for them, as J. B. Priestley wrote, her work was more like "*asperges vinaigrettes* [than] a chocolate sundae" (*Bio,* 246).[93] Again in her diaries, Dawn Powell sought to explain her technique:

> I merely add a dimension to a character, a dimension which gives the person substance and life but which readers often mistake for malice. For instance, take the funeral of a much-loved family woman, a mother. Treating this romantically, one writes only of the sadness in the people's hearts, their woe, their sense of deprivation, their remembrance of her. This is true, but it is not as true as I would do it, with their private bickers over the will . . . as they all gorge themselves at the funeral meals, as the visiting sisters exchange recipes . . . as pet vanities emerge.
>
> Yet in giving this picture, with no malice in mind, no desire to show the grievers up as villains, no wish more than to give people their full statures, one would be accused of "satire," of "cynicism," instead of looking without blinders, blocks, ear mufflers, gags, at life. (118–19)

Powell believed that her critics did not understand satire when they spoke of it; instead, she said, they were actually speaking of "whimsy" (*Diaries,* 215). And despite the fact that her reviewers too often seemed not to "get it," she came to be proud to be writing satire. In a diary entry of 1943 she wrote that "satire [is] social history," that "the only record of a civilization is satire," especially works like Flaubert's *A Sentimental Education,* which "gives a completely invaluable record of Paris, its face and its soul, its manners and its talk of 1840" (215) and, again, works like Frances Trollope's *Domestic Manners*. Powell created an important record of small-town Ohio during the early years of the twentieth century, and of New York in the first half of the same century. As Carleen M. Loper notes, "Following her wit, the second great gift Dawn Powell left us was her sense of place. If one is feeling nostalgic for an America that no longer exists, for a Greenwich Village of the '30s and '40s, or a mill town in the Midwest, one need look no further than the pages of her novels or diaries" (4).

The novelist wrote of what she observed and what she knew. Possessed of a talent for psychological insight, she was able to capture the inner workings of the minds of the people she was acquainted with, those she observed every day on the streets and in the cafés of the Village, those she had met and lived with in the remote farming towns and railroad junctions of Ohio. She knew about the small-town midwestern nobody and his lofty dreams, his disappointments, his despair. She understood the strivers and the seekers, the liars and the phonies, the rogues and the scoundrels who populated the rat-race worlds of advertising and publishing, theaters and saloons, art and commerce, and so she chose to write about them, just as they were. These characters populate her fiction with an authenticity that put some readers off; perhaps the fact that she presented them so realistically made some of her readers and critics perceive flaws in themselves. Whenever editors asked that she prettify her characters, she would tell them that they did not need to be prettified; still, their response always was, "But yes, . . . they do; before the reader will identify himself, he must be changed so that no one else will recognize him" (*Diaries,* 112). But, for the author, what was the point in writing the unrecognizable? She wanted to write the truth of her characters, the truth as she found it. Regardless of the social status, gender, moral practices, or professions of her characters, Powell longed for reviewers to respond to what she had put on the page or the stage, not to what they wished to see there.

The familiar charge never strayed far from her mind. Even as late as 1956 she recorded a humorous diary entry entitled "The Secret of My Failure." While other authors, she said, would write something like "'Last time Gary saw Cindy she was a gawky child; now she was a beautiful woman . . . ' I can't help writing 'Last time Fatso saw Myrt she was a desirable woman; now she was an old bag . . . '" (356). She would not romanticize the truth. "I believe true wit should break a wise man's heart," she once said.

"It should strike at the exact point of weakness and it should scar. It should rest on a pillar of truth, . . . The truth is not so shameful that it cannot be recorded" (Josephson, 28). For Powell, writing was always about just that: telling the truth.

～～～～～～～～～～～～～～～～

She finesses her way into your heart with fresh charm—[reading her] is like revisiting an old friend, or making a new one.

—Ann Geracimos, 1

～～～～～～～～～～～～～～～～

In 1981, nearly two decades after Powell's death, the first full-length study of her life and works was written. Judith Faye Pett, in her dissertation "Dawn Powell: Her Life and Fiction," interpreted Powell more kindly than most of the novelist's contemporaries did. Perhaps it is the distance of years and the changed attitudes of Pett's generation that enabled her to perceive the compassion in the author's portrayals as opposed to what had previously been perceived as vitriol, disapproval, and dislike. Pett recognized her "empathy, her sympathy for her characters" even while the novelist was simultaneously able to "see through or anticipate the results of their actions" (66). For Pett, Powell "accepts the world as it is" rather than seeking to change it. As Gail Pool wrote in 1990, Powell never made "life or people out to be any better than they are. Her great talent was for evoking so precisely what—in all their humor and sadness—they are" (20). In 1990, Michael Feingold explained that Powell's "complexly acid vision was never wholly appreciated in her own time, perhaps because she reflected her time too accurately. Butterflies, even after they're preserved and pinned, can't be expected to wax enthusiastic about the woman with the net. How lucky the 1990s are that Powell's multicolored collection . . . has reached the light again, in all its brilliant hues" (14). Reading Pett, Pool, Feingold, and the reviewers who follow them, one cannot help but think that Powell had been born several decades too soon.

   A slightly earlier posthumous commentary on Powell, this one written in 1973 by her friend Matthew Josephson, spoke of the writer with an eye to posterity. "The good humorists dealing with the comedy of manners play a most useful part in helping us to see that which is real and that which is sham in our social behavior," he wrote. "Casually, in a tone of levity, her books told the plain truth about the changing mores of the urban American during a long span of time extending from the 1920s through the 1950s" (19). It well may be that the upheaval of the times contributed to the discomfort that many Powell contemporaries felt as they read—or did not read—her novels.

More recent critics are generally delighted with Powell. Comparisons with Waugh persist: into the 1990s, the New York novels would be compared to his *Decline and Fall* and *Vile Bodies* (Feingold, 13); another recent commentator says, "Think of [Powell] as a homegrown Evelyn Waugh, with an added soupçon of Yankee asperity" (Marcus, 1). Joseph Coates writes, "Rediscovering a good but neglected writer is both exhilarating and depressing. Here is this terrific novelist, Dawn Powell, a contemporary of Hemingway and Fitzgerald and more prolific than the two put together, who has left a whole shelf of funny, entertaining books that few had ever heard of before Vidal" (3).[94] *Library Journal* calls Powell "one of the great American women writers of the twentieth century [who] at her best is better than most, male or female" (60). Novelist, columnist, and art critic Philip Hensher, writing in the *Atlantic Monthly* in 2001, concurs: "Powell is a supremely deserving candidate for admission to the Library of America, a writer of consistent and startling pleasure, cruelty, and ingenuity. Next to her the celebrated wits of the Algonquin look self-conscious and willful, their exercises in pathos whiny and thin . . . Powell belongs on the shelf with the masters of the novel" ("Country," 135). The ballyhoo, once again, had begun.

THE DAWN POWELL REVIVALS

For decades Dawn Powell was always on the verge of ceasing to be a cult and becoming a major religion.

—Gore Vidal, "Dawn Powell, the American Writer," 1[95]

Two or even three Powell "revivals" have taken place in recent decades, the first precipitated by an editorial in the fall 1981 issue of the *Antioch Review*. Editor Robert S. Fogarty had asked several well-known writers to name a forgotten author who should be recommended to readers of the *Review*. Two of the five he questioned, Roger Angell (writer and stepson of E. B.

White) and Gore Vidal, replied simply, "Dawn Powell." In the brief interview that follows, Vidal said that Powell is "as good as Evelyn Waugh and better than Clemens" (400), high praise indeed—and, in fact, maybe praise too high to be easily swallowed.[96] Half a dozen years later, as we have seen, Vidal again lauded the writer, this time in a sustained commentary published in the *New York Review of Books,* which later appeared in the reissue of Powell's final novel, *The Golden Spur.* It is in this seminal essay that Vidal referred to Powell as "our best comic novelist" (L). He went on to say:

> But despite the work of such cultists as Edmund Wilson and Matthew Josephson, John Dos Passos and Ernest Hemingway, Dawn Powell never became the popular writer that she ought to have been.[97] . . . In her lifetime she should have been as widely read as, say, Hemingway or the early Fitzgerald or the mid O'Hara or even the late, far too late, Katherine Anne Porter. (1–2)

James Wolcott tells of busily rescuing long-neglected Powell volumes from dusty shelves and mouse-infested back rooms just before Vidal wrote his essay, Wolcott's aim being to "write a piece that would place Powell in her proper berth" (42). But then the Vidal piece appeared, and Wolcott, not having yet finished amassing his collection, knew that he had been trumped. In 1989 David Streitfeld of the *Washington Post* credited Vidal with almost single-handedly bringing Powell to our notice (before Tim Page came along), saying that, "if there's no Dawn Powell revival soon, you won't be able to blame Gore Vidal. He's done everything except hawk her books on street corners" (X15). The Vidal essay aroused enough interest in Powell that by the early 1990s New York's Yarrow Press had reissued the first of the two Powell novels it would release. Vintage Books, a division of Random House, in 1989 published three works in a Quality Paperback Book Club edition, *Three by Dawn Powell,* introduced by Vidal. He admitted that he felt "incredibly smug" and "proprietary" ("Queen," 17) about these releases. One only wishes that he had written about Powell earlier; if he had, perhaps he would have rescued her all the sooner from her long existence as "a secret handshake among the chosen few" (*Boston Globe,* "Dawn Powell Has Arrived," 3).

Though Powell's reissued novels received fine notices upon their re-release, this first "revival" soon lost steam. According to Philip Hensher, writing in the *Spectator* in 2002, "Many of the best American writers," among whom he includes Dawn Powell, "somehow 'don't count'" ("Groping," 30). And for British reviewer Nick Rennison, the novelist "may well be the best-kept secret in twentieth-century American literature and the one most worth unlocking" (II, 1).

~~~~~~~~~~~~~~~~~~~~~~~~~~~~

By the mid-1990s, the second revival had begun, this time thanks to Tim Page, who has not only sung Powell's praises in many a locale, but who wrote the only published biography of the author, brought out a collection of her well-received diaries, and edited and issued her remarkable letters. Even before all this activity, Page was responsible for the 1994 collection *Dawn Powell at Her Best*, a hardcover volume of two of her novels,[98] several short stories, and an essay, along with a useful introduction. Page, as a newsman, knew that for this first reissue to receive any serious critical attention, it would have to be published in hardcover. The collection received so much favorable notice that at Page's urging Vermont's Steerforth Press later reissued twelve of Powell's novels, a collection of her short stories, and four of her plays, all in paperback editions and all to much critical notice.

Terry Teachout, writing in 1995, summed up this next revival: "Every decade or so, somebody writes an essay about Dawn Powell, and a few hundred more people discover her work, and are grateful. And that's it. Few American novelists have been so lavishly praised by so many high-powered critics to so little effect" ("Far," 3). He added that Powell "remains today what she was a half-century ago: a fine and important writer adored by a handful of lucky readers and ignored by everyone else" (3). "If there is any justice," he continued, "she will soon receive her due" (6).

A few years later, in a 1999 essay entitled "Big Lights, Big City: Dawn Powell and the Glory of Revival," Heather Joslyn found Powell's works noteworthy not only because of their sheer volume but because they were "both of and far ahead of her time." She wrote:

> Her body of novels form a continuing social history of the
> American Century's first half, depicting how restless searchers
> left their flyspeck rural hometowns and flooded into their
> country's big cities, how they reinvented themselves there, and
> how they inevitably re-created the gossipy insularity of the
> villages they'd escaped inside the foreboding concrete canyons
> of their new frontier. ("Bright")

Following the Steerforth reissues, Page saw to it that The Library of America release nine of Powell's novels in two volumes.[99] Lauren Weiner of the *New Criterion,* originally hesitant to believe that another "full-fledged Powell revival [was] in progress," came by 1999 to see "the evidence piling up" and finally to "accept the idea," adding that two of Powell's novels, *A Time to Be Born* and *The Locusts Have No King,* "deserve to be on a short list of the best comic novels in American literature" ("Fruits," 23). In a lengthy 2002 essay praising the novelist, Alice Tufel noted that this second revival "is a dream come true too late" (155).

But the revivals, short-lived or no, have made something of a lasting imprint. Today Powell's reissued books are readily available in bookstores and on online auction sites, though most of the first editions, which once were to be found in used book stacks for as little as a quarter apiece,[100] have now been snatched up by collectors and are being offered at steep prices. Some of Powell's novels may in fact be brought to the movie screen: filmmaker David Mamet is said to have purchased the film rights to two of them (Loper, 4), and award-winning filmmakers Ivy Meeropol and Mark Campbell completed a screenplay of *The Happy Island,* which they were in recent years said to be shopping around ("Ivy").[101] A decade ago Angelica Huston was working on bringing out a film based on a Powell book, and Julia Roberts has been said to have had some interest, but nothing has come of any of it.

To Charles McNulty, it seems that she "has been 'rediscovered' so many times that nearly every age tries to claim Powell as a contemporary" (2), while Michael Rogers calls her "the comeback kid" ("Golden," 160). The *Christian Science Monitor* notes that the "compassionate and sharp-eyed" Powell "keeps turning up on the lists of the underrated" ("Great Reads"); and Erica Jong, who polled "250 or so distinguished writers and critics" to put together a women's fiction list, found Powell ranked in the top 100 (35). The novelist is included in 2002's *Invisible Giants: 50 Americans Who Shaped the Nation but Missed the History Books,* and Terry Teachout's well-received 2004 collection of essays leads off with "Far from Ohio" in her praise.[102] She is sometimes mentioned in the Sunday *New York Times Book Review:* to name a few occasions, in 2005 she appeared in Randy Cohen's article "We'll Map Manhattan" and in its follow-up article a month later. In the same publication, Thomas Mallon in 2008 regretfully referred to Powell and fellow New York writer Helene Hanff[103] as "sharp, gallant characters . . . women clinging to New York literary life, or its fringes, by their talented fingernails" (15). In a 2004 review of a new book—*Boomtown*, by Greg Williams—Chris Lehmann noted that, when Williams makes a certain point about New York City, readers "can almost see Dawn Powell nodding faintly in assent" (C.04), a comment placing Powell in the position of novel-writing authority on New York; another book reviewer called Gloria Emerson, the author of *Loving Graham Greene*, "a delicious cross between Dawn Powell and Martha Gellhorn"[104] (Russo, Review). A Maryland bookstore owner recently told me that late cartoonist and award-winning *American Splendor* screenwriter Harvey Pekar was an ardent Powell fan and collector. An article celebrating the 180th birthday of Ninth Street headlines Powell over all the other artists who have lived there, including such notables as Marianne Moore, Elinor Wylie, S. J. Perelman, Bret Harte, Edna St. Vincent Millay, and many others (Loschiavo, 2). In another recent *New York Times Book Review*, Morris Dickstein called Powell the Village's "wittiest chronicler" (9), while for the *Village Voice*'s Toni Schlesinger, the very words "Greenwich Village" make her "think of Dawn Powell throwing one back" (2). Nick Dennison includes Powell's *A Time to Be Born* in his two-part article, "Reading the City: Old New York." The series, an exploration of novels that bring Manhattan to life, links her works with those of more famous novelists such as Henry James, Edith Wharton, Steven Crane (I, 1–3); and Henry Roth, John Dos Passos, and Damon Runyon (II, 1–5). Ross Wetzsteon devotes a chapter to Powell in his book *Republic of Dreams: Greenwich Village, the American Bohemia*;[105] and Alice Sparberg Alexiou, in her 2006 biography of Jane Jacobs, foe of Robert Moses and noted preservationist of city neighborhoods, includes Dawn Powell as a familiar Village "luminary" (22, and *passim*).

Powell's name frequently turns up even when one is not expecting to find it: for example, perusing the "About Us" link on the Peccadillo Theater Company's website, I stumbled upon this item: "Peccadillo concentrates on the era of the well-made play, a period of sparkling wit and sophistication in comedy as well as deepening realism in the drama. It encompasses such diverse and, sad to say, little-known American playwrights as Sidney Howard, Philip Barry, William Inge, Dawn Powell, and many, many more" (1). True to their word, the Peccadillo Theatre Company in March 2001 produced Powell's 1934 comedy *Jig Saw* under the direction of Dan Wackerman, and a year later New York's Sightlines Theatre Company also staged it. For *Village Voice* theater critic Jessica Winter, the play, this time staged as written, "hardly lacks for whiskey-lubricated one-liners" though it "evokes less the droll chamber music of Powell's contemporary Noel Coward than the cacophony stirred by the recent revival of *The Women*." Powell would detest being compared to Clare Boothe Luce, whom she famously satirized in her 1942 novel *A Time to Be Born*. But these New York productions were not the first revivals of the play: in 2000, Los Angeles Classical Theatre Ensemble Antaeus staged it in a production directed by John Walcutt, and even before that, in 1997, it had been restaged at Long Island University (Parks, 1).

~~~~~~~~~~~~~~~

The Peccadillo also produced *Talk of the Town*, an original musical comedy about the Algonquin group; and *The Ladies of the Corridor*, Dorothy Parker and Arnaud d'Usseau's weepy 1953 drama (McNulty, 2). I ran across the following mention in a review of Broadway's 2004 revival of Ben Hecht and Charles MacArthur's comedy *Twentieth Century:* "Just a footnote: you know, most urban literature of this time—by the likes of John O'Hara, Dawn Powell, F. Scott Fitzgerald and Dorothy Parker—was very, very hip. This play, with its snappy dialogue, modern thoughts about sex and adultery and cynicism about show business, could be set in 2004 instead of 1932 and no one would notice" (R. Friedman, "Anne," 3). It seems as if, in theatre circles at least, Dawn Powell's name had almost become a household word.

Extracts from Powell's diaries appear in 2000's *The Assassin's Cloak: An Anthology of the World's Greatest Diarists*, in Phillip Lopate's *Writing New York*, and in Teresa Carpenter's *New York Diaries, 1609–2009*. Seeing that Carpenter had included so much of Powell in her 2012 book, I wrote her to ask why. She replied,

> I'm sometimes asked to pick my favorite diarists from this
> collection and I usually demur out of a sense of literary courtesy.
> But I'll break ranks with courtesy in this instance to say that
> Dawn Powell is emphatically top-tier. She was a woman who
> knew so much sorrow—alcoholic husband, disabled son,
> personal struggles. . . . Yet in the end it's her extraordinary
> resilience and vitality that make her diary entries so compelling.
> In her personal writings, sorrow is eclipsed by a constant stream
> of ideas for novels and stories all of which sparkle with wit and
> insight into the human condition. Her off-the-cuff vignettes
> of Greenwich Village, which she called her "creative oxygen,"

are more vivid than photos, and her often ruthlessly spot-on portraits of New Yorkers are classics of the genre.

Though Powell has been named one of the "extraordinary diarists of our era" (Levinson, 107), more often of course she is acclaimed for her novels. Lewis M. Dabney, in his biography of Edmund Wilson, placed Powell among the ten novelists who "helped define the literary and intellectual life" of this country in the last century (6). The bookseller Powell's Books, reviewing the Library of America's issues, called her "a rediscovery of rare importance" (2), while the *Library Journal* noted that the collection placed her among our finest writers, where she belongs (Rogers, "Dawn Powell Novels," 160). For *New York Times* critic A. O. Scott, Dawn Powell is "a writer we can no longer imagine ever having forgotten" (B10).

One can imagine her impatient response, "It's about time!"—softened
with a rueful laugh, of course.

—Margaret Carlin, 1[106]

By 2000, Powell's work had begun to appear in a few anthologies and some college course syllabi as well. Not only does Ross Wetzsteon's *Republic of Dreams* include her, but she appears as a character in Vidal's 2000 novel *The Golden Age,* in which the writer describes her as "a round little woman with squirrel-bright eyes" (284). Vidal called her last published work, *The Golden Spur,* one of his five favorite postwar novels ("True Gore," 1–2). A course at the New School, called "Dawn Powell's New York," was offered by Professor Theresa Craig in the fall of 2003 (*New School,* 44); and her work has been included in a course called "Urban Myths and the American City" at Columbia University's Barnard College. Powell friend and emeritus Professor William Peterson of Southampton College, Long Island University, who once taught at the novelist's alma mater, together with Tim Page presented a symposium for the centennial of Powell's birth at Cleveland's Case Western Reserve University in 1996; and in 2006, the sesquicentennial of the founding of Lake Erie College, all freshman arrivals were given copies of *My Home Is Far Away* in celebration of its most famous alumna.

In its premiere performance, Powell's *Women at Four O'Clock,* along with *Jig Saw, Big Night,* and "several dramatic adaptations of Powell's short stories," was staged by Sightlines Theatre Company, at the Seventy-Eighth Street Theatre Lab in New York, from January through March 2002 in a festival named "Permanent Visitor: A Festival Celebrating Dawn Powell in New York." Musical Theatre Works staged an adaptation of Powell's 1942 novel, *A Time to Be Born* (Horwitz, 45), written by Suzanne Myers (*Redeemable*, 1). And *Walking down Broadway*, another Powell drama never before produced, debuted at New York's Mint Theatre in late 2005.

Literary tours of Powell's remaining haunts and residences are conducted from time to time; and her effect on popular American culture has even reached 1980s and 1990s television: *Seinfeld*, the program once thought to be "too New York" by television audiences and producers alike (Boudreaux, 1), may in fact owe something to Ohio-born Powell. At least three episodes closely echo certain incidents in her *Turn, Magic Wheel* (71), *The Happy Island* (121), and *The Golden Spur* (*passim*). The novelist has been linked to other television programming: *Chicago Tribune* writer Mary Schmich calls Powell's New York novel *A Time to Be Born* a forerunner of the HBO series *Sex and the City*[107] (4C.1); and Rory, the erstwhile college student in *Gilmore Girls*, is shown in one episode to be reading Dawn Powell's collected works, thanks to Tim Page. Radio, too, has recently featured Powell: on January 29, 2005, WOSU radio program *Ohio Arts Alive*, of Columbus, Ohio, "paid tribute" to the author in a special broadcast featuring radio host Christopher Purdy, Tim Page, and two of Powell's now-deceased cousins, sister and brother Rita and Jack Sherman. Selections from *The Bride's House, A Time to Be Born, Come Back to Sorrento*, and *Turn, Magic Wheel;* certain *Diaries* entries; and the first act of *Big Night* were read (Purdy, "Christopher," 1). In April 2005, her short story "Can't We Cry a Little," a "humorous look at radio's Golden Age," was read during the eightieth-anniversary tribute to the New York Public Radio station WNYC ("Women with Attitude," 1). The story was read again on September 24, 2006, at New York's Symphony Space and broadcast on National Public Radio Station WBFO, this time in "celebration of the short story" (WBFO, 1–4).

Additionally, discussions about and readings from Powell's novels and plays have in recent years been held in various New York City locales and elsewhere; writers including Susan Minot, Francine Prose, and Melissa Bank have appeared at bookstores such as the Housing Works Used Book Café in Soho to speak about Powell and to read from her novels (Russo, 1). Marian Seldes, Michael Feingold, and Fran Lebowitz have given readings of Powell's works at the Algonquin Hotel, an irony which surely would not be lost on our novelist, who sniffed that that crowd did little more than "spend their lives preventing each other from working" (*Diaries,* 209). America's great stage actress Irene Worth (1916–2002) read from Powell's novels on at least two occasions in New York, once at Joe's Pub in Greenwich Village; Professor William Peterson has since the 1990s presented public lectures on Long Island about the novelist (Finalborgo, 9); and Tim Page has spoken on her at such locales as the Museum of the City of New York, New York University, and in numerous Greenwich Village bookstores. John Strausbaugh's 2013 publication, *The Village: 400 Years of Beats and Bohemians, Radicals and Rogues,* mentions Powell throughout.

Today, interest in Powell is climbing again. In 2010 the ReGroup Theatre Company helmed by Allie Mulholland staged a reading of *Big Night* at St. Luke's Theatre in New York and presented a talk on her work and that of other Group playwrights at Symphony Space in 2011; in November and December 2012, they produced the comedy off-Broadway, also in Powell's original version. *Jig Saw* was recently restaged at the Riverside Arts Center in Ypsilanti, Michigan, in December 2013, by Nan Bauer; Tim Page and Carol Warstler were on hand to introduce the play. Page remarked that ""Dawn Powell's fizzy, dizzy *Jig-Saw* comes to brilliant and exhilarating life in [this] production!" In late 2012 Page offered her original diaries for sale, prompting much attention in such publications as the *New York Times* and the *New Yorker* and in social media sites. A short while later Columbia University purchased the volumes, to much media notice, including a piece by John Williams in the *New York Times* which stated, quite rightfully, that "Page has done more than anyone [else] to champion her work." Powell was featured in a 2011 discussion of Group Theatre playwrights at New York City's Symphony Space; her friend and portraitist, Peggy Bacon, was in 2012 featured in an art exhibit at the Smithsonian in Washington, DC; and her novel *A Time to Be Born* was not only chosen that same year as a selection of the *New York Times'* "Big City Book Club" but a few months later named by literary blogger Nathaniel Rich as one of the finest novels of World War II; he stated that "it doesn't have a single gun" in it yet it "captures the viciousness and madness of the homefront." Contemporary writer Whitney Otto, perhaps most famous for her novel and the film adaptation of *How to Make an American Quilt,* told me in a 2013 e-mail that her 2002 novel *A Collection of Beauties at the Height of Their Popularity* had been partially influenced by *The Wicked Pavilion* and that she did not fail to speak of the Powell novel while on publicity tours. Her 2012 book, *Eight Girls*

Taking Pictures, similarly contains a sly nod to Powell (289), who also receives much attention in *Playing Smart: New York Women Writers and Modern Magazine Culture,* Catherine Keyser's 2011 publication. Historian John Joseph delivered a well-attended speech on Powell on December 11, 2014, entitled "Dawn Powell: An Often Overlooked Literary Great," under the auspices of the Greenwich Village Society for Historic Preservation. Most prominently, perhaps, on June 2, 2015, Powell was presented a prestigious award from Rocco Staino and the Empire State Center for the Book. In October of the same year, David Earle, amasser of Powell's earliest short publications, wrote "Dawn Powell, Flapper Stories, and the Pulps"; and Terry Teachout published an essay, "Little Miss Wolfsbane," on October 13, 2015, in response to David Pomerantz's, Robert Nedelkoff's, and Tim Page's Facebook announcement that a previously unknown recording of Powell's voice on a radio show of October 9, 1939, had surfaced. In April 2016, R. Scott Evans, Senior Vice President of Lake Erie College's Institutional Advancement and Chief of the President's Staff, along with Lake Erie College English professors Jennifer Swartz-Levine and Adam Stier, hosted a celebration of Dawn Powell scholarship at her alma mater at which Marcy Smith and I spoke. The activity continues.

Yet despite all this praise, despite all this activity, I have still encountered few readers who have heard of Dawn Powell. Perhaps this work will help to shine a little more of the spotlight squarely on Powell; perhaps it will help bring her out of the "perpetual dusk" in which she has too long languished (Wolcott, 42). For novelist Lorrie Moore, it seems not at all unusual that yet another revival might be required for the author to receive her due, for "during [Powell's] own lifetime, her struggling though productive career seems to have been in constant semi-revival" (1). As we have noted, some activity around Powell is beginning again. Perhaps now the time is finally ripe for Dawn Powell.

CHAPTER THREE

"Every Artist Writes His Own Autobiography"

The Diaries, Letters, Short Stories, and Criticism

As for New York City, it's the only place where people with nothing behind them but their wits can be and do everything.

—*Letters*, 75–76[1]

Because all of Powell's novels are to some extent autobiographical, those studying her would do well to acquaint themselves with the biography as they approach her fiction. For that reason, among others, it is fortunate that she left us the great many letters and diaries she did, for they help to inform our understanding of what she was attempting to accomplish in each novel, assist us in measuring what she thought she had achieved against what critics then and now believe she did in fact achieve, and shed light on the ways in which certain autobiographical events as they appear in letter or diary are transformed into fiction. Edited by Tim Page, both diary and letter collections have met with praise: Gerald Howard, an editor at Doubleday, calls *The Diaries of Dawn Powell, 1931–1965* "one of the finest interior portraits of the novelist's art and temper in our literature" (10); and of the *Selected Letters of Dawn Powell, 1913–1965,* novelist Lorrie Moore says, "So current and alive is Powell's epistolary voice, even in the earliest letters, that one is tempted to suggest that what we think of as the contemporary American voice—in journalism and the arts—is none other than hers: ironic, triumphant, mocking and game; the voice of a smart, chipper, small-town Ohio girl newly settled in New York" (2). As soon as Powell arrived, she cheerfully settled in. A 1931 letter from her to her cousin Jack Sherman praises the city breathlessly (*Letters*, 75): for the writer, it was a place where anything was possible, where humble beginnings did not matter, where a young poverty-stricken nobody from a tiny midwestern town had every opportunity to make her dreams come true.[2]

The Diaries, according to critic Bill Buford, revealed that "Powell had a brilliant mind and a keen wit, and [that] her humor was never at a finer pitch than in her diaries. And yet her story is a poignant one—a son emotionally and mentally impaired, a household of too much alcohol and never enough money, and an artistic career that, if not a failure, fell far short of the success she craved. All is recorded here—along with working sketches for her novels, and often revealing portraits of her many friends (a literary who's who of her period)—in her always unique style and without self-delusion." This evaluation of Powell's diaries, in so few words, is as spot-on an assessment of this edition of her diaries as any to date.

With the publication of Tim Page's biography of Powell, and with all of her best works now back in print, it would appear that Dawn Powell has clearly "arrived" and taken her deserved place in American letters. Her remarkable *Diaries* will stand as one of her finest literary achievements; indeed, they are among the finest achievements of the genre.

Of course, Tim Page's *Dawn Powell: A Biography* also assists readers in this undertaking. Praised as "meticulously researched, well written, and sympathetic," the biography does "a superb job of establishing [Powell's] right to an honored place in the pantheon of American letters" (Bing, 61). Today's readers and students of the author are fortunate to have these three sources available to them. They have proven indispensable in providing a window into the working mind of the author.

THE DIARIES OF DAWN POWELL, 1931–1965

The thrills of a writer's diary

—Susan Salter Reynolds, 10

If it is true, as A. A. Milne said in 1919, that diaries are "so rarely kept nowadays" because "nothing ever happens to anybody" (A. Taylor, ix), it would follow that because so much *did* happen to Dawn Powell, she had little choice but to record it all. Or perhaps she kept a diary because, as the narrator of 1962's *The Golden Spur* says, people "who have no one they trust to understand them" keep journals (94). Her own diaries, which are "poignant, sometimes devastating, in tone" (Lopate, *Writing*, 538), read like a *Who's Who* of the theater, art, and literary worlds: famous names from Stella Adler to Thomas Wolfe appear and reappear, yet the diaries are much more than calculated jottings meant to impress or amaze. Diary anthologist Alan Taylor maintains that "the best diaries are those in which the voice of the individual comes through untainted by self-censorship or a desire to please" (ix), just as the voice does here. The *Village Voice* remarks that "the brilliant" diarist Powell never "samples the consolations of dishonesty—a true miracle" ("Our 25," SS23). The diaries not only record her many encounters with the rich and famous but also register the ordinary, the mundane, the frightening, the embarrassing, the devastating—everything, it seems, but her intimate life. Family matters, personal worries, money troubles, childcare woes, drunken brawls, health problems are given as much if not more attention here as are weekends with Libby Holman (182), parties with Lillian Hellman (355), or dinners with Langston Hughes (445). At their best, the diaries delight with witty character vignettes, overheard conversations, intuitive observations. The frightful, the comic, and the tragic all mingle among the pages. As Terry Teachout says, "there is much heartbreak in these diaries, and more mirth" ("Far," 5). A disturbing entry of 1933 reads

> The shock of my life today. This little tiny constant pain in my heart, the X-ray and Dr. Witt says, is a tumor or cyst over it and between the lungs. Nothing to worry about, he says, just a question of waiting. And waiting for what? . . . Nothing to worry about! . . . I walked down Madison Avenue not looking in shops for the first time because I thought it extravagant to buy or even want things for so short a while. It doesn't matter what the corpse wears. (69)

If the entry sounds self-pitying, the next one, four days later, says simply, "Finished play 'Jig-Saw'" (69). Powell had taken no time off to lament: despite the terrifying news, the disciplined writer continued working. A few pages later, readers are treated to a taste of something quite different, one of countless examples of the "mirth" Teachout mentions:

> To dinner at Catalan's[3] with Sue[4] and Esther[5]—down under
> Brooklyn Bridge. Lots of fun with some men eager to be gay.
> One told me he ran a column. "Where? I'll read it," I said.
> "Don't be silly, Baby, you never read a word in your life," he
> said. In fact by his comments I judged I looked more a fine lay
> than an intelligentsia. He said to Sue, "You're a waitress, aren't
> you, sister?" and since anybody would rather look like a tart
> than a waitress Sue was secretly mad at me.[6] (76–77)

Powell moves from one entry to the next with ease, one day wretched, the next joyous, sometimes a combination of the two, much as she moved from the tragedy of her own life to working on yet another comic piece. Richard Selzer, reviewing the *Diaries* in the *Wilson Quarterly*, praises her "intuition for the relationship between tragedy and folly" (77), as readers see in the following passage. Writing of an overly talkative woman whom she has just met at a cocktail party, Powell at first wishes "to escape the incessant bombardment of her chatter" (114), then softens at hearing of the woman's insane son:

> People were very gay. It was odd for two women in the middle
> of this confusion, sandwiches and martinis politely being passed
> . . . to find that strange bond in common—a 14-year-old only
> son—one 20 years ago and the other now—quivering on the
> brink of a nightmare future. I understood then her incessant gay
> chatter—for 20 years she had sparkled and chattered to drown
> the roar of her own tragedy, a little boy raving mad. (115)

The *Diaries*, widely varied in subject matter, mood, and tone as they are, provide a living, colorful portrait of Manhattan and its inhabitants, all its delightful multiplicity mirrored in the reach of the prose. That Powell could so easily in the space of a day or two move from paralyzing dread—"Fear is such an utterly disrupting force—fears of no publisher, fear of cringing once more before debtors, fear of being trapped in the Middle West again and dependent on relatives" (100) to the ludicrous: "At Lafayette, Berkeley Tobey,[7] [age] 50, begged us to drink to Eloise, his very young wife, who is at last to have a baby. 'Whose?,' we all wondered, as we drank reverently" (100)—is remarkable and at the same time understandable. For Powell, as she said many times in her journals, "the oxygen of humor" (456) was the only thing that made life bearable.

Powell herself ruminated on the habit of diary writing in an entry of February 5, 1954:

> Virginia Woolf's diary. People keep diaries because they don't enjoy exposing themselves in conversation and furthermore they trust no one to understand. As soon as a writer finds a group that does understand him he stops writing and starts hamming. In diaries, revealing the innermost soul, the entries stop when anything interesting happens or whenever the writer is happy. Diaries tell nothing—chips from a heroic statue. (335)

But Powell's diaries reveal more than she knew, or more than she was prepared to say, as readers clearly see.

A brief, unsigned *New Yorker* review of the *Diaries* sums the volume up nicely:

> Socialist theatre, all-night parties, advice-dispensing taxi drivers, perfume girls at Bergdorf's: as a diarist, Powell was an urban magpie, and a little bit of everything ended up in her journals. They are also brimming with agonizings, professional and domestic, and razor-sharp remarks ("Lou feels that a cold wife who has a headache is a pure one, a high-class one.") But, as much as anything, these diaries read like a love letter to the city itself. (120)

Yet for all their entertainment value, the diaries provide a view into the mind of the writer, concerned as they are with depicting "the lonely struggle of an artist driven to create" (Begley, 7). The *Village Voice* calls Powell's *Diaries* not its favorite book of journal entries but its "favorite book about books" ("Our 25," SS23). Still, not everyone praised them: the composer and diarist Ned Rorem, in an 1999 interview called "The Art of the Diary No. 1," was asked whether he admired Powell's diaries, which were located in plain view on his bookshelf. Rorem answered, "There are certain things I can't get the point of. Bagels, for instance. Why do people like them? I can't get the point of Berlioz. I can dislike a composer, while admitting what others see in him or her. But not Berlioz. Likewise Dawn Powell" (McClatchy).

Most other commentators disagree, among them Teachout, who says that, from the very first entry, the diaries are not only a pleasure to read but are in fact "a writer's notebook, concerned less with earthshaking events and true confessions than with the raw material of what later became her novels" ("Far," 4). And so I turn to them here, not only to be entertained, not only to learn about the life, personality, friends, and associates of the woman who wrote them, but to learn something about Powell's creative process. The diaries, "an engrossing if painful account of a writer's life" (S. Keen, 25), allow readers to observe the author as she plots and strategizes, includes and discards, works and reworks, writes and rewrites. For example, as Powell begins thinking about *Turn, Magic Wheel,* readers of the diaries can clearly see her thoughtful plotting of the novel, her testing out of the many scenes and sketches that she may or may not some day include in this book or the next, and events from her life that she later will transform into fiction.[8]

In "A Diamond to Cut New York," a 1995 *New Yorker* article attributed to the long-deceased Powell, the unnamed columnist describes the included diary selections, which were chosen by Tim Page, as "vignettes of the bohemian low life and the literary high life, and evidence of how one woman managed to fit an entire city into her classic social satires" (104). Reading the diaries, one is able to see the ways in which the city both shapes the novels and informs them. The vibrant Manhattan becomes a character in her best New York novels and in her diaries as well.

Powell's journals may aptly be termed "A Writer's Diary," as Leonard Woolf titled Virginia Woolf's private writings, for "that's exactly what Powell's diary is, a workshop, where the author is practicing her chops" (Dyer, "After Dawn," 3).[9] Indeed, Powell's diaries are of much value in their own right, certainly not only for shedding light on her fiction but as a fine example of the genre: Phillip Lopate, who includes entries from Powell's diaries in his anthology *Writing New York,* finds her an exceptional diarist (xx), while Page in his introduction cites their "extraordinary value as autobiography, literature, social history, and psychological study" (ix). Like any good diary collection, this one offers not only scholars but general readers valuable insight into Powell's life and craft.

SELECTED LETTERS OF DAWN POWELL, 1913–1965

The letters of Dawn Powell are brave, funny, and smart as hell. You'll wish you could write her back.

—John Waters[10]

The *Selected Letters of Dawn Powell, 1913–1965,* which Tim Page in his introduction calls "the record of a courageous, dramatic, and productive life" (ix), assists my examination of the novels, and particularly my examination of 1925's *Whither*, in part because there are no diaries of that early period to turn to. The adult Powell did not begin keeping a proper diary until January 1, 1931. Before that time, beginning sometime in the same year the first novel was published, she had begun keeping "diaries of sorts," though they were "little more than appointment books, with terse commentary thrown in here and there" (*Diaries*, 4). So if diaries are lacking for a given period, we happily have this collection of "epistolary wit" (*Newsday*), which is full of delightful, often lengthy accounts of her impressions of the city and its inhabitants along with the author's hopes, dreams, observations, adventures, encounters. The letters, spanning forty-two years—1913 through 1965—cover eighteen years more than the diaries do, though they lack the emotional range of the diaries.[11] In addressing her correspondents, Powell most often left her blacker moments unremarked. Lorrie Moore finds the "lightheartedness" Powell brings to her letters, in spite of her serious personal woes, "the utmost generosity" (2). Powell did not wish to burden her friends, acquaintances, or family members with her most serious difficulties. Indeed, Richard Bernstein writes that "one of the strongest elements of these letters . . . is their steadily cheery tone, the absence of references to domestic travails" (1), while Page explains, "If Powell's diaries reflect the emotional turmoil that was such a large part of her psychological makeup, her letters tend to show the witty persona she constructed as a shield" (*Letters*, ix–x). Though she expressed her darkest troubles in her diaries, "throughout [the letters], she tends to put a comical gloss on her tribulations, with the tears of things peeking out through the cracks" (Bernstein, 1). The humorist in Powell would never allow her to sound gloomy for long: as the reviewer for the *New Yorker* observes, the letters' "darkest moments are almost reflexively transformed by her supple wit" (137), so much so that that the volume reads as "a glorious and supremely funny record of her long struggles and . . . lasting triumphs" (Marcus, 1). Powell preferred to present a happy face to the world, much like the characters in *Angels on Toast*, who, she writes, put up a "jovial, openhanded, wisecracking front that is so seldom let down that they themselves aren't sure what's under it" (*Letters*, 110). Though she knew exactly what remained hidden underneath the front she had created for herself, she was determined not to allow others to see it.

The *Letters*, like the *Diaries*, have been well received, Lorrie Moore regretting the lateness of their release: "One cannot help believing that if

[Powell] had been male and Ivy League educated, her career would never have fallen into disarray—not with 15 novels—and we would have had these letters years ago" (3). An anonymous reviewer in *Publishers Weekly* calls the letters

> A posthumous triumph . . . in many ways the perfect record of a difficult life lived with pluck, intelligence and verve. . . . [They] record a sense of humor, a political acuity and a down-to-earth genius for friendship, love and getting by that is nothing less than invigorating. The great flaw of this volume is that there isn't more of it. . . . What letters we have may win Powell even deeper admiration than *The Diaries of Dawn Powell.* (1)

Like many of the diary entries, some of the letters have been printed elsewhere: a letter Powell wrote to John Dos Passos describing Gerald Murphy's funeral, for example, appears in Linda Patterson Miller's *Letters from the Lost Generation* (341), but not in the *Selected Letters of Dawn Powell.* Howard Mansfield, editor of the 2006 volume *Where the Mountain Stands Alone: Stories of Place in the Monadnock Region,* includes excerpts from a 1949 letter that a peevish but funny Powell wrote to Joe from New Hampshire's MacDowell Colony. Originally published in Page's *Selected Letters,* it appears in Mansfield's collection under the title "And Not So Well for Others" (285), as Powell considered life in the artists' colony too rigid for "so lax a person as myself" (286).

Unfortunately for readers approaching the fiction, few letters mention *Whither,* the first novel, at all; none shows her working at it or plotting it. Nonetheless, small episodes or character sketches first seen in the letters will emerge in a later novel or play, some in fact in *Whither.* One incident recorded in a letter of 1918 appears several years later in her first novel. Just two months arrived in New York, Powell wrote to her college friend Charlotte Johnson:

> [A man] asked where we were on the subway and because I smiled back he grabbed my arm and told me he had just inherited half a million dollars from an uncle down in the Honduras and it was his guardian, the vice consul for the Honduras, that he was now on his way to. He was so handsome! And so young! And so—gee! He came to see me twice, then his boat left for the South and I know I'll never see him again. (33)

In *Whither,* a friend of main character Zoe meets just such a young man, at a soda fountain instead of in the subway, but the story is the same. Also, in *Whither,* some elements of the main character's voice and tone are not unlike the very young Powell's.

Another passage from the same letter appeared half a dozen years later in the writer's 1931 play *Walking down Broadway.* It seems that Powell either had an uncanny memory—a gift she furnishes alter ego Marcia with in the autobiographical *My Home is Far Away*—or that she kept copies of the letters she sent. The following episode recounted in the letter reads much as it does in the play:

> It makes me dizzy to think of all the warm friendships and Passionate Affairs I've been through in three months.[12] . . . And all the men say "I love you" and look at you with long wistful "I-surely-am-hit-now" gaze and you kiss them and say this is the first time I've ever cared like this and then you never see each other again. (33)

Several additional passages in the letters will turn up in the later novels as well, all of them providing a glimpse into Powell's personal life, her skills at observation, her disciplined writing habits. The keen sense of humor for which the author is known surfaces in the letters again and again also. For example, on hearing the news of her grandmother Julia Sherman's recent marriage, young Dawn writes from college, "You can imagine how surprised I was just now to learn from Auntie May's letter that I had a Grandpa born all of a sudden. In fact I had to sit down and be fanned. But of course I am very glad, since my grandparents are rather scarce—your being the only one up until the fatal hour Wednesday" (7).

Years later, in a hilarious letter to Dos Passos, Powell wrote:

> . . . We have been boycotting [the Brevoort] all summer but it is very expensive. It began one day when a few friends on the terrazzo started going to the Gents' room through the window instead of the formal door and the waiter and the papa-waiter refused all drinks so we boycotted it and went to the Lafayette. The next day, as we were sitting on the terrace, boycotting again, a big man wheeled a little baby past and Coby Gilman said, "Why, what a cunning little son of a bitch." So the big man shook his perambulator at us and said, "If you wait till I

get this little bastard home I'll settle with you for calling my child a son of a bitch," at which he wheeled it stormily up the street shaking his fist at the same time while the little snort screamed and dangled by its snaps. (88)

The letter continues in this vein for some time, ending only once Powell, having related one ludicrous mishap after another, writes, "This is all the fault of the Brevoort. So we are organizing boycotters all over the world—we have even a group who are boycotting the Brevoort from the Australian bush" (88–89). As in the *Diaries,* the bright portraits, sharp humor, drunken incidents recorded here add up not only to rich material for the novels but also to agreeable diversions for the reader of Powell's delightful *Selected Letters.*

~~~~~~~~~~~~~~~~~~~~~~~~~

A decade after this volume was published, a half dozen letters and other items from Powell to Gilman appeared in a Literary Miscellany at the William Reese Company in New Haven, Connecticut. This find is a major one, given that Page notes in his introduction to the *Selected Letters* his disappointment that "only a scant four letters to Coburn Gilman seem to have survived, though he was one of Powell's closest confidants for many years" (xi). The letters sold for amounts ranging from $600 to $4,000 each; a first-edition Hemingway novel, inscribed "somewhat drunkenly" to Powell ("to Dawn, from where all the characters in this book are drawn— Ernest Hemingway"), sold for $1,500.00; and an "unpublished, illustrated manuscript," called "The Teen Age / Murder Book / by Aunt Bossy Powell / For Children Between 5 and 7:15 / Quiet Please," went for $7,500. The letters from Powell to Gilman are tantalizingly described: I reproduce a partial description of one of the letters here, given that the Powell/Gilman relationship is of interest to many:

> 382. Powell, Dawn. Autograph Letter, Signed. New York / Dated only "Monday." Ca. 1930.
> A high-pitched, possibly somewhat inebriated personal letter from Powell to one of her favorite drinking buddies of the time, and eventually, for much of her remaining life, one of her closest intimate friends, "Dearest Coby . . . signed "Love, Dawn."[13]

Thanks to Tim Page, I now have copies of those letters in their entirety and intend to reproduce them fully at a later date.

SHORT STORIES, ESSAYS, AND REVIEWS

Talk about ambition, story ideas, etc.—you do a lot better
when you're among people you know.

—*Letters*, 39

Page notes in his biography, "Although Powell wrote well over a hundred short stories during her lifetime, only a few dozen have been identified to date" (338). Aided by Internet resources unavailable when Page began conducting research for his biography, I have located about a dozen more published short pieces that to my knowledge have never been republished. Powell contributed short fiction frequently to the *New Yorker*, particularly in the 1930s: one such un-republished story, "Bon Voyage," came out in April 1933; it was written with recognizable Powell humor. A spring allergy sufferer, unable to sleep,

> experimented desperately with all manner of sleep-inducers. She counted sheep but always stopped at five, since it was ridiculous to suppose that in these times anyone could afford more than five sheep. She might as well stop at one, and even then she realized perfectly that it wasn't a real sheep but two men fixed up to look that way (17).

Another un-republished *New Yorker* item I located, "The Daisy Chain," appeared in September that same year. In it Powell demonstrates her satiric sensibility and again jabs at snobbish consumerism and at the all-knowing young New York career girl:

> Finally they decided on 146, since Elinor could have her shrimps there, and Violet could be seen in a suitably expensive light by her newest client, a Mr. Bule, and what [newcomer] Sarah preferred didn't matter anyway. In the taxi, the two business-women examined Sarah rather critically, and Violet suggested a darker lipstick and tying those ribbons on the left shoulder rather than right in front.
> "Look, Honey," commanded Elinor, taking both hands to yank Sarah's hat around, "this is the way to wear that hat" (19).

Powell would go on to publish at least five other short pieces for the magazine, four in 1933: the above-mentioned three and "Blue Hyacinths." (We cannot be certain, as she sometimes published under pseudonyms.) Other *New Yorker* stories include "Artist's Life" (1935), which in its tension between observer and observed seems something of a precursor to her novel *Turn, Magic Wheel*; "Can't We Cry a Little"; and "The Comeback"; they and "Blue Hyacinths" would be reissued in the collection of short stories selected by Powell herself, 1952's *Sunday, Monday and Always*. "Such a Pretty Day" would be republished there and in two other compilations: *Short Stories from the New Yorker: A Collection of Sixty-Eight Notable Stories*, in 1940; and in Tim Page's 1994 collection, *Dawn Powell at Her Best*.

Earlier, in the 1920s, Powell was publishing short stories in *Munsey's Magazine*, three of which I have located: "The Little Green Model" (February 1924); "Precious" (January 1928), and "Orchids for Rosanie" (March 1928). Powell sounded upbeat in a 1922 letter to Aunt Orpha May about having had a story accepted by the magazine, but by November 1928 she was complaining to her aunt that "like a fool I'd been signing something with *Munsey's* from time to time which gave them all rights" (68). After publishing two final pieces in *Munsey's* in 1928, she ended her involvement with that periodical. She added in the same letter to her aunt, "I wouldn't even have a word to say if they sold it to the movies. The best magazines don't do that but *Munsey's*, it seems, gets away with whatever it can" (68).

I have also turned up several other short stories, essays, and reviews that before now had not been identified, among them the short story "Elegy," published in *transition* 8 in November 1927 by Paris's Shakespeare and Co. The periodical has been called

> the most important of all the "little magazines" that popularized the expatriate community's works. This issue, like most of them, reads like a "Who's Who" in its table of contents, featuring among others James Joyce ("Continuation of a Work in Progress"—later published as "Finnegans Wake"), Dawn Powell ("Elegy"), William Carlos Williams, Gertrude Stein, and poems by Andre Gide, Alfred Kreymborg and others. (*transition*)

Notably, Powell's name appears second only to Joyce's.

I found the politically left "Dynamite in the Office," which was issued in *Coronet* in 1938; "Enter Two Girls, Laughing" published in *Harper's Bazaar* in January 1939; "I'm Glad She's Happy" in a 1939 *Redbook*; a piece in the *Partisan Review* called "Radio's Gift to Art," reviewing *Fourteen Radio Plays* by Art Oboler; a book review in a 1945 issue of *Tomorrow* called "Two Historical Novels," about *Young Bess* by Margaret Irwin and *The Violent Friends* by Winston Clewes; another review, called "Mary Petty Presents," in a 1946 issue of the *Nation;* an essay, "Speaking of the Younger Generation," in *Harper's Bazaar* in August 1949 (discussed later in this chapter); and a hilarious story, "The Nefarious Triangle," which appeared in *Today's Woman* in November that same year. In July 1950, an issue of *Flair* included a short essay by Powell called "Vision of Don Juan," published nowhere else, to my knowledge. Of the piece, Cowles says Powell "began by looking homeward to the first self-styled ladies' man she ever encountered, [and] brought him up to date through some of the latter-day variations she observes from her downtown New York vantage point." The first sentence is unmistakably Powell: "I first saw Don Juan sitting in a boardinghouse parlor of Shelby Junction, and he was sitting as close to me as you are" (24).

Other finds are a curious little story featuring a bar, a lobster, and a lion called "A Greenwich Village Christmas Idyll" in the *Chicago Tribune* in 1963; and the seriocomic "Weekend in Town," printed in the *Saturday Evening Post* in the year before her death. That story features two young women, roommates who get along well because "they wore different size clothes," again in a line reminiscent of *Whither,* written nearly four decades earlier. The girls in the story had "good jobs and a really charming apartment overlooking a garden on West Twelfth Street. It was fixed up like a decorator's dream with 'gravy'—the latest in sample fabrics . . . and the newest in gadgets" (58). Consumerism was rarely far from Powell's mind.

Recently, an online resource called "The FictionMags Index," edited by William G. Contento, posted a list of Powell stories it had located. David Earle, of the University of West Florida, has "found just about all of [her] pre-1930 stories from various pulp magazines—it amounts to 15 or so stories, all pretty wonderful and very flapperish" (Earle, personal e-mail) Professor Earle kindly sent me copies of two: one, published in *Breezy Stories* in 1921, called "And When She Was Bad—" and the other, "Not the Marrying Kind," about which a cryptic Powell diary notation, dated April 6, 1925, reads: "Letter about 'The Marrying Kind' saying 'This Dawn Powell writes so attractively I hate to return her story.' He did" (*Diaries,* 5). It is unclear who the "he" was.

But still, decades after the biography appeared, many if not most of her short works remain elusive; though scattered mentions of these pieces appear throughout her letters and diaries, they are often mentioned in passing, without date or name of publication, making them all but impossible to trace.

POWELL ON SATIRE

The enjoyment of satire is that of nine-pins—seeing the ball strike truly and the pins go down.

—Diaries, 75

Writing the truth, for Dawn Powell, was always most important. She wrote that "truth seems to me the most beautiful form of art in the world" (*Diaries*, 154), and the best means of telling the truth, for Powell, was satire. Powell's habit of telling the truth in her comedies earned her the charges of cynicism she too often heard from her critics (see chapter 1). Of course her satires were sharply funny, too. As Amanda Vaill says, "Powell's gift" was "not to repress, not to transcend, but to tell the truth and then to laugh, however ruefully" ("Laughing," X06). As the novelist said over and over again, the truth was what she was always after. Today, many critical commentators understand that point: "Readers are first attracted to Powell's books because they are funny," Richard Dyer writes, but "later they realize that they are funny because they are true" ("After Dawn," 37).

Seeking to explain in her diary the difference between satire and romanticism, Powell wrote simply, "A man endows a hospital in a small town; actually his *motive* is political and social advancement in the town. His *vision* is helping his fellow men in their suffering. Emphasis on the one is satire, on the other romance; both are true and truer than the middle course of 'realism'" (118). Not much later, in a 1940 *New York Times* interview with the author, Robert Van Gelder sought to assist Powell as she attempted to explain her writings up through *Angels on Toast*. Introducing the New York cycle, Van Gelder wrote, "They are very witty satires that, perhaps unfortunately, satirize those people who, to the bulk of the public, must seem the stuff that dreams are made of—fashionable chanteuses, radio big names, advertising contact men, successful commercial artists, popular playwrights, mistresses who have attained Park Avenue addresses" ("Some Difficulties," 102). For Van Gelder, and for many others as well, Powell too often breaks hearts, shatters dreams, crushes expectations. Fully aware of the charge, Powell explained, as Van Gelder notes,

> The way of the satirist is made difficult by the fact that "you both confuse and anger people if you satirize the middle class. It is considered jolly and good-humored to point out the oddities of the poor or of the rich. The frailties of millionaires or garbage collectors can be made to seem amusing to persons who are not millionaires or garbage collectors. Their ways of speech, their personal habits, the peculiarities of their thinking are considered fair game. I go outside the rules with my stuff because I can't help believing that the middle class is funny, too." ("Some Difficulties," 102)

Though Powell sometimes satirized the very wealthy, as she did in *Turn, Magic Wheel*, for example, more often it was the commonplace advertising man or the young secretary on the make who captured her interest and at whom she pointed her pen. Powell more often than not chose to focus on the regular folks she saw about town.

In her journal of the same year she repeated dictums she had heard over and over again:

> The rules for satire as laid down by reviewers are purely materialistic. Let no mockery interfere with the budget! Flay with "good-natured fun" the antics of the poor or the rich, but never say the pleasures of the middle class are a little ridiculous, too. The middle class comes in large families, and if you must record them, say they are earnest; say they eat simple apple pies and honest roast turkeys; say they till the soil, quibble over wills, snub new neighbors, juggle their accounts, cheat their partners (through family necessity), disown sons for unsavory marriages—but show that these vices are necessary, and are accompanied by worry, harassment and groans, never by laughter. Say that these sins (if sins they be, since they are at least *solemn* sins) are done with dignity, unlike the sins of the rich or the very poor. (*Diaries*, 180)

Like her artist friend Reginald Marsh, she most often preferred portraying the "not glamorous or affluent New Yorkers, but those of the lower and middle and lower classes. It was the Bowery bums, burlesque queens, Coney Island musclemen, park denizens, subway riders, and post-flapper-era sirens" (B. Haskell, 6) who captured both her imagination and Marsh's. These people were her focus, her family, the people about whom she cared and whom she understood. Marsh and Powell were well acquainted with each other and with each other's most frequent subjects: in fact, Marsh would illustrate the cover of Powell's 1948 novel, *The Locusts Have No King*.

> It is through her "wonderfully incisive satire"
> that her portraits always convince.
>
> —Tom Sellar

As much as the author longed for more positive commentary, she nevertheless refused to bow to the wishes of her reviewers or the public and sought instead always to refrain from romanticizing her characters or their motivations. As always, Powell would "draw her people with accuracy and honesty, refusing to assign to them noble intentions when they have none" (Sexton, 7). Because writing satire and telling the truth were so closely related for Powell, and because the author fancied herself nothing if not a satirist, writing what she knew was so important to her that she would always base her novels on some sort of autobiographical reality. In 1935, while writing *Turn, Magic Wheel*, she confided in her diary, "Since I can write so fluidly and with such pleasure about real people . . . it seems increasingly an effort to step from this reality into a storybook world. On the other hand, I hate to use real people and hurt them but I have reached the point where I must sacrifice my tender feelings for reality. It's a decision against personal life for the crueler pleasures of artistic exactness" (98–99). Readers will see the same ambivalence at work in *Turn, Magic Wheel*, where Powell-like novelist Dennis Orphen sometimes regrets having cruelly exposed friend Effie Callingham, but in the end both authors' decisions to write the truth wins out.

Powell, understandably, chose to write about subject matter that spoke to her. For example, she often referred to Balzac as one of her favorite novelists, and comparisons with Balzac surfaced in commentaries by Warfel (345) and others, including Gore Vidal (see chapter 1, above) and Glenway Wescott (*Diaries*, 285). Powell's Ohio works tell the tale of provincials at home, often longing to escape; and her New York cycle features similar provincials having made their escape and working to make it in New York. All of her New York novels feature outsiders like Powell herself—those who have come to the city from small-town midwestern locations, full of impossible dreams. Her most interesting characters are those who strive but never do make it: the losers, the graspers, the drinkers, the misfits, the homeless, the heartbroken, the nameless souls who wander the city carrying crumbling suitcases and broken dreams. Powell's "heartaches of the street" (Broyard, 33), wretched as they often are, nevertheless remain hopeful, clinging to their dreams despite long odds. Understanding and sympathizing with her characters as she does, they always ring true.

Satire was her mode, and satire, Powell wrote again and again, was a recounting of the truth. She realized that her favorite literary technique was also her most effective weapon for exposing folly and vice; she maintained in her diaries that "the lashing of . . . evil can only be done by satire" (*Diaries*, 213). She prided herself in being, so far as she knew, "the only person" in the early 1940s who was "doing contemporary social satire" (213). For example, the novelist felt a certain satisfaction in having roundly "slashed" Clare Boothe Luce in her recent book, *A Time to Be Born*, for she felt that such wickedness as Luce had later executed in her smearing of Henry Wallace (*Diaries*, 213n), U.S. vice president under Franklin Roosevelt, must at all costs be exposed. Though the incident occurred after her novel came out, the fact that Powell had ridiculed Luce in her book made her believe that at least her satire had damaged Luce's credibility.

But Powell was generally not a political writer. More often her satire was reminiscent of the comedies of manners of previous centuries, though hers were stingingly contemporary. In her diary she contemplated the fact that, in "modern writing," too many authors "avoid [writing of] contemporary manners":

> In the last century, Thackeray, Dickens, Edith Wharton, James, all wrote of their own times, [so] we have reliable records. Now we have only the escapists, who write of happenings a hundred or three hundred years ago, false to history, false to human nature. Among contemporary writers, only John O'Hara writes of one very small section of 52nd Street or Broadway. We have Hemingway, who writes of a fictional movie hero in Spain with the language neither Spanish nor English. When someone

wishes to write of this age—as I do and have done—critics shy
off—the public shies off. (188)

Later she said that when asked why she wrote "this or that," her answer
most often was that she felt "a sense of historical duty to get a picture of a
fleeting way of life. Probably began with my youthful joy in vignettes of ancient Rome or Greece, which made life real instead of re-embalming dead
life" (*Diaries*, 452). The truth for Powell came from what she knew from
first-hand observation, what she divined from her extraordinary gift for
psychological perception, what she had turned over and over in her mind
and written about in her diaries or letters. To depict those she knew and
those she saw about her, she looked neither to the history books nor to her
imagination as much as to the world she lived in, the streets, the saloons,
the shops, the offices, the cafés. Her fiction was not about romancing or
beautifying; the truth, for Powell, needed no makeup, no surgical treatment,
no sleight of hand. As she explained in her diary, "'Satire' is the technical
word for writing of people as they are; 'romantic,' the other extreme of people as they are to themselves" (118). However painful, she maintained, reality
was never too horrid to be faced squarely:

> True gaiety is based on a foundation of realism. All right, we
> know we're dying, we know we're poor, that is off our minds—
> we eat, sleep, make merry but we are not kidding ourselves that
> we are rich and beautiful. . . . There is only sorrow in people
> making believe—sorrow and sordidness in stories of [an]
> invincible, Peter Pan fairy-godmother world. Gaiety should be
> brave, it should have stout legs of truth, not a gelatine base of
> dreams and wishes. (*Diaries*, 162)

Gaiety, delight, humor all derived from simply telling the truth. She
wrote characters and their motivations as she saw them: "whether writing
about the rural heartland or cosmopolitan Gotham, she gave it to us straight
like a pitchfork in a haystack or a well-chilled martini, hold the vermouth"
(Roberts, 2). The delighted reader of Powell's novels witnesses all at once
the truth of her observation, her insightful understanding of her subjects,
the empathy and tolerance with which she exposes her targets. "As natural
and skillful a satirist as American literature has ever produced" (Howard, 1),
Dawn Powell left her readers two gifts: her lilting novels of Ohio, and her
satirical novels of New York.

Young Dawn Powell with hand on heart.
Used by permission of Tim Page and Estate of Dawn Powell

Young Dawn Powell in profile, ca. 1920s.
Used by permission of the Estate of Dawn Powell

Lobby card for *Footlights and Shadows,* a 1920 film starring Olive Thomas and Ivo Dawson. Powell appeared in the film as an extra.

Ernest Truex and Spring Byington onstage in 1934's *Jig Saw,* produced by the Theatre Guild. Used by permission of the Associated Press

Powell friend and portraitist Peggy Bacon, ca. 1920

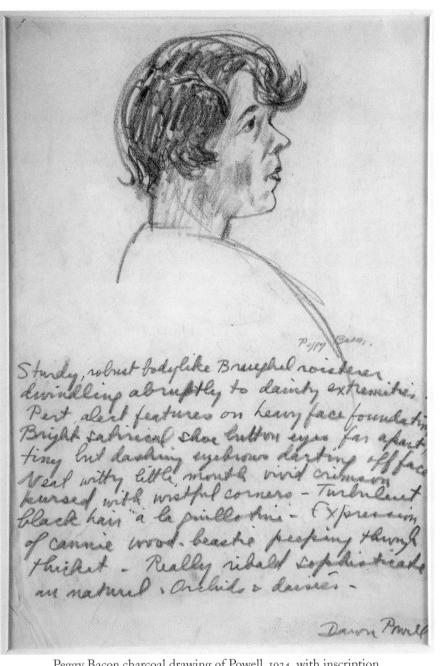

Peggy Bacon charcoal drawing of Powell, 1934, with inscription.
Used by permission of Kraushaar Galleries, Inc.

Peggy Bacon charcoal drawing of Powell, 1934.
Used by permission of Kraushaar Galleries, Inc.

Peggy Bacon charcoal drawing of Coburn "Coby" Gilman, 1934.
Used by permission of Kraushaar Galleries, Inc.

Dawn Powell's "Perkins" vs. "Calhoun"

Peggy Bacon drawing of cats Perkins vs. Calhoun, Peggy Bacon's cat.
Used by permission of Kraushaar Galleries, Inc.

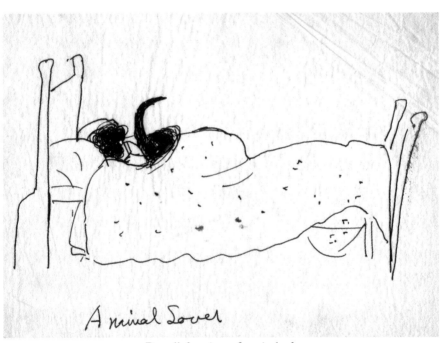

A minal Lover

Powell drawing of cat in bed.
Used by permission of Tim Page and Estate of Dawn Powell

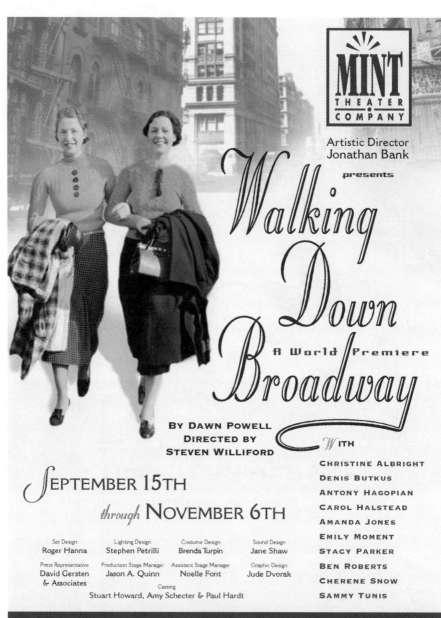

MINT
THEATER
COMPANY

Artistic Director
Jonathan Bank

presents

Walking Down Broadway

A World Premiere

BY DAWN POWELL
DIRECTED BY
STEVEN WILLIFORD

WITH

SEPTEMBER 15TH

through NOVEMBER 6TH

CHRISTINE ALBRIGHT
DENIS BUTKUS
ANTONY HAGOPIAN
CAROL HALSTEAD
AMANDA JONES
EMILY MOMENT
STACY PARKER
BEN ROBERTS
CHERENE SNOW
SAMMY TUNIS

| Set Design | Lighting Design | Costume Design | Sound Design |
| Roger Hanna | Stephen Petrilli | Brenda Turpin | Jane Shaw |

Press Representative	Production Stage Manager	Assistant Stage Manager	Graphic Design
David Gersten	Jason A. Quinn	Noelle Font	Jude Dvorak
& Associates			

Casting
Stuart Howard, Amy Schecter & Paul Hardt

Tues., Wed., Thurs. at 7:00; Fri. & Sat. at 8:00, Sat. and Sun at 2:00

To order tickets call (212) 315-0231
Or visit our on-line Box Office: www.minttheater.org

Flier for *Walking down Broadway,* produced by Jonathan Bank and New York's
Mint Theater Company, 2005. Used by permission of Jonathan Bank

Playbill featuring *Big Night* from the now demolished Maxine Elliott Theatre, January 1933

Flier for *Big Night*, produced by Allie Mulholland and ReGroup Theatre, December 2012. Used by permission of Mikiodo Media

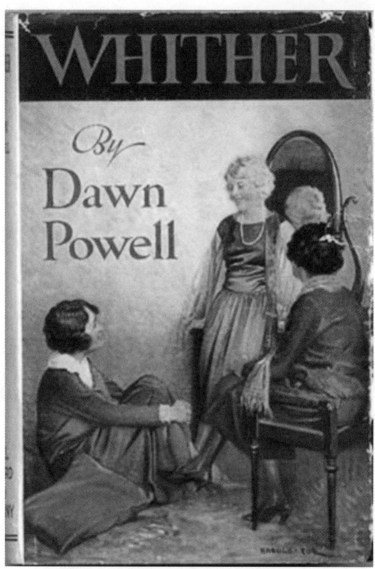

Whither, Powell's first novel (1925), in dust jacket

CHAPTER FOUR

"MIGHTY THINGS FROM SMALL BEGINNINGS GROW"

The Early New York Novels, 1925–38

Powell's first three New York novels—*Whither; Turn, Magic Wheel;* and *The Happy Island*—achieved varying degrees of success, the second receiving the greatest praise of the three. Though Powell herself would likely omit *Whither* from this grouping, I include it here because it provides a point of departure from which to examine the other novels in this early period. Many themes and concerns that appear in the first book will resurface in future works, as will Powell's skills at characterization, her psychological insight, and her satiric voice, which are apparent from the first. The author's loathing of this first effort and the fact that she never repeated certain novelistic events again, such as the "happy ending," reveal much about her literary development.

WHITHER, 1925

Learning New York

Even twenty years after *Whither* was published, Powell's critical view of her first novel had not softened. Rereading it, she "was horrified at how completely hopeless and utterly devoid of promise it was—far worse than what I had written at 13" (*Diaries,* 221). Unfortunately, what she had written at thirteen no longer survives, so we cannot be sure. In any case, the very existence of the novel would trouble her for decades. According to Tim Page, she hated it so much that "she spent the rest of her life buying up copies of it and destroying it wherever she found it" (Purdy, "Dawn"), one reason for its scarcity.[1] Though, as noted in chapter 1, the novel did receive some kind notices upon its release, Powell remained adamant that it was dreadful. The author had learned a hard lesson on its publication: that one must always write what one knows. The first novel's failure kept her from setting another novel in New York for eleven years; the next five would be set in the Ohio of her youth. It was only with a great deal of trepidation and careful planning that Powell undertook to write her second New York novel, *Turn, Magic Wheel,* which was published in 1936.

Writing *Whither,* Powell was still young and inexperienced. Begun in 1922 when the author was just twenty-five years old, the novel does not yet display a fully developed satirical voice, though suggestions of that voice do emerge. The writer had not yet lived in Manhattan long enough to represent it as knowingly or as confidently as she would a decade later. I know of no evidence to suggest that she had yet begun the habit of working and reworking, of meticulously recording her observations, sensations, and understandings, of planning and re-planning, that she demonstrated while writing her later works. Her letters will include some character sketches and incidents she wrote home about that will later appear in her fiction, but little more. Still, the first novel succeeds on some levels: its characterizations are detailed and precise; its focus is cleanly split between marriage and career, that early-to-mid-century conundrum; and the author's sense of humor is evident from the beginning. Describing one of the craftier girls at the boardinghouse, Powell's narrator says, "Fania had been engaged for years to some faraway 'Ralph.' [The engagement] had not altered her conduct a great deal, except that she spread her little infidelities over several men, under the impression that there was loyalty in numbers" (88). Such lines are clearly Powell's, as are these from another boardinghouse resident, Maisie, on the difference between working and not: "From what I see, I gather that having a career means going around hunting for a job. I'm the only person here, I guess, that works. All the rest of the girls have careers" (13). Anne T. Keene remarks that in *Whither* one already sees traces of Powell's "characteristic satiric tone, mordant wit, and unforgiving eye for the foibles of middle-class Americans, whether they lived in the middle west . . . or were newly arrived Midwestern émigrés to the big city of New York, desperately seeking sophistication" (232). Pett shares the opinion: "Even in this earliest effort, Powell's rambunctious satire and her gift for subtle irony shape what appears to be a conventional, popular novel" (207). Not only does the novel give an indication of Powell's sharp wit, her talent for creating character, and her gift of satire, but, again, it includes themes and concerns that will resurface in her future novels of Manhattan, principally those of provincials in New York, their quest for success and material wealth, and their dogged perseverance in the face of defeat.

Like most of Powell's fiction, *Whither* is autobiographical; both Tim Page and Marcelle Smith Rice, author of the 1998 dissertation "Split in Two at the Crossroads" (and of the later work *Dawn Powell,* published in 2000 by Twayne's United States Authors Series), consider it Powell's most highly autobiographical novel with the exception of the Ohio work *My Home Is Far Away.* One of the most striking features of *Whither* is that the author seems nearly as green here as her protagonist does; the title sounds a cry for direction. And while the choice of setting might suggest, as Page does, that Powell was "a convinced, passionate New Yorker from the start" (*Bio,* xiv), she nevertheless might have been wiser to have set her first novel in the midwestern region she knew so well. The Ohio works, on the surface very different in tone and in style than the New York novels, satisfy more than this first book does. As Rice says, "Powell wasn't far enough away from her vision of New York to write about the reality of New York, and her provincialism gawks across the novel" (145).

Still, like any good English major, Powell did adhere to writing what she knew, aside from her choice of larger setting. The main character seems much like the novelist in many ways: like Powell, Zoe Bourne has arrived in the city from a small Ohio town, here the fictitious hamlet of Albon, having fled the unhappy home of her father and stepmother, just as Powell had done years earlier. Zoe settles into a woman's boardinghouse on the West Side of Manhattan, just as Powell did, and finds work in publicity, as Powell did. Additionally, Zoe has no more than "twenty dollars in the world" when she arrives in New York (6), much like young Dawn, who had arrived in Manhattan with only fourteen dollars. Both young women wear their hair fashionably bobbed; both are in their early twenties; both petite and dark. Like Powell a "clever sort" of young woman, Zoe means to become a famous novelist or playwright, but unlike Powell she feels that most other types of writing are beneath her. The novel includes a scene in which Zoe acts as an extra on a movie set, just as Powell herself had done, in 1919, when she appeared in the silent film *Footlights and Shadows*,[2] starring Ziegfeld-girl-turned-film-star Olive Thomas[3] (*Letters*, 40) and leading man Ivo Dawson.

Page surmises that Powell's dislike of the novel may have stemmed from its "brazen incorporation of raw autobiographical material that she never went on to transform into polished fiction" (*Bio*, 70), and what he says may be partly true. Still, I would argue that she has transformed many of the more important autobiographical elements of this book into polished fiction, though the novel misfires for other reasons (discussed below).[4] For example, the largely unsentimental[5] and clear-eyed Powell, who viewed the world "with an unhappy child's uniform skepticism and macabre intimations" (Updike, "Ohio," 271), was neither as naive nor as filled with romantic nonsense as is young Zoe, who dreams of a Prince Charming–style husband in a way that neither Powell nor any of her important future characters ever would. The author's difficult early years had convinced her that a thorny future awaited her: in her journal to the imaginary Mr. Woggs, the very young Dawn wrote, "I must make myself strong for the knocks that are to come"[6] (Warstler, 24). Her troubled childhood had taught her that happily-ever-afters were found only in fairy tales; as a result, Dawn Powell would never write such an ending again.

Another quality of Zoe's that differs from the author's is that the naive, starry-eyed young character complains that, despite her dreams, in New York she "never, never would have been taken on as editor" because "people are so nasty about experience and degrees and things" (30), irony oozing from the lines, though not from the character's mouth. Powell, who had earned her bachelor's degree from Lake Erie College in 1918, understood the necessity of a college education in finding a worthwhile position in such a competitive place as New York, while Zoe has spent only one year in college (108).

Finally, and most important, Powell is not made of the same flimsy stuff that Zoe is: the character is a nonwriting writer,[7] to Powell a laughable if not loathsome character type that crops up again and again in her work, from her first novel to her last and in her diaries and letters as well.[8] In fact, it is not until late in *Whither*, when aspiring nonacting actress Margot confides in her, that Zoe even sees that she is "like Margot, spending her time waiting for something great to come to her. . . . They were alike. She was as blind and stupid as Margot" (215). Margot wishes to act but never does;

despite many offers, she has accepted none, believing them all to be beneath her. Zoe, of course, fails to write a word.[9] Clearly unimpressed with such types, Powell, in a single instance of many, confides in her diary the tale of one John C. Mosher, *New Yorker* columnist and film critic,[10] who, "like so many other gifted young men about town," has "slipped somehow into one of Henry James' lesser mantles, assuming with authority the role of Dean of Letters, without going to the bother of writing" (109). In Powell's final novel, *The Golden Spur,* readers meet a character very much like Powell's Mosher: an editor and aspiring novelist who nonetheless never puts pen to paper, saying that it is his "foolish perfectionism that made his stories too good to sell or for that matter even to write" (73).[11] In her letters Powell often ruminates on the same topic, finding those who occasionally write hardly better than those who write not at all. Even such a famed writer as Ernest Hemingway seemed to Powell, who always worked six to seven hours a day, to be squandering his talent. She said disparagingly that he "is stated (by near and dear) to work two hours early each day, then spend rest of day talking steadily to Anybody" (*Letters,* 169).

So Zoe, flawed character that she is, proves little different from the boastful nonwriting writers who earn Powell's scorn.[12] Though the character has arrived in the city full of romantic notions of becoming a famous playwright or perhaps a novelist, she never gets around to writing a single word other than the inane copy she produces for the advertising agency for which she works, a position she gets by mere accident and good fortune rather than by diligence or even inquiry. After business hours, in her free time, Zoe does not once even put pen to paper;[13] neither can she concentrate on *The Tree of Heaven,*[14] the novel she purports to be reading, sufficiently to prevent it from dropping to the floor as she indulges in foolish daydreams (30). May Sinclair, author of the book Zoe pretends to read, was long a champion of women's rights, a writer concerned with female development; in the novel Zoe is reading, Sinclair writes of women working together for a cause, drawing on her own experiences as a reporter and nurse's assistant during World War I. Zoe's letting the book slip from her fingers suggests that she is in danger of leaving her higher hopes and fonder ambitions behind.

Zoe, brand new to New York, has already begun to lose sight of her loftier aims. Within days of settling in to the boardinghouse, she longs to "have excitement every night the way [roommate] Julie does, and suitors and dances, and pretty clothes, and things like that" (31). She has already fallen

into the trap of material desire that the advertising capital of the world so
adeptly encourages—the trap into which most of her fellow boardinghouse
dwellers have also fallen.

Shortly after Zoe drops her book, she is readily persuaded by fellow
roomer Amy Bruce, "her hair dazzlingly marceled and freshly hennaed, her
eyelashes newly mascaraed, her lips garishly red and her eyelids rouged . . .
her hose . . . accentuat[ing] ankles and legs that had better been left unre-
vealed" (33–34), to take a walk up Broadway, purportedly to Evart's Drug
Store for "a frosted chocolate" (34). Of course Amy on this Friday evening is
after more than an ice cream soda; the adventure that ensues involves a ride
in a green touring car to Pelham Heath[15] with two strangers, Chuck and
George, whom Amy has just picked up on the street. Returning with them,
Zoe, riding in the front seat, turns around to see "George and Amy locked
in one another's arms." She feels "hot and ashamed" over such a "cheap, sordid thing" (42). The reader expects that perhaps Zoe will learn a few things
from this encounter, but when the girl arrives home sometime later, only
to find that her frequently betrothed roommate Julie has yet again broken
off one engagement in favor of another, Zoe thinks ruefully that "if men in
New York didn't like her any better than Chuck had,[16] she certainly would
never be engaged" (43). From as early as the novel's third chapter, it is apparent that what Zoe wants is not a career but a husband. In the next several
chapters Zoe focuses all her energies on acquiring the wiles, the wardrobe,
and the accessories she believes she needs to capture a man. Men, money,
and merchandise are virtually all that are on her mind.

Throughout *Whither*, Powell furnishes Zoe with several examples of the
kinds of writer she might become, though the character never takes it upon
herself to seek out any of them. First, fellow boardinghouse tenant Maisie,
of her own accord, introduces Zoe to the house's own writer-in-residence,
self-described "hack" writer May Roberts who, like Powell, "works like a
slave" (26–27) to pay the bills. As Maisie introduces the two, she says of
Zoe, "She wants to know how you became a successful writer—you know,
how to get a job on the magazines and work up to fame" (25). May is one
of many hardworking writers whom readers meet in Powell, an admirable
type who counterposes the less industrious sort one meets nearly as often.
When Zoe asks May if what she is busily writing is a novel, the older girl
replies, "A novel? Good Lord. Whatever put that idea in your head? Syn-
dicate stuff is my line. Fashions, household hints, little poems, jokes, trade
suggestions—everything" (26). In response to May's offer to recommend

the girl to "the editor of the *Dry Goods Economist,* Zoe's face plainly and tactlessly revealed her disgust at the idea" (27). Sizing Zoe up, May now sees straight through the young woman: "If you're a born artist you'll go some place and starve and write, but you don't look that kind. You want baths and nice neighborhoods and decent friends and salads and beaux and orchestra seats in the theater more than you want to write plays" (28). Zoe claims that she does want to be a playwright, to do "something in a big way," to which May, sounding very much like the author, replies: "You [don't] want to do anything big . . . you're just like all the rest of them. You just want to *be* something big. There's a difference. You don't want to do anything. None of you would do a stroke of work to get the thing you think you want" (27). May warns Zoe that she can either starve or write the schlock that pays the bills, to which suggestion an oblivious Zoe reacts in horrified disbelief. Powell throughout her lifetime wrote many pieces simply to pay the bills.

If May Roberts represents one type of writer Zoe might become, the copywriters at the advertising agency where Maisie works suggest another. Again, Zoe has not endeavored to meet any other writers; she has not even tried to find employment for herself. Maisie has all but forced her to take on work as a file clerk at the advertising firm where she works and where Zoe will meet copywriters Bill Cornell and Christopher Kane. Like the author, and like May Roberts, Bill Cornell is a hardworking type who often stays on after hours. Powell writes, "Zoe had a suspicion that he was one of those hundred per cent American go-getters that one read about in the success magazines" (44). Such industriousness, which Powell very clearly finds attractive, is acceptable to Zoe only because Mr. Cornell is "good looking enough to be forgiven for it" (44). The girl seems surprised if not disappointed to see him eyeing the jar of cold cream on his desk as "an object of most profound consideration" (44) as he attempts to write a piece about it for an advertising campaign; she would much prefer that he were fondly gazing on her.

At the same agency, another writer, Mr. Kane, mistakes file clerk Zoe first for a stenographer and then for a copywriter, to which a flattered Zoe responds, "I'm not—yet, but I'd like to be . . . I'm just filing now to—to get a line on the firm's policy" (47). Later she muses, "So that was how one found a career. You didn't seek it or fret over it, but simply waited and let things drift until suddenly the goal appeared" (48). Again, young Zoe is getting the wrong message; again, she refuses to act, as always preferring passivity to action, unlike her creator. At least Zoe has descended a notch from her snootier self, for now she comes to realize that "she hadn't known she wanted to be an advertising writer. She thought she wanted to become a playwright, but when the one was so far away and the other so near . . ." (48). Her thoughts trail off.

Despite her earlier beliefs, she now decides that a copywriter's job is a fine one, especially if one does not have to go searching for it. Never one to work hard to achieve her dreams, Zoe prefers merely to allow opportunity to fall into her lap. In this sense, the character could not be more different from the hardworking Powell. Now, having been given an opportunity to work on the Voorhees Cold Cream account, Zoe sets to work writing copy for a full-page ad that is to appear in the *Ladies Home Companion*. In a comic send-up of women's magazines,[17] Powell shows us a Zoe deciding that the ad must "strike the woman in the home right in the eye. Something that would show them beauty was as close at hand as their—well, as their broomstick. Beauty and the Broomstick, Beauty on a Broomstick, Beauty versus Broomstick" (96). The ad that finally runs, as it turns out, does away with the broom idea but inanely keeps the sweeping metaphor. The boss describes it as "just this great sweep of white paper . . . and then . . . at the very bottom of the page in big caps—VOORHEES COLD CREAM FOR THE PORES! Do you see the thing, Miss Bourne? Does it get you? Oh it's big—*big!*" (97).

Not long thereafter, Zoe, who is never again seen even thinking about writing further advertisements, one afternoon witnesses blue-eyed Cornell, on whom she has developed a crush, asking pretty file clerk Peggy out to lunch. Near tears, Zoe hunches over her desk, visibly upset. When Mr. Kane sees her sitting there looking so defeated, the narrator tells us, "the absurd thought struck him that her evident grief might be that of an artist condemned to commercialize her genius" (104). Absurd thought, indeed. Zoe instead is only wishing that she knew what the "something else" Peggy had was, and wishing that she herself knew how to get some of it (101). Not once since the novel's outset has Zoe acted in her own behalf to pursue the career she claims she is after—the sole effort in this direction she has taken has been to board a train from Ohio to New York, an action that occurs before the novel begins.

Soon enough Powell supplies yet another writer type for young Zoe. The protagonist not only has never endeavored to seek out any "real" artist types but also has agreed to accompany Allan Myers, a friend from the office, to the Village to meet some of his artist friends only because she knows that Cornell is listening in as Myers invites her. And so the two visit the

Bank Street studio of Myers's friends, Lucille and Dave, where Zoe meets the "haggard, dark-bearded" Dariel (175), a writer who actually writes. He works day and night, subsisting on Shredded Wheat and water and the occasional can of sardines that Dave tosses his way.[18] Juxtaposing Dariel and Zoe in this manner, Powell highlights their differences; placed beside the "real thing" (172), Zoe is exposed as the poseur that she is.

Having been told that the visitor is a writer, Dariel, interested, asks her, "What do you write?" The narrator then says, "Zoe was confused. It seemed silly to call herself a writer on the strength of a few things that had never been published anyway. She felt somehow humble before this wan, threadbare Dariel" (176). Zoe replies simply "Things," then adds, "I've been in an office several months."

The artist replies, sensibly, "Then you write at night."

Zoe says, "No—I—I haven't written much. I want to write later on, though. I want to be a great playwright."

"The way to be a great playwright is to write plays," Dariel says (176).

Using Dariel's simple words, Powell chides her heroine. If young Zoe ultimately learns that to become a playwright one must endeavor to write plays rather than simply to wait around for someone to come up and hire her to do so, it is a lesson that Powell seems always intrinsically to have known. From her earliest days she loved to write, stationing herself in trees and on rooftops to do so. And though she never had any "intentions of going to New York, renting a garret and starving to death writing stories" (*Letters*, 22),[19] as Dariel does, neither does she neglect her writing, as Zoe does. Even as a young woman, Powell was forever composing, observing, collecting material and squirreling it away. Zoe, of course, is interested in more trivial affairs.

Some time later, having indignantly quit her job over some unsavory rumors about her innocent doings with the married Mr. Kane, and still unable to find a new position, Zoe meets former colleague Allan Myers, who asks her if she has started writing yet. In response, "Zoe looked at him, startled. It was queer that she had never thought of doing that very thing" (251). A short time earlier she had been hoping that "perhaps she would meet someone who would set her to writing plays" (246). Nearly the end of the novel and still it has not occurred to Zoe that *she herself* should set herself to writing. Powell needed no such fantasy person.

Later, out of work, broke, bills piling up, Zoe at last recalls Allan's question and asks herself, "Why shouldn't she, so long as she was destined to starve anyway, starve for the sake of art?" (253). Her roommate is conveniently out for the evening, so she believes she might go home and write in peace. Powell was never one to wait for a roommate to disappear before sitting down to write; when she lived in the Broadway boardinghouse on first arriving in New York, she would take herself to Central Park and write there under the trees. Zoe, however, roommate-free and alone in her room, discovers when finally she puts pen to paper that she cannot write at all. Crumpled papers fill the room, each blank but for a single header: "Cast of Characters" (254). In a fit of frustration, Zoe cries out, "I haven't a thing to say!" (254). Unlike Zoe, Powell had much to write about, and more to say, even when she was younger than her character is. As Rice maintains, "It seems that [in *Whither*] Powell tried to incorporate everything she knew about her early experience in New York City, rather than working out of a few experiences" (155). For Rice, Powell had *too much* to write about, unlike Zoe, who has nothing.

As has been noted, each of Powell's New York novels features at least one aspiring artist leaving her (or his) small midwestern hometown for the city; similarly, all of her Ohio novels feature at least one character longing to escape the restrictive Midwest for the possibilities of New York. Though Zoe often feels discouraged and for a time is so broke that she frets she may lose her room at the boardinghouse, she never once contemplates the possibility of returning home. Other characters, from Margot to Amy to Fania to Julie, also never consider going back where they came from, despite much disappointment, little success, and, in many cases, no talent. However, the occasional character does return home, though almost never happily and rarely for long.[20] This theme will appear in *The Happy Island*, particularly, but it first appears in *Whither:* Miss Tait, elderly resident of the boarding-house where Zoe lives, aspires to write "scenarios" for the stars (113). When she becomes discouraged, however, she says,

> "Sometimes I simply pack my trunks and go back to the Nashville Library. I have a very good position there, but anybody can be a librarian."
>
> "But you always come back to New York," Zoe smiled. Miss Tait sighed.
>
> "Yes, I always come back. It's so foolish of me, you see, to waste my time with books when I could be making twenty or thirty thousand a year writing photoplays. Really criminal to neglect such a chance." (113)

As in all of Powell's writings, her striving characters, like Miss Tait (and Powell herself), never give up, never accept defeat. They might pack their bags and return home for a while, but they invariably return to New York and the opportunities it offers.[21] Despite the crushing blows of negative press and light sales, despite feeling that "every book, every play, every story, seems to have less chance than ever, and the factor of luck seems to have nothing to do with me—merely work to no avail" (*Diaries*, 184), Powell always pressed on. Returning to Ohio from time to time, she always longed to get back to her adopted home. Nowhere else could she breathe as freely as she could in New York. For Powell, one of the primary distinctions between the provinces and the city was that "so much of the country" is all about "open hearts and closed minds." In New York, however, "we have closed hearts first, and minds so open that carrier pigeons can fly straight through " (*Letters*, 132). Open minds were necessary to Powell; the airs and pretenses of America's Middle West she would always find confining.

Despite Powell's great love of Manhattan, both Tim Page and Marcelle Smith Rice find that in the author's earliest novel she is not yet able to write convincingly about it, and Powell herself would agree. Rice maintains that "Powell wrote best when she knew and understood her scene . . . she could not be in a place for a brief period and know it . . . she had to absorb it over time. For this reason, *Whither* falls somewhat short of fulfillment" (145). Some favorite New York locations are visited in the novel; Zoe's roommate Julie is to be married at the Little Church around the Corner, the same church where Dawn Powell and Joseph Gousha had wed a few years earlier. Other haunts, such as the Algonquin Hotel and Bank Street and the Bretton Hall, mentioned in the letters and in the diaries, appear here as well, as does Broadway, the boulevard that intersects the street on which Zoe's boardinghouse and Powell's own are located. But few of these sites are ever described; more often they are simply mentioned in passing. Still, when the novelist does seek to describe, her renderings are often effective, as is this account of the protagonist's view from her office: "Zoe sat with her chin in her hands," Powell writes, "frowning out of the window over Madison Square Park, where peripatetic bootblacks, jobless men, swaggering office girls, pinch-backed clerks floated in noon-hour idleness" (101). Though her descriptions often focus on the people who fill the buildings and the streets rather than on the city itself, they are nevertheless evocative, as in this winter portrait of Washington Square:

> Its friendly darkness [was] relieved by the falling snow which
> swirled around the dim street lamps with increasing speed. A
> party of Villagers, obviously in masquerade costume, passed
> them in front of the little cigar store. A pretty girl in gypsy dress,
> barefooted and uncloaked, stopped and smiled at them. (137)

A description of Pelham Heath satisfies in its focus on location:

> They came within sight of the glittering road house, sitting
> in the midst of a golden-lit circle fringed with limousines and
> taxicabs. Once inside, it seemed to Zoe a fantastic mingling
> of brilliant lights, waiters' white shirt fronts, intoxicating jazz
> music and syncopated couples. (41)

Yet for all its promise, Powell's portrait of New York in *Whither* is of course not as polished as in her future works it would be. Not only does Powell's inability to bring New York to life disappoint both Page and Rice, but her reliance on breathless outbursts from Zoe, followed by exclamation points, suggests for them an immature writer. Page says, "Too often, [the author] is content to sum up Zoe's excitement about her new home with the facile ejaculation 'New York!'" (*Bio*, 72). However, the exclamatory style may instead be attributed to Powell's effort to capture Zoe's naïveté rather than to any serious limitation on the part of the author. In fact, an early letter she wrote to former college classmate Charlotte Johnson suggests that it is not Powell, writing *Whither*, who is stuck at exclamation-point riddled "Stage One," but Zoe:

> I've been "doing the Village" quite consistently lately[22] and feel
> that sooner or later I'll be among 'em. There are three stages
> you go through in regard to the Village. First and foremost
> "Oh-so-this-is-Bohemia!! My dear! Don't you just *love* it all?
> Everything is so—well, so absolutely *spontaneous*, don't you
> know!!! Bohemia—oh thrills!" (*Letters*, 34)

It seems clear that in *Whither* Powell is trying to recapture that "first stage" of Zoe's arrival in the City, that gasping sense of wonder felt by the naïve and inexperienced newcomer, exclamation points included. For the moment, Zoe is too newly arrived to be able yet even to express her awe; instead, she is overwhelmed and tongue-tied. Witness the following contrast between Powell's narrator and Zoe:

> A few lights had come on along the street and sent a defiant, puny glow against the dying sun. The sounds of the city and its hurrying people seemed to have melted into one great windlike monotone that was as vast as silence. "I love it," Zoe whispered to herself. (208)

If Powell's portrayal of New York in *Whither* leaves readers unimpressed, if her manner of conveying emotion is unappreciated, her characterizations, overall, do not disappoint. Powell contemporary Charles Norman singled out the boardinghouse landlady, Mrs. Horne, as a "superbly drawn character" ("Jazz Age," 5), while a nameless *New York Times* commentator, reviewing the novel upon its release, said

> Miss Powell peoples her pages with a variety of interesting and, at times, well-hit-off types. Julie and Maisie, with whom Zoe shares rooms and a "semi-private bath," are deftly constructed; Mrs. Horne, the landlady, really lives and moves, and the men in the book, particularly Hill and Kane, are no interpolated puppets. ("New York Adventures," 19)

The *Boston Evening Transcript*'s reviewer described *Whither*'s characters as follows:

> Julie, the beautiful, the well preserved and the languorous; Maisie Colburn, the impudent; Enna, gifted with a bored mama in the background, who showers clothes upon her daughter in lieu of maternal affection; and a host of others. They are all distinctly different, if their characterization is in many cases shadowy, done with charcoal rather than pen and ink. (S.L.R., 5)

The reviewer ends: "nor in passing should we omit a tribute to the kind heart of the landlady, Mrs. Horne" (5). It is notable that three of the four major reviewers who chose to write of *Whither* upon its publication would praise Powell's ability to create believable characters.

Certainly the rooming house setting and the characters in it come off well, largely because Powell was as familiar with rooming houses as she was with the dreamers and boasters one might encounter there. Readers will recall that Powell's aunt had run a boardinghouse near the Shelby train station and that during the girl's itinerant early years, she and her sisters had often been moved from one rooming house to another. It seems certain that Powell's characters in *Whither* come so vividly to life because the author based some of them on people she had observed. It is clear that she draws on college dormitory life, not far different from boardinghouse life. In an amusing scene, Powell paints material girl Julie rating her roommates according to their wardrobes. Complaining that recent arrival Zoe is "too short for her" because Julie will not be able to fit into the new girl's clothes (15), she agrees that height doesn't much matter when it comes to borrowing "furs and gloves and stockings and hats and things like that," but if she is to impress her latest beau, she needs "a new street suit and a couple of dinner gowns." She asks, "How can I look like a wicked woman when I have to wear the same thing every time I go out with him? If only this girl had something giddy looking. But no" (16). The scene recalls an earlier letter to Auntie May from Dawn at college. Recounting a trip to Cleveland she had recently taken with some classmates, Powell wrote, "I was very stunning (oh yes) in Rhoda's skirt, Hester McLauren's silk waist, Charlotte Johnson's hat and Rhoda's coat" (*Letters*, 9). In *Whither* as at Lake Erie, the struggling girls are also group-outfitted.

In this earliest novel and throughout her writings Powell demonstrates her ambivalence about consumer culture, ridiculing while at the same time understanding her characters' desires for the goods now so plentiful and so glitteringly on display in department store windows and popular magazines. The new culture of buying on credit, too, is lampooned, as are hard-hitting salesgirls in department stores on Madison Avenue, like the one who persuades Zoe to buy a coat she absolutely cannot afford. Using Fania's credit, the unemployed Zoe is pushed to buy the expensive coat and does so, reasoning that, as Julie has told her, a girl can never find a job if she looks as if she needs one. Desire, as Powell knew, is created not only in the sparkling window displays of department stores, which Daniel J. Boorstin aptly calls "consumer palaces," and in the glossy pages of women's magazines, but also, illogically, in the disapproving eyes of salesmen and saleswomen. The image of the sneering salesclerk occurs not only in *Whither* but throughout Powell; for example, readers encounter it in "Such a Pretty Day": "They went through Schwab's because Barbs dared Sylvia to go in. This was a large, cool, dark, swank store and so snooty that Barbs and Sylvia clutched each other's hands to keep up their courage before the hostile clerks" (*Sunday*, Steerforth ed., 65). If the autobiographical Ohio novel *My Home Is Far Away* is any indication, readers might imagine the ragged young Dawn feeling much the same way in the new stores that were beginning to appear during her childhood in even the smaller towns of Ohio (Boorstin, 101). One of Marcia Willard's sister's little friends in that novel has a mother who works at the Fair Store (*My Home*, 25), a department store chain that had started in Chicago sometime after the end of the Civil War and then expanded further into the Midwest (Boorstin, 101). After the sisters and their mother go to the Fair Store one afternoon for dressmaking supplies rather than for ready-made dresses, it gets back to them that the friend's mother had sneered behind their backs, saying, "People without money shouldn't go shopping in a high-class store" (73). Like Zoe, who cannot afford her beautiful new blue coat but buys it anyway, at least in part to appease the scornful clerk, the young sisters's father, who flies into a rage when he learns of the salesclerk's remark about his wife, storms into the Fair Store only to return home with an impractical ready-made dress for her, a black satin number he has bought on credit and cannot afford. Powell sympathizes with the motivation behind both Zoe's and Mr. Willard's actions but at the same time understands its futility: their "that'll show 'em" attitude backfires, wounding not the clerks but the destitute buyers themselves.[23]

Trouble no quiet, kind heart; leave sunny imaginations hope.

—Charlotte Brontë, *Villette*[24]

Powell may have come to loathe her first novel in part because of its fashionable happy ending. Friend and fellow writer Hope Hale Davis remembers that in the 1920s, "the writers in style—even female—showed a woman acting not only most romantically but most honorably as faithful handmaiden to an irresistible male" (16). Perhaps Powell was not yet secure enough in her writing ability to defy this convention, but she also did not paint a main character who was serious enough to achieve her career goals. Zoe longs for male companionship throughout the novel more than she ever genuinely aspires to artistic success; readers never see any real indication that Zoe possesses any talent out of the ordinary. Page faults the closing as the "sort of 'happy ending' that Powell had envisioned for herself" (72), but his suggestion does not quite convince: this same "ending" had already happened to Powell. In 1920, just two years after she had arrived in New York, she had met and married Joseph Gousha and seems never to have had to struggle with any choice between career and marriage. The one promised to assist the other, Gousha vowing to work outside the home so that Powell was free to stay in—or to go out—and write. On the other hand, Page acknowledges that Powell herself seems not to have believed in happy endings, not even as a young girl of seventeen or eighteen. Stories she wrote for the college literary magazine, the *Record*, were often "unusually skeptical and antiromantic for a young woman of that era. Already there are signs that Powell foresaw her future—and that she did not believe in happy endings" (*Bio*, 25).

In this novel, the marriage question first comes up when Zoe pays a visit, for the sole purpose of showing off, to an old Albon chum also relocated in New York. The friend, Allie, is the picture of the happily married, fertile wife—even though Zoe thinks she must have been fired to have decided to marry and give up the good job in publicity she had held. Not given the chance to boast of her good fortune in having been promoted to copywriter at the ad agency, Zoe sulks during her visit. Then, taking her leave, Zoe first considers her friends a couple of "old married pigs" (63), but moments later, almost in spite of herself, thinks that "everybody ought to have babies" (64). She even imagines a funny little advertisement:

BABIES!
The Love Perpetuators!
Burrowing into Your Heart! Sliding into
Your Soul!
Every Baby Represents a Thousand Dollars
In the Bank of Love!
Begin Today! (64)

As it happens, Allie's will be the sole happy marriage in the novel; Kane and his long-estranged wife will divorce by novel's end; a Bohemian couple Zoe meets live together without marrying. Often-engaged-but-never-married Julie says that "get[ting] a man" is "always an exciting alternative to becoming a great artist. When you see failure ahead, the thing to do is to become some man's wife or mistress" (71). The roommate's cynical view of marriage hardly seems to foretell a happy union for Zoe. If Powell provides a series of writer-types Zoe might become, she balances those career possibilities with representations of the types of women the girl might emulate, among them not only Julie and Allie but also the independent and in-charge landlady, the kind but unattractive Mrs. Horne; and Fania, engaged but living far away from her betrothed and dating anyone who asks.

As Judith Pett suggests, it may be that the author was quietly attempting to subvert the standard storybook ending. In her future novels Powell certainly eschewed such endings—and she may not even have believed or meant her readers to believe the one she includes here. Pett supposes that it is subtle irony at work. As Pett reminds us, the novel's final words—"It's love that makes you happy—not another thing" (309)—are spoken by the landlady, "whose face is smeared with cold cream, whose coarse 'touched' black hair is knotted on top of her head, whose flowered purple wrapper encases her robust body and whose nose is red and twitching with excitement. She ought to make the reader laugh. Love is not the sentiment which gives this novel its vitality" (Pett, 207). I have to agree. Earlier in the novel, when a defeated and uncharacteristically "cross" (123) Julie has finally agreed to marry Alphonse, she says to Zoe, "I'm so happy . . . because—because," she ended in a heartbroken sob, "I'm going to be married" (137). Even moony Zoe "had some time ago come to the conclusion that Julie was getting married simply because it looked like a dull season and, besides, she'd tried everything else" (122). Finally, in a café with her fiancé just before the wedding date, Julie finds a man at a neighboring table very attractive:

> Julie was remembering the thrill of meeting new men. It was the only thing that made life worthwhile for women. . . . One speculated, too, on just what type of fiancé one would swing to from the one in hand. Usually Julie swung from Latins to Scotch or British and back to Americans. For instance, in the ordinary course of events, she would go from Alphonse's beautiful romanticism to the humorous practicality of—say, the man at the next table. (144–45)

Several years older than Zoe but still not ready to marry, Julie represents a type of woman who chooses to put off marriage, who does not buy into Zoe's antiquated provincial idea that unmarried women over twenty-five are old maids ready to be "shelved" (107).

It seems certain that Powell had not intended to write a fairy-tale ending. Instead, in a closing that on some levels recalls the subversive "happy" ending of Charlotte Brontë's fictional autobiography, *Villette*, it is likely that Powell, like Brontë before her, had understood that in popular women's fiction the female protagonist most satisfyingly, in the minds of readers, ends the novel happily married—or does she? Lisa Zeidner notes Powell's tendency to favor endings that are "not triumphant or tragic, but qualified and enigmatic" (3); perhaps Powell was attempting here one of the inscrutable endings her future novels would feature. On *Whither*'s penultimate page, Julie, still opposed to the idea of marriage, says that "Men spoil everything" (304). Some might agree, for by novel's end Zoe has neither matured nor progressed; instead, she seems as infantile as ever: "Zoe rested her head, like a drowsy child, against [Kane's] shoulder. Life was so simple" (305). Passive from the novel's outset, she remains so at the end, choosing to leave her fate in the hands of someone other than herself. Instead of being a novel of female development, as is the May Sinclair novel that Zoe lets fall to the floor early in the book, *Whither* is a novel of female stagnation. It seems clear that Powell had not meant the "happy" ending to be taken seriously. After all, early in *Whither* Julie had called Mrs. Horne's establishment a "house of failure" (69). Zoe, like most of the others, is clearly not much of a success.

Whatever the author's intention, the closing does not satisfy. And to charges of her novel's happy ending being conventional and unoriginal, Powell would respond in the future by leaving such endings to others. By the time of 1940's *Angels on Toast*, the words "marital bliss" will be "an oxymoron" (Pool, 20). The *Saturday Review of Literature* commentator said of *Whither* that "the ending departs not at all from the usual" (694); the *Boston Evening Transcript*'s review included a small illustration depicting "a flapper whose cigarette smoke curls up to form the word *Whither* and above the title is the query: Husbanding or Careering?" (Rice, 154). The reviewer asks of the characters in the novel, "Is marriage their only salvation, just as it has been through the ages? What a blow it must be to these enfranchised and advanced young women to have still to face the Victorian lot of their sex!" (5). Powell disappoints the reader who longs for an ending for Zoe other than marriage.

Similarly, the *New York Times* says that what happens to Zoe once she arrives in New York—"hardship, disappointment, and then romance"—also "happens annually to thousands like her" (19). Though what happens to Zoe does and did actually happen annually to thousands of visitors to Manhattan, few such visitors had been painted in American novels and plays by women at that time. Not many works before *Whither* concern a young female protagonist who aspires to leave the Midwest in search of success in the New York art world, though Edith Wharton's Undine Spragg, in *The Custom of the Country*, does move from the Midwest to New York in search of entrée into a higher social class through marriage. Willa Cather's *Song of the Lark* features an aspiring singer going to Chicago from the Midwest, arriving in New York after first traveling to Europe; Louisa May Alcott wrote of a Massachusetts woman writing in the city; several of Ellen Glasgow's characters move from the American South to Manhattan. Certainly after 1925 our literature is filled with hopeful midwesterners arriving in the big city, in stage stories, short fiction, and novels. *So Help Me God*, a play written in the late 1920s by Maurine Dallas Watkins (of *Chicago* fame), features a young Cincinnatian named Kerry who moves to New York for a career on the stage, despite the fact that she has no experience and less talent. But the play, which was slated to open in October of 1929, fell victim to the Great Depression and never did make it to the stage. Collections such as Ruth McKenney's rather thin *My Sister Eileen* come a full decade after Powell's novel, the play on which it is based not until 1940; the same is true of such stage and film treatments as *42nd Street*, written in 1933; Edna Ferber and George S. Kaufman's *Stage Door*, 1937; and others. In fact, *Whither* seems an early version of *Stage Door*, which featured Margaret Sullavan in the lead. Later that year the play was filmed at RKO Studios with an all-star cast, including Katharine Hepburn in the starring role and Ginger Rogers, Lucille Ball, and Eve Arden in supporting parts. Though the play and the film differ from one another in some ways, both are set in an inexpensive boardinghouse in New York, the boarders all women from various small-town American locales who have come to Manhattan in search of wealth and stardom. The boardinghouse, called The Footlights Club in both play and film, is said to be located "somewhere in the West Fifties" (G. Kaufman, 260). The play was based on an actual women's rooming house called the Rehearsal Club[25] located at 47 West Fifty-Third Street from 1918 until the building was razed in 1987. Now the site of the Museum of American Folk Art, the address is in the same West Side neighborhood as Powell's fictional rooming house. The novel's residence hotel is filled with young and elderly women alike who dream of successful careers in an array of creative fields, from writing to music to dancing to acting; the characters in *Stage Door*, also both young and old, similarly dance, sing, act, and play. The boardinghouse, the characters, the landlady and cook, the snappy dialogue, the older woman with her scrapbook of clippings, the meals included in the price of lodging,[26] even the surreptitious "borrowing" of clothes and the squabbling among the tenants seem to owe much to Powell's novel. Further, in the filmed *Stage Door* the penthouse scenes with theatrical producer Anthony

Powell, played by an oily Adolphe Menjou, seem to have been influenced by these pages as well; the out-of-work Zoe, in wealthy theatrical producer Al Schuler's sumptuous hotel rooms, is treated to an elegant meal and then seduced, just as several of the ill-fed young women in *Stage Door* are seduced by producer Powell. There is also the matter of the novel's suicidal Margot, broke and weary of having been strung along for months on end in casting offices (206–7), much like the suicidal Kay, broke and weary of the same things, in *Stage Door*. One wonders whether Ferber or Kaufman had read the novel. It seems likely that one or both of them had; the Algonquin crowd certainly knew of Dawn Powell and her work.[27]

As we have seen, the letters and to some extent the diaries, along with Page's biography and Powell's later writings, work together to furnish us insight into this first novel by Powell. Not a triumph by any means,[28] but more noteworthy than the author herself believed, *Whither* is an indication of the work to come. That in this novel readers see the writer trying things out that she will never try again is of use to those who are interested in tracing the arc of Powell's growth, as are the many themes and concerns shown here that will reappear in her future writings. If the novel is not a resounding success, readers might at least agree with the *Boston Evening Transcript*'s reviewer, who ended his lukewarm review simply, saying that "*Whither* is a first novel, and a very good one" (S.L.R., 5), or with Powell's friend Charles Norman, who said of the novel, "It is certainly a very good effort with many achievements" ("Jazz," 5). Indications of the satiric perception, the ironic sense of humor, and the empathy with which Powell would write her future characters and novels are evident in this first effort.

TURN, MAGIC WHEEL, 1936

In the city, time becomes visible

—Mumford, *The Culture of Cities*, 3[29]

So determined was Powell never to produce another *Whither* that eleven years and five Ohio novels would come between it and her first "real" New York novel. Although it took her several years to compose this work, as early as 1930 she had begun to consider setting a book once again in Manhattan.

Six years before it was published, long before she even set pen to paper, the author had begun shaping in her diaries this new novel of the city. Diary readers may look on as she begins assiduously to plan "the Lila novel"[30] (*Diaries,* 80), as she originally referred to it. In some of her first recorded thoughts on this new book of New York, she wrote, "I will not cheat myself so as to start a novel in which I do not believe," as she had presumably done with *Whither.* "Let it be lousy when it's finished. That's different. But, to save my soul, I hope I never have to undertake a big novel with no faith in it or myself" (27). This time she meant to be utterly sure of it—and of herself. To that end she began meticulously planning it, outlining it, mapping it in her diaries. Determined that this next publication would bring her favorite city vibrantly to life in a way that she had not even attempted in the first, she wrote that it should be "full of [the] delicate sharp outlines of New York of today" (61). Not only had she at last begun to believe that she had come to know the bars and restaurants, the hotels and cafés, the office buildings and the city streets well enough to place her story there, but she at last had also come to know Manhattan's commercial trades and those who worked in them well enough to create a story that could happen, and characters that could exist, no place else. She confided in her diary, "In *Turn, Magic Wheel* I believe firmly that I have the perfect New York story, one woman's tragedy viewed through the chinks of a writer's book about her, newspaper clippings, cafe conversations, restaurant brawls, New York night life, so that the story is tangled in the fritter of New York—it could not happen anyplace else" (106). As Powell said, she meant for New York to serve as more than a simple backdrop to the book; "pacing" the novel "to the city's jagged syncopations" (Gibbons, 143), she literally infused the story with it, the city sometimes reflecting, sometimes imitating, sometimes colluding with the characters who populate this raucous send-up of the Manhattan literary world.

Moreover, as always, she wished for every word of the novel to seem entirely believable. She wrote, "Nothing will cut New York but a diamond. . . . [This novel] should be crystal in quality, sharp as the skyline and re-lentlessly true" (*Diaries,* 84). Many of Powell's contemporaries believe that she succeeded on that count: Peter Burra praised the novel's "complete free-dom from pretense" (72), the *New York Times'* Edith Walton said that "the book on the whole rings savagely true" (7), and Jerre Mangione wrote that Powell's "burlesque has a firm basis of truth" (81). The heavy plotting of the novel in her journals and the decade-long wait to set another book in

Manhattan paid off in the end, producing a novel of New York that for many was free of pretense.

But at the outset Powell had more trouble beginning this novel than any other. Despite her meticulous planning, she wrote that this "New York novel sounded so strained and unnatural as I started it. I could see I was a fish out of water" (*Diaries*, 26), a description that might more accurately fit her writing of *Whither*. Why so much trouble starting the novel, she wondered, especially because "as a rule I have a fine excitement in the beginning" (*Diaries*, 28)? A short time later, continuing in this vein, she wrote: "I could not understand why, with Lila's story so clearly and concisely mapped out, I couldn't whiz right through it" (37). At last she discovered that all the long months of laborious planning had backfired on her: "A novel must be a rich forest known at the start only by instinct," she decided. "To have all the paths marked, the trees already labeled, is no more incentive to enter than Central Park is a temptation to explorers" (*Diaries*, 37–38). Having been so determined never to write another book that she did not wholly believe in, she had belabored this new effort, plotting it at every turn and thereby losing the element of discovery she had enjoyed when writing her previous novels.

So, momentarily setting the New York project aside, she turned to writing the Ohio novel that would be published as *The Tenth Moon*, returning to *Turn, Magic Wheel* only once the former was finished. Gaining some distance from the endless plotting, it turned out, would serve her well: she eventually would come to call it "very likely my best, simplest, most original book" (*At Her Best*, xvii), a distinction she frequently conferred also on the Ohio novel *Dance Night*.

I think this is much my best book, expresses more of my own self than anything else I ever did.

—*Diaries*, 99

The diaries allow readers to see Powell rigorously planning her new novel, to understand her difficulty in beginning it, and also to observe her reflecting on decisions she had earlier made and long since incorporated. In one entry Powell sounds satisfied with her decision to make *Turn, Magic Wheel*'s main character, Dennis Orphen, a man rather than a woman—as she had done before, for example, in the Ohio novels *Dance Night* and *The Story of a Country Boy*. Not only would a male protagonist enjoy freedoms that a typical female protagonist would not, such as being able to walk the night-time city streets alone in relative safety, but the author also found the idea of a principal male character useful for other reasons: "How much sharper and better to have the central figure a man rather than a woman. A man in whom my own prejudices and ideas can easily be placed, whereas few women's minds (certainly not Effie's or Corinne's[31]) flit as irresponsibly as that," she wrote (*Diaries*, 96). In this entry Powell confides that alter ego Dennis Orphen embraces at least some of her own ideas, perceptions, and biases, if readers who knew something of the writer had not noticed on their own. Of course the very name "Orphen" is significant: Powell had long fancied herself an orphan, having at the age of seven lost her mother and having a too-often absent father. John Updike remarked on the similarity of the character's name to that of Orpha Mae, Powell's favorite aunt ("Ohio," 269). Unlike *Whither*, about which few if any novelistic decisions she had made would please her, this novel would earn approval not only from Powell but, as it turns out, from many of her critics.

In the new novel, the New York backdrop is vital to all the scenes she writes: she intended that the book radiate with "the sharp detail [of Man-hattan] as seen by one who sees it seldom but then with desperate longing. The Empire State—Coney Island—the Ambassador or Waldorf—the pat-tern of New York" (*Diaries*, 61–62). The Empire State, as Powell spoke of it in 1931, was still new, construction having just begun in March 1930. Two months after its completion, in July 1931, the author recounted her first visit to the extraordinary new building:

> An evening up on the Empire State roof—the strangest
> experience. The huge tomb in steel and glass, the ride to the
> 84th floor and there, under the clouds, a Hawaiian string
> quartet, lounge, concessions and, a thousand feet below,
> New York—a garden of golden lights winking on and off,
> automobiles, trucks winding in and out, and not a sound. All as
> silent as a dead city. (*Diaries*, 32)

A year later, in September 1932, she wrote of a second visit, this time expanding on her original account:

> It was divinely beautiful and strange up there. Clouds, as
> white as if the sky were baby blue, swam beneath us and stars
> were below us. They glittered through the clouds and the

town lay spread out in its spangles like Christmas presents
waiting to be opened, its clangor sifted through space into a
whispering silence. It held a secret, and when suddenly letters
flamed together in the sky you felt—ah, so that's it. "Sunshine
Biscuits," the message of the city. (*Diaries*, 54)

An adaptation of the two diary entries appears later in *Turn, Magic
Wheel*, the passage expressing the author's own breathless wonder at the
view from atop the building. It would become one of the best known and
most frequently cited passages of any in Powell:

New York twinkled far off into Van Cortland Park, spangled
skyscrapers piled up softly against the darkness, tinseled parks
were neatly boxed and ribboned with gold like Christmas
presents waiting to be opened. Sounds of traffic dissolved in
distance, all clangor sifted through space into a whispering
silence, it held a secret, and when letters flamed triumphantly
in the sky, you felt, ah, that was the secret, this at last was it,
this special telegram to God—Sunshine Biscuits. On and off it
went, Eat Sunshine Biscuits, the message of the city.[32] (156)

In these few lines, the author captures not only New York's gorgeous
decadence but its incessant message of consumerism as well. Given her
history, Powell would appreciate the Sunshine advertiser's good fortune in
that his creation is so brightly visible from atop the world's newest, tall-
est structure, while at the same time she would recognize the irony that
this mundane message of commerce, placed as it is above the glittering
city and among the stars, seemed to suggest profound meanings, to di-
vulge long-hidden secrets, as if it were a veritable message to the gods. Both
Richard Lingeman and Tim Page remark on Powell's having disrupted the
poetic quality of her scene by attaching to it the Sunshine Biscuit message.
Lingeman says, "One perceived her sensing a Symbol bearing down on her
in mid-poetic flight, so she deftly undercuts it. The worst thing is to seem
to be taking oneself too seriously" (40), while for Page the attachment of the
Sunshine ad indicates "a marvelous combination of her brilliant powers of
description and her sort of puckish humor" (Hansen, "Dawn Powell").

But more than that, Powell's advertising image parallels such images
created by other noteworthy writers of the period. For one, Powell's oversized Sunshine Biscuit sign is reminiscent of the giant advertising billboard

depicting a pair of washed-out spectacles in *The Great Gatsby*, Fitzgerald's landmark novel of New York, which had been published in the same year as Powell's much flimsier *Whither*.[33] If we imagine the mortified author of *Whither* in those eleven years between that first novel and this one looking back on earlier releases, we might not be surprised to find echoes of *Gatsby* in *Turn, Magic Wheel*.[34] Fitzgerald writes of the imposing but forgotten billboard:

> [A]bove the grey land and the spasms of bleak dust which drift endlessly over it, you perceive, after a moment, the eyes of Dr. T. J. Eckleburg. The eyes of Dr. T. J. Eckleburg are blue and gigantic—their retinas are one yard high. They look out of no face but, instead, from a pair of enormous yellow spectacles, which pass over a non-existent nose. Evidently some wild wag of an oculist [had] set them there to fatten his practice. (23–24)

Also in 1925, Virginia Woolf's *Mrs. Dalloway* was issued. Woolf includes in the novel an episode during which the word "TOFFEE" appears written across the skies, to the wonder and distraction of those who have come to gaze on the queen, the message of commerce detracting from the pomp of the royal visit:

> So, thought Septimus, looking up, they are signaling to me. Not indeed in actual words; that is, he could not read the language yet; but it was plain enough, this beauty, this exquisite beauty, and tears filled his eyes as he looked at the smoke words languishing and melting in the sky and bestowing upon him in their inexhaustible charity and laughing goodness one shape after another of unimaginable beauty and signaling their intention to provide him, for nothing, for ever, for looking merely, with beauty, more beauty! . . .
> It was toffee; they were advertising toffee. (31)

The Sunshine Biscuit ad, Dr. T. J. Eckleburg's spectacles, and Woolf's toffee sign all illustrate the graphic advertising power of the written word.

Five years after Woolf's and Fitzgerald's novels appeared, William Carlos Williams, in "The Attic Which Is Desire," describes the poet's view as he gazes from his New Jersey attic-studio window to the street below, only to fix his eyes on another message of commerce:

the unused tent of
bare beams
beyond which
directly wait

the night
and day—

Here
from the street

by
* * *
* S *
* O *
* D *
* A *
* * *

ringed with
running lights
the darkened
pane
exactly
down the center
is
transfixed. (325)

Woolf's skywritten TOFFEE notice,[35] Fitzgerald's oversized DR. T. J. ECKLEBURG dump-heap billboard, Williams's neon SODA sign, and Powell's blinking SUNSHINE BISCUIT advertisement are four modernistic signs of a new commerce appearing all at once as if from nowhere, right out of the skies.[36]

In Powell's novel, the Empire State Building functions as more than an awe-inspiring backdrop to the story: it is also somehow complicit in the sexual affair between the commitment-shy protagonist Dennis Orphen[37] and his married girlfriend, Corinne, whom he furtively meets there. If, as Laura Barrett says of Fitzgerald's billboard in *Gatsby*, "the eyes seem to pass judgment on the residents of the Valley of Ashes, or so thinks George Wilson" (10), one might argue that Powell's blinking Sunshine Biscuit ad, too, passes judgment on the nefarious doings of Corinne and Dennis as they

meet under his eyes across the building, the advertising images "contributing to the sense of blindness and deception" in both novels (10).

Yet still the building shrouds the illicit pair in secrecy, elevating them
high above the eyes of the world below, if not of the high-placed Sunshine
ad, while enveloping them in an illusion of innocence: "Clouds as white as if
the sky was baby blue instead of black swam softly about them" (152), Powell writes, again taking words from her journal and adapting them to her
story. Not only the Empire State Building but other glimmering New York
locales will serve as alluring settings and more. As John Updike notes, in
this novel "the city is more than its geography and buildings; it is the secret
eroticism that a place so purely human concentrates, like a perfume pressed
from a thousand flowers" ("Ohio," 271). Readers will see that Manhattan
locales in this novel function in a variety of roles, from confidante, ally, and
accomplice, as here; to mirror, judge, and even rival.

The picture Powell paints of the Empire State Building is but one "in a
succession of quick-firing images" she will continue to provide throughout
the novel; readers of *Turn, Magic Wheel* soon grow "conscious of a sharp
intelligence directing, an uninhibited eye observing" her City and its inhabitants (R. Lehmann, 90). Powell evokes, just as she had so carefully
planned, "the beauty and sheer thrill of New York" (*Diaries*, 80), not only
150 pages into the novel, where her image of the famed building appears,
but in fact from the book's outset, where Manhattan locales serve as aids to
understanding—or misunderstanding—character.

~~~~~~~~~~~~~~~~~~~~~~~~~~~~~~~~~~~~~

Ohio-born novelist Dennis Orphen, whom Gore Vidal refers to as "a male
surrogate for Powell herself" ("American," 10), is insatiably curious, ever watchful.
As Mary Ross, reviewing the novel on its release, writes, "Behind [Powell's
stories] lies the kind of curiosity that goaded Dennis" (8). Perceptively, sounding
exactly as if she had read Powell's private—and heretofore unpublished—
diaries, she adds, "It is that genuine desire to know, I think, which gives her
books the substance and vigor and spontaneity not often found in the work
of an established novelist" (8). As Powell confided in her diary, "Curiosity is a
rare gift, particularly when combined with acute observation, understanding
or perception—not mere nosiness of the baffled ignorant who are only curious
because [what they see] is different from their limited views" (430). One of her
friends, William Peterson, remarked on Powell's "usual watchful, calm reserve"
whenever they met (37), and, in one revealing anecdote, the novelist illustrates

the difference between herself and others: In a traffic jam on a Fifth Avenue bus, the driver told the passengers that this day was to be his last, after twenty-five years. No one responded, Powell says, and no one cared. But she wanted to ask him, "What are your plans? And why have you quit? Or were you fired? Are you glad?'" (*Diaries*, 318). Since the time she was a child, Dawn was always motivated by a desire to know.

New York, a city of perpetual distraction

—*Diaries*, 106

Early in the novel, the ever curious Dennis fixes his eyes on a pert young woman he chances to encounter downtown, attempting to determine her story, to fill in the blanks so that he can understand her from the inside out, as writers, he tells himself, will do:

> Dennis followed the little blonde down Second Avenue, at first absently and then deliberately as she came out of Dolly Raoul's Studio of Stage Dancing . . . high heeled gray suede boots, Russian style, clapping firmly down on the pavement, head with its firm yellow curls exploding beneath the green felt hat, but Dennis found now a conscious coquetry in the rhythmic swirl of her skirt, and disillusioned, he stood for a moment at the Fourth Street corner watching her swish right, left, right, left across the street—What called her to the other side?
>
> . . . She was gone, perhaps into the side gate . . . he would never see her again, never, though already the next encounter flickered on the screen—the Paradise or possibly the Folies Bergere [*sic*], and the cigarette girl leaning her tray on his table . . . A little Turkish cap on her head this time and embroidered trousers, but the same girl, the same sharp nose, same galaxy of tight blonde curls. So you weren't a dancer, so you weren't ambitious East Side but nostalgic Broadway all the time. (6–7)

Here and throughout the novel, New York locations will suggest certain ideas about characters; where they reside, where they work will insinuate, correctly or incorrectly, volumes about them. Witness this exchange as Dennis's friend Effie introduces him to wealthy Upper-East-Side matron Belle Glaenzer:

"Dennis Orphen. He lives near me."

"In Chelsea?" asked Belle.

"No, no—near Union Square," Effie stammered and flushed as if, just as Belle suspected, the fellow was a dubious connection indeed.

"Union Square?" repeated Belle, examining critically Dennis's none-too-impressive figure . . . "Union Square never recommended any visitor yet, young lady. Is he one of those radicals?" (78)

Clearly Dennis Orphen is no radical; in fact, though after his first novel he is categorized as a writer of the proletariat who, like Powell, "satirizes his own class" (200), he is far more conservative than the other tenants in his building: a full-fledged Communist lives right upstairs. While Belle's supposition has its basis in a truth she knows about the city—that radicals have long lived in the vicinity of Union Square—such assumptions, Powell lets the reader know, are frequently incorrect; writers such as Orphen must take pains never to presume too much. Dennis understands that he has been mistaken in his assumptions about the blonde girl he had followed, just as Belle is mistaken in her assumptions about Dennis. Later, readers will see that Dennis is also mistaken in many of his assumptions about Effie, the unwitting subject of his latest novel, *The Hunter's Wife.* The Orphen novel is a sort of exposé of Effie's marriage to and divorce from Andrew Callingham, a famed writer based on Ernest Hemingway.[38] Incidentally, if ever there were any doubt about the original of the Callingham character, Page has quelled it: he has now located a drawing of Callingham done by Powell that looks exactly like Hemingway.

Themes of mistaken assumptions, unfortunate misunderstandings, false impressions, and the idea that no one can ever thoroughly know or understand another person, or even oneself, run through the novel. Perhaps not surprisingly, at the same time she was plotting *Turn, Magic Wheel,* Powell wrote that she had begun to believe that she understood others far better than she did herself (*Diaries,* 28).

The asininity of the critics . . .

—*Diaries,* 63

If in *Whither* Powell had attempted to ridicule the faux artist types she seemed forever to be encountering, here, in this "delightfully witty satire on the New York literary scene, where novelists write novels about other novelists and their novels" (Brickell, 21), she has a field day satirizing the Manhattan literary world she knows so well, by this time having had countless dealings, too often unpleasant, with publishers, editors, agents, book reviewers,[39] and newspaper and magazine columnists.[40] We have seen some of the comments that reviewers and editors made regarding Powell's previous works, comments she almost always considered idiotic. Yet so often did editors, publishers, and reviewers either reprove or ignore Powell's writings that she occasionally, if fleetingly, came to doubt herself. She fretted that her "continued faith" in the "value" of her work was "dogged proof of amateur egotism (they can't *all* be wrong in ignoring me as not up to the Isa Glenns,[41] Ellen Glasgows,[42] Storm Jamesons[43] and other crap writers)[44] and so it's possible my own standards are at fault" (*Diaries,* 68). But in the end Powell remained a staunch believer in herself and in her work; she always returned to her view that it was the others who were mistaken in their estimations of her writing. As Lisa Zeidner says, "Powell retained a lucid assurance about the value of her vision" (2). Not only were the words of critics, publishers, and agents distasteful to her, though; the writings of journalists—"nobody can make a shrew out of a jolly woman quicker than a newspaper man" (*Diaries,* 178)—and columnists, to her mind, were little better: "Columnists—the fawners of all time—work on [the well-known], rebuild them, tenderly nurture them, though later, if they are on the skids (usually financially), they say 'Drink did it' or 'Women did it' or 'Overwork did it" or 'Social climbing did it'—in fact, all the things that made their success are accused of being the causes of their downfall" (*Diaries,* 214). She also had a word or two to say about book advertisements and the publications that print them. In *Turn, Magic Wheel,* Powell's narrator says that real-life personage Louis Bromfield,[45] after reading *The Hunter's Wife,* is heard to mutter a single noncommittal word. That word later absurdly appears in print, along with a few other single-word appraisals, in recommendation of the book:

> ... Announcement in *Publishers Weekly* ...
> On Thursday, April 11
> The Hunter's Wife
> by Dennis Orphen
> What they say ...
> "Fine ..." Louis Bromfield. (107)

Reading her diary, one sees that nearly twenty years later Powell would have something of a real-life adventure with Bromfield again having to do with a single word. She writes that on a visit to Shelby in 1954 she was asked to accompany her aunt and sisters on what they surely considered a chic literary visit to Bromfield's Ohio farm, a trip they likely imagined as somehow in keeping with Powell's heady New York lifestyle. The novelist, however, excused herself from going; she reported that "everyone . . . was stunned and bewildered that I didn't want to accept this honor" (340). When the family returned, her sister Phyllis, who "never got over the thrill" of the trip, reported having asked the great man if he had ever heard of Dawn Powell. "*Certainly,*" he replied (340).

Having by now become all too familiar with "tactless publishers and crass editorial interference" (Wyndham, 39), Powell in *Turn, Magic Wheel* shoots a few rounds straight into the hearts of the city's publishers and editors and their protégés, whose main goal, it seems to her, is not art but profit, not distinction but uniformity, not innovation but reliance on the old, tried, and tired. The novel's publishing executive MacTweed—allusive of Boss Tweed, corrupt New York City politician—is firmly taken to task here. A "comic invention worthy of any in Dickens" ("About This Book," 1), MacTweed, when readers first meet him, is spouting idiocies through nicotine-"stained fangs" (101); later one sees him childishly pounding on his desktop so hard that the children's book editor in the adjoining office is made to spill ink all over her proofs. MacTweed's hands, furthermore, are "tobacco-stained, calloused, the nails ripped off and appallingly unkempt" (104), in contrast to the "large, beautifully tended white hands" of his newest and still hopeful partner in the firm.

Readers next meet an editor and magazine publisher called Okie, name suggestive of small-town backgrounds and small-minded attitudes. Publisher of a weekly called *The Town*, he is "a tiresome red-faced fellow" who "always used one's full name as if it were a title and would fill hearers with awe—not *the* Dennis Orphen, as if he were Al Smith or somebody" (28). Habitué of the famous Fourteenth Street bar and restaurant Luchow's,[46] the "too-too average Okie" (120) obtrusively conducts the German waltz orchestra from his table, first with his finger, then with his knife, and finally with his menu. Accompanying him at dinner are a couple of young blonde women—actresses—who "kept exchanging glances of veiled meaning and took turns borrowing nickels from Okie to telephone wonderful men somewhere else" (31). Obviously, better company is to be found elsewhere, despite Okie's largesse.

From MacTweed and Okie, Powell turns to the subordinate lemming types she finds so plentiful in the publishing trade, the crowds of yes-men to the MacTweeds, the tribes of subordinates to the Okies. Echoing a letter she had earlier written to her Ohio cousin Jack Sherman, in which she says that New York City "is full of standard young Harvard men, all exactly alike—we make fun of them" (76), she absolutely "makes fun of them" here: in a riotous scene, Powell sends up what she considers just so many cookie-cutter Harvard types, whom she refers to as "And Company":

> They all looked alike. . . . Keen, long-jawed, tallish young men
> with sleek mouse-colored hair, large mouths filled with strong big
> white teeth good for gnawing bark or raw coconuts but doubtless
> taxed chiefly by moules[47] or at the most squab, nearsighted
> pleasant eyes under unrimmed glasses that might be bifocal,
> large ears set away from the head like good aerials, large carefully
> manicured hands, a bit soft, and agreeable deep voices left
> over from old Glee Clubs. . . . These And Companys, many in
> publishing, some in their uncles' devious businesses, were all men
> of good taste, and if Semitic were decent enough to be blond and
> even a little dumb just to be more palatable socially. (98)

One particular And Company, Johnson, is the sole And Company given a name, and a common name at that. Although he feebly attempts to break free from the crowd, to set himself apart, primarily so that he might be promoted, he finds that everything he does is mimicked by the others: when he marries a showgirl from *Face the Music*[48] instead of the standard Bryn Mawr girl, so do all the other And Companys (98); when he and his wife have a "little blond baby," it is the same little blond baby "everyone was having that year" (99). Later, deciding "to throw his fellows off the track by lunching at the Vanderbilt or 70 Park instead of the club, they all went to lunch with him—indeed, they were there first, their fine clean-cut jaws uttering well-bred baritone remarks, never too personal, never too witty for good taste" (99). Finally, taking to drinking applejack instead of scotch, Johnson sees that the others "all ordered applejack. He saw them all over the country clubs and town restaurants, he saw them in bar mirrors, rows of clean-cut, spectacled, somewhat adenoidal young men drinking applejack, hats at the same angle . . . they were all the same except for one who had a boil on his neck. Johnson envied this pioneer, this rebel" (99). The only characteristic that sets one apart from the others is a hideous if laughable

accident of nature, certainly nothing of the man's own doing, and a temporary distinction at that.

Johnson at last succeeds in distinguishing himself from the other And
Companys by growing a mustache that is "as large as an anchovy"; the inspiration behind the mustache, however, had come not from his own imagination but from a Japanese And Company he had recently encountered at
the Oriental Wholesale House on Fifth Avenue. To make up for the mustache's small size, Johnson colors it with his wife's eye pencil, leaving it "a
rich emphatic black color" while his "own hair was only hair-colored" (100).
This absurd emblem of difference makes Johnson feel confident enough to
speak up to "his master MacTweed" who at first balks at Johnson's suggestion that they publish Orphen's latest novel. It would hardly be "ethical,"
the odious MacTweed bellows, to publish a novel in which "one author satirizes another" (101). All the while, both the reader and Johnson understand
that MacTweed is thinking of profit and not of ethics: he is afraid only of
perhaps alienating Callingham, a vastly more popular writer than Orphen,
thereby losing out on a potential opportunity to publish the bigger seller.
It is hilarious, too, to realize that Powell is at the same time writing precisely the same sort of satirical novel about just such a famous writer
as Callingham/Hemingway and cheekily imagining her own publisher's
objections to it. And, as it happens, she is not far off track. Farrar and
Rinehart, who had been her publisher since *Dance Night*, initially refused
the first pages of the manuscript of *Turn, Magic Wheel* she had submitted,[49]
John Farrar advising Powell by letter to tear it up and throw it out (*Diaries*,
444), though in the end the company, of course, did publish it. As it turns
out, *Turn, Magic Wheel* would sell more copies for Farrar and Rinehart than
any of Powell's novels had sold for them before or would sell again (*Bio*, 151).

Still, the author had every right to be dissatisfied with this publishing
company that a few years before had done nothing for the beautifully plaintive Ohio novel *Dance Night*, on which she had worked so diligently and for
which she had had such high hopes. A diary entry on its 1930 release says
simply, "*Dance Night* came out with dull thud. Went to country and very
discouraged and weepy" (16). Later, the weepiness having turned to anger,
Powell wrote,

> *Dance Night*—two years work—received less attention
> than my other books because Farrar and Rinehart hate to
> mention anything but "tripe" virtues in connection with their

publications. This is bad because while it sells tripe (Widdemer, Brush,[50] etc.) it only angers a tripe-hunting reader to find he's been misled into something literary. I owe $2100 on the book.[51] (*Diaries*, 23)

Sadly, Powell would never get over either the lack of publicity given her favorite Ohio novel or its resultant dismal sales. For years she would revisit the "crippling" (31) disappointment of *Dance Night* in her diaries, often insisting that it was her best book, always lamenting its absolute failure.[52]

Going up today to get evening dress. In that place . . . perfume girl comes in with trace of Matchabelli to squirt at you.

—*Diaries*, 106

Having in *Whither* and elsewhere roasted the sneering department store clerk whose aim it is to make humble shoppers feel less than adequate, thereby inducing them to spend money they do not have, Powell here returns to the Fifth Avenue world of judgmental shop girls. The aging, fortyish Effie learns that Andrew is returning to New York from Europe at last, though she is unaware that he is coming not to see her but because he feels it is time he makes a publicity appearance and because his latest, one Asta Lundgren, *Premiere Danseuse,* is to be appearing in Manhattan at the Garden Follies[53] (179). Still somehow hoping that he is returning to her, however, Effie shops the fashionable stores in a vain attempt to recapture not only her ex-husband but her youth. Ordering filmy, flimsy, impractically youthful clothing and lingerie, the types of garments Andrew had always wanted her to wear years before but which she never did,

> Effie was brought to a pause by the suspicious interrogation in the salesgirl's eyes. You can't pay for these, said the look, and for whom do you buy these bridal treasures, surely not for your old poor person, modest finances betrayed by ready-made coat, counter hat, bargain gloves, pawnshop antique silver necklace, basement pocketbook. Effie threw up her shoulders haughtily at the inquisition, flung out Mrs. Anthony Glaenzer's name as the charge's name, and then she thought Why, it's true, I can't pay for these things. (129–30)

But like Zoe in *Whither,* like Mr. Willard in *My Home Is Far Away,* buy them she does.

As we have seen, from the novel's outset Powell places her provincial writer character Dennis Orphen in the crowded, vibrant streets of Manhattan, responding to the sights and sounds about him as he broods over his profession, much as Powell forever brooded in her diaries over her own. Having determined that curiosity is the basis of his writing, as Powell herself many times said it was of hers,[54] Orphen walks by "the reading rooms of the Forty-second Street library," where Powell had often gone to write, and seeing "countless people absorbed in books," he wonders "Why absorbed? What do they read? Why do they read it?" When they "look up and away," he asks himself, "what sentence stirred what memories?" (4–5). As Mary Ross says, "The curiosity from which Dennis suffers, the need to know why *this* person does *this* thing, is the stuff of the storyteller's art" (8) and the stuff of Powell's. Always on the lookout for material, having now lost sight of the blonde dancer with the tightly curled hair, Dennis concludes that he will never be as able to get inside the stranger as he could get inside Effie, and so he guiltily excuses his having furtively studied his friend, in fact betrayed her, in order to write his novel.

Effie, as Powell planned her, should be "swift, intense, violently real, moving as a brave, generous, gallant woman, eager to do things to help, bound by her life" (*Diaries,* 87), and she is one of the most remarkable and sympathetic characters in all of Powell. Long-suffering, noble, high-minded Effie, "who had never lied to a living soul, who had never betrayed anyone, had committed no crime in her whole life" (49), is long divorced from famed writer Andrew Callingham.[55] Effie is as innocent a character as Andrew is guilty. He, a preening and performing artist rather than a hardworking one, is plainly neither the kind of writer nor the kind of human being Powell admired, as readers of *Whither* know. Although Callingham does not appear until the end of the novel, we hear of him frequently and come to await his arrival as do Effie and his second ex-wife, Marian, who lies dying of cancer in a Manhattan hospital. The unsympathetic Andy is described by a fellow character as "a big hairy roaring sort of guy—he-man. Loved trying out every woman he met" (35). Readers hear of his exploits and his reputation, but never of the discipline of his writing; instead, he seems to be forever womanizing, posing for photographers, and parading his fame.[56] Powell herself rarely posed for publicity cameras, though she did tell of one occasion on which she succumbed to a photographer's request, only because she found the set-up so hilarious: "Today I posed eating a pineapple at my typewriter for the J. Walter Thompson Agency—the funniest thing I ever heard of, so funny I couldn't help doing it even though Coby thought it was a hideous lowering of myself" (*Diaries*, 71). That instance was an anomaly; Powell generally shied away from publicity of all sorts. James Gibbons remarks that "As much as Powell quite reasonably sought fame herself, she was acutely aware that celebrity can turn writers into Personages whose self-importance blunts their perceptions" (156), much as Andrew's celebrity has blunted his.

Callingham's ever-loyal first wife Effie, who lives under the delusion that some day he will come back to her, is nevertheless the better person. It is her story that Dennis surreptitiously takes from her, her story and, through it, Callingham's, that Dennis without permission tells. Though Orphen does feel guilty about what he has done, he at the same time readily excuses it, trying to convince himself that the novelist is pardoned for such doings, that the literary art requires such trespass.

In addition to events she had witnessed and recorded in either diary or letter and then, transforming them, included in her novels, Powell also included in her journal sketches of the people she happened to meet, later incorporating them in her works. For example, in her diary Powell briefly recounted a second meeting with the male half of a couple she had previously been introduced to: "Party with Vincent Sheean,[57] Coby and Mr. Baby," she wrote. "I asked where was Mrs. Baby (I'd forgotten their names, only remembered that they called each other Baby) and he gravely said 'bust up.' That's what happens to these babies" (39). The couple had captured her imagination sufficiently to eventually become the well-drawn Corinne and Phil Barrow in *Turn, Magic Wheel*. In the novel, at a dinner party celebrating the publication of *The Hunter's Wife*, Dennis's mistress, the dimwitted Corinne, has been said actually to have read the new book. "'Is that so, Baby? You read it, did you?' Phil deferred eagerly to Baby's intellect, as if her having read it showed far more brilliance than merely having written it" (121). Corinne replies, "'I think it's really very good . . . You know, Baby, I think there's a picture in it. It would suit Ann Harding'"[58] (122). After this exchange, Dennis, appalled, "strove vainly to force Corinne's attention so she might see his scorn. *Baby!* So, not only did her husband call her Baby, but she called him Baby, too! . . . Good God! What was he doing here between these Babys?" (122). If no one Orphen meets is safe from his pen, few Powell met were safe from hers.

Like Orphen, Powell guiltily mentioned her writerly habit of spying on friends and acquaintances; like Orphen, Powell excused having done so in the name of art. Contemplating the fact that this new novel was to be based on one or more famous persons, the author wrote that it never-theless "must be burningly contemporary, even libelous if necessary—no words to be spared, no feelings saved, no recognition softened. This is to be the works" (*Diaries*, 96). The book is sharply contemporary, just as Powell had designed it to be: Rosamond Lehmann, for one, noted upon its release that the novel is "microscopically contemporary and immediate . . . *Turn, Magic Wheel* is a section of that harsh, ugly, strident thing called Life" (90). Another reviewer found the book "an ultramodern novel for sophisticated readers" (*Booklist*, 155). Further, Powell's prophetic words, above, echo her descriptions of Orphen's book, *The Hunter's Wife;* certainly no feelings will be saved in its writing. Though on one level Orphen is ashamed of his having betrayed Effie, the novel supplies worse types who, in comparison, might help assuage his guilt: far less principled than Orphen are the novel's money-hungry publishers who will go so far as to try to convince Effie "to deny that the book had anything to do with her" (95), hoping to protect themselves from the financial loss a potential lawsuit would cause them. At the bottom of the advertisement in *Publishers Weekly*, in fact, they had resorted to printing the following lie:

> "All the characters in this novel are highly fictitious" (107).

More than a scorching satire of the publishing industry, however, more than a *Whither*-like tale of provincials struggling in Manhattan, *Turn, Magic Wheel* is a novel of longing and reminiscence, of empathy and grace, of love and loyalty, of shattered dreams and broken hearts. Teachout calls the novel "a glittering comedy of manners in which [Powell's] mature self comes instantaneously into focus from the first page onward" ("Far," 5). As the jacket blurb on the 1999 reissue says, "Powell's famous wit was never sharper than here, but *Turn, Magic Wheel* is also one of the most poignant and heart-wrenching of her novels" ("About This Book," 1). After having met with so many disappointments, her novels so often panned by critics, ignored by buyers, she said, during the planning phase of *Turn, Magic Wheel*, "I will do real people, relentlessly, truly, unmasked—now I have nothing to lose" (*Diaries*, 88). The novel is a story of personal invasion and disclosure, of laying hidden truths bare, an issue Powell wrestled with for decades, as her journals and letters attest. But it is an issue that many writers struggle with: Joan Didion, for example, notes that writers are "always ratting somebody out. . . . [to do so, they] must be possessed of a certain amount of ruthlessness" (Beha). This "ratting out" is precisely what Orphen does to Effie in a heartrending scene. Upon learning that he has been secretly studying her, learning of the book he has been writing about her and her ex-husband only just before it appears in bookstores, she trembles at the thought of exposure. Rather than react in anger, however, she calmly tells him, "You don't mind if I hide for a few days after the book comes out, do you? I mean—you know—I hate people finding out that Andy deserted me, that's all. I'd rather they just went on thinking we—well—were temporarily away from each other " (23). Dennis stares at her in disbelief, then explodes with, "Is that all? . . . Why everyone's always known that he walked out on you, if that's all that worries you about the book. Hell, Effie, that's no news to anybody!" (23). He storms out, angry at himself, angry at her, in fact "angry at the whole mess" (24), leaving Effie wounded and alone:

> Waiting quietly until the slamming of the front door showed he had gone, hands clutched together in her lap, a little hole in her mind where the bullet had gone through—"everyone has always known he walked out on you"—and nothing to put in its place but an old swimming pain, that same almost-forgotten pain of smiling gaily at the party, eyes fixed on companion—don't turn, don't wince, don't pale, don't show you see Andy pulling the blonde girl out onto the balcony with that veiled excited look in his eyes. . . . She stood up astonished that legs could support this heavy stone, legs marched out the door, one, two, one, two, downstairs one flight . . . down one flight more into the vestibule, and stop, turn, look. There was the card on her mailbox:
>
> Mrs. Andrew Callingham
>
> It had been there and on all her mailboxes for years, secretly shaming her before the world. It was incredible that she had not realized its mocking pretensions before, somehow it had seemed only loyalty, it was to show Andy she bore no grudge. . . .

She pulled the little white card out of the mailbox and turned it over. On the back her trembling fingers printed in pencil—

Miss Effie Thorne

—and put it back in place. (25–26)

Effie's hurt is palpable, her delicate sense of honor wounded. *Turn, Magic Wheel,* far from simply a scathing, gay romp, includes some of the haunting, lyrical qualities for which Powell's Ohio novels are known but for which her New York novels generally are not. Page, too, discovers the melancholy air in the work, noting that although the novel is a "dizzying, hilarious send-up of Manhattan literary life," it is at the same time "so funny and so sad, so riotous and so realistic, so acute and yet so accepting in the portrayal of flawed humankind" (*At Her Best,* xx–xxi). At the same time, of course, in it Powell exposed friends, acquaintances, and business associates who she knew would recognize themselves in its pages, though it no longer seemed to matter.[59]

If in Powell's first novel Manhattan failed to come alive, there is no mistaking that in *Turn, Magic Wheel* it becomes a living, breathing character that preens, poses, strives. As Richard Lingeman says, "New York [is] the central character in her novels about the city, and she evoked it as memorably as any of her contemporaries" (40). In an animated portrait of a not-quite-topnotch midtown saloon that attempts to appear to be what it is not, just as so many of her characters do, Powell's narrator writes, "It was like all of the wonderful secret places Okie discovered in the Broadway district, little places with their own special crowd, tail ends of the theater, fringes and pale copies of more celebrated circles" (159). The bar, a low-budget joint where the proprietor serves also as the night's entertainment, is likewise populated with "pale copies" of "more celebrated" types. In one of dozens of comic portraits of tiny, peripheral characters, Powell writes,

A large policeman-type tenor walked slowly about the floor, singing in a rich honeyed whine; this was really the proprietor, easy enough to guess, for even while he was somberly whining "A boyuh—ahnd—ah gurrul—war dahncing"—he kept a keen eye on the bartender to make sure no cheating was going on, and

> when he was not warbling, this shrewd fellow (called 'Sammy'
> to suggest the affectionate esteem of the Broadway crowd)
> stood in the outer vestibule bowing welcome to new arrivals but
> fixing eyes on an innocent mirror upon which the bar activities
> were remirrored, all of which the bartender knew perfectly well,
> having been warned by the Cuban hat-check girl. (159)

The author's *restaurateur* is the very image of one depicted in Caroline Ware's documentary account, wherein a certain New York nightclub's "proprietor stood by the door greeting everybody, eying all newcomers and making announcements" (253), and presumably a type familiar to the nightlife-loving Powell.[60] Only the mirror is absent. In the novel, the bar itself is an accessory, an abettor, implicated in the watching while all the time understood by the watched. And if the barroom mirrors the bartender's doings, it also mirrors the striving, posing, grasping attitudes of its customers:

> That Boots was Tony's girlfriend was patent from Tony's all-
> enveloping princely possessive air, and from the girl's discreet
> manner, a special arrogance that could pass for "class" and small
> wonder she should adopt this air, for Tony, with her, became
> doubly the aristocrat, triply the aloof patrician; his pointed
> absorption in her declared defiantly her worthiness for the
> honor, and permitted her to share in his own private privilege of
> snubbing her friends. (159–60)

Powell always had a clear eye for the shallow pretensions of imposters and pretenders whom she encountered in both country and city; in her novels, as Frederic Morton notes, "no pretense escapes her" (5). She loathed affectation as much as she loathed anything else: witness, for example, this irony-drenched sketch of Clare Boothe Brokaw, not yet married to Henry Luce:

> Recalling Selma Robinson's[61] episode with the rich Clare
> Boothe Brokaw, whose book *Stuffed Shirts* she was publicizing.
> Like any young ambitious woman, she was flattered at having
> lunch with Miss Boothe. A real person. Nothing phony about
> her. Hates her whole crowd, just like we do, despises society,
> just a real girl. Chums. (Meantime Clare milking Selma for
> publicity, has her up to meet people, tells her gossip about
> them—hates them all, a real genuine person.) (*Diaries*, 175)

The entry continues; Brokaw's sham behavior is fully uncovered, Powell's distaste for it clear. Such sketches appear throughout the *Diaries;* open the book to a random page and chances are good you will find another such portrait of pretense. Some pages after the entry on Brokaw, Powell having recently taken an "incredibly silly and kindergarten" position as book reviewer at *Mademoiselle,* she wrote:

> Then lunch and this usual but new business of people *I* know
> but am sure don't recognize me waving to someone behind me
> and bowing and finally coming over and saying "Well, well,
> *Dawn!*" I am still so amazed at the brazenness of people—
> completely New York people—who only remember you when
> you've gone into your fourth printing. (*Diaries,* 207)

That which she perceived as the arrogant condescension of the wealthy was also loathsome to Powell. Never having fully recovered from the judgmental snubbing she had met with so often at the hands of the better-placed small-town Ohioans she had known in her youth, she remembered with aversion that in the provinces "you have to hide your low beginnings and pretend everybody in the family is white and can read and write and play the harp," but not in New York. In Manhattan, even if you happen to live in a rat-infested slum, "—well, that doesn't prevent you from being asked to Park Avenue penthouses" (*Letters,* 76). Such an invitation, presumably, would not have been extended to a member of the lower class in any of the midwestern towns that Powell knew.

Additionally, never having fully recovered from the savage cruelty of her wealthy stepmother, she forever in her fiction drew heartbreaking sketches in which needy characters are both rebuked and humiliated by their more affluent neighbors and kin; the diaries, too, record such anguished memories. It is likely that the first case of such extreme parsimoniousness Powell ever witnessed had been that of her well-to-do stepmother, Sabra, who was always "dressed in the finest clothing [while] the girls wore rags" (Warstler, 6). According to Powell, the stepmother enjoyed the "sadistic treat" of making the three sisters "come out on [the] porch" of her large, impressive house "on Monday morning and run wringer or washboard in worn-out Sunday dress (instead of cute bungalow aprons like other girls), in full view of the children playing in the schoolyard so they could mock us" (*Diaries,* 187).

Powell's New York surely had its share of the tightfisted rich as well. For example, the author recalled the story of one Mrs. Ames, earliest executive

director of the artist residence Yaddo where Powell would stay for a time in
the late 1950s and again in 1960 (Page, "Biographical Notes," 479); in fact,
Powell's first visit to Yaddo in 1955 coincided with James Baldwin's (McGee,
131). This Mrs. Ames, a woman who had "accumulated millions," was nevertheless said to be "the most selfish person in the world," so much so that
she would destroy the marriage plans of a young woman to whom she for a
time had planned to bequeath her great wealth upon her death, never having
shared it with anyone else (*Diaries*, 424–25). Such complacent and unchar-
itable hoarders of wealth as the stepmother and Mrs. Ames become transformed in *Turn, Magic Wheel* into the person of Belle Glaenzer, her imposing
Upper East Side residence, and the sleek automobile waiting in front of it:

> Belle's dignified brownstone resolutely pushed its way out of
> the shadow of penthouse apartments on either side, just as her
> respectable old limousine raised its body a few haughty inches above
> the gutter instead of slithering along, daschund style, like the new
> models of the penthouse tenants. A high iron grilling separated this
> decent-person's dwelling from the unworthy passers-by. (69)

The penthouse is so daunting that "the occasional women callers" who
venture there are provoked to "wipe off their lipstick, pull down their skirts
a little more" (69). Belle is very much an intimidating, imperious edifice
herself, as Powell's narrator describes her:

> In a huge black plush chair, in a ring of grisly bluish lamplight
> sat Belle Glaenzer, a vast dough-faced shapeless Buddha in
> black velvet that flowed out of the chair and spilled its inky
> folds into the du Barry roses of the carpet. There should be an
> emerald in the middle of her forehead, thought Dennis, and a
> great cabochon ruby glittering in her long-lost navel. (75)

Belle, "the meanest, stingiest old woman of all the mean stingy old
women in New York," is quite literally "eating herself into the grave" (79):

> Belle's tapering hand fumbling among the chocolates so
> lovingly, choosing her pet very slowly, very carefully, as if she
> were in no greedy haste, no indeed, as if it were nothing to her,
> that rush of ecstasy to the tip of her tongue the instant sugar
> touched it. The robber fingers withdrew reluctantly from the
> candies with only one treasure but with it in her mouth her eyes

> continued to keep passionate watch over the others. Be happy,
> little coconut fondant and almond paste, Belle's adoring tongue
> will soon appreciate you, too, all in your turn. (80)

The character's overindulgence in sugary treats, coupled with her refusal to donate to charity, exposes the ugliness of greed, excess, and selfishness that Powell would always find intolerable, especially after having as a child lived with a woman so miserly that when Dawn and her sisters asked if they could make "hot-water soup" of "hot water, salt and butter," she would coldly refuse them (*Diaries*, 187). Excessive spending of any sort she found contemptible: for example, her play *Jig Saw* painted "a rather scathing picture of idle women spending their husband's money or alimony in New York apartment hotels, shopping one day and taking the stuff back the next, hoping for Something or Other to fill in their days without their expending any energy themselves" (Peterson, 38). On another occasion, having just returned from having had lunch with Pauline Hemingway, Powell said that her friend, recently divorced from the famed novelist, "seemed sharp-edged, too eager, brown and desperate. . . . She should have a cause, beyond Saks Fifth Avenue" (*Diaries*, 203). Her distaste for Pauline's ex-husband's behavior surfaced as well; Powell had no tolerance for those who would use others or their money to achieve their own ends. Hemingway, she wrote, before the imminent divorce from Pauline, was "play[ing] on present wife's rich uncle's cultural passion, so that uncle upbraids niece for not holding him and is set to receive the supplantee of his niece and thus add to the cruelty" (182).

Powell examined her own materialism as well: "Very queer about material things and avarice. There are people whose lives are dedicated to acquiring what they never had, then there are those who are only . . . greedy . . . in hanging on to what they have. Jack[62] has a little of both, but I have the latter. I've never gotten over my surprise of owning what I do—and with each added convenience comes an accompanying passion for hanging onto it" (*Diaries*, 59). Unfortunately, for various reasons Powell often would be unable to hang on to her possessions. One day she wrote simply, "Fire in beautiful new sofa due to Joe's falling asleep with cigarette" (*Diaries*, 207). In her last years she had very few belongings left at all. She and Joe had been forced to move from their 35 East Ninth Street apartment in 1958 for being behind on their rent and because the building was to be converted into co-ops. Renters who wished to stay were required to purchase their units, an expense the couple could ill afford.

Preparing to move, Powell listed her meager inventory. She had a few boxes of signed first editions from such friends as Hemingway and Dos Passos, and the following:

> One hall desk, oak.
> Doll heads in carton and dolls. Secretary desk.
> Three straight chairs.
> One large dirty rug.
> Three small dirty rugs.[63] (*Diaries*, 389)

Page tells the tale poignantly: "At a stage in her life when she should have been feted and honored as one of America's great writers," Powell was essentially homeless, "forced to seek shelter in a series of seedy residential hotels" (*Bio*, 268). Moving into the first in a bleak series of residence hotels, she was unable to carry with her even the few items she had managed to hold on to. William Peterson, visiting Powell at the rather run-down Madison Square Hotel where she and Joe had moved upon his retirement, recalled her talking for some time about her "habit of gleaning useful articles, even furniture, from the things that New Yorkers throw out, depositing them on the sidewalks to be carted away by the garbage men. She had recently found a sturdy armchair, upholstered in imitation leather, and pointed out that her husband was sitting in it" (37).

But when she was flush, she was generous, often lending money and taking care to repay sums she had borrowed. On one occasion, having just received a check from an undisclosed source, she recorded that after having paid doctor and dentist bills for Jojo, she lent substantial sums to friends Dos Passos, Bill Rollins,[64] and LeClercq,[65] gave $200 to her younger sister, and repaid debts she owed to friends (*Diaries*, 89). Such a figure as Belle Glaenzer would be detestable to Powell, who understood the horror of poverty and the obligation of charity.

I am very fond of my novel—hope other people are.

—*Diaries*, 99

Upon its completion, delighted with the way the book had turned out, Powell nonetheless steeled herself for a slew of negative reviews, having by now become used to them. Apprehending that the new novel was unlike all her previous publications, Powell expected that the "critics who have never given me more than a paragraph or two of dignified praise will suddenly, in attempting to describe their displeasure over this book, recall with delight my other great works. I expect unfavorable, even insulting, reviews, but long ones" (*Diaries*, 112). If you are going to lambaste me, she is saying, at least give me adequate consideration. Too often her novels earned only slight, one-paragraph mentions, as in, for example, the *New Yorker*'s "Briefly Noted" columns. Happily, *Turn, Magic Wheel* earned Powell some of the best notices she had ever received, and some lengthy ones at that. First of all, for the critics, this newest novel of New York showed Powell equally comfortable writing about Manhattan as ever she was writing of the small towns of Ohio. The New York she has created here comes so vibrantly to life that Edith H. Walton, familiar with Powell's Ohio novels, wrote that "Miss Powell is as wickedly at home in the city as ever she was in the hinterland" ("Ironic," 7). And reviewers remarked on the new novel's being far different from what they had come to expect from Powell:

> The stream of consciousness, no longer that tide we have known
> [in the Ohio novels]—dreaming, hesitating, scattered with soft
> nostalgic lights and perfumed petals, now and then disappearing
> underground—different indeed from such a tide as moving seems
> asleep, comes rattling, roaring in from every side. (R. Lehmann, 90)

In this novel the city never lets its presence be forgotten, as here:

> Dennis . . . watched the rain twinkling over the city, drops like
> golden confetti quivered over street lamps, they dribbled over the
> window ledge, made quick slanting designs across the pane, blurred
> the illuminated letters across the street—HOTEL GRENVILLE.
> On the glittering black pavement legs hurried by with umbrella
> tops, taxis skidded along the curb, their wheels swishing through
> the puddles, raindrops bounced like dice in the gutter. (224)

Once again an illuminated sign, this time a hotel sign, calls brilliant attention to itself, just as the Sunshine Biscuit sign had commanded attention from atop the Empire State. This passage, one frequently included in commentaries on the novel, is for Margo Jefferson an illustration of the way in which both Powell's characters and her story remain "afloat on the sounds and sensations, the dash, squalor, and ugly beauty of the city" (4). It is also reminiscent of some of William Carlos Williams's early poems and their focus on everyday images of New York, as in "The Great Figure":

AMONG the rain
and lights
I saw the figure 5
in gold
on a red
firetruck
moving
tense
unheeded
to gong clangs
siren howls
and wheels rumbling
through the dark city.

(*The Collected Poems*, 1:174)

Both Powell and Williams evoke striking images of the dark city in the rain, each painting car and truck wheels splashing through the wet streets, each portraying the riotous sounds and scenes of New York. Although Williams and Powell are almost exact contemporaries—he was born just three years earlier than Powell and died two years before she did—and though they knew many of the same people, among them Ernest Hemingway (Baker, 127), e. e. cummings, Malcolm Cowley, and Matthew Josephson (Carr, 266–67), and lived not far from one another, they seem not to have been personally acquainted. Not a single mention of Williams is to be found in any of Powell's exhaustive journals or letters, and Page turns up no connections between the two writers in his biography.

Considering Powell alongside other American women writers as he evaluated *Turn, Magic Wheel,* the novelist's contemporary, Jerre Mangione, compared her favorably with Parker and Tess Slesinger, finding Powell "more promising" than the others in that, "as an experienced novelist, she has developed a sense of structure, shown in her ability to go beyond the *bon mot* and invent characters and situations that are comic in themselves" (80). If Powell's contemporaries found much to like in the novel, today's critics all but uniformly admire it, one representative commentator saying that "no one better understood the mythic Manhattan siren call than Dawn Powell" (Sellar, 1). Others note the complex combination of wit and pathos in the novel: "Some readers see this book as a sharp, unremitting satire. I find much more," including "real sympathy and under-standing," in this "beautiful portrait of New York in the mid-1930s" (R. Friedman, 2).

Turn, Magic Wheel was Powell's first novel to be issued abroad, and on its publication in England, it created a stir. Powell confided in her diary that the "reception" she received in England "pleased her more than anything" else had done for quite some time (125). In a letter that British publisher Michael Sadleir[66] wrote to the author, he thoughtfully included a note he had received from Helen Waddell,[67] which thrilled Powell. The note read, "I have just finished Dawn Powell's *Turn, Magic Wheel;* it is the same kind of experience as watching Elizabeth [*sic*] Bergner[68] act for the first time. Odd, to discover again the Comic Muse in Radio City, sorrowful, impish and wise. I do congratulate you"[69] (*Diaries*, 124–25). Waddell's words of praise appeared on the British edition of the book. At last Powell was receiving some richly deserved acclaim.

In a less formulaic ending than is *Whither*'s, Powell here has brought Dennis to the point of aiming to become a nobler, more decent man, one deserving of the love of such a one as Effie. But this sort of change is not really possible, not in this novel, not in Dawn Powell. The book's last lines find Orphen succumbing to the unexceptional charms of the vapid Corinne. Obviously unable to live up to the high standards that Effie, to his mind, would require, he resumes his familiar pattern:

> On the steps of his apartment house a little figure in a white raincoat loomed like a ghost in the dark. It was Corinne.
>
> "I've made up my mind," she said, "I'm going to leave Phil and live with you."
>
> "The hell you are," said Dennis.
>
> But he was enormously glad to see her. She took the burden of high resolutions off his back and he drew a great breath of relief. He kissed her.
>
> "Come on in out of the rain," he said. (228)

THE HAPPY ISLAND, 1938

The bachelors of New York in the Satyricon style.

—*Diaries*, 119

In *The Happy Island,* Powell's third novel of New York and her second written in the 1930s, she attempted to follow the unprecedented success of

Turn, Magic Wheel. By now it had become clear that she wished to branch out, to attempt something new in her novels. The Ohio works had expressed all that she had to say of her birthplace, for the time being; but her Manhattan was rich with material that no one else was writing, at least not in the way she would write it, and Powell was determined to set it down in lively print, a print especially lively because at this time she was "speeding her brains out on diet pills" (Page, telephone, March 7, 2013). Having by now lived for many years in Greenwich Village, an area of the City that, since at least 1890, has had a large homosexual population (Chauncey), Powell had come to befriend many gay men-about-town, among them the *New Yorker*'s John Mosher and the nightclub performer Dwight Fiske. As Page says, "Through Dwight Fiske, she became popular within a circle of gay men . . . who in fact made up a disproportionate percentage of her coterie" (*Bio,* 97–98). Powell also counted many lesbian women among her close friends, including Esther Murphy, well-known in the New York of her day as a scholar and brilliant conversationalist, but, if she is remembered today, it is largely "as Gerald Murphy's eccentric, pathetic sister, a marvel who became a spectacular disappointment" (L. Cohen, 8). Powell recalled having lunched one day with Esther, who apparently did not stop talking at all. As their lunch visit ended, Esther said to Dawn, "Oh, but you were going to say something." Powell replied, "Yes, I was going to say, 'Hello, Esther'" (L. Cohen, 10). Powell was also friendly with other lesbian women, among them "Cheryl Crawford, Djuna Barnes, and especially Virginia Pfeiffer" (*Bio,* 162). Crawford, a founding member of the Group Theatre, had been the director of Powell's first produced play, *Big Night;* Pfeiffer was the sister of Hemingway's second wife, Pauline Pfeiffer Hemingway; Djuna Barnes, American novelist, was the author of the hugely popular *Nightwood,* for which T. S. Eliot wrote an admiring introduction. Taking an early journey into relatively unexplored fictional territory, Powell wrote this novel as honestly and as fearlessly as she would any other.

Buoyed by the success of her previous novel, Powell seemed fearless as she began planning in her diary the work she intended to title *The Joyous Isle.*[70] She wanted this new novel to be a story in the *Satyricon* style, referring to Petronius's lively and sardonic portrayal of the excesses and social manners of the Imperial period of ancient Rome. It is well known that F. Scott Fitzgerald modeled Jay Gatsby's lavish dinner parties after those given by Trimalchio, protagonist of "The Banquet" in the second volume of the *Satyricon.* Powell's novel updates Petronius to the café society of 1930s Manhattan.

Page writes in his introduction to *The Happy Island* that it is "among the first books written after Roman antiquity that is peopled with gay and bi-sexual characters but is neither a hate tract, a psychological study, an apologia, a plea for tolerance, nor an under-the-counter titillation" (vii). As Page suggests, Powell was attempting to write something few had written before, a highly comic romp. Djuna Barnes's hugely popular novel *Nightwood* of just the year before had featured a lesbian couple and a male transvestite, but that work ends punishingly, unlike Powell's devilishly comic novel, one reason, perhaps, that the former was more palatable to readers than *The Happy Island* would prove to be. It also demonstrated, again, Powell's fearless determination to write what she wanted to write, leaving her fears of publishers, readers, and critics as far behind her s possible.

While planning *The Happy Island,* Powell let future readers of her diaries in on the secret of the real-life inspirations behind two of her principal characters, something she rarely if ever did. Even throughout all the detailed planning of *Turn, Magic Wheel,* she never once in either her *Diaries* or *Letters* came out and said that her Andrew Callingham was based on Ernest Hemingway; it was not until four years later that her diary made the source of that character clear, if the novel itself had not (180). But planning *The Happy Island,* which island of course is Manhattan, she sketched two of her main sources, Dwight Fiske and John Mosher, close friends of one another and of her own, making it clear that they would form the basis of two characters in the new book (*Diaries,* 119).

Dwight Fiske was a well-known nightclub entertainer with whom Powell had often collaborated on suggestive skits and songs for his bawdy act. Though the two had been close, Fiske had temporarily lost Powell's friendship in 1932 when she determined that he was "unscrupulous and heartless and thoroughly materialistic" (*Diaries,* 55). She seemed none too pleased with him the next year, either, when his *Without Music* was published, though he dedicated the book to her. The dedication reads, "For Dawn Powell, through whose inspiration many of these stories came to be." In response, Powell wrote that, though he "deserves his success," at least half of the stories he included in the book had been co-written by her: "Of the 25 stories I did a large part of 13, so it seems bitterly ironic that the reviewers (like Stark Young[71]) who were so savage about my play[72] should rave so about lines (usually mine) from this book" (*Diaries,* 73). A dedication rather than partial authorial credit was less than she deserved.

If Powell had been angry with Fiske, however, her anger was short-lived. As if returning the favor, she dedicated *Turn, Magic Wheel* to him, though he had not helped her to write it as she had assisted him with his stories. By 1937 she was accepting invitations from him to "come up to Cape Cod" (*Letters*, 99), in 1935 and as late as 1953 she was still occasionally collaborating with him (*Diaries*, 107; 327), and in 1956 she described him to another acquaintance as "a very dear old friend of mine" (*Letters*, 230). Clearly the relationship had survived its earlier difficulties. Like Hemingway before him, Fiske had presumably forgiven her, too, for her fictionalized portrait of him. At any rate, here in the diary planning the new novel, Powell recorded Fiske neutrally, calling him simply "the theatrical success," always with "adoring people around" (119). Born in 1892 in Providence, Rhode Island, Fiske, an entertainer who leered and jeered at his audiences, was aptly "christened King Leer" in *Variety* for "emblazoning every nonsubtlety with winks, grins, shrieks, and mock-dramatic silent-movie-styled accompaniment" (Gavin, 21). In a letter to Dos Passos, Powell described Fiske's brand of "sophomoric" entertainment (Gavin, 22) in this way: "Dwight Fiske tells stories at the piano which drunken rich people scream about—realizing they'd betray their mental age if they frankly admitted they didn't think much of them" (*Letters*, 84). Page portrays Fiske as a man who "embodied a certain stereotype of the witty, sophisticated, self-deprecating homosexual, a type that was viewed as both daring and fundamentally 'safe' in the years between the world wars" (*Bio*, 59); Gore Vidal refers to him simply as a sort of sub-standard Noel Coward ("American," 10). Powell's impressions of Fiske and my own understanding of him help to inform my insight into the ways in which Dwight Fiske, gay male nightclub performer, becomes Prudence Bly, bisexual female nightclub singer. If in *Turn, Magic Wheel* Powell transformed her observant, Powell-like novelist into a man, here she transforms a male artist into a woman.

Writing about Fiske's reaction to Powell's fictionalized portrait of him, Bill Reed says, "According to urban legend, he was somewhat miffed at his involuntary 'sex change' and complained to Powell, 'You've turned me into a woman!' To which Powell reportedly replied, 'It isn't the first time that's happened and it won't be the last'" (2). This "urban legend" Reed reports has a basis in truth: Powell herself wrote in a letter to her British publisher, Michael Sadleir:

> There are no portraits in *The Happy Island*. Aside from fear
> of libel suits,[73] I find no profit or pleasure in straight portraiture.
> There are frequently snatches of this or that person cautiously

pinned to other persons' bodies and love-lives, and it is true I
have changed one real man into a woman, but as he has done
this himself so often I cannot see that he should object, and
have furthermore combined him with two other people. (103)

Just how the words of this letter would one day form the stuff of urban
legend is anybody's guess. More than the stuff of legend, however, the letter
is illustrative of Powell's technique of characterization, explaining how she
constructs characters by borrowing traits from one person and attaching
them to another.

He who expects nothing is never disappointed.

—*The Happy Island,* 22

Hailing from the fictional town of Silver City, Ohio, Prudence Bly, readers
learn, had an unhappy childhood during which, much like her creator, she
learned to expect nothing from anyone. Her childhood reads like a slightly
fictionalized account of Powell's own: Prudence is brought up by a grandmother; Powell, as readers will recall, by her mother's eldest sister. Prudence's grandmother owns the local flour mill; Powell's father had worked
in such a mill once his second wife had persuaded him to "retire" from his
sales position. When working as a traveling salesman Powell's father was
rarely home; Prudence's father, too, seldom comes around. A vignette from
the novel that sounds like something straight out of Powell's childhood
provides a bit of insight into Prudence's character:

Once her father, an admitted ne'er-do-well, on a rare visit
home, promised her a little blue Swiss watch if she would stop
biting her nails for three hours. Prudence, aged nine, sat in
the hall not biting her nails for three hours, and then he never
gave her the watch at all. The incident conditioned her to a
lack of faith in humanity and provided her with a rather wry
philosophy. (19)

Not surprisingly, as soon as she is able Prudence leaves Silver City and
lands in Pittsburgh, where she takes a job as a waitress in a railroad diner.
There she meets a sailor who teaches her to play the accordion; she begins
making up songs with such titles as *Queen Helen and the Gypsy* and, "thus

equipped," believes that she is ready for New York (21). Upon arriving in the
Village, Prudence lands a singing gig "at a speakeasy on MacDougal Street"
(21), a stepping stone, she believes, to the Big Time.

From the moment she arrives in Manhattan, Prudence, whom Gore
Vidal refers to as "the most carefully examined of Powell's women" ("American," 12), creates herself anew from top to bottom. The narrator says, "She
erased Silver City and overnight invented a new personality into which she
stepped and like her grandmother kept this dress on day and night" (22).
Soon the uptown crowd has discovered Prudence at her downtown *boite;* as
her repertoire grows, so does her reputation, and so does her popularity.

Prudence, who at novel's end has returned home to Silver City, realizes
almost at once that she must go back to New York, as if the city were her
very lungs (261). Like *Whither*'s Miss Tait before her, like Dawn Powell herself, Prudence is unable to resist the siren call of Manhattan. "Some people
aren't complete away from their city," the character says, "as a musician is
nothing without his violin. So New York was my instrument, or I was its.
A fish out of water is a dead fish, not a neurotic or an irritable fish, but a
dead fish" (261). Powell also, as readers have seen, never felt fully alive when
away from Manhattan. Following a visit to Ohio to see her relatives, Powell
wrote, "Glad as I was to see everyone, I had not the slightest desire to be
always among 'em. No. My happiness was highlighted by the consciousness
of being able to fly out into the World again at once" (*Letters,* 39). That
World, of course, was New York City.

The two are similar in more ways than these, however: Prudence is
possessed, like Powell, of a clear, unromanticized vision of all that surrounds
her. "The wisdom [Prudence] had was for human failings, of sin, corruption, and betrayal; none of these surprised her, and she loved the world
accepting this" (230). In what seems to have been a black mood, the novelist
confided, "I realize more and more how instinctively pessimistic I am of all
human kindness—since I am always so bowled over by it—and am never
surprised by injustice, malice or personal attack" (*Diaries,* 65). Certainly her
difficult childhood had prepared her for such a worldview; nevertheless, as
her novels attest, she remained sympathetic to her fellow human beings,
understanding their virtues as well as their shortcomings. As she said many
times, she loved humanity, warts and all, which is not to suggest that she
was above pointing out the warts—nor was Prudence. Both Powell and the
fictional character possess a sharp tongue, a gift for the *bon mot.* Matthew
Josephson wrote that in much of Powell's work "there is usually introduced

a female personage . . . speaking in the ironic style of the author herself. The nightclub singer in *The Happy Island* is such a one" (43). In the novel, Prudence often "slew with a neat epithet, crippled with a too true word" (45); Powell, too, was known for the same type of slaying, sometimes at drunken parties, more often in her satirical novels of New York.

Songs My Mother Never Taught Me

The Prudence Bly character owes something not only to her creator but to Dwight Fiske[74] as well. Powell believed she and Fiske had much in common: she wrote that the two of them early on "decided that we had the same sour, realist angle on life—[which] was why we were so fond of each other and worked so well together" (*Diaries*, 76). Prudence's unrefined nightclub act is certainly reminiscent of Fiske's—in fact, Powell's having written much of Fiske's material might have spurred her to imagine *herself* as a female Dwight Fiske. The narrator tells us that as Prudence builds her repertoire, she adds "a new libelous number called *Miss Jollypins Gets the Sailor*" (128), the title of the tune sounding not unlike the name of a ditty one might expect to find in Fiske's repertoire, just as her first tune, "Queen Helen and the Gypsy," sounds Fiskean. Actual titles of songs in Fiske's act, as taken from his book *Without Music*, include "Two Horses and a Debutante," "The King and the Queen," and "Malaga, the Grape Girl" (Fiske, 29; 140; 16), many of them, we will recall, written by Powell herself. A pair of lowbrow entertainers always driven to do whatever it takes to make it, Dwight Fiske and Prudence Bly in that sense are much alike. Give the customers what they want, regardless of its nature; forget Real Art. Powell noted that she was sometimes tempted to follow Fiske's example and forgo her higher ambitions, promising herself, "From now on, by God, I am determined to distort every thought into the tawdry easy lines the world can applaud" (*Diaries*, 74). But she would never allow herself to do any such thing.

One might describe Prudence as "unscrupulous and heartless and thoroughly materialistic," just as Powell had earlier described Fiske; if he will attempt to manipulate Powell and others for his own needs, Prudence similarly will try to manipulate others. Powell, explaining why she has come to consider her friend, in 1932, so "unscrupulous and heartless and materialistic," said that Dwight was forever sending her "affectionate telegrams [that] humiliate me by their thinly veneered desire for me to do something for him"

(55), in much the same way that he had "maneuvered" and "fought" his way to success (73). Prudence is the same manipulative sort, demanding much of her audiences and friends, including unwavering loyalty and support, though she gives little in return, including not much in the way of talent. "Isn't Prudence amazing?" one acquaintance, Van Deusen, says. "Very slight gifts to offer but so very insolent, you know, she doesn't care what anyone thinks, so you of course you have to go on thinking she's wonderful" (63).

Van Deusen, a hard-drinking, out-of-luck but nevertheless likable fellow, also seems to have originated with one of Powell's closest friends: Coburn "Coby" Gilman. Matthew Josephson has noted that Coby's "remarkable capacity for alcohol and the tone of his speech are accurately . . . recorded in passages of Dawn Powell's novels" (39), though he fails to mention which ones.[75] A heavy-drinking, down-on-his-luck sort, Coby, like the character, at all times retains his regal bearing despite his shabby clothing. Van Deusen, when readers first meet him, is riding on a bus from Ohio to New York:

> The older man across the aisle with the ingratiatingly fixed
> smile and the natty green fedora brushed his suit carefully with
> a small whisk broom. He shook out a threadbare fawn-colored
> topcoat which had been rolled into a pillow on the trip and
> arranged it over his left arm to conceal the frayed lining. . . .
> . . . Mr. Van Deusen drew on chamois gloves, which, with
> the tilted hat and deftly revealed blue pocket handkerchief,
> transformed the disheveled bus traveler into a dangerous man-
> about-town for all to see. (1, 3)

The portrayal might very well describe the threadbare but elegant Coby, whom Powell had long believed would make a brilliant subject for a novel character. "I sometimes think," she said, "that a writer could become immortal merely as a chronicler of Gilman" (*Diaries*, 164). Though she never did reveal whether Coby had actually served as the basis of any of her characters, he did bear a striking resemblance to Van Deusen:

> On a bus with Coby, a very pretty and richly dressed girl got
> on and everyone was silent with obvious admiration. Coby
> turned around. "I suppose you're going to sit with her," I said.
> "Yes, do you mind?" he said. "No, but just how will you start the
> conversation?" I asked. "I will simply bow, doff my hat to the

ground," he said with a courtly gesture, removing his battered hat—"and say, 'Pardon me, have you seen my new hat?'" (*Diaries*, 176).

In is perhaps no coincidence that at the same time Powell was planning *The Happy Island* she was writing in her journal about Coby at more length than ever before, especially of his Van Deusen–like struggle with the bottle: "On his complaint of all [his] salary being spent on liquor he was told he should have someone parcel him out $2.00 a day—which he agreed was a fine plan, he could manage on $2 a day in addition to his salary, but who was going to give him this $2 a day—would I?" (*Diaries*, 122). Directly from that entry Powell began discussing the new novel: "Going to make *The Joyous Isle* a long book . . . should be flowing, fluid, full of good dishes as John [Mosher] and Dopey see them" (122). On the same page Powell spoke of Coby's frequent resolutions to stop drinking once and for all: "He wished he could go on the wagon, was outraged on being told he could do so if he had any will power. Will power? He had the most amazing will power in the world, it was *amazing,* that will power of his, the only thing was, it was completely futile" (*Diaries*, 122). Van Deusen, too, is possessed of an "amazing" will power, but despite months of sobriety, he always resumes the old habit of going on benders for weeks if not months at a time. At one point in the novel, Prudence is "furious" with Van, who has disappeared just as she has slated him for an appearance at Town Hall. She cries, "I get the manager, a press agent, provide money for the hall—everything for Van to come back; and just the day he's to sign things and make final arrangements, he vanishes . . . out on one of those annual benders of his" (122). "We won't see him again this season" another character adds (122). Van Deusen, as it turns out, is not only a drunk but a nonperforming performer, resembling the many nonacting actors and nonwriting writers one so often encounters in Powell. Coby, too, had failed to live up to his abilities; he told Powell he often felt like a failure: "All my life I've arrived at the station just after the Orient Express has left," he told her (*Diaries*, 175). The same could be said for Esther Murphy, who never finished writing anything she began but who could hold forth brilliantly on myriad subjects; and the brilliant North Carolina–born *New Yorker* writer Joseph Mitchell, who, after twenty years at the magazine, saw his once "Olympian" productivity "dwindle to a trickle—from 13 articles in 1939 to a magisterial five during the entire decade of the '50s" (Bailey, 18). Though Powell remained steadfast friends with Murphy, Mitchell, and Gilman, she still had little tolerance for their shirking of what she saw as their responsibility to their talent.

Even when Coby was on the wagon, unhappy things happened to him: as Powell said, "sobriety makes one an easy prey to catastrophe. Last night as he gloomily ate a salad at Margaret De Silver's,[76] Canby Chambers's[77] horrible spaniel modestly chewed up half Coby's jacket. It was a new suit he had been saving up to buy for a year" (*Letters*, 130). What new clothes he managed to purchase for himself became tattered in no time, again reminding us of the raggedly debonair Van Deusen. In the end, readers empathize with both the character and the man, as Powell writes them, despite their weakness for drink and their frayed though dashing exteriors.

These new young men come to conquer the city

—*The Happy Island*, 5

Readers have seen that in Powell's New York novels, many of her provincials arrive in the city with little more than their dreams. In *Whither*, Zoe Bourne arrives with some twenty dollars, little talent, and less real ambition; in *Turn, Magic Wheel*, Dennis Orphen arrives with a good deal of talent and a work ethic alien to Zoe, though he will sell a friend down the river for a good story. In *The Happy Island*, some characters will arrive with little or nothing, others, however, with a great deal. The shabby Van Deusen, whom Prudence likes only because he has been "an eyewitness to" a former beau's "devotion to her" (42), forever arrives in Manhattan and then leaves again with even less than he came with. "I've come here half a dozen times to make my fortune," Van Deusen tells a younger first-time arrival to New York, whom readers come to know as Jefferson Abbott, aspiring Ohio-born playwright. Van adds, "Sometimes I come by plane and leave by bus, but it's the other way around this time" (3). Even though his fortunes have shrunk, even though he is forever treated shabbily by both Manhattan and its residents, Van Deusen always returns, much as *Whither*'s Miss Tait, thirteen years earlier, was habitually drawn to come back. Like Powell, her typically undaunted characters try their luck again and again, despite the odds stacked against them. Phillip Lopate speaks of the city's "addictive, temptress quality, which ensnares newcomers and convinces them—no matter how much they may suffer at its hands—that no place else will do" (*Writing*, xix). Powell often spoke of her own "addiction" to the city; and clearly the homeless Van Deusen is similarly addicted to New York. The novel's Jefferson Abbott, however, is addiction-proof.

The playwriting newcomer is unlike the pianist Van Deusen, who brings not only a serious drinking problem to New York but a drink-induced spuriousness: playing piano at a recital, "his voice grows perceptibly more affected under Scotch as some voices do" (33). Jeff, who neither drinks nor becomes anything other than what he already is—"devoid of humor" (124), arrogant, blunt, and, to his mind, always right—might actually possess the talent and the work ethic to succeed in Manhattan, though he comes to despise the place, its denizens, even its theater. Prudence, who arrives in the Village with little talent, through sheer will and ambition will succeed, though her aims are hardly lofty. As it happens, Jeff Abbott and Prudence Bly hail from the same small fictional Ohio town; in fact, in earlier days she had had a serious crush on him. But he is something of a small-town snob, a quality with which Powell is familiar. He has the ugly superior attitude, "the surly hostility of these new young men come to conquer the city. You would deduce from their pose they expected to conquer it by slugging it into a stupor" (5), the novel's narrator says. Jeff sniffs at virtually everyone and everything he encounters in New York, including Prudence Bly and her lounge act. As another character, Dol, says, "Jeff was astonished that I had heard of his old playmate in the big city. I got him here to the [nightclub] door, he took one look around, said it looked too awful, and, if [Prudence] could stand this sort of place now, he didn't want to see her. Ran right out" (64). Dol, who has generously brought Jeff to Manhattan, giving him a place to stay free of charge while he reworks his play, "had looked forward to seeing New York through young eager eyes; but young Abbott's self-absorption to the utter exclusion of Gotham glamour had made the gesture foolish" (65). The "sublimely humorless" (Vidal, "American," 12) Jefferson Abbott will be the sole important character in Powell to return to the heartland and complacently remain there.

Although Jeff is a character for whom Powell has provided no source, like Prudence he seems in part loosely based on the author. As an Ohio-born aspiring writer who comes to Manhattan to seek his fortune, and in his attitudes toward columnists and "failure," he is very much like the author, as I noted in chapter 1. The critics having roasted him after the opening of his play, the determined Jeff is left unscathed. The reviewers, not surprisingly, have objected to the sordidness of his characters, as they have long objected to Powell's, causing Jeff to exclaim, "I'm not a writing beauty doctor who fixes up old chins and souls to gratify the customer's mirror" (118). Instead, he says, he paints people precisely as he sees them, just as Powell always said she did. The narrator of *The Happy Island* intimates that true beauty is not to be found in perfection anyway. Prudence Bly, regarding the face of her gorgeous but drunken companion, Jean, one evening, thinks, "One look was enough . . . for there was nothing unknown here, no other quality suggested beyond the patent virtues of contour and hue, no hint of magic, no twinkle of malice. Here was Beauty Clear, and it was not enough. The treacherous eye must hunt furtively for a mole, a dimple, or even a fascinating wart" (14). Both Prudence and Jeff have such a treacherous eye, as does our author. But Jefferson Abbott is humorless and much grimmer, much less likable than was Dawn Powell, and he is not at all enamored of the city, a most unfortunate quality to the author's mind.

If Prudence Bly is based at least partly on Dwight Fiske, if she and Jefferson Abbott are based at least partly on the author herself, the character Dol Lloyd[78] is based closely on John Mosher, and the subordinate character Bert Willy on an anonymous, unattractive "dope." In her diary, Powell wrote,

> John Mosher, unattractive to women, silent in the home,
> finds balm in getting the pale silent young man in borrowed
> evening clothes away from Dwight. He has him in his home
> where he encourages him to go on with his cooking, gets
> him Escoffier . . . brings him home little gadgets, egg slices,
> canapés, entertains, proud of his pompano in fig leaves, his
> duck *a la presse.* John talks, educating him culturally; Dopey
> listens, says salad too wet. Gloomy, naturally ignorant, lazy,
> unattractive young man. (119)

The proud and generous Dol working so hard to please such a dour young man tugs gently at the reader who comes to care about Dol if few characters in the novel ever do. Given this portrait of Mosher's gloomy young friend, it is small wonder that Powell refrained from divulging the source of the inspiration behind Dopey; chances are good, too, that she had neither cared to learn the real fellow's name nor to remember it, finding the pejorative nickname a suitable handle for this insolent young man who was attractive to such a polished aesthete as John Mosher. It is possible that the character she calls Dopey was a composite of many of the younger men always to be found accompanying Fiske or Mosher about town.

Mosher, who in 1926 had become the first film critic on staff at the *New Yorker,* is today remembered as an "urbane" and "extremely sophisticated" fellow who was "witty, perceptive, and informed by a deep and tolerant knowledge of the world," as his colleagues at the magazine described him in his obituary (72). The character Dol Lloyd, like Mosher, is sophisticated and urbane, if a heavy drinker and something of a snob. At the parties he regularly throws for his friends, his friends' friends, and a good assortment of hangers-on, he is regularly to be found sitting "in the big yellow wing chair by the fire smiling fixedly and ignoring his guests" (226). Despite his snobbishness, the portrait Powell paints of Dol is one of the most sympathetic that readers find in her New York novels, while the portrait of his companion Bert is as unsympathetic as any she ever drew.

Not only does Powell often create characters out of more than one "real" person," but she sometimes splits one "real" person into a couple of different characters. Highly amusing is the portrait of peripheral character James Pinckney, with whom Powell has good fun; like Dol, he seems to have been based, at least in terms of the following particular characteristic, on John Mosher:

> Johnny Mosher was over at Dos'. He talks and feels about
> himself as a very dear eccentric aunt and wherever he goes
> watches his own amusing reactions as if he were his own pet,
> too precious to be left in the baggage car but rather to be
> tenderly borne on the lap. When he went alone through Europe
> he was not going alone, he was taking that amusing fellow
> Mosher. (108)

This same odd quality surfaces in James Pinckney, who watches himself wherever he goes, who hears stories from others and rehearses the retelling of them in his mind, forever envisioning his audiences' reactions to his anecdotes and his own reactions to their reactions. When Jean, Prudence's female lover, says of Jefferson's play that "it made me absolutely quiver. It wasn't good, of course, but it made me quiver" (125), a departing James heads for the elevator, where "his lips were moving convulsively" in anticipation of retelling the story. "Oh, it absolutely made me quiver! It definitely made me quiver! ... And the platinum toenails, thought James, above all I mustn't forget the platinum toenails!" (125).

Death be not proud

—John Donne

Near the end of the novel, the charitable Dol suddenly dies, at about the age of fifty, just as Mosher, in a peculiar coincidence, will also die at fifty.[79] The fictional character is seated as usual in his yellow chair by the fire, again throwing his usual party, again wearing a stiff smile, but this time the smile is stiffer than usual. He is soon quietly escorted out and deposited in his bedroom, with the help of the caterers, so that the party will not be spoiled. Once the guests realize, days later, that Dol had actually died during the party, they think it terribly vulgar of him to have done so, even though the corpse had been carried off so that the guests were none the wiser. Dol has died precisely the way Mosher had long wished not to die; Powell's friend had always hoped to go out slowly rather than suddenly, decorously rather than offensively (*Diaries*, 109). In the novel, after the truth comes out, the party guests are repulsed: "It was bad enough to have Dol die, but to have him drop dead right in the middle of a party— even though it was his own, and he had a perfect right, and make so many people feel uncomfortable was so unlike him, so gauche, so lacking in taste as to be almost unforgivable" (227–28). For Michael Feingold, Dol "is Powell's epitome of everything that's good, wise, and generous about Manhattan, and his death . . . is an apocalyptic signal of the chaos that's going to turn the city temporarily sour with the onset of World War II" (14). A few years later, in 1942's *A Time to Be Born,* the war will intrude on and transform not only all the future novels of Dawn Powell but also her beloved New York.

This death scene in the novel and the attendant murmurs of the disgusted guests echo details of the sudden death of one young partygoer named Lilla Worthington, about whom the author had recently written in her diary. The devastating entry, which appears only six days after the diary entry identifying Mosher, Fiske, and Dopey as character sources, reads novelistically, Powell, ever the artist, first setting the scene in rapid-fire, fragmented images:

> Lilla Worthington, who died at the Brandt's[80] cocktail party.
> The rainy day. The elevator strike so the streets were crowded

with strikers, picketers, rain, cold, blowing off hats and umbrellas inside out, taxis stuck for hours on sidestreets . . .

The pretty, sweet-faced Miss Worthington and I tried to remember where we met. I had never seen her at the Brandt parties as they rather dislike having their underlings in the home socially. A few minutes later she was standing talking to other people—a commotion, a slight exclamation, she was on the floor. Window raised, wet cloth brought, suddenly Carl picked her up and carried her into another room, her curly curly head dangling over his arm, strange animal gurgling noises coming from her. . . . People looked at each other with expressions of mingled polite concern and natural distaste for the bad manners of the thing. . . .

. . . The hostess, still in her new hostess gown with trailing train, carefully matched slippers, rushed over to a hotel with mink coat over her arm. It was the dead woman's party. (120–21)

The reactions of the partygoers in both diary and novel are much the same, all the guests clucking over the bad manners of the one dying at a party rather than demonstrating any real concern or sympathy for the deceased. Powell's view, as always, is a dark and mordant one, the novel scene clearly echoing the diary.

As grisly a crew of merrymakers as ever stayed up after curfew.

—*Time*[81]

By novel's end, not much has changed. Steve, Prudence's erstwhile boyfriend, has returned to her and she to him. The characters have remained the same, if only a little the worse for wear. Steve, in the novel's closing scene, says to Prudence, "Did I tell you you never looked lovelier?" The narrator's voice immediately interjects, echoing Steve's unspoken thoughts: "It was a lie. Prudence's looks, he reflected with some surprise, were quite gone. She really looked as hard as nails" (270). In a frightfully realistic if unromantic ending, the two lovers remain together, though neither harbors any delusions about the other.

In the end *The Happy Island* did not receive the high praise that *Turn, Magic Wheel* did. Most of its reviews were mixed, commentators lauding some qualities of the novel but censuring others. For the most part, contemporary reviewers found the book too cutting and too cynical, its author once again too concerned with "lowlifes" to have produced a novel of much interest. The old criticism had returned; the same lines that greeted her play *Big Night* greeted this novel. An anonymous reviewer in *Time* magazine wrote that the characters in Powell's latest publication are all a bunch of "astute backbiters, arrogant neurotics, expert philanderers, and just plain dopes,[82] they are radiant with phony public gaiety, abject with private jealousy, self-pity and hangover broodings which they pass off as philosophy" ("Café Society," 70). Again Powell would insist that it was not her fault that the night-time figures she so often encountered behaved this way; she was not a writer who set out to glamorize or beautify the people she met, nor was she one to write fantasy. She set out to write a satire, and a satire she delivered; obviously if the human beings she encountered were all perfectly noble, she would have no reason to write satire.

Frequent Powell reviewer Edith Walton wrote, "The world of *The Happy Island* is not . . . quite the world of Mr. Beebe's[83] diligent chronicles. Society, so-called, is rather conspicuously absent. What one has left is a strange lunatic medley of real and would-be celebrities, all eager to forget their out-of-town origins" (7). To which remark one would imagine Powell irreverently responding, "And your point is—?" But Walton's review was not altogether negative: she wrote also that "If we are to have novels about that none too alluring phenomenon known as café society, it is well that Dawn Powell should write them. She has the sardonic wit which is needful for the job; she is quite immune to the glitter in which her giddy worldlings move" (7). Walton went on to add, "With a few exceptions, notably the tragic Dol Lloyd—there is hardly a character in the book who seems really human. . . . Somehow or other, Miss Powell's material has betrayed her. One is left with a covert suspicion that it was hardly worth her time" (7). Of course, the point of satire is not necessarily to create wholly believable characters but to shine a light on their folly and wickedness. For some reason, an exasperated Powell felt, reviewers simply did not understand her. Following the release of *The Happy Island,* having read the reviews, Powell reflected on her novel, describing it as

> A picture of people ordinarily envied as Glamorous Idlers and
> showing up—not their immorality, which is always fun—but
> the niggling, bickering meanness of their life—not the great

gorgeous Cecil B. DeMille idea of corruption, a pagan rout
that any imaginative person would like to get into, but a story
of miserly, piddling souls without one great, generous glittering
vice to their name. (*Diaries,* 151)

Portrayals of tragic transgressions or of quiet nobility were welcome in
our American literature, it seemed to Powell, but renderings of everyday
squabbles, small vanities, and petty betrayals were not. Clearly the critical
responses to her novel displeased her, but, remarkably, no sooner had she
finished penning that secret response to her critics than she began, in the
very next paragraph of that same diary entry, planning what would become
1940's delicious *Angels on Toast.*

CHAPTER FIVE

"An Affecting Self~Portrait of the Artist in Middle Age"

The Middle New York Novels, 1940–48

If the 1930s, Powell's most prolific years, saw notable change and growth in her writing, the 1940s witnessed perhaps her greatest artistic progress to date. The three New York novels in this period, 1940's *Angels on Toast*, 1942's *A Time to Be Born*, and 1948's *The Locusts Have No King*, are among the most accomplished of her publications, the latter two enjoying the most acclaim of the three, and *A Time to Be Born* earning the highest sales. I include *Angels on Toast*, Powell's hybrid New York/Chicago novel, with the New York novels for reasons already named, among them that many scenes take place in Manhattan, and its wit is more akin to that in the New York works than in the Ohio. Despite her troubles, Powell's writings soar in this middle stretch of her career. In this decade she not only wrote the three above-mentioned novels, but she also produced her beautifully haunting fictional autobiography, 1944's *My Home Is Far Away*. In the year preceding its publication, she wrote the following, which appears as a memorandum in Page's *Selected Letters of Dawn Powell*:

> "The Man in the Balloon" is Part One of a three-part book to be called *My Home is Far Away*.
>
> My last four novels have been satires on contemporary society. The present book seeks to show the basic illusions and innocence that become fruit for future satire. A child and a

century grow up together. This is a story of growth, of people, town and knowledge flowering, bad and good together; of simple turning complex, of complex inviting destruction to resolve it once again to simple. Here is the blind quest for home in people and the belief that the return to simplicity solves everything. (119)

But she returns to satire in the following three works.

ANGELS ON TOAST, 1940

〜〜〜〜〜〜〜〜〜〜〜〜〜〜〜〜〜〜〜〜〜

A blistering and hilarious story of latter-day Babbitts on wheels.

—Charles Poore, "Diversity," 19

〜〜〜〜〜〜〜〜〜〜〜〜〜〜〜〜〜〜〜〜〜

From the time of *Turn, Magic Wheel* in the previous decade, Powell was seen meticulously planning and outlining her future novels in her diaries. Unfortunately, however, while writing *Angels on Toast* the author had suspended the habit, but diary readers do see her wasting little time, as usual, in moving from one novel to the next. It is as if she were literally unable to rest between writings, and, as Page notes, she was still high on amphetamines during this period. A diary entry of May 31, 1938, states simply, "Finished *The Happy Island* at 6:25 this evening" (145). As always she was working at the same time on a variety of other projects, including a play called *Every Other Day;* another drama, to have been a version of her Ohio novel *Dance Night;* and several short stories (*Bio,* 168). And soon she was already mentioning the next novel: "In the new book," she wrote, "I propose another provincial angle—the businessman on planes, trains, buses, private cars, whose business axis is New York; whose homes are Iowa, Chicago, Detroit, Pittsburgh, Alabama" (*Diaries,* 151). This germ of an idea would eventually become *Angels on Toast,* a book she would write more quickly than any other of her New York works, determined that her hurried writing would translate into a sense of headlong urgency in the pages of the novel.[1]

For a time while writing *Angels,* Powell was able to escape from home to hole up in seclusion at Coney Island's Half-Moon Hotel (*Letters,* 104). The Half-Moon, which was known as Coney Island's own Statue of Liberty (Gray, "The Half-Moon," 1), may be likened to a symbol of liberty for the author herself. Staying there, she was freed from the niggling interruptions of daily home life. Unfortunately, however, the respite was not to last for long: Jojo's needs and visits from her Ohio relatives would recall her home. Her nineteen-year-old son, who had thrown "an unusually serious tantrum" during that time (*Bio*, 171), had to be hospitalized again. Yet the ever-industrious Powell had lately taken on yet another project: a WOR-AM radio show called *Music and Manners* with Anne Honeycutt[2] (*Letters*, 107). Still, she continued working on her novel; as Page says, *Angels on Toast* began "slowly, surely, amid strife and distraction . . . [to take] shape" (*Bio*, 172). The fast-paced book would obviously have been completed even more rapidly than it was had Powell not been faced with so many disruptions. She had earlier told her editor as much in a letter dated October 14, 1939: "I had hoped to have finer news for you at this time about the book" (*Letters*, 107), but, she added, unfortunately the radio program had got in the way. Notably, she did not tell her editor of any other reasons for the delay, forever circumspect about her personal troubles. Still, perhaps her work with the radio show would one day provide her material for another book, she told him hopefully.

About the new novel Powell wrote to her editor, "I wanted to catch people as I heard them on trains and buses and bars, let them do their own story without any literary frame whatever, without explanations, without author's tricks, in fact without writing. The effect I was after was the after-effect. . . . I wanted to convey the sense of speed, changing geography with no change in the conversation, the sense of pressure behind the ever-evanescent big deal" (*Letters*, 110). It seems that because she had decided that no authorial interference would come between the novel and its characters, she had also determined to refrain from any notebook plotting; such heavy plotting might become heavy plodding, interrupting the rushing speed with which she hoped to infuse her novel. As a result, the diaries provide comparatively little inside information aside from the initial entry included in this section's introductory paragraph and a few other brief entries. At any rate, the author believed that she had to write this next novel "fast and intensely since the mood had to be preserved" (*Diaries*, 220). If the novel is to move quickly, to rush headlong as a train rushes, it must not be impeded by too much systematic thought or previous arrangement.

From the outset, the story, sans "author tricks," begins chugging along, as the train in which the two businessmen characters are riding begins to move:

> There was a bottle of Robinson's B. E. B. right in Lou's bag
> but Jay Oliver wasn't interested.

"The hell with cooping up here in the compartment," he said. "Let's go down to the club car. I like to see people."

"I don't," said Lou. "I got things on my mind."

The porter brought the ice, glasses, and soda.

"Okay," sighed Jay. "I might as well stick around a minute."

He sat down and kicked his shoes off. They lay on the floor jauntily toeing out, reddish brown, sleek, very much Jay Oliver. He crossed his stockinged feet on the seat opposite and viewed them complacently, marked the neat way the crimson clocks in the gray hose matched the herring-bone stripe in his blue suit. (1)

The prose of this first passage breaks, the rhythm of the movement is staccato, until it begins to pick up as Jay kicks off his shoes. Very soon, as the train begins to move at full speed, so do Lou's thoughts, and so does the movement of the prose. Thinking back on his departure from home just a short time before, contemplating his wife's reaction to learning that he is about to leave town again after having been home but three days, Lou remembers how it had all gone down:

He explained how tricky his New York contracts were and how he had to keep feeding them in person—telegrams and telephone calls were never effective, but while he was talking she quietly rose and left the table, her coffee and the toast she had just buttered, untouched on her plate. He had always been glad Mary had been so well brought up that she wouldn't dream of making a scene, but this silent indignation could get your goat just as much as a couple of plates flying through the air. He started to go after her, then shrugged, you can't let these things get you. When he called out good-bye to her a few minutes later there was no answer from behind the closed bedroom door. . . . Outside he looked up at the bedroom window, half-expecting Mary to be there waving good-bye, but the shade was drawn to shut out the sun—that meant she had one of her headaches—those headaches, he suspected, that came from controlling her feelings too well. It annoyed him now that such a little thing as his wife's unusual parting mood should cross his mind when he had so many important things to think of—a lot more than old Jay could ever guess. (3)

The passage continues in this vein, the reader hardly pausing for breath as the train flies headlong through the midwestern afternoon. In this single rapid-fire paragraph, readers begin to understand quite a few things about the often absent Chicago businessman Lou Donovan and his repressed wife, Mary, before they have even met her.

In brief, the novel concerns two "latter-day Babbitts," as Charles Poore says ("Diversity," 19). Lou Donovan and Jay Oliver, two successful midwestern businessmen, travel the rails frequently, most often to New York. Of course the two midwesterners are more at home in the Windy City than they are in Manhattan, and Powell most effectively paints them there in a delightful rendering of a Chicago watering hole she calls "a fourth-rate joint" named the Top (161). Sharp-eyed *Chicago Tribune* writer Joseph Coates convincingly identifies the Top as "the old Club Alabam on Rush Street as it was until at least the 1960s" (3). Not knowing for certain, however, whether Powell had ever actually been in Chicago, I asked Tim Page, who replied, "She probably visited Chicago at some point—[her husband] Joe's sister, [Isabel Hofmayr], ended up living there, and there is a real verisimilitude to *Angels on Toast*" (e-mail, November 16, 2006). Powell almost always painted real places rather than fictional ones (though she generally changes the names) so that her knowing readers might immediately recognize the locations.

In *Angels on Toast*, both male protagonists are married and both own luxurious automobiles, fancy clothes, and tastefully if impersonally decorated suburban homes furnished with all the latest conveniences. But something is missing from their lives—the two men cheat on their wives with at least one if not several other women; both are hard-drinking, smooth-talking big shots with barely a conscience between them. The novel's telling title comes from a line in the book: Lou and Jay, celebrating yet another successful business transaction, take their New York mistresses out for a celebratory dinner on the town. Lacking in refinement, like the Sinclair Lewis character, Jay and Lou "made fun of culture because they didn't have any" (48). Jay's girlfriend, Ebie Vane, "had kidded the pair of them the other night at dinner, the night she brushed off Mrs. Kameray" (48), Lou's latest.

> "What'll you have baby, a steak?" Jay had asked.
> "A steak for God's sake," she had mocked. "These two
> bums clean up a fortune today and they can't think of anything
> better than a steak to buy for us."

"Anything you say, baby," Jay said. "You can have quails on toast by just lifting a finger."[3]

"That deal today is nothing," Lou said. "By the time we're through, old dear, we'll be buying you angels on toast." (48–49)

Later, alone in her apartment, Ebie remembers Lou's words. "Angels on toast, my eye" (49), she says. Ruing the day she had ever met Jay, she regrets her folly in having given up her genuine artistic talent for love and empty promises and nights out at the Rainbow Room. She realizes that "the fault was her own for giving up her simple old life as a real artist—work away even if it takes years! That's what she should have done" (50). Ebie is yet another sorry soul who has squandered her talent and thrown up her ambitions for less important things: a married boyfriend, some fancy dinners, a good table at the latest floor show with a classless out-of-town rube her New York crowd would have sneered at (50). Obviously the "angels" of the title is ironic; these two men are in fact the antithesis of angels, and they are quite removed from class. That they believe that the height of chic in restaurant dining is any dish followed by the words "on toast," likely a less sophisticated cousin of the French term *en croute,* underscores what to Powell is their midwestern naïveté.

Ebie Vane's mother, like her daughter a Manhattan transplant from the Midwest, lives "in contented genteel squalor" (Vidal, "American," 13) in a cheap downtown establishment called the Hotel Ellery. In a prescient portrait of what is to become of the novelist herself some two decades later, Powell's narrator shows the elderly residents of the Hotel Ellery, down on their luck, whiling away their time there drinking low-cost Manhattans, just as Claire Van Orphen in Powell's last book will do. Vidal says that the hotel, which "broods over the novel," serves to "evoke lost time in a way that the novel's bumptious contemporary, early talking movies, don't" (14). As always, in *Angels on Toast* the author's portrayals of Manhattan locations ring true. Here Powell preserves in print a lost New York for all time, just as she will do in her final two novels, *The Wicked Pavilion* and *The Golden Spur.*

Writing again to her editor, Powell claimed that in *Angels on Toast* she was not satirizing the American businessman, that the novel's main characters Lou and Jay were not "representative of anything but Americans at high pressure" (110). However, most commentators would insist that she was in fact satirizing American businessmen, although to read the letter is to become convinced that she was at least not satirizing a certain school of them. Powell added, "I could certainly satirize the businessman, the average business success," as readers know she could, "but such a pompous, Dale Carnegie,[4] the office-is-a-holy-thing, success-is-holy, etc., type would not interest me" (110). Powell's businessmen in the book are far removed from the Dale Carnegie model. So one might say that she is satirizing her own brand of American businessman.

June 3, 1940: Tea with Max Perkins

—Diaries, 177

Though Powell had discontinued, at least for the time being, her habit of planning her novels at length in her journal, fortunately for us she wrote several highly detailed letters about her book to her new editor, Max Perkins, a few extracts from which I have shown. By this time she had put her years at Farrar and Rinehart behind her, having for so long been disappointed in the previous publisher for having brought out five of her books and her play *Jig Saw* to so little consequence. At last she had sought new representation. As Page says,

> *The Happy Island* marked the end of Powell's association
> with Farrar and Rinehart. The author was discouraged by
> her sales, which had begun to climb with *Turn, Magic Wheel*
> and then dropped off again sharply with the new novel, and
> she decided to publish elsewhere (her editors at Farrar and
> Rinehart, mystified by her evolving style, were probably not
> sorry to see her go). As it happened, she landed exactly where
> most serious American authors of the time wanted to be: at the
> august firm of Charles Scribner's Sons, with editor Maxwell
> Everts Perkins. (*Bio,* 167)

Powell was both delighted and optimistic about coming aboard Scribner's, "work[ing] enthusiastically" (*Bio,* 168) on her new novel while looking forward to collaborating with the legendary Perkins. She would dedicate *Angels on Toast* to him, and she would name a beloved cat for him.[5] Clearly, from the beginning Powell had high hopes for her new publishing company, even though the advance she received from Scribner's was far less than the advances she had been used to receiving from Farrar and Rinehart. She was given "only a thousand dollars apiece for her next three novels, as opposed to the twenty-five hundred she had received" for each of her two previous novels (*Bio,* 168). Not only did she accept that cut in pay when moving to Scribner's, but she seems to have received curiously few benefits from the new outfit: "Almost the only privilege allowed by Scribners publishing me is one of using their store where the clerks are unusually nice, presided over by a fine, huge, book-loving Belgian who knows more about literature than anybody in the editorial department" (*Diaries,* 278). Page believes that the author "must have decided that being in understanding and creative hands was worth" the reduction in payment and perks (*Bio,* 168). Aside from mentioning the lack of benefits at the new publisher's, Powell remained curiously silent on leaving Farrar and Rinehart and joining Scribner's; her diary of those years is peppered with tiny passages such as "Lunch with Max Perkins," but little more (177). Her letters speak directly to Perkins but rarely about him.

In one such letter from Powell to her new editor, the author politely noted that while Perkins surely knew best how to present her new book, perhaps her explaining herself would nonetheless assist him in so doing. After detailing for him the authorless quality of the novel, she wrote,

> You, the reader, say, hear a strange conversation in a bar. You are not particularly interested but you idly note that the girl is fairly hardboiled, dyed blonde, maybe a tart; the man has a middlewestern voice, is middle-aged, big, a good-looking man. You think you have dismissed them from your mind but in the back of your mind for weeks you speculate about them— what did she mean when she said that? where were they from? what was their relationship? what a funny crack to make—and suddenly this unknown couple has influenced your own life— their lives flower in your mind, complete people emerge from just a dozen or so words. Good or bad, you don't know, but at least they live. If you saw them again someday you would almost rush up and speak to them. (*Letters,* 110)

Not only did Powell provide Perkins a fine insight into her design for the new novel, but her letter provides readers a glimpse into the way her own curiosity operated. Curiosity, for Powell, was forever the realm of the novelist; without it, there would be no new material to sniff out, and without new material, there would be no story to tell.

Behind every successful man is a woman, and behind her is his wife.

—Groucho Marx

If the above letter to Perkins suggests that Powell had not based her characters in *Angels on Toast* on any particular persons of her acquaintance, as she did in *Turn Magic Wheel* and *The Happy Island,* that suggestion would be incorrect. Though she did not name in either her diary or her letters the individuals on whom she had based her characters, she did acknowledge, in an interview with Robert Van Gelder, that her inspirations for the figures in *Angels on Toast* were in fact real-life acquaintances of hers. First, concerned that some people she knew might think that they recognized themselves in the book, she told Perkins, "I will need one of those 'None of the characters in this novel are drawn from living persons' or whatever it is" (*Letters*, 110). Then, as Van Gelder wrote,

> Since she has shown her [businessmen] as selfish, tricky and
> drunken, unfaithful to wives and mistresses and friends, she
> said that she had worried quite a bit as to what the reactions of
> the persons on whom her characters are based would be, and
> had found comfort only in the hope that the models (being
> no great readers) never would get around to the book. ("Some
> Difficulties," 102)

The author later reported that some persons of her acquaintance—some of her own extended family—believed that they had seen themselves in the novel, though she neglected to mention whether their assumptions were correct. It seems that the wife of Powell's husband's brother, reading the book almost immediately on its release, had at once begun to suspect that at least one of its "angelic" traveling businessmen had been based on her husband. Powell wrote: "Harry Gousha. His wife read *Angels on Toast* and started accusing him of being the model. At the train a special telegram waited for him: 'Why are you always so secretive about your trips?'—first indication of suspicions roused by character" (*Diaries*, 181). Though the writer rather coyly had no more to say on the matter, it seems she may in truth have at least partly based the character on her brother-in-law. Certainly Harry Gousha frequently traveled to New York on business; certainly he had done very well for himself, for he tooled around during the Great Depression in a "fantastically sumptuous new Cadillac" (*Diaries*, 70), employed servants (181), and seems in every other way to have been as wealthy as any Lou Donovan in the novel. Powell also may have based this character on Harry Gousha's good friend, Harry Lissfelt, "a great pal of Joe's and a successful businessman who lived in New York and died about 1944" (Page, telephone, 2007).

Although Powell had spoken of her brother-in-law as a source in her journals, she did not supply any insight into the personality of Harry's wife, though Harry did, for what his perception is worth: "Hell, she's always been suspicious," the brother-in-law supposedly told Powell of his wife, "letting herself go, lying around in a negligee one week to the next, thinking up things to be the matter, no makeup, her hair wild, eyes popping out. . . . I come in from after a six weeks' trip—'You never take me anyplace,' she says, looking wild" (*Diaries*, 181). Sounds as if Harry was quite the storyteller. Whether these words were actually Harry's or Powell's one will never know, but the description goes on from there. It seems that the wife was guilty of incessantly whining about a variety of imagined ills. "Nag, nag, I'm a sonofabitch, a bastard, the lowest thing on earth—that's how it begins as soon as I get in the house—no matter how long I've been away" (181), continues the entry in which Powell is purportedly recording Harry Gousha's words.

Powell has certainly supplied a couple of fleshed-out characters in the novel who sound not unlike Harry's unnamed spouse, obviously a bored and lonely housewife with nothing to do and no husband at home to do it with. The author, who had no patience for such indolence, would likely not have had much sympathy for the wealthy Mrs. Harry Gousha, if this portrait of her is in any way accurate. In any case, if Harry's wife had spied her husband in the pages of *Angels on Toast*, she might also have recognized something of herself in the representation of businessman Lou Donovan's wife, Mary, who sometimes stays in her room for days at a time with a headache, venturing nowhere (140) and feeling "desolately left out" of things (152). Or she may have spied something of herself in the far less sympathetic portrayal of Flo, Jay Oliver's wife, a busybody "hellion" known for "swinging her axe around" (148). If either woman more closely resembles the portrait of Mrs. Gousha that appears in Powell's diary, it is Flo Oliver, a crass, classless, and loud woman who surprises her husband's train as it arrives in New York, rather than the more refined, rather silent, and fully repressed Mary Donovan, who would never condescend to mention to her husband any suspicion of infidelity, let alone attempt to catch him red-handed as Flo does Jay.

When friends playing a game of bridge mention to Mary Donovan that her husband's pal Jay has a girlfriend in Manhattan, Mary immediately understands that her own husband does, too. But Mary is so tight-lipped that Lou "never had to listen to what went on in her little mind, and she never asked him what went on in his" (140). She at once realizes that "she would never mention it, she could never ask him, she would never spy, whatever suspicions she might have would have to freeze up inside her along with the evidence" (136). A character like Flo would leave such a telegram as Mrs. Harry Gousha had left for her homebound husband, but Mary Donovan would be quite unable to do so.

Powell in her diary briefly described the novel as being concerned with "love and ambition, two cliché ideas" (176), though she makes the tale unique. In her hands a story of love and ambition will concern "different kinds of love—different kinds of men and women, different kinds of ambition, and the rubber relationships that are not rubber but that sometimes break instead" (176–77). This same image of brittle, easily breakable relationships is repeated almost verbatim in the novel: Although "people think relationships are made of rubber and stretch and give to every crisis," the narrator of *Angels on Toast* says, it is nevertheless "a shock to find that they can snap in two like a glass thermometer" (185–86). The male-female relationships in the book are likewise so fragile that with a slight gust of wind they might break apart like any delicate piece of glass. If the novel's unhappy women "are like army followers—they don't know where the army is going or what for, but all they know is they have to keep up with it or lose" (*Letters*, 111), as Powell told Perkins, they try as best they can to keep up, though their attempts are in vain. The book's narrator tells us:

> In the dead of night wives talked to their husbands, in the
> dark they talked and talked while the clock on the bureau
> ticked sleep away, and the last street cars clanged off on distant
> streets to remoter suburbs, where in new houses bursting with
> mortgages and the latest conveniences, wives talked in the dark,
> and talked and talked. (97)

Their desperate chatter, of course, serves no purpose. Their husbands are already lost to them; the men remain in the marriages for appearance's sake only. "Jay and Lou with their big respect for marriage," Jay's lover Ebie thinks ironically. "Doing anything they pleased on the side but keeping up the great marriage front" (51). That a woman like Mary Donovan should even want to stay in a marriage with such a one as Lou Donovan might seem curious. But Powell provides the reader with insight into Mary's background, thereby allowing the reader to understand the character's inability to let go of her marriage. Lou had been her only love, "the only one she had ever wanted"; she cherished the way that, in the beginning of their relationship, he would "look steadily at her when they went out together until her gaze fluttered to meet his, having her own happiness consist in curbing his desire . . . it was the way she was, it was her own version of passion" (184–85). Even worse, for Mary "it was frightening to wake up in the morning and know that love did not last, no matter how it was treated" (185). She had not changed in the six years they had been married, and her feelings for her husband had not changed. So why had his for her? Why indeed, asks Powell's narrator. "Why should anyone feel that a great truth is hidden from him when it is written all over the sky that nothing is permanent?" (186). Adrift in happier memories of better days, Mary cannot bear the thought of losing—or of having already lost—her husband.

A short time after the novel's release, Powell wrote in her journal that another female character in the book had been based on a real-life acquaintance of hers. Group Theatre director/producer and lifelong Powell friend Bobby Lewis had a girlfriend during the period, a young beauty from Mexico named Maria de Ferreira. Before readers of the diary learn that she is to be a character model, they meet the "charming toy" there, the "tiny, childish and naughty-faced" Maria who, "drunk, eyes shadowed with pure childish fatigue . . . fell asleep in the cab, gardenia still fresh in her hair but drooping down over one eye" (*Diaries,* 170).[6] Of her becoming the inspiration for a character in the novel, Powell somewhat later wrote,

> In *Angels on Toast* I changed my nasty refugee Trina to look like pretty, sweet little Mexican Maria, flowers in hair and all, and by thinking of the character as Maria, instead of the shrewd, self-centered original model, was able to make an attractive person, unhampered by author hatred.
>
> At Maria's this night, I was therefore startled to hear her talk in Spanish over the phone to someone Bobby jealously explained was Maria's Cuban bandleader[7]—for that was exactly what I had invented for her in the novel. (*Diaries,* 180)

This occasion was yet one more instance of "startling" authorial prophecy, it seemed to the writer (180–81). But thoughts of prophecy aside, the sympathetic Powell preferred to feel no animosity for her characters (unless they were hateful, as is Belle Glaenzer in *Turn, Magic Wheel*), so she would rather reinvent the character by modeling her on someone likable. Trina Kameray, the Maria-based character, is one of Lou Donovan's lovers, an immigrant from an unnamed European country who rooms with Jay Oliver's girlfriend Ebie. After Trina suddenly tells the forty-one-year-old Lou that she is twenty-four, the narrator says, "He didn't answer. She was twenty-eight, he knew. She had started being twenty-four a week or two ago and he suspected it had something to do with the young Cuban bandleader she had found in Havana" (189). Just as his wife Mary is suspicious of Lou's doings when he is away from her, Lou is suspicious of Trina Kameray whenever she is out of his sight. He can never be sure of Trina; had Powell not made her at least somewhat appealing, readers likely would not have fully believed in his interest in her nor in her attractiveness to other men; and if they did not believe, they simply might not have cared.

But while Trina therefore is painted in attractive colors for the most part, not all the novel's unmarried female characters are as positively rendered. Powell's razor-sharp depiction of a lesser character kills in a phrase: "Honey was a virgin (at least you couldn't prove she wasn't), and was as proud as punch of it. You'd have thought it was something that had been in the family for generations" (53). Peripheral characters, because readers need not be much concerned with them, are fair game, while characters close to Powell's heart and therefore to the reader's own are much more sympathetically drawn.

An ear novel, if you like . . .

—*Letters*, III

As we have seen, *Angels on Toast* opens on a train, just as so many of Powell's novels do: as Gore Vidal observes, trains in Dawn Powell "go everywhere on earth that is not home" ("American," 17). Here the train is heading swiftly to New York from the Midwest, where businessmen Lou Donovan and Jay Oliver reside with their wives, though the men are much more frequently on the road—or, more accurately, on the rails—than they are at home. Tim Page finds that in the book "Powell captures some of the rushing breathlessness that makes *Turn, Magic Wheel* so appealing" (*Bio*, 173), which is precisely what she had intended. The novel as she envisioned it needed to be fast moving, had to suffer as little narrative intrusion as possible, needed to directly communicate the voices of the characters and the brisk movement of the train. As the author explained to Edmund Wilson, the book was to be quite structureless, "built almost entirely on conversations—an ear novel if you like—with the implications left for the eye of the reader, and the conversation not a means of exchanging ideas or private dreams but a 'line,' every person having a 'line' as his protection of giving away any part of himself" (*Letters*, 111). Her businessmen forever have a selection of lines at the ready from which to choose, not only to call on while selling their wares or setting up their deals or excusing their behavior to their wives, but also when attempting to impress the various "other women" they are forever meeting up with, just as the stereotypical used-car salesman, pickup artist, and con-man will eternally have theirs. Such lines, of course, are meant to conceal rather than to reveal, as Powell well knows; they serve to deflect close attention rather than to invite scrutiny. The fast-talking talker is not attempting to communicate, one realizes, but instead to play games of smoke and mirrors.

Although Powell remained uncharacteristically silent in her diary on planning the novel, she was typically vocal on its release. Just before it went to press, she was momentarily stunned while looking over the proofs to find that some rather odd additions had been made to it. She wrote jocularly to Max Perkins,

> When my proofs arrived and I found you had taken such great
> editorial liberties as to insert in my novel a large chapter on
> the life of William Morris I was a little startled but deferred as
> usual to your better judgment. I decided this was the "strong
> serious undercurrent" referred to in the catalog and probably
> gave the book the class angle Scribner's has always insisted
> upon in its fiction. (*Letters*, 108)

Soon enough a messenger boy from Scribner's arrived at Powell's apartment to retrieve the Morris chapter, to which arrival the writer responded with characteristic wit, "I am beginning to fear that critics will reproach me for not mentioning William Morris, and perhaps I might put a little note about him somewhere or at least mention his life in my bibliography" (*Letters*, 108). Always aware of the idiotic objections commentators would make, she seized this opportunity to make sport of the error. But her mood darkened just a week before the novel was to come out. In an entry that

Page calls a "despondent and affecting self-portrait of the artist in middle age" (*Bio*, 172), Powell wrote,

> I never realize how lost my defenses are until the crisis comes
> and now I only want to run and hide. A new book coming out
> no longer rouses any hope. As the day approaches, I look at the
> book section and think with a sudden horror that this is the
> last Sunday I will be able to look at a book review without sick
> misgiving—no review, bad review or the patronizing review of
> another illiterate lady reviewer.[8] There is a dreadful week now
> of the usual worst fears ahead, and after that the nervous, weary
> effort to pick up and begin again after another disappointment.
> (*Diaries*, 179)

She feared that her hopes once again would be dashed, that the familiar sting of failure would hit her between the eyes yet another time. A few pages earlier she entered an equally heartrending note:

> In spite of pleasure of Max Perkins' editorial work on me, now
> that the book is to come out the usual deadly hopelessness
> and weariness comes in. The lack of any ad or announcement,
> the silence from publishing end, the all-too-familiar signals of
> another blank shot, and once again the weary packing up and
> readying another book—never understanding why I am unable
> to follow the arrogance of my writing with an arrogance of
> personality[9] or why the luck should so unfailingly fall elsewhere.
> (*Diaries*, 177)

No matter with which house Powell placed her work, her novels still met with indifference from editor, publisher, agent, advertiser. As it happened, the publishing company for which she had had such high hopes had even made an error on the dust jacket. "Jay Donovan," it said, "was one of the boys that put across big deals" ("World," 7E). Unfortunately, Jay's last name is Oliver; Lou's surname is Donovan. Some critics both then and now ascribe Scribner's rather careless error to Powell, alleging that the two businessmen are so interchangeable that it is no wonder the advertisers got it wrong. To my mind, however, Jay and Lou are distinct, as are their wives. Still, regardless of any proffered justification for the error, Powell surely might have expected better from her supposedly top-flight new publisher. One might suppose a careless or hurried reviewer might confuse the character names, but the author's own high-toned publisher? Powell remained silent on the mistake until her next novel, *A Time to Be Born*, was about to be released. She wrote then to Perkins in "an unusually testy letter" that may well never have been sent (*Letters*, 116n), "I hope the jacket for my new book is a plain lettered one without figures, and I should like to check the copy on it, since the last jacket had characters mixed up in the blurb" (*Letters*, 116). Not only because of the mistake on the dust jacket, though, Powell's high hopes were once again dashed. Even though she had graciously accepted far less advance money than she had ever received in the previous decade at Farrar and Rinehart, parlaying the loss into greater hopes and renewed if not manic energy, she was once again disappointed in the careless handling the book received and in the inadequate publicity that greeted its release.[10] If the American Dream has it that hard work will pay off in the end, why was it that Powell's hard work rarely seemed to pay off at all?

Powell's novels have progressed steadily from Ohio sunshine to Manhattan madness.

—Morris Gilbert, 40

Happily, the book did receive some favorable notices, despite its having come out, like each of her previous publications, with little or no fanfare. Edmund Wilson's friend, the esteemed film critic Otis Ferguson,[11] had positively reviewed the novel, and Powell appreciated his commentary, as she wrote to Wilson. However, she added that "the faults of construction he noticed were not there at all," for, she told her friend, there had been no construction to speak of in the first place (*Letters*, 111). But Ferguson's review was all but a rave, with a slight reservation or two; it is curious that Powell should focus on the qualifications in it rather than on the good it might do her. Ferguson wrote, among other commendations, that

> Dawn Powell is one of the few writers with a first-class wit who has the kind of understanding that combines appreciation with analysis, a curious ear and eye for everything that goes on, with an endless capacity for getting around. The logic of her general background is good, and her characters so natural in it that they continue acting like heels without stirring resentment. Miss Powell has an eye like a hawk but also the quality of forgiveness,

> which is actually a good deal rarer in novelists than it is in real
> life. ("Far from Main Street," 599)

Powell seems unreasonably defensive in her reaction to Ferguson's kind and perceptive review.

Like Ferguson, a few other critics contemporary to Powell mentioned the structureless quality of the novel, not understanding, as Powell would have it, that the author had left her story structureless for a purpose. An unnamed reviewer in the Massachusetts journal *Springfield Sunday Union and Republican,* for example, said that "Miss Powell writes lively dialog, especially where themes of the thin-ice type are concerned. . . . She gives the impression of having known people like Jay, Lou, Ebie and the dull Chicago wives of the two amorally inclined men. But the novel lacks a coherent and plausible narrative. It rambles from New York to Chicago and other places" ("World," 7E). Unfortunately, the reviewer missed the idea that as the trains rumble and hurtle along, so do the businessmen, and so, therefore, does the story.

Charles Poore's review in the *Times,* however, was positive:

> Miss Powell's novel is . . . a warm-hearted and yet singularly
> penetrating conversation piece about raucous, expansive men
> of affairs who shuttle constantly between New York, Chicago
> and points south or west, who are constantly in hot water with
> their wives, mistresses and competitors, who, in short, inhabit
> a wit-and-glitter world where . . . morals are so loose as to be
> practically detached. We may piously deplore their existence,
> but Miss Powell makes us believe it. ("Diversity," 19)

Though not at all the lengthy, attentive sort of review Powell longed for, it nevertheless praised both the book and the author. Other reviewers were not so kind. The *New Yorker,* in its "Briefly Noted" column, briefly noted the book, calling it "unabashedly trivial but rather entertaining" (95), the commentator referring to the perceived worthlessness of her characters. "Trivial," "pointless"—Powell had heard it all before.

Robert Van Gelder, one reviewer who sometimes faulted Powell for her "worthless" characters, had asked Powell the reason behind the "pointless" types she was so well known for. In reply, she first "wondered how many people out of an odd lot of a hundred wouldn't be rather pointless," then added, "I'll bet if you walked through an office at 5:00 in the afternoon and asked people working there, "What is your aim in life?" most of them would be up against it to give you an answer'" ("Some Difficulties," 102). More often, she said, they would be thinking only of immediate concerns, such as remembering to buy toothpaste or to meet up with friends. For the same reason, Powell felt it disingenuous to write books full of characters who strive to accomplish heroic goals.

Powell's contemporary Rose Feld, in not only a positive but a rather lengthy review, wrote,

> With the exception of Mary Donovan, all the characters are
> on the make, and if they are not sweet and beautiful they are
> devastatingly real and human. Miss Powell pulls no punches,
> plays no favorites. When the little comedy she develops with
> acid acumen is finished, as far as the book is concerned, there
> are neither victors nor spoils. They're all ready to start over
> again with the same problems, the same shabbiness of spirit, the
> same greed. ("Novels of New York," 12)

Of course they are. Powell was not in the business of mending souls or of creating unrealistic, ideal types; instead she was in the habit of pointing out the foibles and faults of the regular Joes and Janes who populate our land-scape with far more regularity than the heroic sort found in so many other novels do.

Feld, one of few commentators to give adequate space and thought to her review of *Angels on Toast*, was one of few who understood and in fact described for her readers the differences between Lou Donovan and Jay Oliver as Powell drew them. Lou, Feld recalled, had begun his career work-ing as a hotel bellhop, then done a stint in vaudeville on his way to the big time of Chicago business. Jay Oliver, in relation to Lou, is given limited background; less successful than Lou, he is "in cotton" but has more of a taste for the ladies than even Lou has: "Jay had lots of girls, and how could he help it, traveling around so much, but Ebie was the one he really loved" ("Novels of New York," 12). Furthermore, Feld recognized and expounded on the differences between the two businessmen's wives, Mary and Flo— the wives they have chosen suggesting significant differences in the men's tastes and temperament as well.

On *Angels on Toast*'s first re-release in 1990, Gail Pool, who devotes sub-stantial space to her review, finds much to like in the novel. She understands Powell as many commentators of the writer's own day did not. "In writing about lovers and spouses, insiders, outsiders, and eccentrics, Powell did not make life or people out to be any better than they are. Her great talent was for evoking so precisely what—in all their humor and sadness—they are" (20). She too notes the distinctions between Lou and Jay, remarking that "unlike his friend Jay Oliver, long involved in an affair with Ebie Vane (who actually loves him), Lou has fooled around only with nightclub women who mean nothing to him" (20). Pool remarks also that "the novel's central comedy has an edge, and the ending is not a conventional wrap-up. These characters can no more easily escape their predicaments than we can ours, and not because Powell has set them up. She is too fine a satirist for that. She quite succeeds in her claim . . . that 'my characters are not slaves to an author's propaganda. I give them their heads. They supply their own nooses'"(20).[12]

To Powell it often seemed that her characters were busily writing their own stories, intently creating the scenarios that would lead them more often to failure than to success. True to form, the characters in her next novel of New York, 1942's searing *A Time to Be Born*, come bearing all the rope they need—and then some—to do the dirty job themselves.

A TIME TO BE BORN, 1942

A scheming, self-promoting Ice Queen with the soul of a hedge-fund trader.

—Robert Lingeman, 40[13]

By the period of *A Time to Be Born*, Powell had come into her own. In this dishy and dark tale of disagreeable characters clawing their way to the top against a backdrop of impending war, the author was at her satirical best. Still working with Max Perkins, Powell (or Scribner's) had again included what by this time had become a common caveat in her works: "All of the characters in this book are the invention of the author and have no living counterparts."[14] This novel, which she dedicated to intimate friend Coburn "Coby" Gilman, concerns a powerful newspaper publisher and his beautiful, conniving wife who, it so happens, is also a successful playwright, novelist, and political speechmaker. For the most part, Powell's contemporary audience, from publishers to publicists to the buying public, were convinced that her characters Julian Evans and Amanda Keeler Evans had been based on Henry and Clare Boothe Luce, though Powell for years would claim that neither of the Luces had inspired her characters.

In her diary of October 1940, the author is first seen thinking about this new novel. Her previous book, *Angels on Toast,* had just been released, yet Powell was already at work churning out another idea:

> Book. New York during the invasion. Eggs thrown at Willkie in Detroit. Accents on the bus. Waking up with pressure on head. In London there is bombing. 87 children lost. A story of ambition against a background that is constantly torn down. The young men—idle, poor, no jobs to look forward to, drinking a little beer—apathetic because what chances are there for optimism? None of the "Welcome To The World, It's Yours To Conquer" of other days. . . . Their girls more and more going over to older men, their own fathers, because they have the money. (182)

Here Powell says nothing of the Luces or of any other character inspirations. She earlier had said that her "plan has always been to feed a historical necessity" (*Diaries,* 151). Following the initial entry on what would eventually become her fifth New York novel, she fell silent, even less forthcoming than she had been on *Angels on Toast.* In fact, not another word would she write in her journal about the new book until after she had completed it, and even then she wrote of it very little, perhaps less than of any other novel save *Whither.* Fourteen years after the book's publication, however, she would confide in her diary:

> I have been denying for years any basis in *A Time to Be Born* for the general idea that it is Clare Luce. I swear it is based on five or six girls, some known personally and some by talk, and often I changed the facts to avoid libel with resulting character a real person evidently and libelously Luce-ian. I insist it was a composite (or compost) but then I find a memo from 1939— "Why not do novel on Clare Luce?" Who can I believe—me or myself? (356)

Attractive as the journal account is, Powell is being disingenuous here, especially when one considers the fact that years earlier, in 1942, she had written to her editor that "I had a friend of [Henry] Luce's at 20th Century

Fox read the galleys and he said it was nothing like Luce but very like Clare B. but he didn't see how a lady who made her living satirizing other living characters could sue for being satirized. He said the character was hers but none of the facts" (*Letters*, 115–16). The writer, her publisher, or both might have been concerned about a potential lawsuit from the Luces. Biographer Page says that it is evident that "Powell knew just what she was doing all the time" (*Letters*, 116n), but her repeated insistence not only in 1942 but as late as 1956 that she had "changed the facts" might explain why she had always claimed that her model had not been *precisely* Clare Luce. And, as has been previously noted here, Powell often used not one but several figures as sources for a particular character, so she may have had more than one woman in mind as she painted the Amanda Keeler/Clare Luce character. If so, she might more consistently have said, as she does above, that the character had been a composite, that it had not been based on Clare Luce *alone*.

Powell's contemporary Beatrice Sherman believed the author, writing that the novel's disclaimer "should be accepted without question, for while Amanda may remind the guileless reader of several ladies on the New York scene, not one of them could equal her prodigious career. Nor does Julian seem a photographic representation of any one of a number of self-important gentlemen whom he might chance to resemble in some way" (6). Certainly, Powell was never one to write "photographic representations" of anything; she was, first of all, a novelist, not a journalist. That Powell was sending up Clare Boothe Luce is clear, though she had a few similar noteworthies in mind as well.

In a letter by Dawn Powell that Tim Page lent to Sylvia Jukes Morris for her biography of Boothe Luce, and which Morris kindly photocopied and sent to me, Powell clearly states that her portrait of Amanda Evans had been *partially* based on Ms. Luce. With Mr. Page's permission, I reproduce the entire letter here:

> 35 East 9th Street, New York City November 1, 1944
>
> My dear Mr. Miller:[15]
>
> Ever since my novel A TIME TO BE BORN appeared two years ago Clare Booth [*sic*] Luce, with her genius for publicity, has been claiming that she is its heroine. As a matter of fact a great many of her bosom friends called or wrote me to berate me for not getting the facts right. One lady called me and indignantly demanded how I dared write that Clare was thrown out of her house by Harry?—I had thinly disguised

it, she stated, by calling my heroine Amanda Evans and her husband Julian Evans. She said it was an outrage and all due to the time Claire (or Clare) was thrown out of her suite at the Ambassador by hem A.C. Blumenthal[16] who was paying her bills but was mad at her on discovering Baruch[17] had palmed her off on him after ten years of supporting her. Why, said the bosom friend righteously, did I not get the facts right? Another bosom friend called up and said my newspaper man Kenneth Saunders was a very unfair picture of Pare Lorentz[18] who was NOT a drunkard when Claire was keeping him and even if I meant Dudley Murphy[19] it was all unfair to Claire.

I assure you in complete candour the book was a work of fiction and I have never been interested in taking one single person complete from life. The character was made up of a number of ruthless, man-eating, money-grabbing, beauty-selling modern career women and I used occasional bits of gossip about all of them. At the time I was writing it Mrs. Luce was not as conspicuous as the others but by the time the book appeared the others had dimmed out and she was very much in the limelight. Curiously enough it was the completely invented situations in the book that struck her friends as the inside story. I got extremely bored with her friends thinking I would waste my good gifts on such a dreary, totally one-dimensional insignificant little creature as Mrs. Luce. However, by the time they had unfolded the True Facts I DID have enough sordid, unbelievably slimy material for a book on a lady Nero. Such people thrive on even the worst kind of publicity and I think all decent people can do is to decry the power and influence of such. Certainly women of talent should be rewarded properly and from what I hear Miss Connors[20] is relying totally on her own brains and personal abilities, instead of the brains, power, and riches of someone else. I wish her every success but I cannot provide any documentation on the evil of her opponent. My advice is to get in touch with all of Mrs. Luce's bosom friends who appear only too glad to reveal her past. It seems to be something, too!

Very truly yours,

DAWN POWELL

In this letter an apparently frustrated Powell insists that her portrait of Amanda Keeler Evans had been a composite.

Powell's old friend Matthew Josephson believed that the Amanda Keeler character had been based on a woman "whom Dawn may have known from her school days in a country town of Ohio" (41–42).[21] In fact, years later, Powell would remark that old college friend Charlotte Johnson was thrown when reading *The Locusts Have No King* because she did not recognize any of the characters as "Lake Erie girls," so accustomed was she to seeing one or more of the school crowd in Powell's books (*Letters*, 153).

Gore Vidal, who had known both Dawn Powell and Clare Boothe Luce, had the following to say: "Even Dawn Powell, our best mid-century novelist, had it in for Clare. Dawn herself had enjoyed almost no success from her novels and plays; then along comes what she regards as a dilettante beauty who takes Broadway—and all the other ways save the strait and narrow—by the proverbial storm. Dawn parodies the Luces as Julian and Amanda in *A Time to Be Born*" ("Woman," 73). If Powell disliked Boothe Luce, she was not alone; the subtitle of Vidal's essay reads "Why Did They All Hate Clare Boothe Luce?" Ms. Luce had not been much liked in her own time, and, to some degree, she is not too fondly remembered in ours.

As I noted in chapter 2, Powell had once congratulated herself on her portrait of the novel's female protagonist, saying, "Clare Luce made such evil use of her Congressional power [that] I was glad to have slashed her in my last book" (213). These words, coming not from the fourteen-year distance of the coy "whom should I believe?" entry, instead appeared only a year after *A Time to Be Born* was published. Here Powell clearly admitted that it was Ms. Luce whom she had skewered in her book; here, too, the novelist was appalled by what she considered Boothe Luce's malevolent behavior in having attacked Vice President Henry Wallace. Clare had railed at Wallace's international political views, pronouncing them nothing but "globaloney"[22] as she attempted to further her isolationist ideology (*Diaries*, 213n); and in so doing she had clearly infuriated Powell.

Vidal himself was none too fond of Boothe Luce; in this same essay he cheerfully repeats "the story that most enraged" her (72), even though he reports that she had forever tried, unsuccessfully, to squelch it. The story in question had to do with Clare Luce's having met with the Pope at the Vatican. A recent convert to Catholicism, Clare was seen incessantly "haranguing the Pope, who kept saying, over and over again, but Madam, I *am* Catholic" (72). She told Vidal that the story was an invention, adding, "It's not like me anyway," to which Vidal responds, "But, of course, it was" (72). In the same essay he speaks of her conniving nature, her ruthless ambition, her plastic surgery which even extended to her having had a statue of herself re-chiseled to match her new look. Also, according to both Vidal and Sylvia Jukes Morris, whose biography was the impetus for Vidal's article, Clare Boothe had told a friend, "I'll marry for money ... Lots of it ... Damned if I'll ever love any mere man. Money! I need it and the power it brings, and some day you shall hear my name spoken of as famous" (Vidal, "Woman," 73). In the next line, Vidal likens Clare Boothe Luce to Scarlett O'Hara, one of American literature's most famous spoiled brats.

Vidal endeavors, in fairness, to speak well of Boothe Luce—suggesting at one point that had feminism been more widely embraced during her time she "might have been admired as what she was, a very tough woman who had so perfectly made it in a man's world" (72). For a moment he even compares her to Hillary Clinton, though he immediately takes it back: "But then, as one thinks of Hillary Clinton, perhaps not—of course, Hillary-haters are mostly men, and the men of long ago were fetched by Clare" (72). Biographer Morris seems hardly fond of her subject, writing of the "dark undercurrents of deceit, ruthlessness, and narcissism in her personality" (overleaf); her being "ever more enamored of luxury" (304); her legendary cruelty and conceit; and her many detractors, among them Dorothy Parker, Irwin Shaw, Franklin Roosevelt, and others.

Attempting to answer the question that he himself had asked—"Why did they all hate Clare Boothe Luce?"—Vidal rather facilely attributes her unpopularity to that oldest of motives: feminine jealousy. He writes that Clare Luce "was too beautiful, too successful in the theatre, in politics, in marriage. . . . It was the women who wanted to do her in" (72). But surely there were countless other beautiful and successful women in New York who did not inspire such fervent jealousy or hatred. Perhaps Powell's fictional take on Boothe Luce might better explain at least one contemporary woman's viewpoint, and perhaps jealousy did have something to do with it. In any case, as Roger K. Miller says, the novel is not only interesting in and of itself but "worth a special look because of the way in which characters can be traced to real personages familiar to Powell" ("Reintroducing," E8), though he stops short of naming them.

In the novel, Powell-like Ohio-born character Ethel Carey, arriving for the first time at Amanda's luxurious Fifth Avenue mansion, initially "flatters herself on her great-hearted lack of envy" at seeing the impressive structure in which her former school chum resides, then excuses the feeling away as "rather a normal sense of justice. Why did Amanda Keeler get everything out of life and not Ethel Carey?" (6). Though the narrator has established that Ethel is seething with envy, the character is determined not to name the sensation jealousy, for she had always "hated to do any one the favor of being jealous" (6). Call it hatred or jealousy or what you will, Powell had her reasons for disapproving of Clare Boothe Luce, just as the novel's characters have more than enough justification for disliking Amanda Keeler Evans.

The best years of no one's life.

—Gore Vidal, "Dawn Powell, the American Writer," 15[23]

In the beginning of the novel, after Powell has first set the stage—New York on the threshold of World War II—she next introduces Amanda Keeler, or, rather, lots of Amanda Keelers. The image Powell paints here is not of a distinct individual but instead of one of any number of cold-hearted strivers:

> This was an age for Amanda Keelers to spring up by the dozen, level-eyed handsome young women with nothing to lose, least of all a heart, so there they were holding it aloft with spotlights playing on it from all corners of the world, a beautiful heart bleeding for war and woe at tremendous financial advantage. No international disaster was too small to receive endorsed photographs and publicity releases from Miss Keeler or her imitators, no microphone too obscure to scatter her clarion call to arms. Presented with a mind the very moment her annual income hit a hundred thousand dollars, the pretty creature was urged to pass her counterfeit perceptions at full face value, and being as grimly ambitious as the age was gullible, she made a heyday of the world's confusion. (4)

The singular (rather than the plural) Amanda Keeler, the narrator tells us, is the type of woman who "rode the world's debacle as if it were her own yacht and saved her tears for Finland and the photographers" (4).[24] As I have shown, Powell had no tolerance for posturing or pretentiousness[25] of any kind, certainly not for the sort that would result in such shameless profiteering as readers see here. If her Andrew Callingham, the preening Hemingwayesque character first introduced in *Turn, Magic Wheel,* had inspired her disapproval, a character who would parade about while profiting from the victims of war would earn her utter disdain. Callingham, readers will recall, returns to New York from his long absence abroad not to visit his dying second wife but instead to swagger before a throng of photographers. The same character makes an appearance in this novel, as does Dennis Orphen; the Luces are both great admirers of the former, a fondness that indicates the shallowness of their characters. Like Callingham, Amanda is ever ready for a photo opportunity. Having promised to appear at a benefit for young children rescued from the London slums, she at the last minute attempts to back out of the engagement, crying to her secretary, "'Telephone them that I can't possibly. I'm worn to the bone with that thing'" (64). When her secretary, Miss Bemel, reminds her that scores of photographers will be there, she immediately reconsiders: "'All right. I suppose I could spare a few minutes. I ought to do that'" (64). Throughout the novel Powell, as usual, roundly condemns affectation in all its guises. Sara Mosle says that "in this wicked comedy of Manhattan manners, Powell strips her characters (and the beds they lie in) of all pretensions" (39). Rather than having stripped them of their pretensions, however, it seems more to the point to say that Powell has placed those pretensions under a microscope, illuminated and enlarged them for all to see, and in so doing not only shown them as laughable but stripped them of their potency.

The self-serving, posturing Amanda Keeler had some years before moved to New York from her birthplace in the lower-class section of Powell's fictional Lakeville, Ohio;[26] readers learn early on in the novel that she intends to use her old hometown acquaintance, the apparently benign Vicky Haven, as her protégée, if only to further her own nefarious aims, primarily to deflect attention from Amanda's having an affair with another man, Ken Saunders. Amanda uses the younger midwestern woman as "a springboard to freedom . . . a perpetual alibi, a private cause that [her husband] Julian could not touch" (59). Use others as she might, Amanda, however, reflects that "they would soon find that Amanda Keeler was not to be used" (78). She was certainly never one for the Golden Rule: having stolen Julian away from his wife and demanding fidelity from him, Amanda nevertheless continues her extramarital affair with the cast-off Saunders.

Ms. Keeler's old school chum Vicky Haven, one of the "brighter young women" of Lakeville, had been at the age of twenty-six doing pretty well for herself, at least by Lakeville's standards; she owned her own small real estate business, was well thought of in the town, and sometimes was even asked to speak at her college's Alumnae Day. Vicky, like everyone else, the narrator says, considered herself smarter than average but "it sometimes surprised her that she was so dumb about the simplest things, such as understanding politics, treaties . . . the use of oyster forks, service plates, back garters on girdles, the difference between Republicans and Democrats, and the management of a lover" (40). Not the brightest of women, she is nevertheless good hearted and good natured, and in that sense she serves as a perfect foil for Amanda Keeler. Still, kind and harmless as Vicky may seem, she is far from perfect; Powell neither sentimentalizes nor plays favorites with her or with any of her other characters. After all, as Sanford Pinsker of the *New Criterion* writes, "Life had turned Powell into a tough cookie, one who saw others with an unblinkered eye" (67). In true Powell fashion, each character's strengths and weaknesses are laid out clearly, without sugarcoating, faults in plain view. For example, after Vicky tells herself, "There's no doubt about it; the female mind can't hold anything very long," the narrator blithely comments on the character's tendency to "blame her own shortcomings on the entire sex" (40). And though young Vicky had been an honor student at Miss Doxey's grammar school, "knowledge scampered through her brain as if it had been warned to get out within twenty-four hours" (40). But at least Vicky retains her memory—she is bright enough to wonder at how her old school friend, the now wildly successful writer Amanda Keeler Evans, had in ten years' time "transformed the opportunist into the scholar" (41). After all, when Vicky had known her, Amanda had been far more interested in "getting faculty favors without too much work" (41) than in actually learning anything. Amanda had first become famous as the author of a "sword and lace romance" (3–4) called *Such Is the Legend*, noteworthy primarily as "a happy escape from the prospect of being bombed" (Sherman, 357). Having been brought to public notice by Julian's huge publicity machine, the book is a runaway best seller, and even if Amanda did not actually written it herself, who was to know?

It is here that readers first meet the aforementioned Ethel Carey, another transplant from Lakeville, as she rides the train in from Ohio to Penn Station. Ethel congratulates herself on having come to Manhattan on behalf of Vicky Haven, even though she is certain that to Amanda's mind both Ethel and Vicky are unimportant little nobodies no different from thousands of other unimportant little nobodies whose "crime" was that they "had no news value" (5). Because her unfortunate friend Vicky has been made miserable over a recent breakup with a boyfriend who has run off and married another woman, Ethel decides that if she appeals to Amanda to find their friend a position in New York, Vicky might more readily recover from her distress. But, Ethel wonders, can such nobodies as Vicky Haven properly ask to be assisted by such important personages as Amanda Keeler Evans? Ethel and Vicky, after all, are now very far removed from Amanda and her ilk—as evinced by the fact that the war offers great opportunities for the Evanses, while it offers these poor souls fresh from Lakeville "no promotions, no parades, no dress uniforms, no regimental dances—no radio speeches, no interviews, no splendid conferences. What unimportant people they were, in this important age!" (5). So when Ethel Carey questions whether she has done the right thing in coming to see the important Amanda at a time like this, the idea so preys on her mind that, once arriving in New York, she "finally solves her indecision by having a facial at Arden's" (5). The author here returns to one of her favorite topics: the way in which department stores, beauty salons, in fact all the palaces of consumer culture serve to distract, to placate, to persuade us that spending our money within their walls will make us feel better about ourselves. Here as in novels from *Whither* through *The Golden Spur* Powell sends up the American Dream, which for the author too often manifested itself in a headlong pursuit of all the latest styles and fads, the newest appliances, and a stack of notes, bills, and baubles to store away in jewelry boxes and safe deposit boxes. The women of New York, on the verge of this country's entry into World War II, were more preoccupied, as Powell saw it, with new fashions than with news forecasts, more impressed with the expensive outerwear of such a one as Amanda Keeler than with her inner nature. In fact, "Ladies clubs saw the label on her coat and the quality of her bracelet and at once begged her to instruct them in politics" (4), though of course Amanda is no authority on the subject. And of those who actually *were* listening at all to the harrowing journalistic reports of the day, too many of them, à la Amanda Keeler Evans, were listening to them with a cold ear to profit. As the narrator says:

> This was a time when the true signs of war were the lavish
> plumage of the women; Fifth Avenue dress-shops and the
> finer restaurants were filled with these vanguards of war. . . .
> The women were once more armed, and their happy voices
> sang of destruction to come. Off to the relief offices they rode
> in their beautiful new cars, off to knit, to sew, to take part
> in the charade . . . off they rode in the new mink, the new

emerald bracelet . . . they quiver[ed] for the easy drama of the trenches. (2)

Similarly, in a letter of the same time Powell wrote to Bruce Bliven, writer and later editor for the *New Republic* (*Letters*, 114n), she disparaged the role of "the church supper" in encouraging the view that "the starving Chinese, the ragged prisoner of war, the orphan can only be helped by as many people as possible putting on their minks and sables and eating more than they want" (115), just as any child growing up in the postwar United States often heard at the dinner table, "Clean your plate; people are starving in China!" Powell's dead-on satire, her cutting, wicked humor bites into every line of the novel. As she points out, not only does our excess not assist the needy, but our vanity in pretending that it does serves no purpose other than to assuage our guilt. American consumerism, following the Great Depression of the previous decade, was alive and well in the wartime years of the 1940s, the tony citizens of New York as well fed then as always. If the message of the city was to "Eat Sunshine Biscuits," then spreading them with caviar—for the war effort, of course—might have seemed an even better idea.

Time to Be Born—Started January 1941

—*Diaries*, 196

The October 1940 entry in which Powell first brought up her idea for the new novel was one of few mentions of the book in her diaries. Because she did not discuss in her diaries either her plans for or her process of writing the book, we are fortunate to have a rather extended synopsis of it in a letter she wrote to the Scribner's publicity department. Determined, it seems, that the publisher not make any errors on the dust jacket of her new novel as on the previous one, the author took it upon herself to let the publicity people know precisely what the work was about and to give them an idea of how they might best present it. One may recall that after the misprint on the dust jacket of *Angels on Toast* Powell had asked Perkins to see to it that her new jacket came out in simple plain letters and without figures (*Letters*, 116). As she had requested, the first edition of *A Time to Be Born* features a rather plain-looking half-blue, half-black dust cover on which are printed the following words: "An exhilarating and keenly perceptive novel of contemporary

American life, manners, aspirations and morals. The pungent and merciless portrait of a 'career woman' who knew exactly what she wanted—which was everything." As Powell had asked, the jacket contains no character names, no figures, and, happily, no errors; moreover, some of the words had come directly from Powell's own synopsis of the novel. Whether or not Perkins had granted her request to approve the jacket copy—and it is not clear that Powell's written request had ever reached him at all (*Letters*, 116n)—it does appear that the publicity department had at least read the novelist's own synopsis of the work:

Author: Dawn Powell

Novel: About 75,000–80,000 words

Title : *A Time to Be Born* (from Ecclesiastes)[27]

Amanda Keeler had this advantage over her rivals: she knew exactly what she wanted and that was Everything. Representative of the new order of career woman, Amanda exploited every detail of her feminine equipment to solidify her position, and armored herself further by a marriage to the powerful newspaper owner Julian Evans. At 30, Amanda had all the wit, fame and beauty that money and publicity could buy; even the coming New War couldn't detrain her, for she adjusted her ambition to the times and rode the world's debacle as if were her own private yacht. (*Letters*, 112–13)

A Time to Be Born is the darkest of all Powell's New York novels to date, though the postwar *The Locusts Have No King* will be even darker. Here, the impending war has cast a shadow on the mood of Manhattan and dampened the spirit of its citizens, as the book will make abundantly clear. However, despite her friendships with such political figures as Floyd Dell, John Dos Passos, and John Howard Lawson, Powell was largely apolitical and agnostic. According to William Peterson, "Her own chosen role, observant and amused chronicler, made her avoid fixed ideas and ideologies. She remained extraordinarily open to new experiences, people, and ideas. Firmly rooted in her culture, she was nevertheless open to change" (42). As Jacqueline Miller Rice remembered, "Dawn didn't think politically. It was John Howard Lawson who brought her into the Group Theatre to do her play *Big Night*. He became one of the Hollywood Ten. But Dawn didn't care about politics. At least they weren't the main event. . . . And when Dos Passos went from the left to the right, that made no difference to Dawn either. He was her friend" (Guare, x). Sanford Pinsker calls her a woman who was "as comfortable with Communists as she was with fat cats" (68), and John Strausbaugh reports that when the once-leftist Dos Passos and Cummings turned into "stalwart Republicans in liberal Greenwich Village, upsetting many of their cohorts," Powell "stuck by them" (181).

But early on she did write at least one short story that reads as decidedly politically left: a piece called "Dynamite in the Office," printed in a 1938 issue of *Coronet* with the header, "By the time the lunch was over, the radical shoe was on the wrong foot." Still, Powell, political at this time or not, could not help speculating about what the United States' involvement in the war would be or what the consequences of its involvement would bring to both the world of her novel and the greater world beyond it. Her synopsis continues:

> With Amanda's honestly ruthless activities as a center
> theme, this novel tells of the hectic period just before and
> during the early stages of the New War. The imminence
> of world disaster sped the momentum of Manhattan life—
> individuals, seeing their personal careers about to be scrapped
> on the war heap, flung themselves as did Amanda into the
> business of "getting theirs" before the crash.
>
> Into Amanda's perfectly organized success machine comes
> a younger woman, equally talented, but with no gift for self-
> exploitation. It suits Amanda's new plans to make Victoria her
> protégée, and this odd friendship gives opportunity for contrast
> between the normal, shy, ever-futile young woman . . . and the
> shrewd, high-handed Amanda. . . .
>
> The background is New York from 1938 to the present,
> showing the effect on private lives of the rising war, with the
> women, as ever, riding ahead to meet it. (*Letters*, 113)

From the first page of the novel, the reader understands that this book will be unlike any of Powell's previous books. "You woke in the morning with the weight of doom over your head," the narrator says, echoing the words Powell had used in that first diary entry when she had begun planning the new book. "You lay with eyes shut wondering why you dreaded the day," she says. Had you just had a terrible nightmare? you wonder. Then, "fully awake, you remembered that it was no dream. Paris was gone, London was under fire, the Atlantic was now a drop of water between the flame on one side and the waiting dynamite on the other" (1). The rest of the world was at war, and it was only a matter of time before the United States would be at war, too. The narrator continues: "Day's duties were performed to the metronome of Extras, radio broadcasts, committee conferences on war orphans, benefits for Britain" (1). War was everywhere, it was unavoidable, it interrupted the flow of everyday life. War had even infiltrated the pages of Dawn Powell. Normally, readers did not turn to Powell for her political views or for her "historical insights, though they add heft to her books." Instead, "we read her for laughs, for her ear for gossip, her satirically skewed vision, her generous, comic view of life" (Lingeman, 40). But in this book we read her for all those things *and* for her stunningly accurate backdrop of New York during the beginning stages of World War II. As Vidal said in his appraisal of Powell and the novel, "I know of no one else who has got so well the essence of that first war year" ("American," 15).

In Powell's view, too many Americans seemed unsure of what awaited them but nevertheless stood ready to try their hands at gaining what they could from a world turned topsy-turvy. As the novel makes clear, "This was no time for beauty, for love, or private future; this was the time for ideals and quick profits on them before the world returned to reality and the drabber opportunities" (2–3). Beatrice Sherman, reviewer for the *New York Times Book Review,* agreed: "[This] book is mighty timely, for no one, even on the sidelines of this war, can fail to see that a number of people are exploiting its possibilities for profit to themselves as if it were a happy windfall or a special godsend marked 'personal'" (6). For those less caught up in schemes ready-made for profiteering, it was as if hope had ceased to exist. The novel tells us, "There was no future; every one waited, marked time, waited. For what? On Fifth Avenue and Fifty-fifth Street hundreds waited for a man"—as readers shall see, the very man about whom Powell would speak to her publisher when explaining her book (*Letters,* 178)—"on a hotel window ledge to jump;[28] hundreds waited with craning necks and thirsty faces as if this single person's final gesture would solve the riddle of the world. Civilization stood on a ledge, and in the tension of waiting it was a relief to have one little man jump" (2–3). The entire city seemed to have become immobile, frozen in time, waiting. Citizens shared a feeling of dread, a sense of hopelessness. Artists, too, feared for the future, so they turned to writing of bygone days, a habit Powell decries in her novel:

> This was a time when writers dared not write of Vicky Haven
> or of simple young women like her. They wrote with shut eyes
> and deaf ears of other days, wise days they boasted, of horse-
> and-buggy men and covered-wagon Cinderellas . . . they made
> ignorance shine as native wit, the barrenness of other years and
> other simpler men was made a talent, their austerity and the
> bold compulsions of their avarice a glorious virtue. (3)

In her diary of the same period Powell similarly complained, "Now we have the escapists who write of happenings a hundred or three-hundred years ago, false to history, false to human nature" (*Diaries*, 188). As always, Powell was after putting down the truth; in this novel, she aims also to place it in its historical moment.

Remind me to tell you of the time I looked into the heart of an artichoke.

—All about Eve

Into this confused prewar fray stride Amanda Keeler and her crowd, the world a plum ripe for their taking. If Amanda and her husband are poised to take advantage of the age, others are at the ready to step into the Evanses' shoes. According to Rose Feld, not only has the author drawn a convincing portrait of a cold-heartedly ambitious "woman of the hour," but she has also "been successful in creating sympathetic little people with modest desires who serve as instruments of her downfall" ("Glitter Girl," 5). In one sense sweet Vicky Haven from Lakeville turns out to have something in common with a character who will appear in our popular culture about a decade later, Joe Mankiewicz's not-so-naïve-as-she-seems Eve Harrington of the 1950 award-winning film *All about Eve.*[29] When Amanda dusts off old flame Ken Saunders, the beau she had jilted to marry Julian Evans, to serve as Vicky's escort, she never imagines that the two will one day fall for each other. As one commentator more bitingly notes, "Ken might have gone on being a tame cat indefinitely but for a quiet little country mouse named Vicky who gobbled him up when Amanda was busy riding the crest" ("Feast," 116). Though Ms. Keeler has brought Ken around to serve her own ego—basking in the light of his devotion to her, she remembers that he "used to be her applause" (75)—her pride is wounded to the quick when she fears she has lost him to the unsophisticated Miss Haven. But Ken, who has been intimately involved with Amanda for some three years, so dislikes the woman she has become that he compares sleeping with her to "being in bed with General Motors" (130). The lovelorn Vicky Haven and the ill-treated Ken Saunders discover they have much in common, including the fact that when attending Amanda's affairs they are forever "linked together by being the two nobodies in a drawing-room of notables, all uttering notable remarks" (133). Eventually, they begin meeting for lunch from time to time, and then even for dinner. By novel's end, the two are swearing their undying devotion to one another, but Powell's narrator throws a hitch into the scene.

Another Harrington-like character who would take what Amanda has for her own is Ethel Carey, the other Lakeview native and good friend of Vicky Haven's. Much less tractable than Vicky, Ethel will not tolerate the snubbing she receives from Amanda. Unlike her more amenable friend, who believes that it is "every one's duty to keep out of [Amanda's] royal path, cower in the background as much as possible lest the goddess be sullied by some ordinary human touch," Ethel refuses to be Amanda's "toady" (170). Out to dinner one evening, Ethel, angry that she has never been invited to one of Amanda's fashionable parties, hilariously "attack[s] her dainty squab with a savagery that might indicate the bird had pulled a knife on her first" (170). Not one to be outdone, Ethel imagines herself revealing all the unsavory facts of Amanda's hidden past to the goddess's elite New York circle. Revenge for this Lakeview Nobody would be sweet indeed.

Other characters, too, would gleefully oust the Evanses and take their place if ever given half the chance. As the *Time* reviewer notes in 1942, "The secretaries, flunkies, ghostwriters inside the publisher's mansion, the throng of harpies and climbers beating on his door, all share Amanda's and Julian's cold-blooded social and financial ambitions in miniature" ("Feast," 116). In fact, all of them soon enough "gang up" ("Feast," 116) on their dear Amanda once her disloyalty to her husband is discovered; all watch in fascination as the ice queen's pretty little empire comes crashing down; all happily wait, Eve Harrington style, for their chance to supplant her.

Delays, hard work, no check . . . money owed and promised back to friends—heckled by everything—cat sick—icebox on blink.

—Diaries, 194

If Amanda Keeler had it all, at least for a time, Dawn Powell herself seemed to have had it all, too, during this period–but her "all," unfortunately, was a pile of woes that seemed almost insurmountable. Though the author remained tight-lipped in her journal on *A Time to Be Born,* she and editor Perkins were still very much in contact by letter as she was writing the novel, just as they had been while she was at work on *Angels on Toast.* In fact, from the time that the author first proposed a title for her latest book until the time it appeared on booksellers' shelves, the two regularly corresponded. Even after Perkins's death in 1947, Powell was discussing by letter the by then five-year-old novel with her new editor at Scribner's, John Hall Wheelock.[30] Looking back, she said, "When Perkins asked me what the plot/general idea would be of *A Time to Be Born* and I said, 'It's about that man on the ledge of the Gotham [Hotel] about to jump off, only that has nothing to do with it,' he nodded as if it were all clear as a bell to him and away we went" (*Letters,* 178). As Powell would have it, she and her editor had understood each other on a level that transcended even language. But another editor, Harrison Smith,[31] viewed Perkins differently: "The reason all authors regard Max Perkins as the greatest editor," he said, "is that he's deaf and doesn't hear all the tripe the bastards are saying" (*Letters,* 225). Cowley corroborated the fact of Perkins's deafness, writing that the editor "is almost totally deaf in his left ear, a fact he doesn't like to explain. The right ear is sharp enough for telephone calls or face-to-face conversations but not for table talk or business meetings" ("Unshaken" I, 33). It is amusing to think that, instead of Powell's having enjoyed a deep, innate understanding of her editor, and he of her, Perkins had simply been unable to hear a word his client was saying. Fortunately, for the two of them as for us, Powell and Perkins quite often communicated by letter.

A year into writing the book, Powell wrote to her editor to say that "the novel has been a great relief," large writing projects always offering her a respite from her cares and a way of managing her demons. She added, "But it seems to get longer by the minute or else I'm getting shorter. I am working very rapidly on it, but I wish you would give me a definite last-minute date. With a supply of Benzedrine, cocaine, marijuana and black coffee I could probably finish it by the end of the month, but if this speed is not necessary, let me know" (*Letters,* 114). Unfortunately we do not have Perkins's response, if Powell ever received any, but we do know that this letter to him was written in February 1942, and the work was already being reviewed by September of the same year. It is certain that she was working quickly; her diary reveals that she had begun the novel only in January 1941 and that it was in the publisher's hands by the summer of 1942, very swift work by any calculation. The rapidity with which a piece is written is clearly no measure of its literary value, but such manic speed does suggest something about the author, especially given that Powell's time and attention were spread so thin among so many different projects and problems. Between the outset of 1941 and the summer of 1942, she was busily thinking back on more painful days, contemplating if not reliving the grim memories that would inform her most autobiographical novel, 1944's *My Home Is Far Away*. Moreover, diary readers see her considering a musical version of *Angels on Toast*, sleeping little, advising young playwrights, wrestling with illness and nightmares, and contemplating fame, fortune, and critics in the space of the first two months during which she had begun *A Time to Be Born*. Not only was she already so fully occupied, but she was suffering from a lack of self-confidence, as she disclosed in a diary entry of May 30, 1941:

> This is a period of no compass, no base, no program of ideas
> for work, no courage to see them through. A complete play
> ready to be written but a panic about using the time for such
> a gamble—as if time was on a budget and must be properly
> apportioned. Short story ideas get started and then fumble as
> memory of past flops make brain uncertain. (*Diaries*, 192)

Still Powell managed at this dark time to press on, to write not only one but two novels and several short stories while considering a play. The two novels would be in fact among the finest that she would produce. And if the troubles she recounted here do not seem sufficiently discouraging, she neglected to mention the difficulties of living with her hard-drinking husband and their troubled son. In another diary entry of the period Powell sounded as if she was at least half-heartedly considering leaving Joe, to whom she had by then been married for more than twenty years:

> Fear is the basis in love loyalty. Fear to break off for fear
> the next will not be as good or as permanent or that the old
> will do too well without you. Women don't leave a drunkard
> as often as is reported. The drunkard, being maverick, can
> always get other women and besides there is the maternal
> he arouses—also the sex interest since he is likely to be a
> different person every time. (192)

Powell was facing myriad troubles at home. Tim Page writes that her son, Jojo, who had again been residing with his parents, suddenly "fled coatless one day into a Manhattan blizzard, leaving her frantic with worry; it took two hours to find him, and the next day he was readmitted into a sanatorium" (*Bio,* 186). As the author recorded the episode in two running diary entries beginning on April 9, 1942, "Jojo ran away this morning, no coat in freezing rain and snow, with no money, intending to look for a job at an employment agency." Perhaps the young man had overheard his parents squabbling over money and wanted to help. Powell continued, "[He] went berserk in afternoon, [we] had to give him epsom salts bath, luminol [a bar-biturate used to relieve anxiety or tension], icebags, etc." (*Diaries,* 199). The next entry said simply, "Jojo back to sanitarium—ran away, went berserk again this morning" (199).

To add to her difficulties, Joe's drinking was escalating so alarmingly that he was often completely incoherent and was growing increasingly ir-responsible. At this time Powell confided in her diary that "I still have a se-cret passion to live alone and work. I could . . . live in a $12 a week furnished apartment, live on $25 a week altogether instead of this massive overhead that Joe and I run up" (195). Though her husband earned a very good salary, he was notorious for mismanaging his money, preferring to blow 150 1940s dollars in an evening at the Rainbow Room or the Stork Club[32] to spend-ing it in any more sensible ways, despite the enormous costs of Jojo's care and the family's other considerable expenses (*Diaries,* 179; *Bio,* 142). The couple had recently moved again, this time into relatively elegant quarters at 35 East Ninth Street; the apartment came "complete with a mezzanine overlooking the living room" from which Dawn and Joe "would occasion-ally send up *Romeo and Juliet* for amused guests" (*Bio,* 178–79). Their new digs, less expensive than their previous apartment had been but still more than they could easily afford (*Diaries,* 202), were just a stone's throw from Powell's favorite café, in the Hotel Lafayette, where, one may recall, she for decades held court with painters, musicians, fellow writers, and other assorted admirers.

At least in part because of Powell's and Gousha's club-going habits, as she told Malcolm Cowley, the couple's finances by this time had sunk so low that "she could look out the window and see her own checks bounc-ing" at the Lafayette (Josephson, 23). So broke were they that Powell was even ready to accept an invitation to return to that most detested of places, Hollywood. On this occasion the studio offered to pay for her to go out in style—"via Stratoliner"—to work on "dialoging *Du Barry Was a Lady*" (*Diaries,* 194), the 1939–40 Broadway production that was being made into

a 1943 Hollywood vehicle for Red Skelton, Lucille Ball, and Gene Kelly
(Crowther, 1). Concerning a nightclub singer, dancer, and hat-check boy,
the film might have benefited from Powell's nightclub know-how, but she
was unable to free herself from her radio commitment. She said that it was
"just as well" that she was unable to go, for she would have had "trouble getting ready cash on a Sunday to take out there" (194). Where she would have
gotten that ready cash even on another day of the week remains a question,
for clearly the couple's finances were in serious trouble: "The gray busy rainy
sky I love, and would like to be out under," she wrote. "But weather, sky,
night, sun, wind, rain, or friends are forbidden when there is not money. . . .
There is the empty purse, too—a walk, an impulse to use a phone, a bus,
buy a newspaper, and these are impossible. . . . Out of doors so forbidden
to the poor and the desperate; for us, there is no time, no sun, no daylight,
but the endless crouching over a typewriter" (195). Nevertheless, despite her
mounting troubles, despite the gloomy voice of the diary writer, the novel
soars, a testament to Powell's work ethic and her ability to shut out all but
her talent. Page, too, finds it "extraordinary" that she had been able to create
a novel "so airborne and exhilarating" (*Bio*, 186) at such a difficult period.

Further disappointment awaited Powell once her novel was issued.
Again, her hopes for her new publisher were dashed when the company
submitted an unsuitable promotional piece for it. Her previous publisher
Farrar and Rinehart had always irritated Powell by touting her works as
little more than harmless, escapist romps; Scribner's was now committing
the same offense. In response, the author wrote a letter to Perkins that may
well never have been sent; in it the author, never much good at speaking
up for herself, sounded unlike her normally taciturn self. Though she was
outspoken in her diaries about perceived injustices, she was much less so
in her personal correspondence. Page notes that the letter "does not exist
in the Scribner collection at Princeton," as most of Powell's other letters to
the publisher do, and "the only known copy is a carbon in the Powell papers
at Columbia" (*Letters*, 116n). On first reading I thought precisely the same
thing: that this letter sounded unlike any correspondence Powell ever had
sent—or ever would send—to Max Perkins. She wrote,

> I do not like at all the approach called to my attention recently
> in *Publishers Weekly* [the same periodical at which she had
> poked such fun in *Turn, Magic Wheel*], which refers to the
> book as "slightly wacky" and uses other deprecatory phrases

that would come better from an angry reviewer than from the
publisher. There is nothing wacky in the book, nor is there
anything to be gained by suggesting it is a jolly little book
for the hammock. It is serious satire in the way Dickens or
Thackeray built satire—the surface may be entertaining but
the content is important comment on contemporary affairs.
(*Letters*, 116)

Try as she might to distinguish this new book from her others, try as
she might to see that her readers would understand that her pointed barbs
were not just silly humor but significant contemporary commentary, nothing seemed to work. We may recall that Powell had had the same complaint—voiced in her private diary, though, not in her letters—about the
way her previous publisher had mishandled publicity for her novels, assign-
ing them, as she said, "tripe virtues" (*Diaries*, 23) that she did not believe
they possessed. Her note to Max Perkins continued:

There are very few American writers today who are writing
satire on the present age—or on any age for that matter—and
if I did not think such work was important I would not engage
in it. I am sure there must be readers for a novel whose mood
follows the tempo of the news they are reading, even though,
like the news, it does not always take the point of view they
would prefer. That is why I think the book's contemporary
scene value should be stressed, and if it is "slightly mad," it is
merely reflecting the times. (116)

Having aligned herself with such an august house as Scribner and Sons,
she was disappointed to find that she still had to contend with unsatisfac-
tory publicity.

***

*It is not the critic who counts. . . . The credit belongs to the man who is
actually in the arena, whose face is marred by dust and sweat and blood.*

—Theodore Roosevelt

***

A Time to Be Born, which would sell more than nine thousand copies—more
than any other Powell novel had sold to that date (*Bio*, 191)—would earn its
author some of the best press of her career. Unfortunately, however, to Powell's mind there were still a few commentators who would misinterpret or

misunderstand. As Sanford Pinsker notes not only of *A Time to Be Born* but of Powell's entire New York cycle, "Readers"—among whom, one may assume, he includes reviewers and advertisers—"in short, got her wrong—not only failing to see the uncompromising realism that went into her depictions of Manhattan café life, but resisting Powell's efforts to capture people as they actually are" (67). One such resister, it may be said, was Diana Trilling, who for a time was the *Nation*'s book critic. *A Time to Be Born* is one of the two novels that spurred the war of words between Trilling and Gore Vidal briefly mentioned earlier. In her review of *this* novel, Trilling wrote that Powell's "description of the women's magazine formula for how to cure a broken heart, her picture of women girding themselves for war, [and] her analysis of contemporary literary trends" were "not only funny [but] they convince us of the educated no-nonsense intelligence that lies behind them" (244). She added that Powell possessed "a first-rate satiric talent." Despite the praise, however, the reviewer went on say that the book "falls apart . . . in the middle" (244). In Vidal's celebrated 1987 *New York Review of Books* article on Powell, he objected to Trilling's criticism, causing her to attempt to explain herself in a letter to the editor of the same publication. Her letter in turn led Vidal again to object. The main points of the argument are as follows: Trilling in her letter strives to demonstrate that Vidal has conflated two of her Powell reviews into one and accuses him in so doing of having misrepresented her, Diana Trilling. The Vidal review with which Trilling takes exception is his review of this novel; in it, among other things, he had noted that while Powell normally directed her gaze on the "boozy meritocracy of theatre and publishing and the art world and whatever 57th Street was and is," the story is different here. In *A Time to be Born,* Vidal says, Powell "takes on the highest level of the meritocracy (the almost nobles) in the form of a powerful publisher and his high-powered wife, based, rather casually, on Mr. and Mrs. Henry Luce" ("American," 15). He then adds a blast directed at Trilling: "At last Powell will have a fling at those seriously important people Diana Trilling felt she was not up to writing about" (15). In her letter Trilling explains that Vidal's "tony people" reference had been not to Trilling's review of *A Time to Be Born* but of her commentary on Powell's later novel, *The Locusts Have No King.* But Vidal, who believed that both novels represent some of Powell's finest work, would have none of it. He insisted that he had represented Trilling's views faithfully. "Surely I did not 'misrepresent' Ms. Trilling," he wrote. "She felt that Powell's witty books finally fail because she did not write about tony people; yet when I described *A Time to Be Born,* all about the Henry Luces and other top people, I said," he repeats, "that Powell was, at least in this book, 'having a fling at those seriously important people Diana Trilling felt that she was not up to writing about'" (2). One can imagine Dawn Powell grinning impishly at the thought of two such esteemed personages as Diana Trilling and Gore Vidal poking each other in print over their estimation of her novels.

Other critics, then and now, agree with Vidal that this novel is one of Powell's finest to date. Many Powell contemporaries wrote positive commentaries, as the following extract from Rose Feld's review in the *New York Herald Tribune* demonstrates:

> The difficulty with reviewing Dawn Powell's new novel, *A Time to Be Born,* is that, first of all, you want to quote from it continually. To say it's brilliant, it's witty, it's penetrating, it's mature isn't enough. You want to prove it by giving examples but then, having chosen your quotes, you find they do not add up to all the book holds and means. Because there is something more in this volume than the exercise of a mind that is as daring as it is keen; there is emotional flavor and pungency which make it greater than an intellectual tour de force. ("Glitter Girl," 5)

Feld's point about wanting to quote from Powell's novel continuously was echoed thirteen days later when Diana Trilling said virtually the same thing: The author "cries out to be quoted," Trilling wrote, "not one sentence at a time, either, like . . . 'She was thirty-two, but she looked like a woman of forty who was so well-preserved she could pass for thirty-two,' but for whole paragraphs and pages" (244). Many reviewers since Feld and Trilling have found this same point to be true; whether they are reviewing her novels, short stories, plays, diaries, or letters, they say the same thing: the author is eminently quotable.

Other Powell contemporaries praised the book as well; according to Tim Page, "This was probably the moment of Powell's greatest celebrity, and she relished it" (*Bio,* 192). But Powell remained curiously silent on the moment in both her diaries her letters, which move directly from explaining to Max Perkins what she would like to see on the cover of *A Time to Be Born* (116) to discussing her next novel, *My Home Is Far Away,* a book, she said, that "seeks to show the basic illusions and innocence that become fruit for future satire" (*Letters,* 119). There at last we have it: Powell attributing the satire she wrote directly to her tragic childhood. But she never seems to have celebrated *A Time to Be Born*'s success—at least not on paper.

Another positive review, this from the *New Yorker*'s "Briefly Noted" column, said:

> [It's] the story of how a brutally egocentric career woman goes about getting what she wants, which is, quite simply, the whole earth. The book is enormously funny and the humor, which could easily have been an end in itself, manages to do some very neat blasting, not only of the stuffed shirts and careerists who are the main characters, but of pretentiousness in general. The material is of the kind that lends itself to slick, urban writing, which the author avoids with a sort of mocking wisdom. (59)

Beatrice Sherman noted in the *New York Times Book Review* that Powell's "wit is sharp, shrewd and biting, and it finds a pretty mark in the stuffed shirts, male and female, of *A Time to Be Born*. . . . Miss Powell has done a fine piece of satiric and witty writing on the Evans pair. . . . One would hate to be speared on the shaft of her wit, but it is a joy to see Amanda and Julian get theirs" (6). In the end, however, the review veers toward the familiar complaint: "You may lament the lack of anything verging on integrity or nobility in Miss Powell's cast of characters," Sherman says, "for she takes delight in shooting the props out from under every sort of illusion, but you can't help but be delighted with the skillful way in which she does it" (6). Finally, Sherman recommends the novel as "an antidote for overindulgence in inspirational or romantic books" (6). Though Sherman's review was slightly more positive than not, Powell's latest novel did receive its share of mixed notices. One commentary of particular interest reads,

> When the ladies start to take their hair down, it's time to take cover. This year's fictional revelations of the weaker sex show them as anything but Dawn Powell. Amanda Keeler Evans adds a new feline to the clever gallery already sharpening their claws on the printed page.
>
> Witty, caustic and amusing Amanda certainly is, but she is far from an honest person or an honest characterization either. Miss Powell seems to have sacrificed completeness for cleverness, and Amanda becomes a portrait of a successful career woman at her hypocritical worst. But that worst makes clever, brittle comedy under the author's facile style.

> Author Powell's comments on New York at the peak of pre-
> war frenzy are shrewd, and her analyses of the social and moral
> consequences of Amanda's income level group go almost deep
> enough. (*Boston Daily Globe*, 19)

Luce-owned *Time* magazine also featured a friendly review. Possibly
written by James Agee or Whittaker Chambers (Page, telephone, 2013),
both of whom were reviewing books for the magazine in 1942, the essay
ends with the following lines: "Cracks and gags are Authoress Powell's spe-
cialty. This novel crackles with them. As social comment, it is a feast of
peanut brittle" ("Feast," 115). The Luces must have been unaware, for the
moment, of the skewering they had received in the novel's pages.

Lauren Weiner, in her lengthy Powell study "Metropolitan Life: The
Novels of Dawn Powell," finds that, ultimately, "we are even moved to sympathy for Amanda, rascal though she is" (36). It is no small accomplishment
that Powell had made such a detestable creature into a sympathetic figure
by novel's end. By 2012, the novel had received further attention: it was chosen Big City Book Club's selection in January of that year, and on May 25,
Nathaniel Rich chose to write of the novel in his blog, "The Daily Beast,"
calling it "one of the most enjoyable novels written about World War II
despite the fact—or is it *thanks* to the fact?—that not a single battlefield
appears anywhere in it, nor any weapon more deadly than an ice pick."

Perhaps it is not surprising that Powell left no record of her feelings
about the reviews her latest novel received. We know that she had objected
to the advertisement her publisher had put out for the new novel; why, then,
should she assume that the book reviewers would get it right? No longer
much concerned about what her critics had to say about her, or at least pretending not to care, she simply moved on. Upon the publication of *A Time
to Be Born*, the writer turned her attention to the other book she had been
working on, the Ohio novel *My Home Is Far Away*, and to its sequel, which
Powell sometimes called "Marcia," sometimes "the Marcia book," and
sometimes "Book II." Immediately upon *A Time to Be Born*'s release, Powell
traveled home to Ohio. While there, seemingly too restless to remain in her
past any longer, she soon began plotting her next New York book which,
years later, she herself would call "an admirable, superior work," one that
demonstrates "indubitable development" (*Diaries*, 270). The book of which
she was speaking would become her decidedly accomplished 1948 novel,
The Locusts Have No King.

THE LOCUSTS HAVE NO KING, 1948

~~~~~~~~~~~~~~~~~~~~~

The Algonquin Round Table, or "The Poison Squad"

~~~~~~~~~~~~~~~~~~~~~

Dawn Powell's sixth New York novel is partly based on the members of the Algonquin lunch crowd who, to the author's mind, stood in each other's way and prevented one another from producing the work they might otherwise have produced.[33] As she made clear from the time of her first novel, she had no tolerance for nonwriting writers and even less tolerance, if less were possible, for those who would prevent an artist from working. As usual, the idea for this book came to Powell long before she actually began to write it: as much as a year before the publication of 1944's *My Home Is Far Away,* the Ohio novel that would immediately follow *A Time to Be Born,* she had told herself,

> I could write a novel about the Destroyers—a third for *Turn, Magic Wheel* and *Happy Island*[34]—that cruel, unhappy, ever-dissatisfied group who feed on frustrations (Dorothy Parker, Wolcott Gibbs,[35] Arthur Kober,[36] etc.). . . . They have perverted their rather infantile ambitions into [the] destruction of others' ambitions and happiness. If people are in love, they must mar it with laughter; if people are laughing, they must stop it with "Your slip is showing." They are in a permanent prep school where they perpetually haze each other. (*Diaries,* 209)

Two years later, on May 23, 1945, after the Ohio novel was published, she wrote in her diary, "I think I need to do a fast modern novel like *Happy Island*" (242). The somber and personally heartrending *My Home Is Far Away* had left Powell ready to return to the more comic style of her New York series. The next diary mention of what would become *The Locusts Have No King*[37] appeared three months later, in August 1945: the quick entry said simply, "Decided (or re-decided) to do New York novel and out in country began notes again on it" (245). Like Marcia in *My Home Is Far Away,* who never forgets a thing, Powell had not forgotten the idea about literary destroyers she had first dreamed up more than two years earlier.

~~~~~~~~~~~~~~~~~~~~~

At the same time that Powell was beginning her new novel, she endured the loss of her beloved cat, Perkins, immortalized in a drawing by Peggy

Bacon. On her cat's death Powell wrote what Tim Page says must be "one of the most loving farewell tributes to a pet ever recorded" (*Bio*, 202). Her very first pet had given her the kind of unconditional love that she received neither from her father, her alcoholic husband, nor her troubled son. She wrote, "My dear cat Perkins died today—very sweetly, very quietly, daintily, a lady wanting to give as little trouble as possible. . . . Finally she lay on the balcony, exhausted, in the sun. I heard her choke, and she was in a convulsion. . . . I held her paw and moistened her lips with water. It was unbearable" (*Diaries*, 245). In this portrait of loss, readers are given a brief glimpse into the tender side of Dawn Powell. It was Mrs. Trollope's *Domestic Manners of the Americans* that Powell turned to for solace afterward, as she confided in her diary: "Joe was in the country. I read Mrs. Trollope furiously all night, loving Mrs. T. for coming to my rescue" (245). Presumably it was her razor-sharp eye and gift for telling the truth—perhaps also that it was largely set in Ohio—that soothed Powell as she had "to give up the little soft dead body lying in the chair" to the SPCA who came and removed it. "Otherwise," Powell remarked, "I would have done away with myself" (245).

As for the destroyers, the locusts of both story and title, Powell had in mind the Algonquin group, as she had said. The writer deplored in her diary their penchant for preventing all those who gathered daily 'round the round table and nightly on assorted bar stools from writing other than the minimum needed to earn their weekly paychecks at the *New Yorker* or other publications for which they wrote. As Powell said of the group:

> They challenge each other by being seen at certain parties, places; they are each others' sores and are half-fascinated, half-repelled. They are ruined by not being able to want what they individually want, but must want inevitably what the other wants. They are spoiled nursery children who really want to go on playing with an old clothespin, but seeing Brother happy with an engine, must fight for engine. Winning it, they are discontented, ill-natured. (*Diaries*, 209)

She found the members as a group largely mean-spirited, petty, and juvenile when "going forth all of them by bands," though taken one at a time, she thought, some could be endearing, among them Parker and Benchley.[38] If it might seem that Powell and Parker were anything but friends, the two women did enjoy a pleasant relationship. In fact, the two writers saw quite a bit of each other from time to time and genuinely seem to have liked one another. Both were good friends of the Murphys, for example, and frequently encountered each other at weekend stays there; both too ran in the same circles, despite the one's being located primarily downtown, the other up. Still, Powell disliked being compared to Parker, again, not because she disliked the woman, but because the two were really quite different, especially in terms of productivity. It annoyed Powell that some would actually believe that there could be only one witty woman writer in New York at a time. Page explains,

> Powell's relationship to Dorothy Parker was necessarily an
> awkward one. She believed Parker's celebrity was largely a matter
> of publicity, and she resented it when they were compared to one
> another. Powell's ingrained work ethic may have had something
> to do with her attitude toward her "rival"; from 1928 to 1944, she
> herself produced at least one novel every other year, while Parker's
> far grander reputation was built on her slight collections of poems
> and short stories and some reported one-liners. (*Bio*, 144–45)

By early January 1946, Powell, who had recently returned to New York from a visit home to Ohio, again settled down to work. As she began working on the new novel, she found that it "seemed to flow" and that it served as a "good psychoanalysis," coming, as it did, on the bleaker heels of *My Home Is Far Away* and "the Marcia novel"[39] (*Diaries*, 250). By early March, Powell felt proud to have typed up to page 42 and had begun referring to the new book as "a work of art—a mosaic" (252). Not only would the novel be a send-up of the Algonquin group, but it would also be an affecting love story and an effective novel of postwar Manhattan. Days after worriedly mentioning in her diary the bombings on Bikini, which would be featured in *Locusts*, she wrote, "The book is a . . . New York love story of a triangle marking time. The love story is serious and important and tragic to the people in it, but a matter of cosmic burlesque to all casual outsiders. Therefore the book has a serious main story in the setting of ageless laughter" (254). All of these succinct dairy entries were the beginning of the longer and more complex diary entries that were to come—as were the many letters she would write about the book. The long dearth of diary discussions of new novels had ended, at least for the time being; Powell was able once again to write about a new creation at length, just as she had done with *Turn, Magic Wheel* so many years before.

Nineteen-forty-seven . . . one of the worst years of Powell's life.

—*Bio,* 207

Though in the beginning the writing of *The Locusts Have No King* seemed to be going well, Powell feeling both happy and confident with its progress (*Diaries,* 257), her mood soon darkened. "This book today seemed dry and cold and dull," she noted, "though frequently it seems fine to me. . . . There is little awareness of the city, in spite of descriptions. Smells, etcetera, are much lacking and I again sense the kind of work done by an afraid person, someone so disabled by fear and insecurity and other lacks as to make expression more and more desperately painful" (258). The old doubts were resurfacing, Powell afraid to make a misstep and fearing more unfavorable reviews. She had been particularly troubled by the not-too-positive review of her latest book, the haunting *My Home Is Far Away,* that her old friend Edmund "Bunny" Wilson had published in the *New Yorker.* At first he had had some positive words to say about both the novel and its author:

> Dawn Powell has made out of [her story] a chronicle of small-town Middle Western life that is touching without sentimentality and amusing with only rare lapses into caricature and farce. One of the best things that Miss Powell does is her sordid or shabby interiors, such as the railroad hotel and the rooming house which the girls' grandmother keeps in Cleveland. . . . She gets out of these unpromising backgrounds a humor and a fairy-tale poetry that have something in common with Dickens. ("Novel," 93)

Years later Terry Teachout would, like Wilson, compare Powell to Dickens, always one of Powell's favorite writers, for, as she said, in Dickens readers could without fail "recognize the truth" (*Diaries,* 248). Alice Tufel, too, finds similarities between Dickens and Powell: "She was also an expert at Dickensian characters, able to capture a whole personality in a few sentences, and sometimes in only one, as she does here in *My Home is Far Away:* 'Mr. Taylor . . . was a dried, sandy little man with a long, pointed nose like a rat's, a feature that seemed to fascinate him as much as it did other people, for he was always tugging at it, then squinting down to see if any change had come over it'" (157). Both Dickens and Powell render not only needy children but also the pompous, insensitive adults who surround them, for example, with skill and accuracy. Contemporary reviewer Tom Beer, too, remarks that the novel's "cast of characters is positively Dickensian" (C44).

Wilson's *New Yorker* review goes on, the critic next comparing Powell favorably with Sinclair Lewis, saying that "she takes human life more calmly, more genially, and less melodramatically" than Lewis does, and that "her quality . . . is all her own: an odd blend of sharp sophistication with something childlike, surprised, and droll—a point of view, in fact, very much like that of the alert, dispossessed little girls in this book" (93). Sadly, for Powell, Wilson's essay continues in a less positive vein:

> Miss Powell, like Marcia in her novel, is a born literary
> temperament, with an independent point of view that does not
> lend itself to clichés of feeling, and a life of the imagination
> that makes writing, for her, an end in itself. . . . But, as a writer,
> she has never yet quite grown up. She appeals to the intelligent
> reader, but she appeals, again, like the perceptive little girl, who
> entertains you with breathless dashes of talking but whose vivid
> improvisations betray, by their falterings and their occasional
> whoppers, that her imaginative world has not yet been
> developed to include all of adult experience. (94)

It seems a curious complaint, for Powell wrote the novel from the perspective of Marcia, a young girl no more than thirteen years old by novel's end and just about five at its outset. In fact, critic Beer notes that "the most striking aspect of *My Home is Far Away* is its fidelity to childhood without the sacrifice of grown-up sophistication" (C44). To be fair, Page credits the critic with catching some narrative muddles, but at times Wilson pointed out errors more commonly taken up with editors than with novelists: he objected to the writer's "addict[ion] to such uses as 'imbecilic' and 'normalcy'" (93). Devastated by his commentary, Powell began sinking into despair once again. Her diary reads, "If Bunny's review had been offset by a powerful, favorable one the book would have gotten off. As it is, it is very discouraging to have someone (who actually has told me I'm infinitely better than John Marquand[40] and equal to Sinclair Lewis at his best) do me so much genuine damage. I have enough damage done me already" (237). One can imagine the anticipation with which Powell must have looked forward to her friend's review of the novel for which she had such high hopes. Instead, Wilson's mixed reaction disappointed her so much that it nearly ended their friendship.[41]

But the book did earn some fine notices on its release: to Powell's delight (*Diaries,* 271), Van Wyck Brooks[42] called it "one of the minor masterpieces of our twentieth-century literature" (Josephson, 33); and Ruth Page, in a *New York Times* review titled "Surrey Ride Minus the Sentiment," found it "a considerable accomplishment" (4). In Powell's time the novel did sell fairly well—"probably more than any of [her] other books to date except *A Time to Be Born*" (*Bio,* 200). Today it is among the most popular of her novels, having sold "twenty thousand [copies] and counting fast, with no end in sight" within just three years of its 1995 reissue (*Bio,* 200). In fact, sales were so brisk that Steerforth released it again in 1999. It would be interesting to know the number of copies it has sold by the time of this writing. Today's critics enjoy the novel—one present-day commentator likens it to "striking oil while spading the garden" (Coates, 3), while Teachout, as I noted earlier, considers it "a permanent masterpiece of childhood" ("Far," 6).

Still, having been inured to pain and disappointment since early childhood, Powell knew better than to expect too much from friend, relative, or stranger. If what we know of the author is any indication, we expect that soon she will recover, the nagging doubts will once again go into hiding, and the old assurance will reemerge. Sure enough, a few weeks after this morose entry readers see her excited again over the new *Locusts* novel as she prepares to submit the first pages to Perkins (*Diaries,* 259). She called her book "a Hogarthian[43] record of the follies of our day—Post War. Therefore," she added, planning, "more careful pictures should be given of apartment difficulties, rationing, conservation" (259). From the smallest entry to discussions that go on for pages, Powell wrote much of this new work in both her letters and her diaries, an experience not seen before; either there were diary entries or there were letters, but rarely if ever were there so many of both. In a letter to Max Perkins, with whom she was still working closely, Powell explained the gist of the new work: "Offhand," she wrote, "I would describe it as a follow-up of *A Time to Be Born,* which dealt with New York in the beginning follies of war. This book deals with the more desperate follies of postwar Manhattan—the exaggerated drive to perdition of a nation now conditioned to destruction" (135). For Powell as for others, little about New York would ever be the same after World War II: as she joked to her erstwhile British publisher, Michael Sadleir, "New York is not the same city it was, being overrun now with Americans" (*Letters,* 148). Not only that, but the historic beauty of Manhattan was being destroyed, it seemed, at every turn. "In an age of destruction," Powell wrote, "one must cling to whatever remnants of love, friendship, or hope . . . one has. . . . I refer to the enemy not as Fascism, Communism, Mammon or anything but the plague of destructivism—inherent in human nature but released in magnified potency since the war" (*Letters*, 149). The novelist's general outlook, in late 1947, appears to have grown even darker than it had been at the period of *A Time to Be Born*.

At the same time that she was writing *The Locusts Have No King*, the novel that, despite her dark mood, would become "one of her funniest and most penetrating satires," the author was found "clinging to her work as if to some profound and desperately needed psychological buoy" (*Bio*, 207). Powell was facing near-poverty and poor health, adding to her despair at seeing her city being torn down all around her; and soon enough she would be made to confront other types of loss, beginning with the sudden death of her editor Max Perkins in June 1947. Her last letter to him was a cheery-sounding, longish synopsis of this latest book, which in the note she subtitled "A Novel of Contemporary New York." She told Perkins that it was based, in part, on a Hans Christian Andersen story in which a man, longing for the bygone days of the Dark Ages, mistakenly dons a pair of magic shoes that project him forward to the fifteenth century, to him a vastly more shameful, lawless, vulgar period. Powell referred to *The Locusts Have No King* as the Andersen tale "in reverse" in that it concerns a character, long immersed in medieval studies, who "emerges at last one night in the autumn of 1945 to find New York a strange and terrifying city—the peace, now being celebrated, as sinister as war, as barbaric as the Dark Ages he just left" (*Letters*, 137). The news she received of Perkins's death, several months after writing this last letter we have from her to him, left her stunned, then sad, then ambivalent. She wrote to Malcolm Cowley, "I think I will cry about Max Perkins's being dead only I have a hunch he was so fed up with pushing writers' egos around that he didn't care what happened" (*Letters*, 140). Though at one moment Powell would mourn his loss, at other moments she would point out that Perkins had never been quite the editor she had hoped him to be.

Then, a few months later, on September 12, 1947, a terrible automobile accident left Powell's friend Dos Passos to suffer the tragic dual losses of his wife, Katy Smith Dos Passos, and of his own eye. Powell, saddened, broke, distraught, was ready to do whatever she could to assist her friend. Upon hearing the news, she wrote him a letter that reveals much about her own ways of dealing with pain:

Dear Dos—

I am thinking about you all the time and I find two things to be glad about. One, that you are a writer so that agony is of service to you, cruel as our work is—and another, that you have physical pain to dull the unbearable other kind. I am glad you aren't rich so you can concentrate on some hardiron thing like making money because physical pain and the need of money have often saved me from going crazy. (*Letters*, 143)

Borrowing money from another friend, she arrived at Dos's side in his hospital room in Massachusetts. Later, alone, staring out her Boston hotel room window, the "tough cookie" wrote, "I cried, to my great surprise" (*Diaries*, 264). The normally unsentimental Powell was carried away with grief for her friend. The heartbroken Dos Passos would marry again, two years later, Elizabeth "Betty" Hamlyn Holdridge (1909–1998); in 1950, they would have a daughter, Lucy Hamlyn Dos Passos Coggin. John Dos Passos Coggin, Dos's only grandson, would write me the following note after his mother mentioned Dawn to him as one of Dos's close friends:

My mother doesn't have strong memories of Dawn but she does remember visiting her with Dos and Betty when they would pass through New York City. I think my mom said that Dawn could be tempestuous emotionally. Dos would usually ask around to see if she were in a mood to receive guests before visiting. "Tempestuous," my mother says, is probably the wrong word. "Stressed" would be more appropriate, given the financial hardships she endured later in life and [the] problems [she had] with her son.

If it seems that things could not have gotten any worse at this point, they did. Now, but two months after Katy Dos Passos's death, on Powell's fifty-second birthday her grown son beat her so badly that she was hospitalized for two weeks. "Evidently life gets incredibly more terrifying," she told her diary—"the childish 'foolish' fears of the bogeyman waiting in the dark are sounder than any hope. Beaten—head bashed—knocked down—and the monster face at last revealed was my birthday present today" (267). This time, it was John Dos Passos who came to her rescue, Powell recording that, while she was still "stunned and frightened," her friend Dos "got me [a] doctor, neurologist. Head no better" (267).

Asked a short time later to write an essay for *Harper's Bazaar* on "What's Wrong with the Younger Generation?" she said, in a letter of June 1948, that she had to think of something wrong with them "outside of their being younger" (154). I recently located a copy of that essay, published in August of the following year, now called "Speaking of the Younger Generation." In it, Powell seems more grouchy than witty, writing that the "new model of ambitious young-man-on-his-way" is concerned not with hard work but escape, that "instead of 'Excelsior' printed on his banner is the motto 'Scram.'" The next paragraph is a single sentence: "In fact, Horatio Alger is dead." This irritability we hear in her *Harper's Bazaar* essay is understandable, given Powell's state of mind while trying to write it: a diary entry of August 1, 1948, finds her sounding especially desperate, wrestling with her troubled finances and newly surfacing tax problems:

> Trying to do *Bazaar* article in a state of frigid hatred toward everything—due, I now see, to humiliation of no longer being independent. It affects my whole ability to write anything. To be in the same position that I was at 12—unable to have haircut, soda pop—ridiculous at my age; ridiculous to be unable to help anyone, to repay a kindness, buy a jar of cold cream, to have to ask always. . . . The only sure thing is this article, which must be done with arrogance or not at all, yet even my words I spend cautiously. (275)

Yet her letters and diaries of this period show her as usual having good days and bad, the good ones including evenings out at the still extant Hotel Lafayette. It was here in 1946 that her photograper friend Genevieve Naylor, wife of the painter Misha Reznikoff, took a rarely seen shot of Powell, included here, thanks to Peter Reznikoff, actor, kind correspondent, and son of the couple. Peter remembers himself as a young boy being brought with his mother and father to various locales that Powell would also frequent, Ms. Naylor producing some fine photographic portraits of her artist and musician friends, many taken at the Lafayette and many at Eddie Condon's jazz place. Powell recorded visiting Condon's club many times, beginning in June 1948. As she wrote to Edmund Wilson, "I was terribly flattered to find on my first visit to Eddie Condon's jazz house that the drummer, no less than the famed George Wettling,[44] had a copy of my book [presumably *Locusts*] under his arm" (*Letters*, 154). Powell had good reason to be as impressed: Wettling, "one of the great Dixieland drummers" had "played with Artie Shaw's 1936 big band [and] with Paul Whiteman. [But] the Condon connection was most significant, for . . . Wettling became a regular with Condon on his Town Hall broadcasts and at his club" ("Drummerworld"). He and Powell became great mutual admirers.

Despite her constant writing, despite the fact that her previous novels had been two of her best, despite many fine notices, there still was not enough money to support her and her family. Her primary concern was as always her work, which, as she told Dos, kept her from losing her mind. It seemed to her "as if all forces, particularly treacherously loyal ones, were bent on keeping me from finishing book already at printers" (*Diaries*, 267). But Powell was not one to dwell on her miseries, certainly not in public and never for long.

Dissipation has its dizzy sidelights . . . [Powell's] characters swim in an aquarium of gin, lightly stirred.

—James Wolcott, 46

Powell created her latest cast of characters with sensitivity, and her comic sensibility is as usual intact here. According to her contemporary Jane Voiles, the novelist wrote this group of "graceless cumberers of the earth" with "a calm, curious, and uninhibited eye" (19). First readers meet Frederick Olliver (not to be confused with Jay single-1 Oliver of *Angels on Toast*), a serious writer of dry, scholarly books; Powell herself had often deplored such dreary books' being well received while her own were too often ignored or dismissed. As she once told an interviewer, "There is so great a premium on dullness that it seems stupid to pass it up" (Van Gelder, "Some Difficulties," 102).

Frederick, whom the author named after Frédéric in Flaubert's *Sentimental Education* (*Letters*, 149), comes out from his long hibernation in the Middle Ages "longing to find out what all the bright conversation and chain smoking are about" (*New Yorker*, Briefly Noted: *Locusts*, 102). Of course, as this is a Powell novel, he finds that all the bright conversation is not about much other than empty bragging, heavy drinking, sexual flirtation, and avoiding real work. Like Powell, however, Frederick is interested in more high-minded pursuits than are the barflies, publishing employees, and assorted hangers-on he finds around town. Both he and the novel bear a resemblance to the afore-mentioned Flaubert work and its protagonist: *Sentimental Education* is in part set during the years after the French Revolution, while Powell's is set during the years following World War II. Both male protagonists come to the great cities from the provinces, the Frenchman, a law student, eager to live the life of a Romantic hero; the American eager to write books of a far-gone era. Like Frédéric Moreau, Frederick Olliver is in love with a married woman; like his predecessor, he engages in affairs with less satisfactory women, leaving him, like his French counterpart, disillusioned and disenchanted.

After first meeting Frederick, readers are introduced to a variety of boozy night people, among them a publicity man proud of his latest advertisement for Hazelnut Cigarettes. The ad, he boasts to an uninterested Frederick, features "just a woman's hand holding a flaming match and the words 'Let me give you a light.'" Getting no reaction from Frederick but, like any good advertising man still determined to capture his indifferent listener's attention, he adds, "the match play[s] like a searchlight over a pack of Hazelnut Cigarettes up in the sky. It's good, damn it, if I do say so myself" (4). The advertisement is reminiscent of Powell's earlier rendering of a "searchlight" message "up in the sky": the flickering advertisement viewed from the top of the Empire State Building she had written of in *Turn, Magic Wheel.*

A short while later, readers meet the object of Frederick Olliver's interest, Lyle Gaynor, the successful, coddled, and married playwright who is "softer and truer than most" female characters in Powell (Bullock, 6); and Dodo Brennan, the delectably delicious yet idiotic sex kitten who will rival the classier woman for his affections. Yet Dodo is neither as flat nor as stereotypical as this brief description makes her sound; Powell fleshes her out. James Wolcott says that though "Frederick . . . could be peeled off a cologne bottle,"

> [Powell's] starring and supporting women are never less than
> individual. What an array! Enough varied hedonistic types to
> launch a Chaucerian caravan. Even the pettiest have dimension.
> Dodo . . . seems a harmless ditz at first, a curvaceous kid. . . . But
> as the novel proceeds she emerges as a shrill, selfish succubus, a

shallow swallower. Powell can't abide those who leech from life, who deaden the party, yet she doesn't make a Mother Superior frown of dismay. (48)

We have seen that Powell rarely frowned at her characters; she understood striving, failure, and disappointment too well to sit in judgment. The few characters who earned her contempt were the cruel, the ungenerous, the gluttonous Belle Glaenzers of the world. But while Powell seems somehow to reserve her judgment of the character, readers do find Dodo disagreeable; like Powell's impression of some members of the Algonquin crowd, this New York transplant "batters away at [others] with public jeers at their work and jubilantly pursues a course of humiliating and teasing them that invigorates, debilitates and somehow appeals to their sense of the preposterous so that they feel oddly protective and sorry for her" (*Letters,* 149). It is known that Dorothy Parker's friends at the Algonquin felt oddly protective of her, and, the name "Dodo," preposterously, is a derivative of "Dorothy."[45]

The character Lyle Gaynor is also well-drawn, Powell presenting her "with an almost shocking photographic accuracy" (Bullock, 6). Playwright Lyle seems to have something in common with the novelist character Dennis Orphen of *Turn, Magic Wheel* (who makes a return appearance here), and, by extension, with novelist/playwright Dawn Powell herself. When Lyle is disappointed that her lover has broken a date with her, she reflects that his having done so is her own fault: "Very well," she muses, "it served her right . . . for cutting up friends and lovers into stage dolls and walking them through her pasteboard plots. Maybe they wanted to make their own plots. Maybe she had always been so blindly sure that she had lost the capacity to observe" (45). For any writer, such a loss would spell disaster. The thought of it terrifies Lyle, just as it would have terrified the author, who prized the twin values of curiosity and observation above all other writerly gifts. For Lyle Gaynor as for Dawn Powell, "her work . . . was her love and her necessity" (41). In a romantic moment Lyle considers leaving her husband for Frederick, but then wonders, "Would she love him if his demands prevented her from writing, if his dislike of the stage obliged her to give up its gay tissue-paper people, its fantastic but dear extortions?" (41). Powell has not raised this question—must marriage for women spell the end of work outside the home?—since *Whither.*

In this postwar period many working women were back in the home, leaving jobs that were to be taken over by returning soldiers. The period itself was one in which the old questions about a woman's place were being raised again. Powell found in the new New York a telling change not only in buildings but in attitudes. As she complained in her diary after a visit uptown to the Bretton Hall, which she had first presented to readers in *Whither,* New York by then had become "much changed since 1920. Rules of conduct are different . . . ladies not allowed at bars in some places but must sit at tables" (258). The constraints of the 1950s were beginning to trouble her.

If Lyle Gaynor resembles her creator at times, the character's lover, Frederick Olliver, is also in some ways a match. Despite James Wolcott's very funny cologne bottle comment, above, Frederick, like Lyle and Dodo, is well drawn. The introspective, reclusive protagonist is not a wooden creation but something of a wooden personality. Not gifted at socializing or even at expressing himself vocally, he nevertheless, like his creator, "had always had a detached literary curiosity about the strangers he passed" (98). If Frederick is not the most exciting character in town, Powell surrounds him with many more invigorating if less cerebral types. As Michael Feingold humorously says, this novel concerns "a slightly dull, earnest-minded young hero" and his "bumpy ride on the beautiful-people roller coaster" (13).

We have seen, especially in *The Happy Island,* that Powell would sometimes break a single real-life person into two characters, understanding that opposing traits might often coexist in "real" persons but would seem unrealistic in fiction. In this novel the author is up to the same device: the more effusive and social Lyle has much in common with the gregarious, outgoing Powell, while the silent and reclusive Frederick, serious minded and devoted to his work, suggests the other side of the writer's nature. Like Powell, Frederick, who despite "all his brains could barely make enough to eat" (69), refuses to play the game that the more successful and often less hard-working writers play:

> "You are so determined to have a difficult life, aren't you?" Lyle
> said quietly. . . . "A little courtesy, a little interest in human
> beings, would make everything easier for you. But you would
> rather have your difficulties so that you can stay bitter and oh,
> so misunderstood. . . . Does your artistic integrity require you to
> be rude to [publishers] Tyson Bricker and Beckley, anyone who
> could be valuable to you?" (34)

Powell was similarly averse to seeking out publicity, to currying favor with those in a position to help her; "playing nice" with advertising men, publicity agents, publishers, reviewers, newsmen and newswomen was simply unbearable to her. Instead, she always preferred to "let her work do the speaking for her" (Ohioana, 2) and often was bitingly sarcastic to those who might have helped her. Edmund Wilson believed that part of the reason for her lack of success was her failure to court publicity; in one typical response to him in 1945, she wrote: "I do not want to chum up with editors, producers, critics, Teacher or Boss in any form. That is the enemy, and any pretense of equality, socially or any other way, is poppycock. I admit their right to vote and spawn, however" (125). If Powell was to be misunderstood and undervalued, at least she would be misunderstood and undervalued on her own terms.

Moonlight on Rubberleg Square

—*The Locusts Have No King*, 57

The author, "dazzling in her descriptions" (Dirda, "Satyricon," X10) of not only character but location, describes in the early chapters of the novel a fictional locale she calls Rubberleg Square, a "mythical, mystical" (*Bio*, 208) Greenwich Village setting so full of bars, clubs, and saloons that by dawn few patrons are able to stand on their legs, filling the place with a "high percentage of weak-kneed pedestrians" night after night (3). The Square comes alive at midnight, hard-drinking "regulars" already in attendance drinking rye and water—five cents cheaper than soda—at their favorite watering holes; myriad on-the-wagon types "suddenly rearing up in their sheets" to fly out into the night for one cocktail; Broadway theatergoers after a dull play "smitten with an irresistible craving for the proximity of barflies, wastrels, crooks" (57). Rubberleg Square each evening at this hour roars "to life with the sound of running feet," drunks moving from the Blue Bar to the Red Bar and back to the Blue, from the Florida Bar to the America's Bar to the New Place, all of them the "same bar, same Bill, Hank, Jim, Al pushing Same-agains across the same counter" (57). We are given views both inside the taverns and out, given brief but memorable portraits of an array of characters in various stages of inebriation, such as "a gentleman in somebody else's hat [who] balances himself carefully down the middle of Avenue of the Americas, as if it was a slack wire, his head thrust forward like a hen's, his arms flapping, his knees buckling, he tacks from curb to curb and finally flutters into the safe cove of 'BAR' like a clumsy pigeon" (58).

Into this sodden scene drifts scholarly medievalist Frederick Olliver, who, having "just emerged from seven years' burial in the dead ages" (2), finds it almost terrifying. The character begins to feel like the Andersen fairy-tale dinner guest who had put on the wrong shoes "and stepped into another age" (2), as Powell had told Max Perkins he would. Out of his element and unlike all the other creatures of the evening, Frederick causes at least one barkeep to think that "maybe he speaks a dozen languages, but he doesn't speak ours" (5). That thought seems perhaps a sly nod to Dorothy Parker, whose oft-quoted words about a female acquaintance alleged that "she speaks eighteen languages but can't say 'no' in any of them."

Other features of the drinkers in the Square evoke other members of the Algonquin group. Frederick, wherever he goes, encounters "advertising men all weeping into their Bourbon of happy days when they were star reporters on the Providence *Journal*. . . . Sometimes these men . . . were not with wives but with stylists, camera ladies, women's-angle-women from their office, all emotionally fulfilled by making fat salaries, wearing Delman shoes and Daché hats,[46] and above all being out with The Office and talking shop" (3–4), just as the Algonquin crowd was known to do. The drinkers here, whose "nightly chore, harmless and gratifying" is "the weighing of disaster and heartbreak" (*Letters*, 149), are an unhappy if jovial lot. They are forever burying real thoughts and genuine feelings under the next barb. Among this group of "the name and fame conscious" are those who "may make their mark in print but never scratch a genuine emotion" (*Kirkus Reviews*, 64). As for the "women's-angle-women" whom readers meet in Rubberleg Square, one may recall that Dorothy Parker had first begun her New York career by writing advertising captions for women's clothing and accessories. Parker was likewise known to carouse day and night with the men from her office. Having early on begun with such hard-drinking colleagues as Robert Benchley and Robert Sherwood to frequent Prohibition-era speakeasies after and even during working hours (Teichmann, *Smart Aleck*, 103), she soon developed a taste for liquor that to her death she never lost. If Powell's fictional admen and newswomen sit around drinking and "talking shop," they also sit around not writing, not fulfilling their artistic ambitions, while jealously making sure that their colleagues, like themselves, do not produce.

Not unlike the peripheral characters of the novel who sell their creative souls to Madison Avenue or to Forty-Fourth Street, Frederick, too, eventually reaps the dual rewards of money and fame once he "surrenders" his loftier dreams (*Letters*, 138) to go to work on a lowbrow comic magazine called *Haw*, if only to be able to afford squiring such a one as Dodo about the Village. And to earn further funds, he takes to teaching night classes at the League for Cultural Foundations (78), a nonsensically titled school that enrolls "middle-aged students anxious to get an idea of what it would be like to have an idea" (80). The League is Powell's parody of The New School.[47] If serious-artist Frederick can sell out, so certainly can the lesser mortals one stumbles into around town.

Certainly this New York is a much darker place than the New York of 1936's *Turn, Magic Wheel* had been. In the earlier novel, Powell's Manhattanites viewed Europe as a place where American writers such as Andrew Callingham and other expatriates went to sun themselves and lead lives of stylish adventure; by 1948, Europe had become the locus of war, of ruin, of loss. Again, Manhattan itself had changed; no longer as fancy-free as it once was, despite the jubilation everyone felt at war's end, of soldiers proudly returning home, this New York was a much more crowded place, less freewheeling, less innocent. The postwar period left residents confused and fearful in ways they had not been in previous decades; now there were atomic bombs to fear, war machines capable of destruction on a previously unimaginable scale. The world, in Powell's novel, has lost not only much of its naïveté but also its heart; Manhattan is no longer as full of possibilities as it had been in those earlier days. As Tim Page says, "An overriding anxiety over the possibility of immediate annihilation haunts *The Locusts Have No King*, with the terror at last made explicit on the final page" (*Bio*, 210). It is in the final scenes that at last lovers Lyle and Frederick find themselves in one another's arms, each having spent the entire novel involved with the wrong person for the wrong reasons. At last Lyle's husband has left her, Dodo has left Frederick, and readers are given finally the pair alone, unencumbered, together where they have always belonged. But the scene is far from joyful as reality intrudes:

> Lyle, combing her hair at the vanity table, smiled at him. . . . Frederick was idly fiddling with the bedside radio and there was a sputtering of words and confused noises.
> "It's the Bikini test—the atom bomb the elevator man's wife is afraid of," Frederick said.
> "When you hear the words—'What goes here'—that will be the signal—" said the faraway voice, and suddenly Frederick was

filled with fear, too. He went over to Lyle and held her tightly. In a world of destruction one must hold fast to whatever fragments of love are left, for sometimes a mosaic can be more beautiful than an unbroken pattern. (286)

~~~~~~

As Powell had written in both her diary and her letters, this "mosaic" of a book (*Diaries,* 252) would be unlike her earlier works in that it would concern a "noble hero and heroine." Readers would view the pair "not only through their ideas of themselves and each other but through the mocking laughter" of the locusts who "do not even know them" (*Letters,* 149). Their genuine love for one another, which "must be guarded against the Destroyers" (*Diaries,* 266), proves purer and more enduring than any other romantic love readers have seen or will see in Powell. This pair is "something rare in Powell's fiction: a compellingly rendered love match of two sympathetic characters" (Weiner, "Metropolitan," 34). Playwright John Guare, who wrote the introduction to the 1990 Yarrow Press reissue of *Locusts,* says of Powell's ending that it is "a declaration of ironic wisdom and passionate insight" (xi). One of the author's most accomplished novels, *The Locusts Have No King* shows readers a Dawn Powell writing at the height of her powers.

~~~~~~

A good review from the critics is just another stay of execution.

—Dustin Hoffman

~~~~~~

Not long after the book's release, Powell one evening ran into friend and fellow novelist Glenway Wescott[48] in the café of the Hotel Lafayette. First telling her how much he had enjoyed her latest novel, he added, "No one but you is doing for New York what Balzac did for Paris." Of the comment, Powell wrote, "It illumined my whole disorder" (*Diaries,* 285). Her comic New York has something in common with Balzac's Paris of *The Human Comedy,* both featuring recurring characters. She had read and admired the French novelist, as she had Flaubert. Powell's claim, however, that Westcott's words helped her see the thematic continuity of her writing is unconvincing: one doubts that she needed Westcott to point out any such thing. But his words elated her, as did most of the early reviews. Writing to her Auntie May[49] in May 1948, just one month after the book first appeared, Powell sounded jubilant as she enclosed review clippings in the envelope, saying that they had been excellent "from a sales point of view" as well as "for prestige" (*Letters,* 153). The letter went on excitedly to add that "Scribner's has a window devoted to me for a week (May 16)—5th Avenue and 48th Street store" (153), a vision that Jeff Lawson remembers (telephone, October 20, 2012). And, although her regular British publisher had decided not to take the book, calling it "too American," Powell was thrilled that other British houses were bidding on it.[50] The author had good reason to feel delighted; it seemed that finally her hard work was about to pay off, in terms of good pay and good press, as she had told her aunt.

A short five weeks later, however, Powell's hopes were beginning to fade once again. First, it seems that some readers, including Edmund Wilson, had begun to suspect that the outrageous publishing clan of Powell's novel was in fact her own publishing house, Scribner's. The fictional publishing company, run by "the dean of all idiots" (33) and his sons, whom Frederick finds "criminally ignorant" (34), reminded many readers of the famed family-run organization.[51] Powell told Wilson, "Others besides you have spoken of the publishing family in my book being Scribner's so there may be some reason for their restraint in advertising it" (*Letters,* 154). Apparently the publisher's advertising machine had lost steam, leaving a Powell novel once again to struggle on its own. But the author told Wilson that she had not meant the novel's publishing house to suggest her own: "That's what comes of my foxily disguising a wholesale-druggist dynasty and newspaper-publisher family into a book family. It comes out my own publishers" (*Letters,* 154). There is no telling who the druggist dynasty or the newspaper tribe might have been, if either had actually existed. Her words seem more likely another coy attempt to obscure the truth of her inspiration, reminiscent of her repeated declarations that Clare Boothe Luce had not inspired the character Amanda Keeler.

Despite her own publisher's rather silent publicity department, however, Powell's latest book did enjoy some positive commentary. A particularly pleasing full-length review, by Florence Haxton Bullock, praised both Powell and her novel. The review is the closest thing to a rave than the author had received to date. Bullock's introduction reads:

> In *The Locusts Have No King,* Dawn Powell impishly assaults you in your ticklish midriff with the absurd performances of her prime young to middle-aging successful and not-quite-successful New Yorkers. And while you are engaged in wiping away the tears of irresponsible laughter from your eyes over their foolish antics, you feel a sudden stabbing pain and

realize that the merry and merciless Miss Powell has given
you a deep thrust in your own unguarded ribs. The follies at
which she pokes such ribald and satiric fun are in a manner of
speaking your follies too. For the rootlessness of these typical
Manhattanites, and their want of serious purpose in life larger
than the single, selfish one of getting on and up in the world,
are certainly everywhere the weaknesses of these our times. (6)

The essay goes on to describe the cast of characters that populate the
novel and the humor and charm with which Powell has written it. By article's end, readers see that the critic has not missed the pain and sadness that
lurk just beneath the surface of each character's bravado, each bar's glaring
neon, Manhattan's foundering spirit. Bullock writes, "All the while [Powell]
indicates through the bright facades of the [characters'] prides and busy
pretensions the lonely emptiness beneath. For all its merry surfaces, *The
Locusts Have No King* is a sad book, and definitely meant to be that" (6).

In another positive full-length review of the day, Alice S. Morris found
that "the combination of a waspish sense of satire with a human sense of
pathos results in a novel that is highly entertaining and curiously touching"
(1). Then, toward the end of her review, she added, "The justice of Miss
Powell's satire, the clean liveliness of her prose, the human honesty of her
insights, her wit and the neat way she manages a host of characters without
once tripping up the reader in the slightest confusion make *The Locusts
Have No King* an accomplished and engaging novel" (2).

Powell often longed for lengthy commentary, and with *The Locusts Have
No King,* she at last had won it. Many of the reviews were lengthy, many
of them positive; however, among the long pieces was the occasional mixed
review. James C. Fuller, for example, writing in the *Saturday Review of Literature,* enjoyed the novel's "sparks of witty observation" and admitted that
"one reads on and on, fascinated and inquisitive for more," largely "because
Dawn Powell is running the show" (19). But his praise did not go on for long,
Fuller soon faulting Powell's characterizations, her story, even the fact that he
did not believe that what she was writing was genuine, Swiftean satire—but
who had ever said it was? He maintained, "We, living in a tactful age, have
confused wisecracks, caricatures, and ridicule with satire. On cue from Miss
Powell we laugh with delight or embarrassment according to whether it is our
friends or ourselves who have been found out. But it is all in fun, like a family
joke" (19). Fuller missed the darker undertone that others understood.

Most of today's commentators cite the novel as among Powell's best. An uncredited comment on the inside cover of the Steerforth edition says, "To shoot folly as it flies is Dawn Powell's special gift, and no one has deadlier aim." James Marcus refers to the book as Powell's "whip-smart masterwork" (1), and *New York Times* critic A. O. Scott names it his "favorite" work by the author. It "captures the anxious energies of the city in the aftermath of World War II," he writes, beginning "with a young man wandering in the chiaroscuro of the Village at night."

Despite the praise *The Locusts Have No King* received on its publication, and despite its brisk early sales, in the end the numbers were disappointing. Powell casually mentioned that advance sales for the novel were "over 4,000" on the day the book was published, though surely her hopes were higher than her casual tone suggests (*Diaries,* 270). Tim Page, too, reports that at first the book seemed almost to be flying off the shelves, selling well during the first months, but, before long, sales dropped off, and Powell was let down once again. In the end, the book sold only about half as many copies as *A Time to Be Born* had sold (*Bio,* 214).

Perhaps it was the disappointment of yet another misfire, perhaps it was the strain of writing the novel, perhaps it was the hardship of life itself, or perhaps it was a combination of all three that led to what Powell would term her "writer's block." She confided in her journal of July 1948 that she was feeling "incredibly discouraged and bleak about everything, including [Marcia] novel. What use doing another when Scribner's outfit so oblivious? No real life anywhere, except from reviewers who praised—but no decent proofreading, editorship or anything else" (275). Now, despite her many attempts to resume work on *Marcia,* the unfinished sequel to *My Home Is Far Away,* she found herself unable to make any headway on it. Instead, she said, "I freeze in my tracks at idea of writing it" (*Diaries,* 284).

By late 1949, it appeared that Powell had decided to give up on the Marcia novel altogether, at last coming to realize that "it is not necessary to do the nostalgic child book" that Perkins had wanted her to do (285). However, not two months later she was yet again at work on the sequel (286). By 1950, still "blocked and locked" in that novel (291), she had begun to feel frustrated enough to recall that it was a New York book—*The Locusts Have No King*—that had brought her out of *Marcia* before. It had taken her two years to realize what seems from our perspective a simple fact. In the end, an unprecedented six years would come between this novel and her next, 1954's *The Wicked Pavilion.*

Powell, elegant in pearls, ca. 1930s. Used by permission of Tim Page

Powell in staged publicity photo eating pineapple, 1933.
Used by permission of Tim Page and Estate of Dawn Powell

Coburn "Coby" Gilman (*standing*) with Jackson Pollock (*seated at right*) at painter Thomas Hart Benton's summer home on Martha's Vineyard; Rita Benton in white hat. Photo by Alfred Eisenstaedt, used by permission of Getty Images

Clare Booth Luce, whom Powell skewers in her 1942 novel,
A Time to Be Born. Used by permission of Associated Press/Fox

Members of the Council on Books in Wartime, ca. 1943. *Left to right:* Bennett Cerf, founder of Random House; Powell; unidentified; Ludwig Bemelmans, author of the *Madeline* books; and Marjorie Kinnan Rawlings (?), author of *The Yearling*

A coy-looking Powell.
Used by permission of Tim Page and Estate of Dawn Powell

(*left*) Powell in her beloved Café Lafayette, 1946.
Photo by Genevieve Naylor, used by permission of Peter Reznikoff

Powell sitting on couch in her Greenwich Village apartment, ca. 1950.
Used by permission of Tim Page

Powell and husband, Joseph Gousha, 1952, at Tavern on the Green, New York City.
Used by permission of the Estate of Dawn Powell

"The Lost Generation" from a 1963 *Esquire* article by Malcolm Cowley.
Seated, far left to right: Marcel Duchamp, Kay Boyle, Caresse Crosby, Carl Van Vechten,
Dawn Powell, Glenway Wescott. *Standing, left to right:* Malcolm Cowley, Man Ray,
William Slater Brown, Matthew Josephson, and Virgil Thomson.
Used by permission. Copyright Carl Fischer

Powell caricature by David Johnson. Used by permission of David A. Johnson

Powell's close friend Hannah Green, 1974. Also from Ohio, Green met Powell at Yaddo.

Author with Tim Page, 2014. Photo by author

CHAPTER SIX

"EITHER THAT WALLPAPER GOES, OR I DO"

The Late New York Novels, 1954–62

Lafayette almost down, alack . . .

—*Letters*, 210

From 1950 until the end of her life, Dawn Powell would struggle to write as she had never struggled before. Her husband's and her own increasingly serious illnesses, financial woes unlike any they had seen before, the end of the irregular meetings with writer and painter friends at the Hotels Lafayette and Brevoort, and mounting self-doubts all threatened her productivity. Although the author had faced numerous hardships all her life, she no longer found them as easy to ignore, joke about, or write away as she once did. Yet despite her troubles, Powell managed to produce two of her finest works, *The Wicked Pavilion* and *The Golden Spur*, during this period.[1]

THE WICKED PAVILION, 1954

The idea for *The Wicked Pavilion*, which the author wanted to subtitle *A Novel of Washington Square*,[2] came to her during a weekend she spent outside Manhattan. In early 1950 she had gone to stay at Sara and Gerald Murphy's place in Snedens Landing, an exclusive, historic, riverview village in Rockland County, now part of Palisades. Having spent years struggling to get the Marcia novel off the ground, Powell was inspired with the idea for the new novel when she picked up a book of Gerald's. In her diary she wrote, "A lovely, remote time at Murphys'. . . . Gerald reading Sir William Maxwell edition of *The Creevy* [sic] Papers, which I glanced at and became fascinated [with], especially at Mrs. Creevy's letters to her husband from Bath in which she refers to 'that Wicked Pavilion'—the place everyone enjoys till after midnight, drinking so they cannot get up till noon, and then with heads" (289). The "Wicked Pavilion" of Eleanor Creevey's letters reminded Powell of her favorite old haunt, the café of the Hotel Lafayette, where she and her fellow artists had met for decades, and that reminder provided the focus she needed for her next book. Two days later she had started writing what she was already calling *The Wicked Pavilion*,[3] having transformed the Café Lafayette into the Café Julien of the novel. "If this [book] goes," she noted in her diary, "it will be due to Murphy weekend—early bed in strange, river atmosphere and without the dull callers" (289). The author was happy to be writing again after two years of frustration.

The Creevey Papers furnished Powell with more than her title and focus on the Lafayette and on its sister hotel, the Brevoort. She wrote that she wished "to convey the complete vivid details of New York life and varied characters not in conventional fiction guise but with the *complete* reality of the 18th- and 19th-century letter writers who told all the inside scandals chattily, informatively, real places, real names, etc." (*Diaries*, 292). Eleanor Creevey's letters to her husband are just the sort that Powell intended to imitate in her new novel: they are expressive, chatty, irreverent, full of scandal and names—and not just any names, but the names of many members of the aristocracy.

Thomas Creevey, whose papers these are, was born in 1768 in Liverpool, to William Creevey, "the merchant of that city" (Gore, xvii); the younger Creevey was a member of Parliament who moved in elite circles. In the same 1805 Creevey letter that mentions the "Wicked Pavilion" that had so amused Powell (a letter written from Brighton, not Bath, as Powell had misremembered), Eleanor Creevey reveals that a particular German baron that evening had been "extremely drunk" and that the Right Honorable John Macmahon,[4] whom Mrs. Creevey familiarly refers to as "Mac," was "even more foolish than I expected" (Gore, 41). Another letter from Mrs. Creevey, written a few days later, says,

> I went to the Pavilion last night quite well, and moreover am
> well to-day and fit for Johnstone's ball, which at last is to be. . . .
> They were at the Pavilion and she [Miss Johnstone] persecuted
> both the Prince[5] and Mrs. Fitzherbert[6] like a most impudent
> fool. The former was all complyance and good nature—the
> latter very civil, but most steady in refusing to go [to the
> ball]. She said she could not go out, and Miss J. grinned and
> answer'd—"Oh! but you *are out* here." (Gore, 43)

The letters go on in this deliciously gossipy manner, their appeal to
Powell obvious. Like the Creeveys, who had known "everybody who was
anybody" in the political world of early-to-mid-1800s Brighton,[7] Dawn
Powell knew everybody who was anybody in the art and literary worlds
of Greenwich Village from the mid-1920s to the early 1960s. One imagines that Dawn Powell and Eleanor Creevey, possessed of similar senses of
humor and talents of observation, might have been great friends.

No good looking around the old neighborhood for
souvenirs of the vanished past.

—*The Wicked Pavilion,* 280

The novelist explained her design for this latest book in a letter to
John Hall Wheelock, her new editor at Scribner's. As with her most recent publications, she was not reluctant to write of the new work in either
diaries or letters. Her note to Wheelock says, "Reading the gossipy letters
of French ladies and all the letters in the *Creevey Papers,* it struck me how
sad it was that the vivid realness of life as described by these ordinary
letter-writers—the customs, the town talk, the scandal . . . was never really done in a novel. . . . I felt compelled to do my own favorite city the
service the old letter-writers did for their times" (*Letters,* 177). And serve
her favorite city she does. New York will be the "heroine" of this novel, for
Powell was determined to "make the city live" (*Diaries,* 305).

From the outset, she captures the way Manhattan appears at first glance to
an awestruck visitor from a small town in Michigan, a young officer on leave:

> Rick Prescott . . . strolled happily down Fifth Avenue,
> finding all faces beautiful and wondrously kind, the lacy fragility
> of the city trees incomparably superior to his huge native

forests. Under the giant diesel hum of street and harbor traffic
he caught the sweet music of danger, the voices of deathless
love and magic adventure.

My city, he had exulted, mine for these few hours at least,
no matter what comes after. He wanted to embrace the Library
lions, follow each smiling girl . . . bellow his joy from the top
of the Empire State building. Wandering on foot or bus in a
joyous daze he suddenly came at evening upon the treasure
itself, a softly lit quiet park into which the avenue itself
disappeared. (11–12)

Later, meeting some friends at the Café Julien, Rick is unable to make
them believe that "his day's adventure had been with a city and not a girl"
(12). Perhaps Powell on first arriving in New York had felt much the same
way that Prescott feels. For Rick, there is nothing more romantic than the
way he feels on first discovering this greatest of cities.

For her depiction of the Julien, Powell said, "I combined the Lafayette
and the Brevoort so as not to step on toes" (*Letters*, 215). The sister hotels,
which the 1939 *Writer's Project Guide to New York* (*WPA*) called "meeting
places of intellectuals" (Gody, 136), had been, as Martin Levin graphically
puts it, "kicked to bits to make way for more up-to-date real estate" (62).[8]
Powell deeply lamented their passing, saying that "with their going a very
special way of life went" (*Letters*, 215). One review of the time stated that
The Wicked Pavilion "has as its hero not a person, but an environment—the
cultural climate of the Fifties—concentrated within the limits of a rendez-
vous called the 'Café Julien,'" adding that it "doesn't require a Hawkshaw[9]
to deduce" the hotels on which Powell had modeled her Julien, for she
changed almost nothing about the legendary locales (Levin, 62).

The café society that Powell had known and depended on for so long
was now becoming a thing of the past. As she explained in an unaddressed
letter, "For writers, artists and [other] people who work alone all day, this
particular café life was almost a necessity. In our work we can't plan a social life too definitely—we never know but what we may get going good
just when we're expected at a dinner. We do know that we'll want to see
somebody—anybody, sometimes—after being locked up with ourselves all
day but we daren't risk tying ourselves down" (*Letters*, 215). She added, a
bit wistfully, that because "this special kind of retreat has vanished . . . I
wanted to re-create it in fiction before it was completely forgotten" (215).
Charles Poore believed that in writing this novel Powell accomplished just

what she had set out to do: she created a dying New York world that in her book remains vibrantly alive ("Greenwich," 29). And Brendan Gill, a noted *New Yorker* columnist who had known both Powell and the Lafayette,[10] remarked that she had captured the café "to the life." He found "the old front room . . . with its tiled floor and marble-topped tables and bleak, bentwood chairs" the same in the novel as he had known them in reality ("Rough," 157). Gill added, "It is not the least of Miss Powell's virtues that her evocation of that lost landmark is both loving and unsentimental" (158), no small accomplishment given the novelist's fond memories of happier and more productive days spent there.

Today the kind of New York café society Powell had so long enjoyed has not been completely forgotten, thanks at least in part to this novel, whose "underlying theme is fragility" (Pool, 20), in that the things we care for are too often taken from us. In this book, a fond remembrance of a vanishing New York, Powell seeks not only to serve Manhattan in the ways she has already mentioned: she seeks to alarm readers into preserving it. In *The Improper Bohemians*, Alan Churchill wrote, "As time has passed, the spirit of a changing Village has been captured in the novels of Dawn Powell who, as a steadfast Villager of the Newer Day, has sought to picture her cherished community in print" (330). More than that, from her earliest New York novels, Powell voiced her dismay at the destruction of historic locations: as early as *Turn, Magic Wheel,* again in *The Happy Island,* and all the way through to her last novel, *The Golden Spur,* her narrators and characters are frequently heard to bemoan the changing face of the city. And, of course, by the late 1940s and the early '50s, the author's beloved Village was literally coming down around her, many lovely old structures being demolished and replaced by tall, inharmonious apartment buildings, just as other sections of Manhattan are today being so transformed. Asked in the early 1950s to fill out a questionnaire about her life and work, Powell joked, "Although it seems that my beloved city is being pulled down around my ears, our own lives seem singularly untouched by progress. I have never had an automobile, Mixmaster, Bendix,[11] a television set or pressure cooker" (*Bio,* 215). Perhaps the passing of her favorite cafés and, along with them, the passing of the café society she had so long turned to had something to do with the paralyzing bouts of writer's block she was experiencing now but had not known before.

Powell, who loved not only Greenwich Village but all other areas of Manhattan as well, lamented both not only the razing of her favorite downtown haunts but the widespread destruction that was taking place all over the city. Outside the Village, she especially regretted the demolition of countless lovely old uptown brownstones to expand Columbia University,[12] a regret she put into the mouth of Dennis Orphen, eternal Powell spokesman. But Downtown was Powell's primary focus. In *The Locusts Have No King* she had ridiculed the New School, which in 1930 had grown to include the Alvin Johnson/J. M. Kaplan building at 66 West Twelfth Street, just two blocks north of Powell's own neighborhood.[13] To make room, workers had mowed down several historic brownstones, one of which had housed fellow Ohioan James Thurber (Naureckas, "11th," 1). The unfortunate destruction Powell had seen going on for decades was in the postwar 1940s becoming more and more commonplace and moving closer and closer to home. E. B. White called the surge in destruction during these years a "boom" (5), his term echoing the noise of the wrecking ball. David W. Dunlap reiterates White's lament: "In the post-war building boom," he writes, "a number of Broadway landmarks were sacrificed for hulking, bulky, glass-and-steel office towers in lower Manhattan and midtown" (9). In "The Lost Pleasure of Browsing," Charles Rosen mourned the disappearance of the many secondhand bookstores in the area; at least one, "the great shop of Dauber and Pine," was lost to the New School. And Philip Lopate speaks wistfully of the few remaining harbingers of a bygone era, those well-hidden "remarkable apartment house enclaves, built during the 1920s and 30s, when city developers still thought it economically viable to erect castles for the middle class" (*Getting*, 85). By the postwar 1940s, however, those days have become but a memory. As Powell's mouthpiece, fictional novelist Dennis Orphen, writes,

> There was nothing unusual about that winter of 1948, for the unusual was now the usual. . . . Universities dynamited acres of historic mansions and playgrounds to build halls for teaching history and child psychology . . . parents were able, by patriotic investment in the world's largest munitions plant, to send their sons to the fine college next door to it, though time and labor would have been saved by whizzing the sons direct from home to factory to have their heads blown off at once. (3–4)

Not only were Columbia University and the New School responsible for much of the widespread destruction of Manhattan, but so were builders of condominiums and apartment buildings. Alice Sparberg Alexiou, after first describing the 1954 razing of the Brevoort, writes of the serious losses that any aficionado of American literature and New York history would find distressing. She laments the 1953 destruction of

> the Federal style Lafayette Hotel on Washington Square South, where writers—Dawn Powell, John Cheever, A. J. Liebling, and Joseph Mitchell[14] were among the regulars—schmoozed around little marble-topped tables in the mirrored-wall café. And along with the Lafayette . . . Madame Branchard's rooming house, 'the house of genius,' that at various times was the digs of Theodore Dreiser, Stephen Crane, Willa Cather, and John Dos Passos [was also torn down]. (50)

It was ironic to Powell that universities would propose to teach history by destroying it, to explain child behavior by razing parks and playgrounds, to finance education through the purchase of war machines that would soon enough slaughter the newly educated. It appeared to her foolhardy that a local university should annihilate so much of its own proud literary past in the interest of teaching it (NYU's proposed expansions continue even today, and Village residents meet often to protest). The destruction of the city had by then become so commonplace that it seemed to the writer that few New Yorkers so much as raised an eyebrow at it. Years before Jane Jacobs, another noted Greenwich Villager, would effectively fight to save Manhattan and the outer boroughs from the bulldozers of Robert Moses (Burns, 514–17),[15] Powell was howling into her novels a message of saving New York, hoping that someone would hear.

Other denizens of New York, before Powell and since, have written similar objections to or regrets about the same kinds of devastation, especially to the artists' milieu of Greenwich Village. Long before Powell came along, Henry James, for one, despaired of the changes occurring in the Manhattan of his day. Introducing a recent collection of James's New York stories, Colm Tóibín finds that "James's writings about New York disclose, more than anything, an anger, quite unlike any other anger in James, at what has been lost to him, what has been done, in the name of commerce and material progress, to a place he once knew" (vii). In 1926, a few decades after James, Powell's erstwhile friend Floyd Dell, once "a major force in American literature . . . a bellwether of literary experimentation" (Roby, 1), wrote,

> This Greenwich Village . . . this tiny refuge for desperate young lovers of beauty, in the midst of the rushing metropolis—

this fragile respite of theirs was already doomed. Greenwich
Village could not remain forever islanded amid the roaring
tides of commerce. Already the barriers were being broken
down; Seventh Avenue was being extended southward, the
new subway was being laid; in a little while the magic isolation
of the Village would be ended. The tangle of crooked streets
would be pierced by a great straight road, the beautiful
crumbling houses of great rooms and high ceilings and deep
embrasured windows would be ruthlessly torn down to make
room for modern apartment buildings. (Dell, 296)

Then, in 1933, Stanley Walker, city editor of the *New York Herald Tribune*, would publish *The Night Club Era,* one of many books fondly recalling
New York's bygone nightclub scene in a sort of journalistic, Prohibition-era
version of Powell's novel; and E. B. White, about the same time that Powell
began *The Wicked Pavilion,* wrote "Here Is New York," a short piece originally published in *Holiday* magazine. In the foreword to the book edition,
White briefly echoed Powell's sentiments about the Washington Square
hotel: "The Lafayette Hotel, mentioned in passing" he wrote, "has passed
despite the mention" (5). Though White did mention the change, John Updike found that Powell "stays loyal to New York with an ardor beside which
that of celebrants like . . . E. B. White appear fickle" ("Ohio," 262). Today,
White's stepson, writer Roger Angell,[16] considers it a "dilemma" (8) that
countless more of the places his stepfather had mentioned in "Here Is New
York" have now been lost, many of them destroyed almost immediately
after the short essay's release. Maintaining that "like the rest of us," White
wanted New York "back again, back the way it was" (15), Angell laments,
"The Third Avenue Elevated, the neighborhood ice-coal-and-wood cellars,
Schrafft's restaurant on Fifth Avenue, the ancient book elevators at the
Public Library, the old Metropolitan Opera . . . all have vanished from sight
and almost from memory" (7–8).[17] In the recent *Downtown: My Manhattan*,
Pete Hamill wistfully recalls the loss of the Brevoort:

I was about 15 when I first looked . . . at the Brevoort Hotel,
rising five stories on the northeast corner of Eighth Street, all
of it painted white, with elegant awnings for each window. . . .
Beginning in 1854, when the hotel was opened, it had provided
rooms for many writers and painters, along with businessmen

and assorted transient peddlers of dreams and desires. Eugene
O'Neill and Theodore Dreiser, Edna St. Vincent Millay and
Edmund Wilson, John Dos Passos[18] and Isadora Duncan. . . . I
wanted to lunch there too [but] never did. . . . In 1952, I went
away to the navy. When I came back, the white hotel was
gone. (160–61)

The sorrow these writers feel at having lost the irreplaceable is almost
palpable. Thanks in part to their voices, much of what remains of historic
New York is today legally protected. Such groups as the New York City
Landmarks Preservation Commission, created in 1965 in reaction to the
destruction of the original and "architecturally distinguished" Pennsylvania
Station and other important buildings, and the Greenwich Village Society
for Historic Preservation, founded as recently as 1980, work to safeguard
New York's historic structures. The relatively new "landmark law" has also
helped preserve some of historic New York (Alexiou, 6). Today, fifty years
after the appalling razing of Penn Station, the following *New York Times*
editorial of the period, "Farewell to Penn Station," is noteworthy:

> Any city gets what it admires, will pay for, and, ultimately,
> deserves. Even when we had Penn Station, we couldn't afford
> to keep it clean. We want and deserve tin-can architecture in
> a tinhorn culture. And we will probably be judged not by the
> monuments we build but by those we have destroyed.

*New York's dolls and dowagers . . . the wastrels, geniuses, artists and
mountebanks whose lodestones are the marble-topped tables of her Café Julien.*

—Charles Poore, "Greenwich Village Ghosts"

Despite the novel's somber themes of impermanence and loss, *The Wicked
Pavilion* is both "witty and serious," Powell's outlook, as Brendan Gill says,
"neither Kafka-black nor Rinso-white" ("Rough," 361). From lively renderings of what soon would be a bygone Manhattan, the novelist next turned
to painting portraits of the characters that fill this "veritable three-ring circus of a novel" (Weiner, "Metropolitan," 40). As intent as was Mrs. Creevey
on capturing the sometimes unsavory reality and the frequent hilarity of
the local inhabitants' daily lives, Powell created characters, both central and

peripheral, with pinpoint accuracy and unrelenting truth. As Poore says, the characters in the Café Julien "are all ghosts of the Twenties, the Thirties, the Forties, destined to join the café presently in gaudy oblivion. But since they do not know it, they are, in Miss Powell's superb necromancy, vividly and superbly alive" ("Greenwich," 29). One may recall that many of the friends Powell drank with at the Lafayette were not only poets, playwrights, musicians, and novelists, but also painters such as Reginald Marsh, Niles Spencer, and Stuart Davis. Additionally, at the Cedar Tavern,[19] which originally had been located near the Brevoort,[20] Powell had known artists Willem de Kooning (*Letters*, 252–53), Jackson Pollock, and Franz Kline (*Letters*, 303–4) and jazz musician Dave Brubeck (*Letters*, 242). This novel, which Katherine A. Powers calls "a perfect skewering of the New York art world of the late 1940s and early 1950s" (N4), features painters as well as writers, many based on the author's own acquaintances, for the novelist "had friends in all circles" (Brownrigg, 2).

Further, at least one character in this book was modeled on a wealthy and famous New York woman, just as Amanda Keeler Evans in *A Time to Be Born* had been based on Clare Boothe Luce. In this case, the model is noted art patron Peggy Guggenheim. The fictionalized Ms. Guggenheim, called Cynthia Earle in the book, is more interested in getting promising young artists into bed than in securing their careers.[21] The artists with whom she is involved consider her a slumming "nymphomaniac . . . [whose] perverse pleasure was in climbing up your dark tenement steps and wallowing in straw ticking and dirty blankets. She could have introduced you into the soft lights of her world but it always ended with her invading yours" (165–66). When first readers meet Ms. Earle, the narrator describes her through the eyes of starving-artist character Dalzell Sloane:

> And the beaming woman . . . was none other than Cynthia Earle,
> Cynthia with new short ash-blond curls cluttering around her
> narrow once-brunette head, which swiveled, snakewise, in a nest
> of glittering jewelry. As her arms reached out eagerly to embrace
> him, the thought leapt between them that he still owed her six
> hundred dollars. (40)

But "Nobody ever pays back Cynthia," fellow artist Ben tells Dalzell, for Cynthia always gets "her money's worth" out of her artists, "never fear" (165).

The idea behind the fictionalized Guggenheim character might first have occurred to Powell in Paris, which she had visited in the fall of 1950.

There she would meet Samuel Beckett, who had been living and writing in Paris since 1937. At the time of their meeting, Powell seems to have had no idea who Beckett was. But her unfamiliarity with him is hardly surprising, given that his best-known play, *Waiting for Godot*, would not be published until 1952, and that it would be four years after their meeting that it would be translated into English. Powell clearly assumed that Edmund Wilson was unfamiliar with Beckett as well, for she wrote to her old friend that she had just met "an Irish writer named Sam Beckett (celebrated as one of Peggy Guggenheim's lovers) who now writes in French" (*Letters*, 192). Corroborating the story of the relationship between Beckett and Guggenheim, Paul Davies, of the University of Ulster, notes that Beckett "was reluctantly involved with Peggy Guggenheim in the early Paris days" (1), himself sounding reluctant to say so. At the time that Powell met Beckett, of course, she was writing—or thinking about writing—*The Wicked Pavilion*. It seems possible that this chance meeting with an artistic former paramour of Guggenheim's had prompted Powell's idea of including a man-chasing art patron in the novel. Later, Powell admitted that in the book "there are characters who may be recognizable to many in the literary and art world (I shall of course deny this and with good reason as some of the people formed their lives to fit the books, it seems to me, instead of vice versa)" (*Letters*, 212). Few of the novel's readers missed the fictionalized portrait of the "female Don Juan," as BBC filmmaker Tim Niel calls Guggenheim, just as few had missed the portrait of Clare Luce in *A Time to Be Born* about a decade before.

In *The Wicked Pavilion*, as in *Turn, Magic Wheel*, Powell cleverly created pathos amid the revelry. Her portrait at the end of the novel of the invisible and unwanted elderly residents being displaced by the razing of the Julien resonates even more strongly than her portrait of the loss of café society. When a hundred-year-old laurel tree at last stubbornly comes down, an old woman cries out, "My poor birds!" (277). The narrator describes the woman as "a rouged and dyed old lady elaborately dressed in the fashion of pre-World-War One. . . . [She] looked at Rick appealingly. 'Their nest was right outside my window and now they're homeless . . . Oh what will they do now?'" she asks. The irony is that the unfortunate woman, along with her fellow "old-timers," soon enough will be homeless like the birds she seeks to protect. A workman says, "a lot of queer old birds" are being "flushed out of their nests" (277–78) as the buildings are being demolished. Rick replies, his words embodying the obliviousness of too many New Yorkers to the plight of the elderly, "I didn't realize people lived upstairs" (278).

Ten men waiting for me at the door? Send one of them home; I'm tired.

—Mae West

Powell expressed, in the same letter, a desire for the book's dust jacket to give "a shock of recognition [to] those who know the place, and a sense of pleasure ahead [to] those who don't . . . like standing in the café door looking around to see who's here and what's new tonight" (212). The jacket, drawn by her old friend and café regular Reginald Marsh, does just that. According to another old friend, artist Louis Bouché, as transcribed by his daughter, Jane Strong: "A lot of us would meet in the café at the Lafayette, drink, laugh and have a good time. There were Alex Brook[22], Niles Spencer, Dawn Powell, Coby Gilman, Charlie and Madge [Knight] Howard[23] and many others. It was always fun to meet there, as you never knew just who would turn up. In other words, it was just like Paris."

In an amusing photograph taken at Carl Fischer Studios, Powell is seen posing with several expatriates, members of Gertrude Stein's "Lost Generation," around a table for an *Esquire* magazine article. According to Malcolm Cowley, "*Esquire* had arranged for all this with the laudable notion of photographing some of the people in the arts who had lived in Paris during the good time that was the Twenties" (77). Though Powell had visited Paris, she certainly had never lived there in the '20s or otherwise; she was included in the photo only because, "When we got back to New York, we looked for her in the French café of the Hotel Lafayette, where the repatriates used to read the Paris papers at marble-topped tables" (77). I spoke on the telephone to the photographer Carl Fischer in April 2014; he easily recalled the photo shoot that day, telling me that this group was behaving like unruly children, all so glad to meet up with one another once again, many after long years apart, that they simply could not keep still. What he says is evidenced in the photograph.

The experience of this café society as Powell describes it—of never knowing who would be in attendance or when—was very unlike the more regulated Algonquin Round Table luncheons at which Dorothy Parker and the other members of that group had spent so much of their time. Brendan Gill discloses that later in life an aging Dotty Parker had finally come to realize that

> The major American writers of the period had not been
> members of any set; they had lived and worked far from the

coterie of self-promoters who gathered under the heading of
the Algonquin Round Table. Hemingway, Faulkner, Lardner,
Fitzgerald, Dos Passos, Cather, Crane, and O'Neill were not
to be found cracking jokes and singing each other's praises
or waspishly stinging each other into tantrums on West 44th
Street. (Gill, "Intro," xv)

Dawn Powell, too, should appear on Parker's list. The café diversion
Powell had so long enjoyed came only for the admission price of a day's
hard work; and the treat was often skipped altogether when the writing
was going well or when other responsibilities called. Still, it was necessary
that artists knew they had a place to go, she said, a place where they might
run into likeminded souls when they were able, and, meeting them, feel
less isolated; it was vital that those who toiled in private could touch a
piece of the real world outside the studios or rooftops where they worked
(*Letters*, 215). As if to distinguish Powell's Lafayette from Parker's Algonquin, old chum Matthew Josephson, in his lengthy 1973 article on the
novelist, movingly wrote,

> I always thought that [Powell] died a little some fifteen years
> before her end when her beloved Café Lafayette closed its
> doors. *The Wicked Pavilion* was her memorial to that historic, if
> not sacred, shrine of artists and lovers. In her book's nostalgic
> epilogue she recreates that happy hunting ground, that little
> world of friendly drinks and conversation that belonged to
> Dawn Powell and her circle. (51)

The respite afforded by the café in the Hotel Lafayette was not about
whatever all those afternoons at the Algonquin round table were about.
Philosophizing about this new era of disappearing café life, Powell said, "I
do not think this sort of casual life would appeal to young people looking
for sheer fun or gaiety, for the pleasure [we had came] from chance conversation and impromptu meetings with a variety of people, some living such
different lives that [we'd] never had a chance to become friends" (*Letters*,
215). While Parker's and her friends' meetings at the Algonquin were rather
insular and regulated, Powell's at the Lafayette were open and spontaneous.
Further, while the former sessions were largely about joking and avoiding
work, the latter were about meeting with other artists to gear up, shore up,
and return to the work awaiting them.

In the Café Julien, as in Mrs. Creevey's Pavilion, much time is spent waiting for something to happen, for some special someone to appear. In the Brighton Pavilion, everyone waits for the Prince to arrive, and, if he does not show, the entire evening goes down as uneventful. As Powell in "an open letter about *The Wicked Pavilion*" (*Letters,* 214) wrote, "In my Café Julien sometimes a person got there too early or too late to find whatever they sought. The lives of these characters . . . depend on just what time they got or didn't get to the Café Julien. Dalzell Sloane, for instance, . . . would have had his whole life changed if he'd waited ten minutes longer, because that was when the big advertising tycoon came in . . . to give him a job. . . . What a difference ten minutes sometimes makes in all our lives" (215).

Even before readers meet Rick Prescott, the narrator reintroduces Dennis Orphen, who, we recall, was first introduced in *Turn, Magic Wheel.* Powell had thought as early as 1940 that she could bring this favorite character back for another novel (*Diaries,* 178); and though, as readers have seen, he appeared in *A Time to Be Born* and *The Locusts Have No King,* his appearances in those works had been only small cameos. Here, he is still not a featured player—Vidal says "he is simply still there, watching the not-so-magic wheel turn as the happy island grows sad" ("American," 18)—though he frames the book. Michael Feingold in the *Village Voice* writes, "Given Powell's dubious view of her deparented childhood, it is probably significant that the most frequently reappearing of these writers, from his debut as the hero of *Turn, Magic Wheel* in 1936 to his last bow in the prologue and epilogue of . . . *The Wicked Pavilion,* is named Orphen" (14). The Powell-like character who returns in several of her novels in many ways serves as a surrogate for and certainly a spokesperson for the "orphaned" author herself. The first character readers meet in this novel, he will also be the last. The book opens with these lines:

> Shortly after two a sandy-haired gentleman in the middle years hurried into the Café Julien, sat down at Alexander's table as he always did, ordered coffee and cognac as he always did, shook out a fountain pen and proceeded to write. Considering that this was the very same man who spent each morning staring, motionless, before a typewriter in a midtown hotel, it was surprising how swiftly his pen moved over the pages at the café table. (3)

The author has given the character the trouble of writer's block in this novel, an issue readers see here in Powell for the first time. If in *Whither* her main character, Zoe Bourne, had been unable to write, it was not because she was suffering from any such condition; it was simply that she was not a writer. Here, however, Powell's alter-ego Dennis Orphen suffers from the same type of writerly difficulties that the author was suffering. Only a change of venue—moving from his midtown hotel room to a marble-topped table in the café—offers him any solution to the problem, just as Powell had hoped Paris would do for her when she traveled there in October 1950. For Orphen, the solution is only temporary; for the author, as we shall see, it was no solution at all.

Orphen will voice Powell's message of loss at novel's end. Vidal notes that for the character, "as for Powell, the café is central to his life. Here he writes, sees friends, observes the vanity fair" ("American," 18), just as Powell had done for nearly forty years at the Lafayette. His favorite retreat by this point having been torn down, Orphen writes, "The Café Julien was gone and a reign was over. Those who had been bound by it fell apart like straws when the baling cord is cut and remembered each other's name and face as part of a dream that would never come back" (281). It was no longer even possible to remain friends with those who caused "the vague feeling" that "here was someone identified with" or somehow even "responsible for the fall of the Julien" (280). It was preferable, and much easier, to try to forget the loss than to face reminders of it.

As only New Yorkers know, if you can get through the twilight,
you'll live through the night.

—Dorothy Parker

While beginning this latest novel of Manhattan, Powell was both relieved and unburdened at last to have moved away from writing the Marcia novel, a semiautobiographical tale of the dreary Ohio of her late girlhood and early adulthood. She was pleased to find *The Wicked Pavilion* progressing nicely, though at the same time she feared losing her ability to write again. "Delighted with new novel," she said, "—so far—as it seems to have already been written in my head waiting for the title (and focal point of the Lafayette) to release it. How wonderful to feel it again—the wheel beneath the hand, the chariot leave the ground. Even though there will be the colossally depressed days, one is happy over that initial sense of power over the instrument" (*Diaries,* 289). She was able to recognize the nature of her own moods very well by that time, having lived with and managed them for so long, but suffering this writer's block had proved a new and different trial. Clearly, she meant to savor the productive moment while it lasted, explaining that she doubted she could "endure another such desert" (*Diaries,* 303).

Despite her elation at being able to write again with relative ease, life was proving difficult for her once more; as she confided in her journal, the conditions under which she found herself working "would absolutely devastate me if I dared be devastated" (292). For one thing, in April 1949 she had come through the terrifying ordeal of having a teratoma removed. Teratoma, from the Greek word for "monster," is a large growth often attached to the heart; someone had told Powell it was a failed twin, a story she delighted in (*Bio,* 219). In spite of, or perhaps because of, the seriousness of the surgery, she characteristically joked about it in a letter to her sisters: "I had nine broken ribs . . . and probably Terry [as she called the growth] would keep cracking them if I let him. I was very glad on hearing of my twin that he hadn't popped out of my chest during a formal dinner party, me in my strapless and him grabbing my martini" (*Letters,* 160). Once released from the hospital, she of course found troubles waiting for her on the home front. Joe was "by now an obvious and debilitated alcoholic" (*Bio,* 215); and Jojo, who still resided with his parents part of the time (*Bio,* 206), needed to be treated with a certain amount of caution after having beaten his mother a few years before. Further, some very bad news from Ohio arrived for Powell at about this time: her sister Mabel Powell Pocock, older than Dawn by only sixteen months, had fallen desperately ill, but her Christian Science religion had made her reluctant to see a doctor. When at last she did seek medical treatment, she learned that she was in an advanced stage of cancer of the uterus (*Bio,* 219). Unfortunately, her diagnosis came too late; Mabel lost her battle with the disease in October 1949. Although Powell said little of her great loss in either diary or letter, Page understands that, as the novelist had suggested in many of her books, "some feelings may simply be too enormous to face" (*Bio,* 219). As if in reaction to Mabel's death, writing became an ordeal for Powell once again.

To escape her troubles at least mentally, the author began thinking of going to Paris "to shake walls of doom away" (*Diaries,* 292–93). Her good friend Margaret De Silver, hoping to help cure her friend of her gloom, had recently given her a round-trip ticket to Paris on the *Ile de France*[24] (*Diaries,*

291); and though Powell had no idea how she would manage to afford the incidental expenses of the trip, she began to hope that some remuneration from her last novel would come in so that she could travel (291). Some weeks later she decided that she would stay in Paris for about two months, "not touring but *living* there, working, and changing my luck" (292). As always, her writing was her priority; perhaps Paris would be the answer to these unbearable, recurring bouts of "block." She hoped that while abroad she would feel "released and free to tell more frankly the true New York stories" (*Diaries*, 294). All those thoughts in mind, on October 14, 1950, Dawn Powell set sail on the *Ile de France* for Paris.

Unfortunately, the trip did her little good. She desperately missed New York, her family, her friends, and her second cat, Fagin, presumably named for the Dickens character. (A photo of Fagin with the author appears on the cover of *The Diaries of Dawn Powell.*) Too, she felt "secretly sunk" when in Paris she received word that the *New Yorker* had rejected her latest short story (*Diaries*, 296), and worse, she got little writing done, other than a stack of lovely letters home to Joe, Margaret De Silver, Edmund Wilson, and one to Jojo (*Letters*, 181–201), the only letter to her son that was previously thought to have survived until Page recently turned up a few more.[25]

Once back in New York, she immediately began making some changes in her professional affairs, most importantly leaving Scribner's, the firm she had recently disparaged as "oblivious" (*Diaries*, 275), and signing on with Houghton Mifflin, where Edmund Wilson's daughter Rosalind Baker Wilson worked as an editor. Explaining her disappointment with Scribner's to Baker Wilson, Powell wrote:

> As sickness slowed up my production [of *The Wicked Pavilion*]
> I wanted to have my [collection of] short stories[26] published
> in order to have more time on the novel, but Scribner's felt
> the novel should come first and later the others. At present
> I feel that my name has been out of print too long and that
> my chances of selling occasional short pieces would be greatly
> improved by publishing the short stories as soon as possible,
> and personally I need the incentive of a greater show of
> confidence to enable me to get *The Wicked Pavilion* done. (204)

Powell next turned to writing letters explaining her decision to part from her agent, Ivan Van Auw, with whom she had signed upon leaving the Brandts, and from her editor John Wheelock. All of this attention to business took her away from her novel writing, as did further domestic troubles: Joe, away on a company trip, had just been injured in an automobile accident. According to Powell, "A business associate of my husband decided it wise to drive his car through a Connecticut stone wall, smashing car, battering husband's leg and sending him home in a wheelchair" (*Letters,* 205). Furthermore, by this time utterly dependent on drink, Joe had taken to treating his next highball as if it were "a medicine ordered by the doctor . . . a digitalis potion" (*Diaries,* 318). And, to make matters worse for the struggling writer, Jojo had been sent back to stay with his parents for something the hospital called "Home Influence." Powell was "gratified to find that I was up to these horrendous demands [of caring for both Joe and Jojo], but it kicked the novel out completely" (*Letters,* 205). Given all her mounting difficulties, it is remarkable that this next-to-last novel got written at all; that it is such a fine piece of work is further testament to her unwavering determination.

〜〜〜〜〜〜〜〜

In April 1953, some ten months before *The Wicked Pavilion* came out, the *New York Times Book Review*'s Harvey Breit was already looking forward to it, grumbling that six years was far "too long" to wait between books by Dawn Powell. When the novel did arrive, Page notes, it was the only Powell book "to make the *New York Times* bestseller list, even if it was only for one week" ("Muse," 53).[27] Powell, for the first time in her career, said, "I have a peculiar feeling about this *Wicked Pavilion* novel—a feeling I never had about my other novels after they were finished. I miss it" (*Letters,* 214).

Charles Poore, who found the book on its release to be "first-rate reading," appreciated the fact that this "suavely sardonic novel of Washington Square" was "haunted by the old Brevoort," he, too, seemingly missing it ("Greenwich," 29). Clearly having enjoyed both reading the novel and now writing about it, he ended his piece by calling the book "a chronicle written with a kind of furious compassion, savage grace, and style, wit and ribald laughter" (29). Powell noted a stepped-up response from the reading public, and Page speaks of the "banner treatment" the novel received from its publisher (*Bio,* 287). Lending libraries were scooping up copies, borrowers after reading it were buying it, and "interest" seemed to be "mounting" wherever Powell went. She mentioned receiving "letters, phone calls, even flowers from strangers," then wrote this amusing account of one particular telephone conversation: "A young playwright called me to say that during his play's opening last week he had done nothing but hole up in a hotel with gin and oysters and the *WP.* He said it would be of interest to science that it was possible to exist 72 hours on gin and oysters and Powell" (*Letters,* 219). Gin and oysters indeed: *The Wicked Pavilion,* "with a total print run of nine-thousand," proved to be one of Powell's "grandest successes" (*Bio,* 245).

But it would almost not be a Powell novel if it did not receive some negative press. Somewhat famously among her readers today, or "notoriously," as Alice Tufel says (155), one of the author's contemporaries, Frederic Morton, complained that Powell lacked "the pure indignation that moves Evelyn Waugh to his absurdities and forced Orwell into his haunting contortions. Her verbal equipment is probably unsurpassed among writers of her genre—but she views the antics of humanity with too surgical a calm" (5). That "calm" with which Powell viewed the antics of her characters is one of her most admirable qualities, at least for present-day readers, for "the essence of her characters is their moral sloppiness—the 'antics' that all human beings share—and the essence of Powell's vision was her acceptance of that imperfect condition" (Tufel, 155). But Morton may have hit upon something when he wrote those words: perhaps her "calm" was precisely the reason that many readers of Powell's day did not quite understand or fully appreciate her. Perhaps they expected the author to disparage her characters, to sneeringly disapprove of them. As I have noted throughout, Powell both understood and sympathized with her fellow human beings, their dreams, their motivations, too well to sit in judgment of them. As Joseph Coates remarks, "A remarkably good-natured satirist, Powell neither denounces nor proselytizes, seems to have no agenda in mind and obviously likes most of her people—not least for giving her such great comic targets" (4). James Gibbons, too, says that, though "the razor-sharp social comedy of the New York novels might be taken . . . as an attempt to instruct by negative example, Powell was averse to moralizing in any form" (147). Not only was her "razor-sharp" humor not to be missed, but neither were her pointed characterizations. Some reviewers compared her favorably with a few of her novel-writing contemporaries: Earle F. Walbridge, coincidentally of Powell's neighborhood Washington Square Library, noted that "Mary McCarthy[28] will have to sharpen her stiletto to equal this" book (1504); while Martin Levin memorably wrote that Powell "at the top of her form should make the majority of her professional colleagues want to sell their typewriters and take up something less taxing" (62).

In one of the least flattering reviews from Powell's day that I have turned up, the author of a brief piece in *Kirkus* complained that *The Wicked*

Pavilion is "a novel of no particular purpose over and above its display of acerb brilliance" (408). The reviewer did note, however, that the book is "an entertainment which if deadly is never dull" (408). Unfortunately, in saying that the novel is of no particular purpose, he revealed that he had missed its overriding message of loss, fragility, temporality.

Today *The Wicked Pavilion* is among Powell's most popular books. Ross Wetzsteon in 2002 called it and its follow-up novel, *The Golden Spur*, "the most accurate, the most penetrating, the most outrageously comic of all the hundreds of novels written about the Village" (516). James Wolcott finds it "one of Powell's best novels" (46), an assertion with which countless others agree. Gary Soto says that, despite the novel's "diverse assortment of self-styled Bohemians," it is clear that the "real hero of the story is Manhattan. . . . Powell obviously is aware that her love for the city and its artistic demi-monde is more foolish than wise, but she never lets the realization spoil her nostalgic evocation of a more innocent era" (10). That the unsentimental Powell understood the irretrievability of the past is clear; still, she would attempt not only to record it but to warn others of the folly of too rashly destroying what might better have been preserved. Readers will see more of this objective in her final novel, 1962's *The Golden Spur*, which many readers then as now consider her *tour de force*.

THE GOLDEN SPUR, 1962

Death darkens her eyes and unplumes her wings,
yet the sweetest song is the last she sings.

—Cicero

The Golden Spur would be Powell's swan song. Eight years would pass between it and the previous New York novel, *The Wicked Pavilion*, though another book would come between the final two novels of Manhattan: 1957's *A Cage for Lovers*, which, as has been noted, is set primarily in Paris and which, as Page says, "had been almost completely disemboweled" by Houghton Mifflin (telephone call, March 7, 2013). The five years that would elapse between *A Cage for Lovers* and *The Golden Spur* were almost an unheard-of space of time between books for Powell,[29] with the exception of the six years that came between *The Locusts Have No King* and *The Wicked Pavilion*, but her personal troubles at this point had grown even grimmer than they had been before. Joe, no longer working, had fallen into ever more debilitating despair, drunkenness, and illness, detesting being housebound and frustrated at feeling worthless. As Powell revealed to an old friend from the early Village days, Cornelius G. Burke,[30] Joe's loss of work "was his REAL death, as it is for most people—worse than cancer or other desperations" (*Letters*, 302). Of course, on Joe's mandatory retirement the couple's finances reached their lowest point; as a result, they were forced to move from one seedy residential hotel to another until August 2, 1959 (*Diaries*, 400), when old friend Margaret de Silver came through with a trust fund for the family on which Powell managed, between paychecks, to live for the rest of her life.[31]

Despite the cheering security that the money brought after years of crushing poverty, it was too late for Joe, who lay dying, more often than not in unbearable pain, in the hospital for a year and then back home again. Soon Margaret de Silver would fall seriously ill as well (*Letters*, 303), the result of having been forgotten while being X-rayed, then contracting a severe internal infection from the burns (*Letters*, 309). Powell would lose both Joe and Margaret in 1962, the same year that her final novel was published. For much of that same year it appeared as if she would also lose her beloved younger sister, Phyllis. According to Page, the hospitalized Phyllis was "desperately and mysteriously ill and thought to be dying" (*Bio*, 291).[32] As distraught as Powell was at the idea of losing her sister, the model for Florrie in *My Home Is Far Away*, she continued to work. Six months before *The Golden Spur* was released, Powell told Malcolm Cowley how exhausting the long years spent writing the novel had been, especially considering that she had had to draw "an iron curtain between my personal problems and the acrobatic necessities of a comic novel" (*Letters*, 301). As she wrote to Burke, "I finally finished [the] novel I started four or five years ago—and, as it was to be completely and classically comic, it required considerable bullish willpower to shut off my life and reconstruct this playhouse every day" (*Letters*, 302). She completed the book at last, she said, only out of the "sheer rage" that Joe's death had prompted (302).

Losing her husband, who had passed away on Valentine's Day, 1962, proved especially difficult for her. Powell recounted a dream she had had of him some four months after his death:

> Dreamed at last of Joe—very vivid and shaking. I was in my
> bed in the street next to the Wanamaker building[33] and he came
> and sat on the bed—saying it was more than he could stand,
> our separation. There were tears in his eyes and I held his head
> and tried to console him but people were passing by on the
> street, staring at us.
>
> In the morning I was sick and shook up—the first chipping
> off of the ice barricade I built up in his last few months when
> he was already gone. "I'm no good to you or myself or anybody
> anymore," he cried out one day in December. "I'm no help to you."
> I said he was—that I couldn't work or live without him to turn to.
> It is true that things do not have much meaning. (*Diaries*, 442)

Difficult as their relationship had always been, troubled as Joe was, the two had forged a strong, unbreakable bond. Losing Joe would haunt Powell for the rest of her days, and her diaries to the end are peppered with brief meditations on his loss. Yet despite all the difficulties she faced in these later years, as Daniel Aaron notes, Powell would never "fizzle out or lose control of her bumpy life, or surrender her belief in the dignity of her own work" (37). This last novel, a story of aging, irrelevance, and loss, is considered by many to be her finest. And, despite the somber themes, it is a wickedly funny book.

During these years, not only was Powell wrestling with the above-mentioned woes, but she found herself facing profound fears and once again fighting a debilitating case of writer's block. She wrote in the last month of 1957 that "the years get worse; work is almost taboo because of memories of past failures" (*Diaries*, 378). As she struggled again with the Marcia book, it began to appear that she might never complete it or any other novel. Then, happily, following the release of *A Cage for Lovers* in England, longtime supporter J. B. Priestley spoke of both the author and her new novel so favorably[34] that Powell credited him with giving her the confidence she needed to write another book of Manhattan: "On receiving Priestley encouragement," she said, "reverted to Cedar idea and started Cedar novel—*The Golden Spur*" (*Diaries*, 381). By "Cedar" Powell meant the Cedar Tavern, longtime Village bar and haunt of many struggling abstract expressionist painters of the day. It has been said that the Cedar (and other such artist hangouts in the Village) "look[ed] like a cockpit where visionaries f[ought] for the world's soul" (Grooms, 10). If the novelist had used the elegant cafés of the Hotels Lafayette and Brevoort as the models for her Café

Julien in *The Wicked Pavilion*, here she turned to the darker, danker, more bohemian—and, in the late '50s and early '60s, still extant in its original location—Cedar Tavern to draw the Golden Spur, "the metropolitan wayside inn" of the novel's title (Poore, "*Golden*," 39).

Elated by Priestley's praise, in which, Powell said, the critic "advised readers to pick up any old books by me and declared he would support any move to republish my former works" (*Letters*, 251), she literally lost no time in getting to the "Cedar novel": the diary entry that immediately follows her jubilation at first hearing of Priestley's comments finds her already explaining, if in fragmented thoughts, the next book's general storyline:

> —minor hero . . . like Dennis Orphen in *Turn, Magic Wheel*—a young man who comes to New York to find his father. He has resisted the man he thought was his father, a conventional stuffy man. On father's death, mother tells him he is illegitimate. She has told him stories of Greenwich Village for years—Sam Schwartz's,[35] Romany Marie's,[36] Three Steps Down,[37] etc. She had a lover—a well-known man, gay artist, [and the character] sees himself at once that way. (381–82)

Many commentators found the storyline an excellent one, especially in Powell's hands.[38] Morris Gilbert, for one, said that in this novel, "the author has hit upon one of the happiest imaginable and most original plot contrivances" (40), a position with which Tim Page agrees: "Powell relays a clear, direct story," he writes, "one of her most perfect, in *The Golden Spur*" (*Bio*, 285). Edmund Wilson, too, maintained that "Miss Powell . . . has constructed here a very neat plot, and for once in her career played Santa Claus and made her hero a generous present" ("Dawn Powell," 235). The "generous present" Powell has given Jonathan is an answer to his question—although, as anyone who knows the novels of Dawn Powell should expect, it is not exactly the answer he wishes to receive.

A Candide out of the boondocks.

—Charles Poore, review of *The Golden Spur*

Briefly, the story concerns Ohio-born optimist and illegitimate son Jonathan Jaimison, who, not only having read his mother's journals after her death but having all his life listened to her stories, happily realizes that at last he has the chance to find for himself a more impressive, less conventional father figure. Discovering a new father, he believes, will enable him to fashion for himself a less stodgy past that will somehow make possible a more glamorous future. As he tells a new friend once he has begun his search, "All my life before this I didn't think I could count on [having inherited] anything but the Jaimison pigheadedness. Now I can be anything. For instance, if my father was a great writer—" (68), he says dreamily, his voice trailing off.

If young Jaimison seeks for himself a new past and ultimately a new future, this book, like its immediate predecessor, showcases the Village with a nostalgia for what has been lost in the name of progress. Jonathan, newly arrived in New York, settles not far from Washington Square and just past a "street of old brick houses with their fanlights over white doorways, trellised balconies of greenery, magnolia trees, vined walls, cats sunning themselves in windows" (5). The picture Powell paints is a nostalgic one; reading the paragraph, one wonders where the old New York has gone. And Powell's narrator soon will tell us. Just as readers learn that Jonathan, "only eighteen hours in New York," already "loved everything" about the City, "every inch of it" (6), he is hit in the eye by a bit of flying rubble, as if to signify the dual ideas that Manhattan is no easy conquest, and that change and destruction in this city of cities are unavoidable. The character soon finds himself "caught up in a crowd around a demolition operation that took up the whole block" (80); it turns out that Wanamaker's Department Store, the longtime Greenwich Village landmark about which the author dreamed following her husband's death, is about to be razed. Looking up, Jonathan witnesses the destruction:

> A giant crane was the star performer, lifting its neck
> heavenward, then dropping a great iron ball gently down to
> a doomed monster clock in the front wall of the structure,
> tapping it tenderly, like a diagnostician looking for the sore
> spot. Does it hurt here? here? or here? Wherever it hurts must
> be target for the wham, and wham comes next, with the rubble
> hurtling down into the arena with a roar. A pause, and then the
> eager watchers followed the long neck's purposeful rise again,
> the rhythmical lowering of the magic ball, the blind grope for
> the clock face, and then the avalanche once more. The cloud of
> dust cleared, and a cry went up to see the clock still there, the
> balcony behind it falling. "They can't get the clock," someone

exulted. "Not today! Hooray for the clock!" The spectators smiled and nodded to one another. Good show. (9)

But the demolition crews will not give up, and eventually the celebrated Wanamaker's will come down. An angry man standing beside Jonathan, "twisting his mustache savagely," tells the stranger, "Destruction is what pays today . . . wreckers, bomb-builders, poison-makers. Who buys creative brains today?" When Jonathan asks why such a vast crowd has come out to see the destruction, the man tells him, "In the first place, this was a splendid old landmark and people like to see the old order blown up. Then there is the glorious dirt and uproar which are the vitamins of New York, and of course the secret hope that the street will cave in and swallow us all up" (10). The man, for a moment wondering whether having paid his Wanamaker bill might have made any difference, in the next moment tells himself, "Well, mustn't get sentimental" (10). Like the mustached man, Powell, before receiving the generous endowment from Margaret de Silver, had for quite some time been unable to pay her bills. As Page writes, by 1957 "the Goushas had no economic security whatsoever—no savings, no income . . . the bills began to pile up, the phone was shut off, and merchants discontinued their credit; demand letters arrived daily . . . but there was nothing they could do about any of it, so after a while, the numbed Powell simply stopped opening her mail" (*Bio,* 267). One wonders whether she, too, had fleetingly wondered whether having paid her Wanamaker's bills could possibly have helped to save the legendary store. Reading this vivid account of the attempted destruction of the store's great clock, the toppling of its grand balcony, one wonders whether the author had been a member of the crowd that day, even whether, like the mustached man, she had fought the tendency to grow sentimental over the store's destruction.

Wanamaker's symbolizes more for both Powell and the novel than merely the changing face of New York, however. The vast department store, housed in a strikingly impressive building, had an equally impressive history and a notable New York significance as well. The store, which had "filled an entire block from Broadway to Fourth Avenue and from East Ninth to 10th Streets" in Greenwich Village (Museum, "Berenice"), was unlike any other; it had "an entrance hall and an art gallery and was even said to have more windows than the Empire State Building" (Gopnik, 94). To construct it, John Wanamaker, salesman extraordinaire, "had purchased the old A.T. Stewart Cast Iron Palace . . . and [in 1905] connected it with a 'Bridge of

Progress' to a new 16-story building next door" (Schoenherr, 4). The Stewart building, which had first gone up in 1862, "is believed to [have been] the
first building in the city with a cast-iron front. A sky-lighted open well in
the center of the old store recalls the days before electricity made good illu-
mination possible" (Gody, 137). The department store's structure was grand;
its interior even grander; and, moreover, it was known for a series of firsts:
it had the first department-store elevator, the first electric wiring, and so on.
Finally, Wanamaker's, having opened in 1896, was brought down in 1956.
This symbol of a more graceful, more opulent era was demolished, according to some sources, after a fire broke out, even though the cast-iron building had withstood the blaze (Museum, "Berenice"); other sources say that
it was already being bulldozed when the fire broke out (Gray, "Sixth").[39] In
any case, the magnificent building no longer stands, having been replaced
by a soulless apartment tower and nondescript office buildings. Yet because
"it was Wanamaker's, more than anyone else, who transformed the department store from a place where women bought stuff to a place where they
simply and necessarily went" (Gopnik, 94), its removal signaled important
geographic, cultural, and commercial changes in the city, therefore providing an appropriate starting point for Powell's novel, a book she felt should
read "like an explosion" (*Diaries*, 394), reminiscent of E. B. White's "boom."
Following the store's demise, the shopping district formerly known as the
Ladies Mile moved over to Fifth Avenue and uptown. No longer was it
considered chic to find "everything under one roof," as one could at Wanamaker's; it had now become fashionable to travel from one store to another,
each located within a short walking distance of the other.

By 1956, two years after *The Wicked Pavilion* was published and six years
before *The Golden Spur* appeared, not only was New York changing but so
was the entire face of the nation. President Dwight D. Eisenhower had in-
stituted his Interstate Highway Project; before that, when interstate travel
had largely meant railroad travel,[40] there had been no K-Marts, no Taco
Bells, no Motel 6's. The proliferation of chain stores, fast food outlets, and
nationwide hotels that grew up along the Interstates changed the face of
the American countryside, homogenizing it, making every Interstate town
look almost exactly like the next. The Village was also rapidly changing,
not only in the physical appearance of its cafés, hotels, apartment houses,
and department stores, but in the look of its population as well. Edmund
Wilson wrote, "In *The Golden Spur* readers see the Village at a point of its
decline that is rather squalid: bearded beatniks and abstract painters have

seeped in among the Guggenheim fellows, the raffish N.Y.U. professors, and the adult-education students" ("Dawn Powell," 233).[41] Powell's view of the "adult-education" students of whom Wilson seems so fond is far different from her friend's: here she takes another shot at them, as she had gleefully done in *The Wicked Pavilion:* "Somber Adult Education students, in town to slurp up enough culture to nourish them through the long dry winter in some Midwest Endsville,[42] sipped beer at the bar and dreamed of a wild Greenwich Village nymphomaniac who would oblige them to forget their careers" (61). And, although the novelist seems none too happy with the overly casual "young housewives in pants and sandals, hair in curlers under scarves" (61) who seemed suddenly to have cropped up all over town, she is certainly less stuffy than Wilson, having acquainted herself with her share of bearded beatniks, abstract painters, and assorted young arrivals to the city. What's more, she bore them no ill will.

But still, she missed her old friends, old haunts, old Village. At one point, late in life, she lamented being the only one of her contemporaries left other than Coby Gilman (*Letters,* 343). Though Dos Passos, Wilson, and others whom Powell had known since the old days were still alive, she had lost such a great many friends by then that at times it must have seemed she was the only one left. Many of Powell's new friends were a generation or even two younger than she.

Not everyone can be an orphan.

—André Gide

Speaking of old friends: Dennis Orphen fails to make an appearance in *The Golden Spur.* Gore Vidal surmises that the recurring character "presumably . . . lies buried beneath whatever glass and cement horror replaced the La-fayette" ("American," 20); Page tells me that Powell once explained that, by the time of this final novel, "Dennis would have been too drunk to show up." But other familiar characters, or character types, do reappear. In the previous novel, as we have seen, Powell had based an art patron character on Peggy Guggenheim, and in this novel she has not yet finished with her. No longer called Cynthia Earle, the hard-drinking, man-chasing art lover is now more appropriately and humorously named Cassie Bender. Powell's narrator tells us she "was forty-three—well, all right, forty-eight, if you're going to count every lost weekend" (206). It is well known about town that "Mrs. Bender had gone into the art racket as an excuse to raid the art quarters of cities all over the world for lovers" (206). Toward her "shrewdly created" (Brophy, 942) artist characters, Powell is equally irreverent. Those hard-drinking, pugnacious, unwashed creatures who spent their days in the fictional Spur, or in the real-life Cedar, were "all modern, in that they were against the previous generation, though generations in art were not much longer than cat generations" (60). As ever, Powell created a cast of characters of all stripes, from the high-placed to the low, from the *au courant* to the passé, from the bright to the dull, from the innocent to the manipulative; for the most part, she provides the reader with "a wonderfully mad gallery of derelicts" (R. Payne, 65).

Notably, book critics of the 1960s, perhaps as a result of having become more used to seeing informal types about town, were less apt to fault Powell's characters than were her reviewers of the 1920s through the'50s. Powell, at this point beyond caring, at least outwardly, about how commentators would fault her, allowed her "wonderful Manhattan talent for seeing through everybody and enjoying them thoroughly in the process" to shine (Terwilliger, 13). In the process she created her latest cast of characters with aplomb and wit and, most of all, with an insider's understanding. In other words, as times changed, her readers became more receptive to the satiric, dead-eyed Powell. As always, in this novel the author's humor surfaces above the sadness, rapid-fire barbs forever punctuating truths. If fashions and hairstyles, language and manners change over time; if elegance gives way to coarseness; if the old indecency becomes the modern propriety; if cityscapes are irrevocably altered and favorite locales destroyed, one thing remains constant: the deplorable, the endearing, the laughable foolishness of human beings. The world and everything in it might change, but as long as people existed, Powell would never run out of material.

~~~~~~~~~~~~~~~~~~~~~~~~~~~~

Although the familiar figure of Dennis Orphen has vanished, his surname and all it might imply has not: Powell introduces in this novel a central female character by name of Miss Claire Van Orphen (40–41). In 1958, upon learning of Priestley's complimentary words, Powell wrote in her diary a brief and cryptic entry: "Did notes on a Cedar novel where I could use myself instead of being driven into hiding" (381). She has decided that she herself can appear as a character in the novel, rather than having to hide behind a Dennis Orphen or other male figure. Was it her age, one wonders, or perhaps a final self-assurance, that led her at last to feel that she no longer needed a younger mouthpiece? Whatever the case, in *The Golden Spur* Powell has transformed Dennis Orphen, successful male writer, into older, less successful female writer Claire Van Orphen. Both have much to do with our novelist. This female Orphen is now "over 60" (46)—Powell herself had turned sixty in November 1956—and she has surely seen better days. Broke, Van Orphen lives in a modest Village hotel; Powell, too, had been rooming in such places while writing much of the novel. Despite the overflowing trunks and shelves that fill her claustrophobic quarters, Claire cannot stop writing (44–45), as clearly Powell, who spoke of overflowing trunks (*Letters,* 134), never could. The character thinks warmly of "lavish days—in the Brevoort banquet suite" (42), which Powell wistfully recalled. But in one way or another it is just as well that those elegant days are over, for neither woman would have had a thing to wear on a visit there (*Letters,* 317).

Claire Van Orphen treats herself to a Manhattan cocktail weekly at a nearby bar where she, her clothing, and her old-world manners are shunned, laughed at, and spoken about behind her back. To make matters worse, a fashionable young woman who works at the hotel newsstand is "always gesturing to her that an under-arm seam had popped or that a top hook wasn't fastened. She further annoyed Claire with her helpful comments that her rouge or lipstick was crooked or too thick, and had she read that rouge wasn't fashionable any more?" (47). In many ways, Powell's touching portrait of Miss Van Orphen and her worn, torn, out-of-date clothing is reminiscent of Katherine Mansfield's 1922 portrait of short-story character Miss Brill. The shadowy existence of the elderly, the unwanted, the lonely is a theme of this novel, as it had been, though less centrally, of *The Wicked Pavilion.* And the matter of the aged and the no-longer relevant is closely related to the matter of a changing New York. As the older parts of a city die, so do its forgotten elderly inhabitants; as a city changes, many longtime residents find themselves forced out, alienated, unable to keep up.

Before Jonathan has had a chance to meet Miss Van Orphen, he asks his has-been writer friend, Earl Turner, about her, to which Earl replies curtly, "Never heard of her." Then, seeing the disappointment in his friend's face, he adds, "She must have been a best-seller in her day, that's why I never knew her" (61). "Never heard of her," of course, might well have been the standard response any young man or woman in the late 1950s or early '60s would have given to anyone who chanced—if anyone would—to ask of Dawn Powell. Most of her novels had gone out of print by then, many of them decades before; her name no longer appeared in news columns or gossip pages; it was absent from collections of or commentaries on American literature; and, as we have seen, the "old-fashioned" cafés where she had once so famously held court had simply vanished. In Earl's line, Powell is making a joke about herself.

Strange new world

At last the naïve Jonathan has his opportunity to interview Miss Van Orphen, hoping she can tell him something about his mother, whom she had casually known so many years before, and in so doing help lead him to his father, supposedly a man of certain fame who used to frequent the Golden Spur. Claire Van Orphen, unable to remember much of anything about the quiet, unassuming young typist Jonathan's mother had been, feels she must give the hopeful young man something—after all, he has kindly bought her a cocktail—so she begins to embellish what she knows and even to make up a few things, to his rapt delight. After a time Jonathan finds that he must leave, but before going he introduces Claire to Earl, who clearly wants nothing to do with her. Then, in a sustained portrait of a Claire who is clearly out of her element but determined not to let on, the narrator of this "murderously comic novel" (Poore, "*Golden*," 39) makes the character sound not unlike the proud, aging Powell herself:

> She could feel the fine self confidence built up by the
> young Jonathan melting away under the bored expression of her
> companion. He scarcely glanced at her, classifying her no doubt
> as a dull family friend of Jonathan's, entitled to the respect
> due her age but nothing more. He looked beyond her to greet
> new and young arrivals, drumming on the table as he smoked.
> Stubbornly Claire took her time finishing her drink.
>   The Spur was filling up with the pre-dinner crowd now,
> all races and all costumes . . . the searching look in the eyes of
> everyone seemed faintly sinister to Claire . . . It annoyed her
> that her hands shook as she drew on her rose-colored gloves
> and that Jonathan's friend should be watching her now.

"Pretty rough crowd for you, I'm afraid," he said.

"Not for me, Mr. Turner," Claire said with dignity. "I find the people most attractive. The blonde girl . . . looks fascinating."

"Fascinating indeed! She just got back from Greece, where she's been living on money she got from selling her baby . . ."

He wanted to shock her, Claire knew, and steeled herself.

"Enterprising, then," she said lightly.

The scene continues in this manner, Claire not letting on that she finds the crowd intimidating, unruly, unattractive, even frightening. She will not let her sneering companion decide that he knows all there is to know about her. When at last she elegantly rises to go, the narrator says, "She would be the stately literary figure that Jonathan assumed her to be, she told herself defiantly, not the timid spinster" (70–72). So adept has Claire been at playing her role that in the end she has even won over the scowling Mr. Turner, who offers to walk her back to her hotel. "The polite gesture," the narrator says, "seemed to surprise Mr. Turner himself as much as it did Claire" (72).

The writer knows this character inside and out; she understands clearly the position of suddenly finding that one has grown old, that one appears to the younger set to be irrelevant and feeble and out of place, unattractive and naïve, unknowing and incapable. In Powell's hands, however, the clever victim of this sort of presumption will win the round, buoyed by her whip-smart sense, her gift for one-up-manship, her psychological know-how. Edmund Wilson found that the novel had been written by an aging author less ill-at-ease than one might have expected her to be: he noted, "I have said that Dawn Powell must be less at home in the 'beat' than in the old Village, yet it is interesting to find that in *The Golden Spur* she has succeeded in modulating without strain from the charming Lafayette café to its so much less distinguished successor, and that the beatnik's dread of the 'square' comes to seem here the natural extension of the old attitude" ("Dawn Powell," 236). Powell's ability to translate the dread of what is un-hip in this newer day of the beats into the same sense of what was not "cool" to her crowd of earlier Villagers—such as uptown versus down—makes her seem very up-to-date, not at all out of place. Brophy, similarly, finds Powell's new-age characters "some of the most convincing bohemians in literature" (942). Like Claire Van Orphen who will not be cowed by the younger, more "with-it" Villagers, Powell could move up in time with the best of them. Her novel seems in some ways so much of the new moment that old friend

Malcolm Cowley, then her editor,[43] had such a "deep, sentimental nostalgia for his old Village days [that] he was disappointed that [Powell's] Village is not what he imagined and is cross about it" (*Diaries*, 398).

Although the fictional writer and the real one have much in common, Claire Van Orphen is a far sadder creature than Dawn Powell might ever have been: the character is much lonelier, more out-of-touch, more passé than ever was her creator.[44]

As early as 1953, a year before *The Wicked Pavilion* was released, the author was already speaking of a future work that would feature a woman who is "as fixed in a fixed old past as a fixed cat" (*Letters*, 211). Clearly Powell was never so fixed in the past, and, as the novel continues, even Claire Van Orphen becomes less so fixed. Ultimately discovering with the help of writer friend Earl Turner that if she simply changes her magazine stories from their old-fashioned "homebody wife is good, outdoor career girl is bad" point of view to the precise opposite, magazine publishers and readers alike will be pleased. Soon enough Hollywood films and television programs come calling on the elderly, once passé writer. Vidal notes that "Powell herself was writing television plays in the age of Eisenhower and no doubt had made this astonishing discovery on her own," another parallel between the novelist and the character ("American," 20). Despite the fact that Van Orphen is able, with assistance, to modernize her magazine stories, she is nonetheless unable to fit in with the strange new world about her. On some levels, it seems that the Van Orphen character might represent a Dawn Powell our author fears becoming. In fact, close friend and one-time literary executor Jacqueline Miller Rice claimed that Powell need not have died from the cancer that killed her. As Rice told John Guare: "She helped her husband wage a long, excruciating battle against cancer, but when it came to her own cancer, she refused surgery. We were sitting in the Jumble Shop on Waverly Place.[45] I told her: 'I want you to live to be a mean cranky old lady with a cane.' She wouldn't listen. Her cancer could have been so easily treated. But she'd had terrible experiences with doctors" (x).

~~~~~~~~~~~~~~~~

As this is a Dawn Powell novel, readers should not be surprised to find that other characters in the book also have much in common with the writer. If the proud and elderly Claire Van Orphen is in many ways like the older Powell, Jonathan Jaimison recalls the young, ebullient young woman recently moved from Ohio in search of a better future. As Robin Friedman says, "Dawn Powell has put some of herself . . . in each of the people in her book—the young Jonathan Jaimison leaving rural Ohio for a new life in New York City, the young sexually active women in the Village,[46] the struggling artists, the aging unsuccessful writer" ("Rediscovered," 5). Powell herself wrote of this novel that it is like "an artichoke . . . each character represents the hero at another time—in another situation—under different circumstances. The fruit opens, seems several people, then closes into One" *(Diaries,* 441). Working as always from what she knew best, the author created wholly believable characters, many based at least partly on herself, and placed them in the rapidly changing city that, despite everything, she still managed to know and love so well.

Sweet Smell of Success

—Ernest Lehman[47]

The Golden Spur, released in October 1962, received some of the best notices of any novel Powell had written. One of the most significant reviews was Edmund Wilson's essay in that year's November *New Yorker,* which Tim Page calls "far and away the most sustained and serious critical appreciation to appear during her lifetime" (*Letters,* 309n). In a letter to her sister Phyllis, an upbeat Powell spoke of the "important *New Yorker* piece—one that sells books since Wilson is the world's greatest critic" (309), an excited Powell overlooking the hurtful comments he had made about *My Home Is Far Away* back in 1944. Elsewhere she wrote that "Viking tells me reviews [are] picking up all over country, due to *New Yorker* Wilson piece probably. Also *Spur* is on final list of National Book Award. And Mrs. Vincent Astor loves book and wants me for cocktails" *(Diaries,* 450). At last Powell was getting some well-deserved recognition, and from a variety of quarters at that— though the applause might have seemed to her to be coming rather late.

The author initially regarded the Astor invitation with some suspicion, confiding in her diary, "Why? Does she think we writers should band to-gether?" (450). Though her words at first seem to dismiss Astor's literary talent, Powell actually found the philanthropist's memoir of childhood, *Patchwork Child,* "quite interesting" (*Letters,* 312), and two years later she would very much enjoy her "charming" novel, *The Bluebird Is at Home*[48] *(Di-aries,* 469). Sounding excited by the standards of the emotions-held-in-check

Powell, she wrote to her niece, "Among other crazy things, Mrs. Vincent Astor asked my publisher if I would come see her as she wanted me to auto-graph some books of mine she loved. So I am going there this Thursday, which means I have to get a haircut and find some dress that fastens and fix my nails and all these things I haven't time to do" (*Letters*, 312). Though she felt she did not have much time to spare from her work, she was delighted to have been invited. Just twelve days later, she arrived for tea at Astor's Park Avenue address (*Diaries*, 450).

Soon thereafter, an elated Powell spoke of receiving "a great deal of publicity about the book" and "much fan mail." Parties were being thrown in her honor, she said, mentioning a particularly "wonderful one given by the Murdock Pembertons, old friends.[49] They had '*The Golden Spur*' painted on their door and about 50 guests, many old friends" (*Letters*, 310).

The new book generated more than publicity, fan mail, and parties, however: Powell was approached by a pair of successful young theater com-posers who asked her to collaborate with them on a musical version of the book, to which proposal she enthusiastically agreed. As she wrote to her sister, "I am now signed up to adapt *Golden Spur* for a musical comedy with two very smart boys—[Charles] Strouse and [Lee] Adams, who did the songs for *Bye Bye Birdie*"[50] (*Letters*, 308). From the start she sounded optimistic and eager, settling in to working "industriously" on the new proj-ect "with these talented young guys who are more original and also more intelligent than the Broadway pros I've been accustomed to" (*Letters*, 310). Clearly the author was enjoying this triumphant moment that had arrived at last, but still she was not tempted to lie around and bask in the limelight: as always, she preferred to get down to work and began digging into this musical version of her novel. Unfortunately, however, she soon grew too weak to continue with the project. The musical for which she had such high hopes would never be completed.[51]

A pure bubble of enchanted comedy.

—Brigid Brophy

Of this final novel Tim Page says, "Had Powell deliberately planned *The Golden Spur* as a last testament, it couldn't have been a much more thorough or appropriate summation of her life's work" (*Bio*, 285). The novel's last words, which tell us that Jonathan "was very glad that Hugow had turned back downtown, perhaps to the Spur, where they could begin all over" (274), seem a bittersweet final phrase. If only the author could turn back time, a part of her seems to say; if only she could begin her journey all over again. Still, we have seen that Powell had refused the potentially life-saving surgery offered her; it is clear, too, that her life had never been easy. So perhaps the thought of beginning anew was not as tantalizing to her as it might appear to readers. The book, which Vidal says might be her "most appealing novel" ("American," 20), is noteworthy for many reasons besides its ending, among them its fleshed-out character portrayals and the psychological understanding for which Powell has been known; its sympathetic if familiar theme of the young provincial arriving in New York and becoming, like the author, "a permanent visitor"; its rich, satiric humor; its themes of consumerism, longing, change, aging, loneliness. And it is all done in the irreverent Powell style though drawn with a defter hand than before.

Charles Poore, writing in 1962, remarked that the novel "should entertain thousands of delighted readers now and in the years ahead—for artistic nonconformity is one conformity that never goes out of style. . . . Powell is, in a way, the diarist for two different yet allied generations: the Lost Generation of the nineteen-twenties and the even loster generation of today" (39).

Despite the warm reviews, Page says that they were "rarely as well placed as an author might have wished" (*Bio*, 287). But along with Wilson's well-placed *New Yorker* essay, other notices turned up in the *Virginia Quarterly*, *New York Herald Tribune Books*, *New York Times*, *New York Times Book Review*, *New Statesman*, and *Saturday Review*. It seems that the notices were rather well placed, and that they should have helped fuel sales, just as Powell had thought Wilson's essay would. Page agrees that the Wilson piece should have inspired sales for *The Golden Spur*: "Certainly such a review *should* have sold books," he writes, "but sadly, it didn't." In the end, the novel barely earned 30 percent of the $2,000 advance Viking had paid for it (*Bio*, 290). Despite all her long years of hard work, Powell would not live to see any of her books earn the kind of recognition she had always hoped they would.

An Updated "Message of the City"

New York City of the late 1950s and early 1960s was still as always about commerce and trade, about banking and Wall Street. In fact, in the four decades that elapsed since the young Dawn Powell wrote her first novel there, the island had become an even more important, more sophisticated commercial center than before. Now, of course, no longer does the quaint Sunshine Biscuit ad rule the skies; no longer does the view from atop the Empire State inspire the kind of breathless wonder it did in 1933. The Manhattan of the 1960s was a Manhattan vastly different from the one of Prohibition and flappers that Powell had encountered when first she arrived there all those years before. In the final years of the novelist's life, New York had become a city of beatniks and coffee houses, growing crime and rising prices, bulldozers and wrecking balls. But its essence had not changed, and its essence will not change. New York remains forever a city of dreamers and their dreams, a city to which midwesterners Zoe Bourne and Dennis Orphen, Prudence Bly and Lou Donovan, Amanda Keeler and Frederick Olliver, Rick Prescott and Jonathan Jaimison are eternally drawn and inextricably bound. Each day then as now hundreds if not thousands of newcomers from Ohio, Wisconsin, Iowa, Nebraska—to say nothing of the hundreds of other nations of the world—pour into the city in search of an elusive something that exists nowhere else, New York's symbolic gates twirling like a massive, perpetual turnstile allowing them entry. As Morris Gilbert says, "The phenomenon that New York is filled and possessed, year in and year out, with successions of provincials who presently become New York's New Yorkers is like a law of nature" (40). All of this—and, as we have seen, much, much more—is captured in the New York novels of Dawn Powell, and nowhere more effectively than in her final book, *The Golden Spur*.

CHAPTER SEVEN

"Turn, Magic Wheel"

The Changing Fortunes of Dawn Powell

An often overlooked literary great.

—John Joseph

In 1962, we will recall, Edmund Wilson famously asked the question that first brought Dawn Powell to the attention of Tim Page, Judith Pett, James Wolcott, and other important commentators. "Why is it," he wrote, "that the novels of Miss Dawn Powell are so much less well known that they ought to be?" ("Dawn Powell," 233). Wilson himself attempted to answer his question the moment he asked it, first mentioning Powell's aversion to publishers' lunches and parties, an aversion that has been well documented here and elsewhere. Like Wilson, Lauren Weiner said that Powell's "unwillingness to bow and scrape" probably cost her more than she knew. Her reluctance to take part in the publicity game that was so well played by, for example, Truman Capote and Mary McCarthy, "meant that the travails of . . . Holly Golightly, not those of Ebie Vane [of *Angels on Toast*] or Amanda Keeler Evans [of *A Time to Be Born*], made it into the minor-league pantheon of books-turned-into-major-motion-pictures. It meant that Mary McCarthy's out-of-print early fiction, and not Dawn Powell's, is today passed from reader to reader in frayed copies" ("Metropolitan," 41). Weiner goes on to say that Powell at her best and even at her less-than-best is still better than

Capote and McCarthy, who "each have a small place in the literary firma-
ment, [while] Dawn Powell has none. It is not an unfairness of Olympic
proportions, but it is still unfair" (41). Though Powell was certainly no wide-
eyed Pollyanna, she still always had faith that her books would one day be
lauded on their own merits, that she should not have to stoop to working
the publicity circuit like some small-time vaudevillian. Unfortunately, as by
now has become clear, she was incorrect. In death, of course, there can be
no easy means of "making it." As the *Boston Globe* notes, "a dead writer is
particularly hard to market because, crudely put, he or she cannot make the
rounds of talk shows or sit for the interviews necessary to sell books. . . . So
the writer needs champions of stature and indefatigability" ("Dawn Powell
Has Arrived," 2), champions such as those Powell so fortunately—and so
deservedly—had and has had in Gore Vidal, Tim Page, and others.

Wilson's article went on:

> No effort has been made to glamorize [Powell], and it
> would be hopeless to try to glamorize her novels. For in these
> novels, she does nothing to stimulate feminine daydreams. The
> woman reader can find no comfort in identifying herself with
> Miss Powell's heroines. The women who appear in her stories
> are likely to be as sordid and absurd as the men. There are no
> love scenes to rouse you or melt you. (233)

Clearly Wilson, the product of a vanished era, seems to have believed
that it was woman's special province to read and to write love stories, but
writing love stories was never one of Powell's primary concerns; even Wilson goes on to say, "But love is not Miss Powell's theme" (233). Still, it
should come as no surprise to recall that the critic preferred Powell's atyp-
ical romance novel, *A Cage for Lovers*, to her Ohio novels or her New York
books: in October 1957, having just finished reading *A Cage for Lovers*—not
only its title but its cover art proclaiming it to be unlike any other of Powell's works—Wilson wrote to Powell, "We have just read your book with
enthusiasm. It seems to me more complete and convincing than anything
else of yours, and is such a complete departure from anything else that I was
rather astonished by it and dare say I might not have recognized your hand
if I had not known you had written it" (*Edmund*, 78). Although Wilson
was more often than not a brilliant and sensitive critic, he was not without
his prejudices or his outdated views, particularly concerning women. As
his most recent biographer, Lewis M. Dabney, writes, "Though [Wilson]

looked up to and fostered intellectual women, in his work he interpreted the struggles of male artists and public figures, playing his part in the generation produced by World War I who challenged the Victorian deference to the feminine" (26). Not only was he not one to play "the deference to the feminine" game, but at times he could be downright intolerant of women. In *The Forties,* for example, he wrote disparagingly of Edna St. Vincent Millay's "continual complaining and having to be comforted," which, he added, "is one of the most annoying traits of women writers: Elinor Wylie, Louise Bogan, Anaïs Nin (Dawn Powell [is] the only woman I know, I think, who doesn't have it)" (288). He demanded certain qualities of his female friends and appreciated Powell's being, in his estimation, "an old-fashioned American woman not far from the pioneering civilization: strong-willed, stoical, plain-spoken, not to be imposed upon" (Meyers, 257). In fact, curiously enough, Wilson fondly told his elder daughter, Rosalind, that Dawn Powell was "actually a man" (*Bio,* 81). He once addressed a letter to both Powell and Cowley "Dear Messrs" and in his closing, once again, referred to the two as "chers messieurs" (*Letters on Literature,* 692).

James Wolcott faults Wilson's well-meaning article for "not doing much to take Powell out of the packing crate" (45); he adds that all the critic really needed to do was to "unbutton his vest and quote" (46) from her novels, echoing Rose Feld and Diana Trilling who so many years before had remarked on the novelist's eminent quotablity. Still, Wilson's quote-free *New Yorker* review did have much in it to recommend Powell to readers such as Page and Wolcott and Pett. For one thing, Wilson declared that "the mind, the personality behind [the books], with all its sophistication, is very stout and self-sustaining, strong in Middle Western common sense, capable of toughness and brusqueness; yet a fairyland strain of Welsh fantasy instills into everything she writes a kind of kaleidoscopic liveliness that renders even her hardheadedness elusive" ("Dawn Powell," 233). Additionally, he complimented the novelist's portrayal in *The Golden Spur* of a departed Village whose passing, again, he himself deeply lamented:

> She has imagined and established for her readers her own
> Greenwich Village world, which is never journalistic copy and
> which possesses a memorable reality of which journalistic fiction
> is incapable. Her chronicle extends from the days of such old-
> fashioned resorts as the Brevoort and the Lafayette, with their
> elegant and well-served French restaurants and domino-playing

> cafés, which encouraged the dignity of love and art and
> provided a comfortable setting for leisurely conversations. . . .
> Her chronicle, perhaps rather her poem, extends from the era of
> this rather tranquil quarter, now almost entirely destroyed. (234)

The paragraph then lapses into Wilson's own deep-seated regrets about the newer Village. Unfortunately, for all the good Wilson's essay eventually did Powell, some of his assertions in it seem to have established a critical pattern not unlike those set by all those bygone critics who faulted her for writing so many "odious" characters. Such a reviewer as John Updike, "an astute admirer of Wilson" (Meyers, xv), in an otherwise highly favorable review builds on the Wilson essay when he speaks of Powell's "failure to cater to the reader's need for wish fulfillment" (271). Similarly, Gore Vidal, who once pronounced Wilson "America's best mind" (Meyers, xv), at first glance might seem to be echoing Wilson when he writes of Powell's "failure to put a down payment on Love" (2), though "Vidal himself winced at Wilson's clumsy footwork" (Wolcott, 46) in the essay. In fact, Vidal is speaking ironically when he says,

> Dawn Powell never became the popular writer that she ought
> to have been. In those days, with a bit of luck, a good writer
> eventually attracted voluntary readers, and became popular.
> Today, of course, "popular" means bad writing that is widely
> read while good writing is that which is taught to involuntary
> readers. Powell failed on both counts. . . . [She] was that
> unthinkable monster: a witty woman who felt no obligation to
> make a single, much less final, down payment on Love or The
> Family; she saw life with a bright neutrality, and every host at
> life's feast was a potential Trimalchio to be sent up. (2)

Vidal's remarks were right on the mark: one of Powell's favorite reads was Petronius's *Satyricon*. As we have seen, she had read it many times and was rereading it shortly before her death, as she reported in a letter to her cousin Jack (*Bio,* 306). The author of the ancient Roman work, which was a satire as its name suggests, ridicules everyone and everything, not for purposes of sermonizing, judging, or reforming, but for amusement, just as Powell always did. Trimalchio, who through hard work and determination achieves enormous financial success, comes to be known for his overly lavish dinner parties.

Even before Wilson raised the question that came, after all, very late in Powell's career, others had wrestled with it, among them J. B. Priestley, who even posited that the trouble might lie in her very name, which he found suggestive of "ultra-romantic magazine serials" (*Bio*, 246). Powell herself, according to Page, believed that her name "conjured up the image of an unsuccessful stripper" (*Bio*, 246n).

Old friend and critic Matthew Josephson, whose astute but less frequently noted essay on Powell appeared in 1973, was another who attempted to determine why Powell was never as successful as she deserved to be. Stating that "Humor is acceptable to the public, but irony does not always make for popularity" (22), he footnoted these next remarks, asking "Can it be that in the USA women are not wanted as satirists? Several years ago Mary McCarthy, the novelist and author of the brilliant and coldly ironical autobiography, [1957's] *Memoirs of a Catholic Girlhood,* was characterized in *Time* as "The Lady with a Switch Blade" (22).[1] Terry Teachout takes Josephson's point a step further, positing that "what kept [Powell] under wraps for so long [was that] nobody thought that a writer so amusing could really be any good, especially if she was also a woman" (Intro, *Dud,* vii). Of course Powell is hardly the only good comedic writer to have been ignored; notwithstanding gender, comic works in general are often put aside: witness the omission of countless comedic films overlooked for Oscar consideration. Writing about the lack of appreciation for twenty-first-century writer Roy Blount Jr., *New York Times*' Jack Shafer says that his subject has been "marginalized as a humorist (like Mencken) because he knows how to write funny" (9). Comedy, satire, in this country, whether written by men or women, seems never to have been a very popular genre:

> George S. Kaufman famously declared that satire is what closes on Saturday night. He might have said much the same thing about satiric novels. Portraiture confined to too small a social space and containing too much acerbic wit generally rings up disappointing sales, excites scant academic interest, and then slides down the memory hole a decade later. . . . Dawn Powell is an instructive case in point. (Pinsker, 67)

Wilson agreed, finding in Powell's novels a satire more palatable to British audiences than to American, placing her comedy "closer to the high social comedy" of Waugh and Anthony Powell "than to any accepted brand of American humor" (236).

While Pinsker sounds certain about the reason behind Powell's lack of popularity, others seem flummoxed as they attempt to explain the neglect of such a profound talent, as Priestley does here. A handful, however, sound more sure-handed, as does Joseph Coates, who suspects that "It is probably the sharpness of her eye as much as anything else that precluded her greater popularity. Her great skill was in showing how people can con themselves into trouble, and every reader will probably find himself somewhere in her gallery of self-deceits" (4). Still, Adam Begley wonders, "Why didn't her books catch on? Was her satire too expert, her wit too deadly? Perhaps it seemed so at the time. To this reader she seems fond and forgiving, even when she detects a mother lode of pure human folly" (7). Like Begley, many other reviewers have noted in Powell a pronounced fondness for her characters, warts and all. That her characters so often raised the hackles of so many reviewers is well known. James Gibbons of the Library of America explains that

> Powell doesn't flinch from the consequences made inevitable
> by the weaknesses of her characters; she has the courage to
> do so without redeeming them in a perfunctory manner.
> It is this, at last, that accounts for the steadiness of nerve
> behind the writing. Her characters' failures, deficiencies, and
> the occasional hard-fought triumphs reveal the depth of her
> tough-minded vision, a vision all the more extraordinary for
> the sparkling surface of the prose. Always sharp, never cranky,
> and with a pagan's delight in the pleasures of this world,
> Powell's work elaborates the human comedy with a vigor
> matched only by its unpretentious wisdom. Much less might
> have been expected from a figure now emerging from so long
> a period of neglect. (159)

Because many lesser lights have in recent decades been unearthed and so extravagantly praised, readers and critics, understandably, will sometimes approach a new discovery with reservation if not suspicion. I, too, was not expecting much when I opened the first Powell novel I read, *My Home Is Far Away*. But five pages in and all my doubts were erased. The only time I felt disappointed in Powell was when I ran out of novels by her to read.

Publicity can be terrible. But only if you don't have any.

—Jane Russell

Also, Powell's publishers rarely spent much time or money promoting her books, and when they did, they frequently got things wrong. One may recall Powell's despondency at the muddle her publishers made of *Dance Night*, for example; her pronouncement, in 1940, that "a new book coming out no longer rouses any hope" (*Diaries* 179); and her despair about "the lack of any ad or announcement, the silence from publishing end, the all-too-familiar signals of another blank shot" (*Diaries*, 177). Margaret Carlin sums it up tersely: "Her fiction earned fine reviews, but for some inexplicable reason, the publicity machines of the time did not turn her into a literary icon. Her books were praised, put aside, forgotten" (1). Each time Powell moved from one publishing house to another in hopes of better treatment, deeper understanding, more accurate publicity, she was disappointed. Farrar and Rinehart let her down, as did Scribner's, Houghton Mifflin, even Viking after Cowley left as editor there (*Bio*, 295). In her last years Powell moved to Bennett Cerf's Random House, which had contracted her next book (*Letters*, 340n).[2] Powell was hopeful about working with writer and editor friend Morris Philipson at Random House, but she would die before the publishing house could either please or disappoint her.

As culturally and geographically specific as Powell's New York novels were, they manage to be timeless and universal.

—Gerald Howard, "How Dawn Powell Can Save Your Life"[3]

That Powell was a gifted portrayer of psychological insight has been established both here and elsewhere; that she was equally gifted at evoking time and place has also been shown. So adept was she at conjuring a long-vanished Village, an unsavory Times Square saloon, or a fleabag Chelsea hotel that some have seen her as dated, as evocative of a bygone era. Yet there is something unquestionably timeless about her vision, her characters, her representations of human nature. As Dos Passos wrote in "A Note on Fitzgerald," a sort of afterword to Fitzgerald's *The Crack-Up*, "It's the quality of detaching itself from its period while embodying its period that marks a piece as good" (338). Michael Feingold finds that although John Guare and Gore Vidal, two Powell supporters, "pay due praise to [her] talents," they at the same time seem nevertheless "to plump for her as the nostalgic spirit of a bygone age" (14). For Feingold, however, "while the names and places of New York may change, [Powell] notated the process of change so exactly that most of her events, suitably re-costumed, could be happening today; her work isn't so much a sentimental paean as a sardonic warning" (14). As was noted here in chapter 5, especially, Powell's last novels were in part warnings against rash redevelopment, mass destruction, displacing the old in the interest of the new—or the young.

Tim Page remarks on the relevance of Powell's works for present-day readers:

> Her novels are both period pieces and absolutely up-to-date.
> . . . The details of Bohemian life—fashions, neighborhoods
> . . . mating dances—may have changed; the spirit has not.
> And somewhere an eager, frustrated youngster, trapped and
> misunderstood in a town that does not comprehend ambition,
> is listening to trains roar through the night—automobiles and
> airplanes, too—and dreaming of cities far away. (Intro, *Dawn
> Powell at Her Best*, xxiii)

The characters who populate Powell's works are as recognizable as if they had been written today; their motivations equally comprehensible; the ways in which they strive, pose, dream as current as this morning's news. Herbert Muschamp in 1998 noted that "Powell would have been 102 years old" that November, "a shocking milestone," he said, given the "freshness" of her voice (1). Like Muschamp, Heather Joslyn finds Powell's writing "so appropriate to our time and place" that "you can't write about American literature these days without mentioning her" ("A Time").

Powell deplored the fate of the "writer of talent or genius" in our culture

> who never makes money and whose shabbiness and usually
> accompanying bitterness, profanity or simple rudeness makes
> him regrettable in the society which makes or breaks artists.
> These are the men [and women?] who must wait for death
> (instead of money) to make them socially desirable, to [see]
> their wit and wisdom collected, their lives exploited by
> weeping biographers and others who find them more palatable

in death than in life, more glamorous as misunderstood
geniuses dying in garrets than as living, bitter talent with
no tuxedo to make their presence acceptable at the PEN[4] or
Stork Club. (*Diaries*, 178)

She realized that she was not alone in her predicament, certainly not
the only talented writer destined in her lifetime to achieve little fame and
less fortune. Whatever the answer to Wilson's question is—and there is no
simple answer—Powell's one-time exclusion from the canon of American literature, her former disappearance from the literary history of New
York, once as complete as the disappearance of the Hotels Lafayette and
Brevoort, has been regrettable, robbing readers of a distinct American talent. Yet despite limited publicity for her books and disappointing sales,
Dawn Powell always worked on, committed to writing her novels, determined to leave behind a record of her impressions of the New York she so
loved. The Message of the City, as it happens, is located not in the Sunshine
Biscuit advertisement in the skies but instead in the Manhattan novels of
Dawn Powell, a series of heartfelt love letters to her adopted home.

NOTES

CHAPTER 1: "ALLOW ME TO INTRODUCE YOU"

1. Many sources put the year of her birth at 1897, Powell, according to Tim Page, having chosen to make herself a year younger at about the time she turned thirty (*Bio*, 77–78). But I would add that many of those born toward the end of any given year find their ages too often mathematically miscalculated, which may be a reason that Powell changed her birth year at that time. Page, however, says that he has caught Powell claiming to be born as late as 1900.

2. Powell wrote fifteen novels, though a few sources give the total as sixteen, counting *A Man's Affair*, the "very stunted novel" (Page, telephone, March 7, 2013) that was a 1957 abridgement of *Angels on Toast*.

3. Occasionally a lighthearted (and not very good) poem will turn up in Powell's journals or in a local newspaper article, but I know of only one serious published poem, "Dead Things," which appears in a 1925 anthology (Cheyney, 75). Clearly poetry was not her genre.

4. This novel, Powell's second (or the one she often called her first), was titled after Lord Byron's 1815 poem of the same name. For a time she had considered calling it *The Dark Pool*.

5. Jefferson ("Characters," 1) is playing on Henry James's words—"So this is it at last, the distinguished thing!"—which James reportedly spoke following his December 1915 stroke, thinking he was about to die (Edel, 2). He died the following year.

6. Two of Powell's novels do not figure into this equation: *A Cage for Lovers* (1957), a dark "Cinderella tale in reverse" (L. Kaufman, 1), set largely in Paris; and *A Man's Affair* (1956), a shortened reworking of *Angels on Toast*.

7. Ruminating on the various kinds of fame that an author might achieve, Powell spoke of "the famous writer who is touted to fame by journalists," the writer "whose actual work is of no importance but rides on personal notoriety," naming Dorothy Parker (1893–1967) as an example of the type (*Diaries*, 178).

8. In response to the *Times* article, Lee Adams (lyricist partner of composer Charles Strouse of *Bye Bye Birdie*, *Applause*, *Golden Boy*, and other musical plays) wrote a letter to the newspaper saying that in 1960 Powell,

Strouse, and he had begun working on a musical version of Powell's final novel, *The Golden Spur,* but that the novelist soon grew too ill to complete the project. Calling her "a tremendous talent" who wrote "funny, funny stuff," Adams added, "The Powell resurgence is long overdue."

9. Vidal's championing of Powell was nothing new. Even in her lifetime, in 1958, Vidal had lectured on Powell at Harvard, calling her "America's only satirist" (*Diaries,* 390). Still, to many it seems he had done too little too late for his friend.

10. Powell admired Vidal, too. She found him to be "a clear, sharply cut, extraordinary individual with a rich articulate gift" (*Diaries,* 338).

11. For more on Powell's short publications in the *New Yorker* and elsewhere, see chapter 3.

CHAPTER 2: "HIDDEN IN PLAIN VIEW"

Chapter title taken from *Hidden in Plain View,* a nonfiction account of the underground railroad, written by Jacqueline L. Tobin and Raymond G. Dobard.

1. Powell's first novel, *Whither,* would be published in 1925, exactly ten years after she made this pronouncement.

2. Like Dawn, young Marcia in the autobiographical novel *My Home Is Far Away* "had read and written almost as soon as she walked and talked" (25).

3. As Oscar Wilde once said, "Life is far too important a thing ever to talk seriously about."

4. Jacqueline Miller Rice (1931–2004) was named executor of Powell's literary estate on the author's death, but because of her own problems allowed the writings to languish, despite myriad requests for information or for permission to reprint. (See *Bio* for a thorough discussion.) It was finally Jack Sherman, Powell's closest cousin, who, at Page's urging, freed the estate from its long limbo. The papers of Dawn Powell have been housed at Columbia University ever since.

5. The issue of abortion was often on Powell's mind. Her play *Walking down Broadway* concerns an unwanted pregnancy ended by abortion, as does her 1942 novel, *A Time to Be Born.* An undated notebook of Powell's includes the following lines: "Women get jobs, get the vote, have their freedom, but there is one thing that never changes—a single girl who finds she's pregnant is still a girl in a jam" (*Bio,* 16).

6. Forbidden to touch any of the books in Sabra's home, Powell says she would frequently escape, while locked out of the house, to a neighbor's "fine rich household with hundreds of books where I read, where I learned to play piano," and where "Mrs. Kahnheimer advised me to read *Adam Bede*" (*Diaries,* 158–59).

7. About twenty years before Woolf's *A Room of One's Own* appeared, young Dawn, writing in treetops (*Diaries,* 229), hid her work but not well enough to keep her stepmother from finding and setting fire to it.

8. In the novel, Marcia finds a "silver-tasseled little whip in the street after the circus parade," which her stepmother "at once appropriated, saying grimly … 'You'll get your whip when you ask for it'" (221–22).

9. Incidentally, although of the three sisters Phyllis had faced the most savage treatment from Sabra, she was more forgiving of their stepmother than her sisters were.

10. All three girls would run away, in turn, each when she was in her early teens. Dawn's youngest sister, Phyllis, endured more abuse from her stepmother than her sisters did as the last of Roy Powell's daughters remaining at home (*Letters*, 131–32).

11. According to David Neal Lewis on Dawn Powell's Facebook page (March 16, 2014), "You wouldn't imagine that such a little town [as Shelby] could support a record label. But it did: http://45rpmrecords.com/OH/Cabut .php, probably since 1965."

12. Powell's beloved younger cousin, John "Jack" Franklin Sherman, would move in with Auntie May in Shelby when his parents died, not long after Dawn had come to live with her.

13. Powell's maternal grandmother, Julia Miller Sherman, who had been widowed in 1903 (*Bio,* 16), would eleven years later, at the age of seventy, marry Jesse Hostetter and promptly close her boardinghouse (*Letters,* 7).

14. A look at the original diaries demonstrates that Powell was a talented caricaturist.

15. At first, Auntie May seemed to have been unenthusiastic about Dawn's desire to go to college. A month before Powell died, writing to her cousin Jack Sherman, she asked, "Do you ever think of how Auntie May would be really baffled that anyone would want to leave Shelby or a job with a Shelby firm? I recall that when I thought of college she hastily spoke to Scott [?] about a job in the telephone office for me" (Peterson, 42).

16. In a 1958 letter to the *Lake Erie Nota Bene,* Powell remembered preparing for her arrival at Lake Erie College, which felt to her like being "shot from a cannon into the strange wonderful planet" that was the school, and having saved "every cent" she earned that summer of 1914 "working on the newspaper [the *Shelby Globe*] by day and ushering in a movie house by night" (*Letters,* 249). Powell did pay whatever tuition she was charged, or in any case she agreed to do so; according to Page, "the college was still chasing her down for money into the 1940s."

17. The two former roommates would meet again decades later when Powell spoke at Lake Erie College. Farnham, who had become a journalist, later visited Powell in New York while Joe was hospitalized (Peterson, 37).

18. Auntie May made quite a favorable impression on Powell's classmates at Lake Erie College when she came for a visit. Powell recounts her friends' saying that Auntie May was "perfectly fascinating" and recalls their looking admiringly at Dawn, "as if I were responsible for her" (*Letters,* 6).

19. Lake Erie College Library Director Christopher Bennett told me in a telephone conversation (August 26, 2006) that campus rumor has long had it that Dawn Powell never paid any tuition because President Small believed that "the college should absorb the interesting ones like Dawn." He did acknowledge that Powell ran the elevator, which he says is still there and in much the same condition it was in Dawn's day, though it has since been electrified.

20. The Shore Club, sometimes referred to as Shorelands, first opened circa 1899, a magnificent location and "an important center of social activity through most of the first twenty years of this [the twentieth] century" (P. K. Smith, 166). By 1940, however, the club was in ruins: "A recent trip . . . finds a deserted and saddened scene. The only buildings that remain are the annex, its windows barred or broken, other cottages and the former P. K. Smith home; a jungle of weeds and thicket over the land where the club house and other cottages [once] stood. The road along the bank has crumbled away, and there is no path to the beach" (Ahlstrom, 168). The property had previously been purchased by the Diamond Alkali Company, a chemical plant in Painesville, which drove salt wells into the land and laid railroad tracks across it (168).

21. The *Lake Erie Record* was originally published five times a year, but in 1917, the paper announced the year before Dawn graduated that "owing to the advance in price of paper, *The Record* will be published four times this year" (January 17, 1917). Presumably the paper shortages during the war had caused the increase. The *Record* remained a quarterly ever after, later changing its name. In 1996, Powell's friend William Peterson wrote of having asked her, in 1958, to write a column for the Lake Erie College literary magazine, now called *Nota Bene*.

22. Obviously not the John Steinbeck play and novel, which were not written until 1937. Powell refers to this drama, probably *Mice and Men* (1902) by London playwright Madeleine Lucette Ryley, as a "new sensation which has set all Europe aflame" (*Letters*, 9–10).

23. A somewhat later description, from a different source, says that Powell shared "the same apologetic, chuckly, half-hesitant manner that distinguishes Donald Ogden Stewart" (Crichton, 84). Although unfortunately no filmed record of Powell survives that we know of, one might get an idea of the charming behavior she is said to have shared with fellow Ohioan Stewart (1894–1980) by viewing him in the rare 1929 Marion Davies early talkie *Not So Dumb* or in 1998's *Robert Benchley and the Knights of the Algonquin*, readily available on DVD. Incidentally, Powell was very fond of Stewart, calling him "a really funny man" (*Diaries*, 163); and Kyle Crichton, similarly, found him "the wittiest man I ever met" (143). Powell's cousin Jack Sherman described her for Matthew Josephson as "pert, petite, and devastatingly witty and

astute" (36). Another description of Powell, late in life, provided by Broadway composer Charles Strouse in a telephone conversation, recalls her in her last years as "smallish, short, chubby, and absolutely delightful" (March 6, 2007).

24. Butterick dress pattern books will appear in 1944's *My Home Is Far Away* as a source of entertainment and longing for the young sisters (14).

25. The Interchurch World Movement was a short-lived "effort in ecumenical cooperation." Its aim was "broadly conceived to include evangelization, education, and social betterment" (Interchurch, 1).

26. The Bretton Hall, once a public inn, still stands at West 86th and Broadway; today it is a residence hotel. Built in 1902, it touted itself as "the largest uptown hotel, with 'all the comforts of New York City's best Hotels at one-third less price'" (Dunlap, 242).

27. Leon Edel surmised that the Bill Brown of whom Wilson speaks was "probably Wilson's Hill School friend William Adams Brown, a member of the banking family (Brown Brothers)" (Wilson, *Thirties*, 242n). But Tim Page, in a telephone conversation with me (October 28, 2007), said that he believes that the Bill Brown in question was more likely to have been William Slater Brown (1897–1997), a Greenwich Village resident and friend of e. e. cummings's who appears as a character in cummings's *The Enormous Room* (1922). The *New York Times* obituary for Dawn Powell describes William Slater Brown as "a hard-drinking, hard-smoking, womanizing writer whose circle of close friends went on to become some of the most prominent figures of 20th-century American letters: e. e. cummings, Hart Crane (the Ohio-born poet who would commit suicide at 32), Malcolm Cowley, Edmund Wilson, Djuna Barnes, Eugene O'Neill, Kenneth Burke, Matthew Josephson, John Dos Passos, and Edna St. Vincent Millay." Readers will notice that many of the artists on that list were close friends of Powell's as well. I agree with Page that this Bill Brown is the more likely friend at Wilson's party. He appears in a 1963 *Esquire* photo of Powell, Cowley, Josephson, Wescott, Man Ray, Virgil Thomson, and other artists and friends. Despite Brown's "hard-drinking, hard-smoking, womanizing" lifestyle, he lived to be a hundred.

28. The Café Royale—"Café Royal," as it is spelled in the 1939 *WPA Guide*—was located at Twelfth Street and Second Avenue; it was a "meeting place of the Jewish intelligentsia" where "vehement arguments [were] carried on for and against a new play, book, or art movement" (Gody, 124).

29. Peggy Brook Bacon (1895–1987), the accomplished Greenwich Village artist, author, caricaturist, and book illustrator, was for years an on-again, off-again friend of Powell's. Judith Stonehill reproduces in her 2002 book *Greenwich Village: A Guide to America's Legendary Left Bank* a delightful caricature that Bacon drew of Powell in 1934. Of the sketch Powell said that "it looked just like me, depressingly enough" (Stonehill, 51). Bacon noted that her subject was "sturdy" with a "robust body like [a] Brueghel roisterer . . . [having]

bright shoe button eyes far apart . . . [a] really ribald sophisticate au naturel" (51). A similar Bacon print was until recently housed at New York's Kraushaar Galleries (50) along with another Bacon print of Powell and one of Coburn Gilman, of whom more later. I am now the happy owner of all three prints. (The gallery's Katherine Degn tells me that she is a Powell fan who owns a Bacon drawing of Powell and one of Gilman.) For an excellent commentary on Bacon's work, see Roberta K. Tarbell's "Peggy Bacon's Pastel and Charcoal Caricature Portraits"; for reproductions of many of Bacon's portraits and drawings, see the artist's *Off with Their Heads* and *Personality and Places*. Sadly, none of Bacon's Powell prints makes it into either of Bacon's published collections, though Powell wrote in passing that her portrait was included in Bacon's 1934 show (*Diaries*, 85). The novelist mentions sitting for Bacon on February 1 of that year (*Diaries*, 83), the same year that Bacon won a Guggenheim fellowship for "creative work in the graphic arts" (Tarbell, 35). For a delightful interview with the elderly Bacon looking back, see Cummings, "Interview."

30. Page writes that compared to her husband, Powell was "downright temperate. . . . Joe indulged in daily three-martini lunches in the speakeasies near his office on Lexington Avenue; after work, he would regularly drink into the night until he passed out" (*Bio*, 53). As Powell wrote in 1930, "Joe tight so much and mentally blurred so it's impossible to talk with him. Makes me sick at heart and so tired emotionally to see him blah-blah drunk all the time with nights of horror that make me sorry for him yet worry so" (*Diaries*, 14). Two years later she would record that "drinking is getting to be a really terrifying thing so far as Joe is concerned" (*Diaries*, 60).

31. Ironically, had Powell passed her afternoons sitting around with the Algonquin set, she may well have written less but been better known.

32. The church's proper name is the Church of the Transfiguration; an Episcopal church, it has long been a good friend of theater folk.

33. For a time in 2007 and beyond, the historic Hotel Pennsylvania was slated to be razed, despite the efforts of many New York preservationists to save it. Happily that fate has at least temporarily been put off.

34. Before working in advertising, Joseph Gousha (pronounced "Goushay") had been a drama critic (*Letters*, 81).

35. The Pen and Brush Club, a nonprofit women's arts organization, was until November 2008 still housed in the same Greek Revival townhouse it had been in since 1923, at 16 East Tenth Street between Fifth Avenue and University Place. The same club would appear in Powell's 1962 novel *The Golden Spur* (41). Unfortunately, the long-lived artists' colony went on the market for $13.5 million when its owners said they could no longer "afford maintenance and repairs" on the old building, which was erected in 1848, though they were "considering the purchase of an alternative property in Manhattan" (Pogrebin, C1). On the organization's website, executive director

Janice Sands says that the Club has indeed found another space, this time in the Flatiron district, and reopened in the spring of 2013. The old Tenth Avenue building is now being converted into a single-family mansion.

36. Powell is referred to as "the underrated writer who was to become Lawson's loving muse" in Gerald Horne's study on Lawson, *The Final Victim of the Blacklist: John Howard Lawson, Dean of the Hollywood Ten.*

37. Canby Chambers (1895–1958) was "a charming, bibulous poet" and friend of Powell's (*Bio,* 58). He was the "longtime love" of Powell's close friend, editor Esther Andrews (see note 5 to chapter 3, below).

38. Margaret De Silver (1890–1962) was a longtime friend of Powell's. Like the author, she had an institutionalized child. An heiress, De Silver would rescue Powell and Gousha from poverty in the 1960s with a sizable trust.

39. Charles Norman related an episode in which he encountered Gousha and Powell in a Village bar: "A few years ago, I went in to the Cedar Tavern—the original one, on University Place near Ninth Street—and saw Joe Gousha in a booth. He was drinking a martini and reading the *World-Telegram* with a scowl. In another booth sat Dawn and Cobey [in various sources spelled alternately "Cobie" and "Coby"] Gilman, glowing with gin and laughter" (*Poets,* 55). See Page's biography for more on the relationship between Powell and Gilman. (See *Harper's Magazine* of December 1926 for a beautifully translated piece by Gilman from the French, called "She Had to Be Right.") Powell's *Diaries* and *Letters* include much mention of him as well, though they never reveal any intimate details. Still, Gilman (1893–1967) was a fond friend and perhaps lover of Powell's who, after Joe's death, remained a close companion, often sitting by her hospital bedside as she lay dying. He would die just two years later, in December 1967.

40. Powell's *Diaries* catalogue her many illnesses, which included anemia, "heart pain," jaundice, pleurisy, the Spanish flu, teratoma, frequent and often serious nosebleeds, high blood pressure, and the cancer that ultimately killed her. At the young age of thirty-four, Powell listed her extensive health woes, saying she could never be a hypochondriac because she could never "think up all the things wrong with me—teeth, sinus trouble, tonsils, rheumatism, tumor, ovarian cysts, and dandruff" (27).

41. Powell is joking here. She was just five feet tall.

42. Powell wrote a heartbreaking short story, "The Elopers," based on her daily bus rides out to Ward's Island to visit her institutionalized son. It first appeared in the *Saturday Evening Post* of August 24, 1963, and was added to the 1999 reissue of her 1952 collection, *Sunday, Monday and Always,* though it was not included in the original volume. The *Post* would publish a second piece of hers, "Weekend in Town," the following year.

43. Although we have no documentation that Powell ever met Fitzgerald, the two shared a good many friends, among them Hemingway and Wilson,

and for a time shared the same storied editor, Max Perkins. Tim Page is "sure she must have met him" (e-mail, December 30, 2008), given the circles the two writers ran in. Dos Passos noted that, in their early Bohemian years in New York, Hemingway and Fitzgerald "were always hovering about" (Horne, 24), and he includes Powell in "this enchanting circle" (24). Andrew Turnbull, Fitzgerald biographer and editor of Scott's letters to his daughter, asked Powell in 1957, as he was researching his subject, about Fitzgerald's relationship with Hemingway, believing that Powell had known both novelists (*Letters,* 244–45). In a 1945 letter to Edmund Wilson, Powell speaks of having met Frances "Scotty" Fitzgerald, Zelda and Scott's daughter (127). Coincidentally, not only were both Powell and Fitzgerald born in 1896, but their only children were born in 1921.

44. In a bon mot Powell surely would have enjoyed, Tennessee Williams (1911–1983), who toiled in Hollywood for a time, said that the scripts he wrote at MGM were little more than "celluloid brassieres" for female film stars (Bray, viii).

45. Decades later, after Powell had published what was to be her last novel, *The Golden Spur, Esquire* magazine asked her to go out to Hollywood to "do a piece" about James Stewart, who was then filming *Take Her, She's Mine,* with Audrey Meadows. The ailing Powell was all set to go, hoping the California locations and expense-account pampering might "bring roses to my cheeks." She had even been "bright enough to ask for more dough" than *Esquire* originally offered, but the assignment was not to be. The film company finished shooting early, and the story was canceled (*Letters,* 320). One cannot help wondering what a Powell piece on Jimmy Stewart would have been like and whether the California climate might have improved her health.

46. Frances Keene (1913–1997), Boston-born American writer, educator, and translator, was a good friend of Powell's (obituary).

47. Other favorite locations to which Powell would sometimes escape to write were the Hotel Traymore in Atlantic City and the Half-Moon Hotel at Coney Island (*Bio,* 168), though not surprisingly she reported missing Manhattan while away. Both hotels have since been razed.

48. Hope Hale Davis (1903–2004), American writer and friend of Powell's.

49. The magazine *Snappy Stories,* which ran somewhat irregularly from 1912 to 1932, has been called "an early example of liberated fiction full of free women" (philsp.com). Powell published at least one story in it, "There Goes the Bride," which appeared in the April 2, 1926, issue. In the spring of that year, Powell wrote to her sister Phyllis, "I have a story in the next *Snappy* and will send it if you're interested in belles-lettres" (*Letters,* 62). She was also published in a similar pulp called *Breezy Stories.*

50. Fleur Cowles (1908–2009), born Florence Freidman in New York City (obituary), was a well-known artist, writer, editor, crusader for wildlife

preservation, coeditor at *Look* magazine and founder of *Flair,* a publication that was and still is considered "the most intriguingly beautiful and creative modern magazine ever published" (Columbia, 1–2). The few remaining issues of *Flair* are highly sought after today. In 1996 a pricy, limited edition of a compilation called *The Best of Flair* was published and soon sold out, although it was republished three years later at the same price, $250. In 1996 Cowles published "an anecdotal memoir" called *She Made Friends and Kept Them,* its issue just preceding the release of *The Best of Flair.*

51. Raymond Orteig (1870–1939) would become famous as the man who put up the $25,000 prize money that Charles Lindbergh would win for his flight to Paris (Hirsh, *Manhattan Hotels,* 99). He was remarkable as a hotelier as well. Having emigrated to the United States in 1882, he began working at the Lafayette, ultimately working his way up to the position of maître d' there. Saving his money, twenty years later he bought the nearby Brevoort, "which had gained a reputation in the late 19th century as a stopping place for titled Europeans" (Turkel, 294), and then the Lafayette, long a favorite haunt of writers and other artists. In a letter to Rosalind Baker Wilson, Powell spoke of "the three brothers Orteig who ran the Lafayette," saying that her book should give them "no reason to froth" (*Letters,* 212).

52. Edmund Wilson tells an amusing story about Niles Spencer (1893–1951), Powell, and Gilman: "It was closing time in the Lafayette Grill, and Cobey Gilman was being swept out from under the table. Niles Spencer had been stuttering for five minutes, and Dawn Powell gave him a crack on the jaw and said, '*Nuts* is the word you're groping for'" (*Thirties,* 621–22).

53. Stuart Davis (1894–1964), Philadelphia-born American cubist painter, said to have been influenced by Gerald Murphy's style of pre-pop art.

54. Powell had known Reginald Marsh (1898–1954) since at least 1930, recording in her diary on July 22 of that year having had "lunch at a swell Chinese place on 14th Street" with him (15). Much later, not long before his death, he would design the jacket of her *The Wicked Pavilion* (*Letters,* 212n); the novel would mourn the demolition of Hotels Brevoort and Lafayette. From June through September 2013, Marsh's works were on display at the New-York Historical Society under the title "Swing Time"; the society has released a book of the same name.

55. The stroke would prove fatal, but Powell fortunately arrived in Ohio before he died (*Bio,* 7).

56. Wilson's letter, written more than three years after Powell's death, shows that his dear friend Dawn was still on his mind.

57. Morris Philipson (1926–2011) worked as editor at many New York publishing houses until he moved to the University of Chicago Press in 1966, where he served for one year as executive editor and then as director, finally retiring in 1999. He wrote five novels and many short pieces of fiction and

nonfiction (Rust, 1–4). On the front cover of his 1965 novel, *Bourgeois Anonymous,* Powell's praise for it reads "Worthy of Aldous Huxley." On the back cover is her comment in full: "Here is a fresh, mischievous approach to the contemporary American reverence for middleclassness. Mr. Philipson's record of an underground group fighting to overcome their natural bourgeois tastes and be individuals is worthy of Aldous Huxley, although the author has his own original brand of satire that should delight the perceptive reader."

58. I speak further of Joseph Mitchell and his book in chapter 6.

59. Clearly, Gilman had always cared very much for Powell; he may once have even asked her to marry him (Wilson, *Forties,* 306).

60. See Edmund Wilson's *The Sixties* or his *New Yorker* article, "Upstate Diary 1960–1970," for a moving portrait of the fatally ill Dawn Powell.

61. On his mother's death, Jojo, forty-four years old and by then a ward of New York State, would be placed under the legal guardianship of Powell's dearest cousin, Jack Sherman, until Jojo's death on Christmas Day 1998, at the age of seventy-seven. Page, grateful for Sherman's generosity and kind assistance, named a son after him. Jack Sherman passed away on May 9, 2007, aged ninety-six. Jack's sister, Rita A. Sherman, having literally been left at the altar on her wedding day (Page, telephone), lived with Jack for much of her life. She died at ninety-one on July 14, 2013.

62. Richard Lingeman says that "the fate of [Powell's] remains might suggest another sad chapter in the annals of America's neglect of its finest writers" (38). After Powell's death, her good friend Edmund Wilson wrote, "I have felt that some part of my own life was gone" (*Sixties,* 490), and in a letter to Dos Passos not long after her passing he told his friend, "I have been rather upset by Dawn's death" (*Letters on Literature,* 657).

63. It was John Treville Latouche (1914–1956), writer, lyricist, and librettist, who introduced Powell to Gore Vidal (*Bio,* 236).

64. Dwight Fiske (1892–1952), well-known nightclub entertainer, author, and recording artist. A performer of "deadpan stream of consciousness monologues," he was discovered by Tallulah Bankhead (Riddle, 1). "In the 1930s, a young lady had not experienced living if she had not seen Dwight Fiske. At every party . . . you had to hear one of his records" (Reed, 2). Fiske's 1933 book, *Without Music,* is dedicated to Powell, who wrote or cowrote many of his stories and monologues, as many as thirteen of the twenty-five included in the above-mentioned volume (*Diaries,* 73). Her *Turn, Magic Wheel* is dedicated to Fiske, and *The Happy Island* features a female character said to be based on him (Reed, 2).

65. Djuna Barnes (1892–1982), American writer remembered primarily for her 1936 novel, *Nightwood.*

66. Edmund Wilson's daughter, Rosalind, who later would become Powell's editor at Houghton Mifflin (*Bio,* 103), was very close to Powell. She

even wrote that she wished her father had married Powell instead of Mary McCarthy: "Mary was never a sympathetic intellect to me. Had my father married Dawn Powell I would have found her sympathetic and someone I really wanted to be with" (Kiernan, 154). But Powell, it seems, had no romantic interest in Wilson, nor he in her.

67. Madame Récamier (1777–1849), "celebrated French beauty, was considered . . . the most beautiful and graceful woman of her day" ("Madame," 1). Her salon attracted the great thinkers of her time, much as Powell's evenings at the café of the Hotel Lafayette attracted many of the most forward-thinking artists and writers of her day.

68. The Johnsons were known for their books and films recounting their travels to Africa, the South Pacific, and Borneo. That year their film *Across the World with Mr. and Mrs. Martin Johnson* had opened; it captured the impish Powell's imagination ("Martin and Osa Johnson," 1–3).

69. Sullivan wrote his year-end "Greetings, Friends" column from 1932 until 1974. Two years later, Roger Angell, noted baseball writer, *New Yorker* editor—and, incidentally, Dawn Powell fan (see section "The Dawn Powell Revivals," this chapter)—took the reins, continuing the tradition until 1998, at which time the column disappeared because Angell found it increasingly difficult to rhyme names. In 2008, however, Angell and his column, both of which the *New York Times* refers to as the "Rhyming Name Dropper," returned. Angell said he had begun to miss writing the holiday poem and had lately been inspired (Garner).

70. Hannah Green (1927–1996) was, like Powell, a novelist born in Ohio; the two women met when both were staying at Yaddo and remained close friends until Powell's death. Author of acclaimed novel *The Dead of the House,* she was married to artist John Wesley ("Hannah Green Papers").

71. *Processional, A Jazz Symphony of American Life,* was a popular four-act play written by John Howard Lawson and published in 1925, the same year that *Whither* was published. Coincidentally, as has been noted, Lawson and Powell would later meet and have a long-term affair, as Jeffrey Lawson remembers.

72. Charles Norman would become a lifelong friend of Dawn and Joe's (*Bio,* 76).

73. Powell, who had heard from a friend that Robinson had mentioned her novel in his column, said she thought it "nice" to have been included in the Ohio paper (*Letters,* 54). It seems, however, that she had not seen his unflattering column herself, or that she was putting a positive spin on it for her correspondent, as was often her style.

74. Robinson's words "snappy fiction" may well be a reference to a popular publication of the day, *Snappy Stories,* in which Powell would be published the following year.

75. *Last Year's Nest* (1925), by Dorothy à Beckett Terrell (n.d.), writer of novels, romances, and religious tracts (Between the Covers). Its dust jacket reads, "When a woman with a grown-up daughter [marries a much younger man], it is a dangerous thing."

76. *Singing Waters,* by Elizabeth Stancy Payne (?–1944). She wrote at least eight novels and other "miscellaneous" pieces (Between the Covers).

77. In print, *Whither* remains scarce, but it is available on Archive.org (https://archive.org/details/whitheoopowe) free of charge, news that would likely exasperate Powell.

78. Today, *Dance Night* is considered one of Powell's finest novels. John Updike, for example, says that it "partakes of Sherwood Anderson's wistful mood of small-town disquiet and projects the blurred largeness of and emotional force of helpless childhood impressions" ("Ohio Runaway," 263).

79. Powell herself called *The Tenth Moon* "a quivering book filled with pain and beauty" (*Diaries,* 214).

80. For more on Powell's short pieces, see the section "Short Stories, Essays, and Reviews" in chapter 3.

81. George S. Kaufman often said that "the newspapers treat both the safe-cracker and the playwright as common criminals," an assessment with which Powell would likely agree (Teichmann, *George,* vii).

82. Powell objected in her diary to the way that even some cast members were interpreting her characters: "I am getting crotchety about their moral, superior attitude about the play: the people [characters] seem to me to be anybody, only their high points are exaggerated. . . . Certainly 'cheap' is not the word for the lowest common human denominator any more than 'brutal' is the word for truth" (61). Obviously Powell sympathized with rather than judged her characters. This same sort of criticism would dog Powell all her life.

83. *Dinner at Eight,* by George Kaufman and Edna Ferber, was first produced in 1932.

84. *Dangerous Corner,* written by J. B. Priestley, an admirer of Powell's later works, had been produced the previous year.

85. Benchley, too, tried his hand at writing for the stage. A project for Fred and Adele Astaire, *Smarty* was scored by Ira and George Gershwin; Benchley worked on the book with Fred Thompson. It proved a dismal failure (Altman, 244).

86. The caption to an Associated Press photograph of Spring Byington and Ernest Truex in the original production (included in this volume) states, "The central figure in the comedy is said to be based on the life of a well known actress." Having never heard that assertion before, I asked Tim Page whether he had; he replied that he had not but added that Powell and famed actress Katharine Cornell had been "briefly close." Still, he was not at all

certain that the play had been based on Cornell or in fact on anyone in particular. Page surmised that the AP reporter might have had added that line on his or her own.

87. Carol Hill Brandt (1904–1984), Powell's literary agent, after Ann Watkins, from 1935 (*Bio*, 92); Brandt represented John Dos Passos, Thornton Wilder, Vincent Sheean, and others (obituary).

88. Richard Halliday (1905–1973), story editor and producer; later husband and agent of Broadway star Mary Martin.

89. Matthew Josephson noted that many satirists, "from Voltaire to Aldous Huxley," have faced "similar charges" (44).

90. Even as astute a theater director and critic as Powell friend and associate Harold Clurman faulted O'Neill for his characters, as so many critics faulted the novelist for hers. About the original 1946 production of O'Neill's classic drama *The Iceman Cometh*, Clurman complained, "The world cannot be represented by a bunch of drunks who fail to do anything" (Canby, 1). However, the award-winning actor Kevin Spacey, who has brilliantly interpreted O'Neill onstage many times, says of the playwright, "[He] had a way of writing about characters who were so personal to him—without any judgment. He just writes them, flaws and all, and lets you make up your own mind" (Haun, 10). Powell had long said the same thing about what she was attempting with her characters.

91. Here Vidal is alluding to Diana Trilling's husband, noted Columbia University professor, essayist, critic, and novelist Lionel Trilling (1905–1975), and his 1947 novel *The Middle of the Journey*. For what it's worth, Trilling's novel opens on a train, as do almost all of Dawn Powell's New York books, but his train is leaving New York and heading for the provinces, while Powell's are always leaving the provinces and heading for New York. Continuing the allusion to Professor Trilling's novel, Diana Trilling (1905–1996) in 1993 published a memoir called *The Beginning of the Journey*, in which she names Dawn Powell as one of the "imposing array of authors" she was given to review, as opposed to the authors "of no interest" whom she more frequently was assigned (338).

92. Frances Milton Trollope (1780–1863), who often published under the name Mrs. Trollope and was frequently called "Fanny," was the mother of famous Victorian novelist Anthony Trollope (1815–1882).

93. Powell did enjoy some success abroad. Her novels generally received more favorable reviews in England than in the United States; her first British publication was *Turn, Magic Wheel*. Today some of her novels have been translated into French, German, Italian, and Spanish.

94. Although compared to many other writers of her day, Powell was exceptionally productive (she wrote and published more works than Hemingway and Fitzgerald combined), today we might think of the prodigious output

of Joyce Carol Oates or John Updike, for example, to which Powell's output might seem to pale in comparison. As for other woman writers, especially of Powell's time and before it, we may recall that in *A Room of One's Own* Virginia Woolf famously spoke of the difficulties peculiar to her sex, stating that what a woman needed to write was a quiet room of her own, money, and preferably no children. The successful woman writer is often childless: of Great Britain's notable female authors, Christina Rossetti, Jane Austen, George Eliot, the three Brontë sisters, and Woolf herself come to mind. On this side of the Atlantic, Edith Wharton, Emily Dickinson, Louisa Mae Alcott, Willa Cather, Dorothy Parker, Edna Ferber, Katherine Anne Porter, Edna St. Vincent Millay, and the afore-mentioned Oates, among others, had no children. The fact that Powell's son was so troubled makes her output seem all the more remarkable. That he would often scream meaningless phrases over and over into her ears as she sat writing, and that she still managed to produce the remarkable work that she did, is almost unfathomable. (Incidentally, not only were the majority of the female writers named above childless, but, like Powell, they were left motherless early in their lives.)

95. Oft-quoted line by Gore Vidal.

96. Nicholas Birns writes: "Sometimes Powell's admirers have done her as much harm as good. Lisa Zeidner, writing in the *New York Times Book Review*, overdoes it when she says Powell is 'wittier than Dorothy Parker, dissects the rich better than F. Scott Fitzgerald, is more plaintive than Willa Cather in her evocation of heartland, and has a more supple control of satirical voice than Evelyn Waugh" (2). For that same reason I did not include that particular Zeidner review in this book, though clearly the critic had good intentions and though I do quote from other pieces by her in this work. I heartily recommend Birns's entire essay.

97. A writer's popularity too often could be double-edged, according to Powell's friend Hemingway, who once said, "If you have success, you have it for the wrong reasons. If you become popular it is always because of the worst aspects of your work." Powell may have agreed.

98. The novels included in *Dawn Powell at Her Best* are *Dance Night* and *Turn, Magic Wheel.*

99. The first Library of America volume includes novels written from 1930 to 1942: *Dance Night; Come Back to Sorrento* (or *The Tenth Moon*); *Turn, Magic Wheel; Angels on Toast;* and *A Time to Be Born.* Volume 2 includes novels written from 1944 to 1962: *My Home Is Far Away, The Locusts Have No King, The Wicked Pavilion,* and *The Golden Spur,* all selected by Tim Page.

100. Tim Page recounted on Christopher Purdy's radio program that when he first became enamored of Powell, he would ask sellers of used books whether they had any volumes by Dawn Powell. "I have never heard of Donald Powell," they would invariably reply (Purdy, WOSU).

101. Hollywood has often been interested in Powell's novels. Upon the release of *A Time to Be Born* in 1942, for example, David O. Selznick offered an option on the film rights, but Powell refused to sell. *The Story of a Country Boy* (1934) had already been filmed, disastrously, as *The Man of Iron* (*Bio*, 137). Tim Page reports that the actress Anne Baxter, who had costarred with Bette Davis as the title character in the 1951 Oscar-winning film *All about Eve*, telephoned Powell to ask about the stage and film rights to *A Cage for Lovers*, though nothing ever came of it (*Bio*, 260).

102. Teachout humorously refers to himself as "a Little Powell Guy," in contrast to his friend Tim Page, whom he calls "the Big Powell Guy" ("About Last Night," 5). In the same article he tells of being thrilled when Page presented him with a gift of one of Powell's "Thurberesque" caricatures (6).

103. Philadelphia-born Helene Hanff (1916–1997), most famous for her 1970 book *84, Charing Cross Road*, had like Powell come to New York to become a playwright. And though she wrote "at least a play a month," she never produced a single one. She did write several other books, though none saw the success of *84, Charing Cross Road*, which in 1987 was made into a film starring Anne Bancroft and Anthony Hopkins. But Hanff "always considered herself a playwright rather than an author. She spent all her adult life in New York working in temporary jobs, such as selling theatre tickets and writing press releases for theatrical agents, in order to finance her writing" (obituary).

104. Gellhorn (1908–1998), the journalist and war correspondent, was Ernest Hemingway's third wife, from 1940 to 1945. Hemingway had left his second wife, Pauline Pfeiffer, for Gellhorn. Pauline was the sister of Powell's close friend Virginia Pfeiffer.

105. Too often, however, Powell is still excluded from such compilations and essays. Though her *Turn, Magic Wheel* features an exquisite tribute to the Empire State Building, which is included in the *Turn, Magic Wheel* chapter below, the writer of a recent *New York Times* article commemorating the building's seventh-fifth anniversary falls back on the overused—and not terribly compelling—lines from the 1957 Cary Grant/ Deborah Kerr film *An Affair to Remember*, seemingly unaware of Dawn Powell (Kingwell, 1–3). The recent *New York, New York: The City in Art and Literature* fails to include Powell, while such less-talented and less-productive writers as Djuna Barnes are included (Lach). The book is introduced by Brooke Astor, a one-time Powell admirer. The recent *Literary Landmarks of New York* (Morgan), too, fails to mention her. In 1996, Daniel Aaron noted: "It does seem strange to find no entry for her in *The Oxford Companion to American Literature*, or in *Notable American Women*, or in Kenneth Jackson's recent *Encyclopedia of New York* and strange, too, that she is not mentioned in Ann Douglas's *Terrible Honesty*, her survey of culture in Manhattan in the 1920s" (37).

106. Like Margaret Carlin, Sanford Pinsker imagines Powell's reaction to her newfound fame: "My hunch is that she is probably laughing sardonically in whatever corner of heaven (or circle of hell) writers are consigned to . . . and also that she will be eternally grateful" (69).

107. In another *Sex and the City* connection, actress Cynthia Nixon, who played Miranda in the series, has been a Powell fan since 2001, after having been introduced to her by the designer Isaac Mizrahi, a fan since 1995. In 2002 Nixon read from *A Time to Be Born* for the Atlantic Theatre Company at a benefit for the three theaters that were putting on the Powell "Permanent Visitor" celebration (Mandell, 5).

CHAPTER 3: "EVERY ARTIST WRITES HIS OWN AUTOBIOGRAPHY"

"Every artist writes his own autobiography," taken from Havelock Ellis (1859–1939), *The New Spirit,* 1920.

1. From a letter dated June 1931 from Powell to her cousin Jack Sherman (*Letters,* 76).

2. Edmund Wilson reported that Powell, who claimed to be part Native American (she was part Welsh and part Irish as well) often "amused herself by talking about" her Indian background, though she said that her sisters were ashamed of it. John Lardner (1912–1958), also part Native American, would jokingly tell her, "Oh, you Ohio Indians are just poor red trash" (*Sixties,* 26).

3. No longer extant Spanish restaurant located near the Brooklyn Bridge, run by old Senor Sebastian Catalan and his wife, Valentina (*Diaries,* 97), both originally from Spain; Powell and her friends frequented it regularly throughout the 1930s (*Diaries, passim*).

4. "Sue" here refers to Susan Edmond Lawson (1895–1997), wife of John Howard Lawson (1894–1977), with whom, as we have seen, Powell likely had an intimate affair. According to Page, "the two women evidently hated one another pretty much from the start, but Powell seems to have been half determined to stick it out and become the other's great friend" (*Bio,* 63).

5. Esther Andrews (1890–1962), editor and writer who had been a close friend of D. H. Lawrence (*Bio,* 58), was a lifelong Powell friend.

6. This line is reminiscent of a comment in *Whither,* in which one roommate says of a fellow tenant and her latest beau, "I'll bet she was mighty flattered when he told her his base intentions. Insults are such a tribute" (91).

7. Berkeley Tobey (1885–1962), a John Reed (1887–1920) associate, wrote for "the original *Masses,* the leading radical organ of its time" (*Bio,* 498). He later married Esther McCoy (1896–1989), noted architectural historian and writer (Dawson).

8. In the diaries readers frequently sees Powell planning two novels, or a play and a novel, at one time.

9. Reading Woolf's diaries upon their release, Powell found them "self-conscious, intense, exhausting, pecking away at her heart, brain, soul" (*Diaries*, 336).

10. John Waters, filmmaker, born in Baltimore. In 1998 he chose Dawn Powell as one of his top objects of interest ("John Waters' Top Ten," 1), later contributing this jacket blurb to her *Letters*. He goes on to refer to Powell as "the wittiest, most terrifyingly personal writer you never heard of."

11. The volume includes letters from Powell to all of her immediate family members save her father. It is more than likely that Dawn wrote to her father, for she always remained fond of him, but we know of no surviving letter from her to him. Given her stepmother's history of burning the girl's writings, it is possible that the older woman destroyed the letters—either before or after Roy Powell read them.

12. This letter is dated December 6, 1918; Powell had arrived in the city on September 2 of that year, so she had been in New York for closer to two months than three.

13. Frank Shea (1888–1954), born in New Jersey, was a bookseller, writer, publisher, actor, and well-known character about Greenwich Village until he and his wife moved to Provincetown, Massachusetts ("The Shop"). Powell must have been confusing Provincetown with Gloucester. Robert Kemp (1878–1959) was a literary critic, as were Floyd Dell, Edmund Wilson, and Lewis Gannett; the last three appear throughout these pages.

CHAPTER 4: "MIGHTY THINGS FROM SMALL BEGINNINGS GROW"

1. The novel is so rare that very few copies are known to exist, and only two are believed to survive in dust jacket. One of those copies belongs to University of Delaware Director of Libraries Susan Brynteson, a Powell collector who is affiliated with Yaddo, the writer's residence where Powell stayed in the late 1950s and again in 1960. Ms. Brynteson kindly sent a photograph of the dust jacket and liner notes to me. The notes read:

> Dawn Powell has traced with her pen a cross-section of New York City life as a young girl finds it, and presents her picture with unusual zeal and piquancy, tinged just enough with satire. Realistic, yet it has beauty, that potent charm so entirely lacking in the vast majority of realistic novels.
>
> What small-town girl alone in New York does not find herself staring life face to face? Even the closest of friends can not solve problems for her, and the impersonal acquaintances, who are scrambling for "Art for Art's sake," because they must amuse themselves, are poor teachers. But Zoe is strong and daring, though too serious in her purpose not to have a difficult

time of it. She drives forward, suffers necessarily, then finds the
way more happily with the uplifting influence of love.

As readers of this work shall see, it was this very tidy and conventional
ending that so troubled Powell. It is noteworthy that the blurb writers actually sound as if they had read the novel, a trouble it seems few went to when
"promoting" her later works.

2. Unfortunately, no copy of the film has ever been located, though I did
find a lobby card for it.

3. Olive Thomas (1894–1920), famed beauty and actress "better known
for the horrific nature of her death" at the age of twenty-five "than for
her thespian talents." She had left her small-town Pennsylvania home
for New York, where she was "discovered by illustrator Harrison Fisher.
Her modeling career led to . . . a spot in the 1915 *Ziegfeld Follies*" ("Olive
Thomas," allmovie.com, 1) and a blossoming film career. In 1917 she married
Jack Pickford, brother of screen star Mary Pickford (*Olive Thomas Collection*). Her gruesome death was the result of her having ingested "bichloride
of mercury after a round of the little cafés of Montmartre" with Pickford
(Farnsworth, 89). It has never been discovered whether she swallowed the
poison purposefully or accidentally. Ivo Dawson (1879–1934) was a British
silent film actor.

4. Tim Page makes no secret of the fact that he disliked *Whither* nearly as
much as Powell did. Still, after reading this book, he told me that my evaluation of the novel made him "*almost* want to read it again."

5. As for Powell's being unsentimental, Glenway Wescott, upon first
meeting her, found her "touching and distinguished," to which Powell replied, "I don't get the 'touching'" part (*Diaries*, 200).

6. In *Sister Bernadette's Barking Dog: The Quirky History and Lost Art of Diagramming Sentences,* Kitty Burns Florey parses this phrase and the several lines
that follow it (108–9). Powell's prediction, as it happens, was not far off the mark.

7. Powell seems to be echoing the famous dictum of Francis Bacon (1561–
1626) here: "Only the foolish wait for opportunities, while the wise create
them." She also sounds much like French writer Jules Renard (1864–1910),
who said, "Talent is a matter of quantity. It does not write one page, it writes
three hundred." http://used.addall.com/New/quote.cgi?quoteNum=115.

8. Author, socialist, activist, Provincetown player, and Powell friend Floyd
Dell (1887–1969) would similarly introduce readers to a pair of "writers who
did not write" in his compilation of short stories, *Love in Greenwich Village.*
Dell's charming book was published in 1926, the same year that he and Powell
first met and a year after Powell's first novel had been issued. Incidentally,
Floyd Dell is portrayed—though briefly—by actor Max Wright in *Reds,*
Warren Beatty's acclaimed 1981 film.

9. Mrs. Horne's boardinghouse has more than its share of dreamy non-doers and no-talents, one of whom is Fania, an aspiring designer. Looking at one of Fania's sketches, Zoe "was surprised" to find that "it was just the sort of sketch anyone might have done, artist or no artist" (69).

10. John Chapin Mosher (1892–1942), editor, short-story writer, and film critic who began at the *New Yorker* in 1926 (obituary); he would serve as the model for a sympathetic but ill-fated character in Powell's 1938 novel *The Happy Island* (*Diaries,* 119). Even his obituary in the *New Yorker* says he produced fiction only "from time to time." He wrote an essay on Scott Fitzgerald for the magazine in 1926, called "That Sad Young Man."

11. Again, as readers shall see, a character partly based on John Mosher appears in Powell's 1938 novel, *The Happy Island.*

12. In this sense nothing like Zoe, Powell would complete three novels and begin her fourth in the 1920s; she also wrote several plays and many essays and short stories during that decade.

13. Powell's recurrent disparagement of these nonwriting types calls to mind William Hazlitt's words, "The only impeccable writers are those who never wrote" (200).

14. *The Tree of Heaven,* by May Sinclair (1863–1946), a best seller on its release in 1917, underwent four more printings in the following year.

15. Pelham Heath Inn was a famous Bronx nightclub where the popular bands of the day performed and from which live shows were broadcast nightly across the country. The club closed in 1952.

16. Though Zoe clearly dislikes Chuck, she is upset that he doesn't like her: "Zoe had no particular liking for either of the two men," the narrator says. "But to have them dare to dislike *her*—" (53).

17. Women's magazines of the day encouraged women to stay in the home and attempted to make housework into a full-time job, even promising them a sort of "social status for unpaid household work" (Scanlon, 68). Powell obviously was wise to the game.

18. In *Love in Greenwich Village,* Floyd Dell wrote that no artist really ever starved there, that friends and café owners would always contribute a sandwich or loaf of bread to the artist, just as Dave does Dariel here (*passim*).

19. From a 1918 letter to her older sister Mabel, written not long before Powell moved to New York.

20. *The Happy Island*'s Jefferson Abbott is the sole exception to this rule.

21. The mythology of the hopeful striver discovering his lack of talent and nobly returning home is not seen in Powell, though our literature is rife with it even through the present period: for example, Woody Allen's 1994 *Bullets over Broadway,* set in 1920s New York, ends with the protagonist, a failed playwright, returning to Pittsburgh to marry and begin a family, giving up all aspirations of a theatrical career. But Allen does have at least one thing

in common with the novelist: in 1948 Powell wrote of a movie actor stepping out from the screen to connect with an audience member (*The Locusts Have No King,* 9), just as Allen will do some four decades later in *The Purple Rose of Cairo.*

22. Unlike Powell, Zoe never "does" the Village except when Myers, Julie, or Kane drags her there.

23. Years after Dawn had escaped to Auntie May's home in Shelby, her aunt often took her to the "most prestigious department store in the state, Halle Brothers in Cleveland," where Auntie May worked as a buyer (*Bio,* 18). The great department store, which featured uniformed doormen, had been established in 1891 (Wallen, 72). Incidentally, Cleveland-born actress Halle Berry was named for the store.

24. From the ending of Charlotte Brontë's *Villette,* which Brontë included largely because her father insisted on a "happy" ending (596).

25. In an interesting coincidence, cofounder of the Rehearsal Club Jane Harris Hall (1877–1956) was a deaconess at the Church of the Transfiguration, or the Little Church around the Corner, where Dawn Powell and Joseph Gousha were married (Church, 1).

26. In Powell's novel, the girls at the rooming house pay fifteen dollars a week, room with one other girl, share a bath with several, and receive two meals a day. In the film, the exact figure is not mentioned (though the proprietor lacks change for the fifty-dollar bill a new tenant gives her), the girls pay by the week, get two meals a day, share a bath, and room with another. When Kathleen Conry lived at the Rehearsal Club in 1966, the fee had been increased only to twenty-six dollars a week; the other arrangements had not changed.

27. Rehearsal Club lore has it that in 1936 or '37 Edna Ferber roomed there, incognito, soaking up material for the play. The role-hungry (and often literally hungry) housemates were devastated, however, when the team of Kaufman and Ferber neglected to hire even one of the actresses from the club for the most insignificant of parts (Conry, telephone). Ferber is frequently remembered unkindly: according to Lee Israel, she was "a scold, a snob, a low-profile dominatrix whose corseted asperity was never far from busting out" (quoted in Mallon, 15). Alexander Woollcott also had some choice words for her. See note 33 to chapter 5 on *The Locusts Have No King.*

28. Although sales figures for *Whither* are not available, Powell noted in her diary that she had earned only $545.00 the year it was published (82). In an interesting side note, F. Scott Fitzgerald recalled telling his publisher, Scribner's, that he "didn't expect" his first book, 1920's *This Side of Paradise,* "to sell more than twenty-thousand copies, and when the laughter died away I was told that a sale of five thousand was excellent for a first novel" ("On *This Side of Paradise,*" 337). Sales of *Whither,* of course, did not come close to that figure. It was not until 1930 that Powell saw sales of a novel of hers approach

it: *Dance Night*, whose sales and reception deeply disappointed her, sold just under five thousand copies on what Powell called its "regular" (first) release, though she reported that its reprint edition sold seven thousand copies (*Diaries*, 106).

29. Lewis Mumford (1895–1990), New York–born writer, was the longtime architectural critic for the *New Yorker*.

30. By October 1934, Powell had changed the name of the main female character from Lila to Effie, as it would remain. It so happens that Powell's Columbus cousin Charlie Miller, on whom she had based the protagonist of the Ohio novel *The Story of a Country Boy*, was married to a woman named Effie (*Diaries*, 204). Powell would then begin referring to the still untitled book as "the Effie novel" (95).

31. Effie and Corinne are the novel's two female protagonists; readers will learn more of them in the next pages.

32. John Updike, in a lecture series he delivered at the Metropolitan Museum of Art called "Art Creates the City," cited this same Statue of Liberty passage of Powell's in the lecture he gave on December 5, 1995, appropriately called "The Glittering City." Updike read another passage from this same Powell novel: "a laundress in the basement yard singing over her clothes-hanging, the swish of a broom on stone and hydrant splashing over cement court, the endless flow of trucks and streetcars and fire engine all translated into a steady throb in the walls of [the hero's] fourth-floor room" (*More Matter*, 83). In his lecture, Powell comes immediately after Fitzgerald.

33. The *New York Times* reviewed *The Great Gatsby* upon its release, praising its "whimsical magic and simple pathos that is realized with economy and restraint" and calling it "a curious book, a mystical glamorous story of today. It takes a deeper cut at life than hitherto has been essayed by Mr. Fitzgerald. He writes well—he always has—for he writes naturally, and his sense of form is becoming perfected" (Edwin Clark). Unfortunately, sales were not good. By 1934, however, the novel was being called "a classic" (Scribner, xiv).

34. Although Tim Page finds that Powell "seems to have taken small interest in the works of F. Scott Fitzgerald" (*Bio*, 145), and a list she wrote in 1953 of her dozen or so favorite novels does not include him, she had seen the Broadway play based on *The Great Gatsby* in 1926 (*Diaries*, 7), and it is almost certain that she had read the novel. Later, in 1959, she would propose to her good friend, the editor Monroe Stearns (1913–1987), that she write a volume on Dickens in the style of Fitzgerald's *The Crack-Up*, "with brief excerpts, paragraphs here and there, comments, descriptions, all adhering to sheer sophisticated comedy as it later was embraced by the smart boys" (*Letters*, 267). *The Crack-Up*, a sort of hodge-podge of Fitzgerald miscellany, had been compiled and edited by Edmund Wilson after Fitzgerald's death in 1940. The book Powell suggested never came to be.

35. Advertising by skywriting, a new technology as Woolf was writing *Mrs. Dalloway*, had just been pioneered in 1922 by J. C. Savage, an English aviator (*Columbia Encyclopedia*, s.v. "Skywriting").

36. At the turn of the last century, "advances in printing technology and a burgeoning economy" led to "an explosion of outdoor advertising" (Gant). For more on this phenomenon, see Fred E. Basten's *Great American Billboards: 100 Years of History by the Side of the Road*. As early as 1914, Loose and Wiles, founders of Sunshine Biscuits, had erected a flashing sign over their nine-story building; it blinked day and night over Long Island City, Queens, and was visible from Manhattan and other locales (*Signs of the Times*, 18).

37. Years later, having reread *Turn, Magic Wheel*, *The Locusts Have No King*, and *The Wicked Pavilion*, Powell wrote that she liked the "hero of *Magic Wheel* best for one thing—[he's a] half-sentimental, half no-good guy" (414).

38. Though various episodes in the life of the Callingham character are based on Hemingway's, much of Powell's descriptive writing in this novel echoes Fitzgerald's.

39. Not afraid to bite the hand that never fed her anyway, Powell here ridicules the *New York Herald Tribune's* book critic Lewis Gannett (1891–1966), Harvard graduate and controversial reviewer (*Turn, Magic Wheel*, 39). Vidal calls him "dense" and "serenely outside literature" ("Queen," 23); Mary McCarthy (1912–1989) found him unqualified to be writing literary criticism (Chamberlain, 1). Though Gannett and Powell had been drinking buddies in her early New York days, they would later have a falling out, Gannett introducing Powell at a party saying, "Dawn's a good girl but she drinks too much and one of these days she's going to do a good novel." Powell retorted, "If I did, you wouldn't know it." She continued to "lecture him," she said, telling him that "if I ever wrote something that he considered 'good' I would know I was slipping" (*Diaries*, 229).

40. On the same page Powell poked fun at Gladys Glad (1907–1983), former member of the Ziegfeld Follies, billed as America's Most Famous Beauty and married twice to drama critic and film producer Mark Hellinger. Called "the great love of Hellinger's life" (Farnsworth, 165), Glad for a time wrote a newspaper beauty column. Coincidentally, or, as Powell might say, "prophetically" (see note 55 to this chapter for Powell's take on "accidental prophecy"), Hellinger a few years later would produce a film of Hemingway's short story "The Killers" (*Time*, "New Pictures," 1).

41. Isa Glenn (1874–1951), Atlanta-born writer. Little new information on Glenn is readily available; a cursory search turns up a 1928 review of her novel *Southern Charm* (*Time*, "Southern Impudence," 1), and an October 2009 review of some of her novels crops up on "The Neglected Books Page" of the website Neglected Books (www.neglectedbooks.com/?s=isa+glenn).

42. Ellen Glasgow (1873–1945), Virginia-born novelist, poet, memoirist, and essayist. Many of her works have been reissued. Of the three women writers Powell names, Glasgow is the best known today.

43. Margaret Storm Jameson (1891–1986), British novelist. Amazon.com shows that one of her novels has been reissued; the rest remain out of print.

44. It would likely cheer Powell to know that fifty-odd years after her diary entry, only two of the three writers she mentions have experienced any of the sort of fanfare that has lately heralded Powell, though Glasgow is still much read and admired today.

45. Louis Bromfield (1896–1956), who hailed from Mansfield, Ohio, was a well-known novelist. Born the same year as Powell, he for a short time had been a grammar-school classmate of hers (Page, "Biographical Notes," 481).

46. Powell knew her city well, not only the Manhattan of her day but historic Manhattan as well. Here, in a scene that fairly rushes by, Powell tosses in a humorous aside. Okie introducing Dennis around Luchow's says, in passing, "That's Victor Herbert" (33). Not another reference to that introduction is made; it seems it is just Powell having a bit of fun, perhaps hoping that in-the-know readers will get a chuckle from it—or it is possible that she is referring to a portrait that may have been on the wall. Those who know the composer Herbert (1859–1924) may recognize that for years he had had a regular table at Luchow's (Dana, 1). Obviously, however, he could not possibly be sitting there then, having died in 1924, more than a decade before the novel takes place. Incidentally, Herbert founded ASCAP at Luchow's (Page, telephone, October 28, 2007).

47. According to Lucius Beebe, the "top-ranking dish" on the "celebrated menu" of Powell's favorite café, located in the Hotel Lafayette, was *moules marinières* (marinated mussels) (*Snoot*, 43). Coincidentally, a Powell story called "Artist's Life," published in the *New Yorker* in 1935, was accompanied by a cartoon about the same dish.

48. *Face the Music*, a 1932 work by Irving Berlin and Moss Hart, was a social satire on the Depression. The play opens "at the Automat, where the recently humbled rich are being forced to share their modest repasts among the hoi polloi," an idea that surely would capture Powell's imagination (Maslon, 1). The show spawned the hit song "Let's Have Another Cup of Coffee" (Jablonski, 152). *Face the Music* enjoyed a much-heralded revival in New York in 2007 (Isherwood, "Let's Put On an Automat!").

49. Powell was "so enraged" at Farrar's letter that she said, "I slammed into completely myself at my most nonconforming and so found myself" (*Diaries*, 444). Afterward, she wrote to Dos Passos, "I can't think of what wonderful revenge to take—whether to stop the novel right now in its middle and take up radio tap dancing, or whether to finish it. I suppose the finest revenge to take on any publisher is to finish it" (*Letters*, 90).

50. Margaret Widdemer (1884–1976), best-selling American poet and novelist. In a 1937 letter Powell wrote to Dos Passos, she jokingly addressed him as Widdemer (*Letters*, 97). Katharine Brush (1902–1952), American novelist and short story writer who penned the novel on which Anita Loos (1888–1981) based her screenplay for the 1932 Jean Harlow vehicle, *Red-Headed Woman*. Later Powell would come to admire and befriend Brush, who died suddenly at fifty of a brain tumor (*Diaries*, 73, 315, 364; *Letters*, 172), and even attended her funeral (*Diaries* 315). In their day, both Widdemer and Brush were far more successful than Powell was, though, with the exception of Brush's short story "The Birthday Party," their writings are largely forgotten today.

51. On April 9, 1930, Powell had signed a three-novel contract with Farrar and Rinehart and received a $3,500 advance (*Diaries*, 14). Previously with Brentano's, which had published her second and third novels, she later would wish she had stayed with them (*Diaries*, 22). *Turn, Magic Wheel* would be her fourth novel with Farrar and Rinehart, though they at first rejected it and later John Farrar told Powell it "probably wouldn't sell" (*Bio*, 151); her next novel, *The Happy Island*, would be her last with the publisher.

52. In a moving diary entry Powell wrote that *Dance Night* was "a rocket that only sizzled because it was rained on. Still wait for the blaze in the sky. It did a very funny thing to me, that dead rocket" (33).

53. Presumably the Shubert-owned Winter Garden, which first opened in 1911 at 1634 Broadway; it had housed the Ziegfeld Follies as recently as 1934 and would do so again in 1936, the same year this novel was published. It had also long featured something called "The Passing Show," its own "answer to Ziegfeld's Follies" (Shubert, "Winter Garden," 1).

54. The idea of a novelist's curiosity would be important to Powell throughout her life. In the year of her death she would write, "Most important thing for novelist is curiosity and how curious that so many of them lack it. They seem self-absorbed, family-absorbed, success-absorbed. . . . I contend that a writer's business is minding other people's business. It is his oxygen, and all the vices of the village gossip are the virtues of a writer" (*Diaries*, 473).

55. Four years after the novel was published, Powell wrote: "Accidental prophecy seems to be part of the writer's job. After *Turn, Magic Wheel*, Ernest Hemingway's married life started turning out that way" (*Diaries*, 180). She maintained that "prophecies" she had written in *The Happy Island* and *Angels on Toast* had similarly come true.

56. At about this time Powell wrote in a letter to a friend of Dos Passos's selflessness, an attribute she much admired, in having found the time to visit an ill friend, Bill Rollins. She says, "Isn't that wonderful? I don't know of any other great man who would do such a thing on his one day in New York on business unless of course photographers and publicity men were present" (*Letters*, 171).

57. James Vincent Sheean (1899–1975) was a journalist, foreign correspondent, novelist, and essayist born in Pana, Illinois. Like a character straight out of Powell, Sheean as a young man had left home for New York without luggage and with little cash, soon finding himself employed at the *Daily News.* In his remarkable career he traveled throughout the world, witnessing and reporting on many of the most important events of the day. He was "one of Ernest Hemingway's favorite drinking buddies."

58. Ann Harding (1901–1981), born Dorothy Walton Gatley in Texas, was "one of the biggest of the big movie stars in the early 1930s" (Parish, 11). Corinne is on to something here: the beautiful Harding was known for playing noble women involved with callous men, as is Effie in both *Turn, Magic Wheel* and *The Hunter's Wife,* the novel within the novel.

59. Hemingway would come to forgive Powell her portrait of him, writing even after the novel's publication to Sara Murphy that he considered Powell one of his best friends (*Diaries,* 471). The two had long known one another: Hemingway biographer Carlos Baker relates a story from 1926 that has his subject, whose "social life was joyously hectic," prowling with a group of friends through the Village streets one night, coming upon Powell's West Ninth Street apartment, and "rapping on the window" till he had convinced her to go with them to Jack Cowles's house. Cowles, a Hemingway friend, is said to have known "dozens of bootleggers" (165).

60. The city's nightlife offered a respite to Powell from the incessant claims on her at home. She wrote, "The perpetual nagging that is the basis of family life [is] the one thing I cannot stand, the thing that will make me run away as it always has. Any barroom brawl is better than the persistent pinpricks of the happy little family" (*Diaries,* 128).

61. Selma Robinson (1899–1977), American publicist, poet, and short story writer (Chasteney, 59).

62. Powell is speaking of Jack Lawson here.

63. It seems material goods were of little interest to Powell, though it is clear that she rarely had much money to spend anyway. According to her niece Phyllis Poccia, "Aunt Mabel and my mother [Phyllis Powell Cook] were interested in material possessions, in collecting things, owning things. . . . [But] Aunt Dawn wasn't interested in all that. She had her possessions—lots of them—but they were in her mind" (*Bio,* 10).

64. Writer friend of Powell's and Dos Passos's, William Rollins (died 1950) is the author of the 1934 "strike" novel *The Shadow Before,* about a workers' strike. Something of a radical, as was Dos Passos in the thirties, Rollins is said to have "disappeared off the scene afterwards" (Wald). Still writing into 1950, however, on his deathbed in July of that year he showed a manuscript to Dos Passos (*Letters,* 171).

65. Jacques LeClercq (1898–1972). One of Powell's closest friends and father of the famed ballerina Tanaquil LeClercq, he was a poet, writer, and

translator (Page, "Biographical Notes," 490). Tanaquil "Tanny" LeClercq (1929–2000), herself a friend of Powell's, was "chic" and "beautiful," even called "Mona Lisa as a *Vogue* model" (C. Barnes, 1). Married in 1952 to George Balanchine (1904–1983), she was "tragically struck down with polio at the height of her career" (Lewis, 105) in 1956.

66. Michael Sadleir (1888–1957), editor/publisher at John Constable Publishing, Ltd., and a fine novelist in his own right, was "Powell's first champion in England" (*Letters*, 91n).

67. Helen Waddell (1889–1965) was a noted Irish medievalist, translator, and novelist (Page, "Biographical Notes," 499). Her *Medieval Latin Lyrics*, which Powell found "heavenly" (*Diaries*, 32), "have always pleased me" (*Diaries*, 124).

68. Elisabeth Bergner (1897–1986), European-born performer considered one of the finest actresses of her time, had just won the 1935 Academy Award for Best Actress in the film *Escape Me Never* ("Exiles," 1).

69. This same blurb would appear on the back cover of Powell's 1948 *The Locusts Have No King* in praise of "Miss Powell's earlier books."

70. Powell originally had wanted to name the novel *The Joyous Isle* after Claude Debussy's piano solo *L'Isle Joyeuse* (1904). The hardworking Debussy (1862–1918) was Powell's favorite type of artist, a diligent and self-effacing sort who provides a fine contradiction to the less industrious, less modest types we meet here. Though the novel was published as *The Happy Island,* its third chapter, which features a Debussy-playing pianist, retains the title Powell had wanted for the book.

71. Stark Young (1881–1963) was a Mississippi-born playwright, theater critic, educator, and novelist (Lloyd, 484–86), author of the "extraordinarily successful" *So Red the Rose* (Cowley I, 34). Unfortunately I have been unable to locate his review of Powell's play, which would presumably have been printed in *Theatre Arts Magazine,* where he began writing in 1919 and which he became editor of in 1947 (485). It might not seem surprising that he disliked Powell's raucous and somewhat racy play, for as the son of a minister he held on throughout his life to the "southern principles" he learned from his father (485). Yet, a gay man himself, he admired what he believed was Fiske's wit.

72. Powell is speaking of *Big Night* here, as *Jig-Saw* would not come out until the following year.

73. Libel laws, always more strict in England than in the United States, were of concern to Sadleir as he contemplated bringing out this novel in England (*Letters*, 103n). However, it seems he voiced no such objections to publishing *Turn, Magic Wheel,* which included a fictionalized portrait of a celebrity far more famous than Fiske. Additionally, this novel is the first of Powell's to include a disclaimer: "The characters in this book are all imaginary."

Perhaps what was so unsettling to her publishers was the idea that many of this novel's characters were gay.

74. Adaptation of the title of the 1955 Dwight Fiske record album, *Songs His Mother Never Taught Him.* The album jacket features a three- or four-year-old boy poring over a risqué magazine, the floor on which he sits littered with a glass of champagne, a bottle of Grand Marnier, and a cigarette-butt-filled ashtray. Page tells me that Fiske's title is a play on a piece written for voice and piano by Antonín Dvořak in 1880, called "Songs My Mother Taught Me."

75. Josephson reveals that Coburn "Coby" Gilman had served as the model for one of John Cheever's (1912–1982) sketches, "The Peril in the Street" (39), published in 1942 in the *New Yorker.*

76. Margaret De Silver (1890–1962) was a longtime friend of Powell's. Like the author, she had an institutionalized child.

77. For Canby Chambers, see note 37 to chapter 2, above.

78. The name "Dol Lloyd" sounds very much like "Floyd Dell": reverse the order of Floyd's first and last names and the two are almost identical. Powell's friend, the writer and socialist Floyd Dell, appears in her diary entries alongside Fiske and Mosher. By 1932, however, Powell had come to consider Dell's talk "pompous and flattened" (*Diaries*, 49); he disappears from the diaries that year, never to return; and he is not mentioned at all in the *Selected Letters.* It seems possible that Powell was thinking not only of Mosher but also of Dell when she created Dol (even though Floyd Dell was quite the ladies' man and not gay), especially as she revealed that her characters are often composites. Later, in her diaries, she would speak of one of Dell's Village hangouts, Three Steps Down (382).

79. Powell's diary records her impression that Mosher is certain that his death is imminent. "He is a faintly funereal wag," she wrote of the then forty-three-year-old Mosher, "expecting cancer with a smile, welcoming decent calamity with great good nature so long as it's something slow and fatal and respectable rather than garish and dramatic" (108–9). In drawing Dol's death in the novel, it is almost as if Powell had again prophesied the future, Mosher dying just four years later. She seemed to believe that she had foretold the future in *Turn, Magic Wheel* when her depiction of Hemingway's marriages breaking up had come true.

80. Carol Hill Brandt (1904–1984) and her husband Carl Brandt (1888–1957) were Powell's literary agents for many years, Carol first coming to work with Powell in 1935 (*Bio*, 92).

81. "Café Society," review of *The Happy Island*, September 19, 1938, 70.

82. Interesting choice of word, Powell having used the very term in her diary to describe the Bert character. If "dopes" fill New York's café society, dopes she will write of.

83. Lucius Beebe (1902–1966), suave man-about-town, journalist, and author of such books on polite society as *Snoot if You Must* and *The Stork Club Bar Book.* Powell, however, has quite a story to tell about him that effactually tarnishes his polish (*Diaries,* 173). See the *Diaries* for more.

CHAPTER 5: AN AFFECTING SELF-PORTRAIT
OF THE ARTIST IN MIDDLE AGE

1. Powell provided a timeline, in a diary entry of 1942, that lists the dates on which she began and finished each of the novels she had written thus far, from *Whither* to the not-yet-finished *A Time to Be Born* (196). It is interesting that the author, who had always disavowed her first novel, should include it in this list.

2. Anne Honeycutt (1902–1989), director of the radio program on which Powell worked and whom she referred to as "Radio Bigshot and generally unreliable efficiency queen" (*Letters,* 106).

3. To Jay this dish oozes class, but it is actually is a middle-American recipe known at least since the earliest decades of the last century. A recipe for "Quail on Toast" appears in *The Home Comfort Cook Book,* circa 1918.

4. Dale Carnegie (1888–1955), author of the 1936 runaway best seller *How to Win Friends and Influence People,* had been born in Missouri and had come to New York where he began the successful Dale Carnegie Courses in communications and salesmanship. The courses continue today.

5. According to Perkins's biographer A. Scott Berg, the handsome and dapper editor was irresistible to the women writers with whom he was associated, though "he had difficulties working with the gender" (522). Similarly, Malcolm Cowley writes that Perkins would often be heard unhappily muttering, "Women, women" (I, 33). Still, Powell enjoyed a good working relationship with him and, according to Cowley, had a "daughterly admiration" for the editor, who was twelve years older than she.

6. The girlfriend Maria became Lewis's wife a short time later: in a diary entry written some ten months after the one cited above, Powell refers to her as Maria Lewis (182).

7. Cuban bandleaders hold a special place in our culture. A decade after *Angels on Toast* appeared, Lucille Ball's Cuban bandleader husband, Desi Arnaz (1917–1986), would be featured in her wildly popular television program, *I Love Lucy,* which ran from 1951 to 1957. Arnaz's mentor, Xavier Cugat (1900–1990), another famed Cuban bandleader (though born in Spain), rose to fame in this country years before Arnaz did. In the 1930s, Cugat and his band became the house band of New York's Waldorf Astoria.

8. Just why she says "illiterate lady reviewer" here is unclear. Powell had at least as many complaints about her "illiterate" or "asinine" male critics and had often been reviewed well by such approving women critics as Edith Walton and Rosamond Lehmann, among others.

9. Rosalind Wilson, Edmund Wilson's daughter, remarked on an NPR radio show on Powell's personal gentleness and charm, which had so surprised those who had come to see her in Boston when Wilson brought her out for a lecture ("Dawn Powell May Usurp Dorothy Parker"). They had expected to encounter a much more acerbic, much less affable woman.

10. Perkins seems to have been ambivalent about advertising. In *At Random,* rival publisher and admirer Bennett Cerf (1898–1971) quotes Perkins as saying, "If [a] car is really stuck in the mud, ten people can't budge it. But if it's moving even a little bit, one man can push it on down the road. By the same token, if a book is absolutely dead, all the advertising in the world isn't going to help. If it's got a glimmer of life, if it's selling a little bit maybe in only one or two spots, it's moving enough to be given a little push" (208). Cerf says he borrowed the line many times, which sounds a bit like an excuse for not spending advertising dollars on certain publications.

11. Otis Ferguson (1907–1943), an accomplished film, music, and literary critic, was on staff at the *New Republic* from 1930 until his early death in battle in World War II. He is considered a major precursor of such renowned film critics as James Agee and Pauline Kael, and he is noted for his appreciation of jazz and its influence on American culture. The collection *In the Spirit of Jazz* "contains his writings on musicians; a selection of his writings on radio, theater, movies, books, and writers; and his autobiographical writings, including some extraordinary accounts of his sea voyages" (Ferguson, card catalogue description of his book).

12. The lines Pool quotes here come from a letter Powell wrote to her British publisher, Michael Sadleir (*Letters,* 150).

13. Richard Lingeman, describing *A Time to Be Born*'s Amanda Keeler Evans, the character who was based on Clare Boothe Luce (40).

14. This disclaimer would be excluded from the 1996 Steerforth Press reissue but retained in the 1991 Yarrow Press edition.

15. Though I have been unable to identify the addressee, he seems clearly to have written to Powell looking for dirt on Boothe Luce in behalf of her 1944 political opponent, Margaret Connors (see note 20 to this chapter).

16. Alfred Cleveland Blumenthal (1885–1957), married to actress and Ziegfeld girl Peggy Fears (1903–1994) from 1929 to 1945, then remarried and divorced for good five years later, was a well-heeled Broadway producer; together with his wife he had made $15 million in the early 1930s coproducing the Kern/Hammerstein show, *Music in the Air.* In *Flapper,* Joshua Zeitz writes of Blumenthal and Fears as very free sexually, on one weekend even "disappearing into a hotel suite" with Charlie Chaplin and silent-film actress Louise Brooks (1906–1985) and not "emerg[ing] until Monday" (254). He records Brooks as saying that "the foursome spent most of the forty-eight hours in a state of undress and complete sexual entanglement" (254). However, nowhere in his

302   Notes to Pages 171–175

history does he mention Boothe Luce, and nowhere in her well-researched book on Boothe Luce does Sylvia Jukes Morris mention either Blumenthal or Fears. It is unclear where Boothe Luce's "bosom friend" got her information.

17. Boothe Brokaw's affair with the married Wall Street tycoon Bernard Baruch (1870–1965), who was said to be the fourth-richest man in America at the time Clare met him (S. Morris, 192), is well documented, though the affair seems to have ended when she married Luce (S. Morris, 276).

18. Pare Lorentz (1905–1992), film director, poet, and movie critic for *Vanity Fair,* wrote in a letter to Clare that he felt his love for her "in every cell, every nerve" (S. Morris, 226). As Powell's letter reports, the two did have an affair in the 1930s (S. Morris, 226).

19. Dudley Murphy (1897–1968), like Lorentz a film director, does not appear in Morris's biography, though he is portrayed in a recent biography as "a bon vivant" who "caromed between film and the other arts, between Hollywood and other cultural capitals—Greenwich Village, Harlem, London, and Paris—hobnobbing with some of the era's leading cultural figures, including Ezra Pound, Man Ray, Duke Ellington, and Charlie Chaplin, and leaving many a scandal in his wake" (Delson, overleaf). I have found no source other than Powell's letter linking the two. Perhaps Morris's second volume (the first ends in 1940) will mention Murphy.

20. Margaret Connors Driscoll (1915–2000), Democratic candidate and opponent of Clare Boothe Luce's in 1944 for her Connecticut seat in the House of Representatives. Despite the fact that Connors was "backed by P.A.C., the President, and many leading New Dealers," Boothe Luce retained her seat in this hard-fought and close-won contest ("New House").

21. Clearly this Ohio schoolroom chum on whom the author might have based Amanda Keeler could not have been Clare Boothe. Boothe, who was born in New York, had spent her early years in Memphis, Nashville, Chicago, and a town in Wisconsin. By 1912 she had moved back to New York (S. J. Morris, 24–40).

22. The witty Mr. Beebe includes a chapter titled "Globaloney Golconda" in *Snoot if You Must,* published in 1943, the same year Boothe Luce made her famous remark. Here he is having a little fun with Mrs. Luce (5).

23. Vidal is alluding to Samuel Goldwyn's 1946 Academy Award–winning World War II film, *The Best Years of Our Lives.*

24. This line echoes almost word for word a line Powell would write in a letter to Scribner's publicity department.

25. The pretentiousness-hating Powell was, according to Charles Strouse, herself "beyond unpretentious" (telephone).

26. The character's birthplace is one "fact of Boothe-Luce's life" that Powell changes, Clare Boothe having been born on West 124th Street in New York (Morris, 15), the character in Lakeville, Ohio.

27. Powell included a few other possible titles here, including *The Almond Tree Shall Blossom* and *The Crackling Thorn,* both from Ecclesiastes, and simply *Amanda* (*Letters,* 112).

28. As Powell had told Max Perkins, the hotel she mentions here at Fifty-Fifth and Fifth was the luxurious Gotham Hotel, "a Beaux-Arts beauty" erected in 1903 that was once one of "the central jewels in Fifth Avenue's Crown" (Riegert, 2). Built with a "façade of limestone and granite, in the Italian renaissance style," it is now the Peninsula New York. The Gotham was and still is, in some quarters, known as the only "fashionable turn-of-the-century New York City hotel to go belly up" (Hirsh, *Manhattan,* 19), largely because it had been unable to get a liquor license from the time it opened in 1905 until it was forced to close in 1908 (Gray, "The Old Gotham," 1). Tim Page pointed me to news reports of the actual suicide that occurred there on July 24, 1938: Wikipedia has an article under the name of the twenty-six-year-old victim, John William Warde, and a recounting of the event turns up in Arthur Gelb's *City Room* (160–62), the *New Yorker,* and elsewhere.

29. *All about Eve* was based on the 1946 short story "The Wisdom of Eve," written by Ohio-raised actress/author Mary Orr (1911–2006) (*Variety,* 1).

30. John Hall Wheelock (1886–1978) was a poet (Cowley II, 34) and Powell's editor at Scribner's following the death of Max Perkins in 1947. He would remain with Scribner's for nearly fifty years (Page, "Biographical Notes," 499). "In two meetings with him," Powell wrote fondly, "I feel closer to him than to Max or any other editor I ever had" (*Diaries,* 265).

31. Harrison Smith (1888–1971), editor and critic; for a time he was president of the *Saturday Review* (Page, "Biographical Notes," 496). Powell had met him in 1930 (*Diaries,* 14).

32. The no-longer-extant Stork Club, a swank, exclusive restaurant and nightclub that opened on West Fifty-Eighth Street in the 1920s, was owned by Sherman Billingsley (1896–1966), father-in-law of *Leave It to Beaver*'s Barbara Billingsley (1915–2010). In its heyday it was "the apex of the social world, the Everest of the Society Climber" (Blumenthal, 3). Newspaperman Walter Winchell (1897–1972) famously named it "New York's New Yorkiest place" (Blumenthal, 9); in 1946, the afore-mentioned epicure Lucius Beebe wrote a popular book called *The Stork Club Bar Book* in which he provided recipes for the many drinks poured at the bar there. The Stork later moved to 3 East Fifty-Third Street but closed in 1965, for "New York changed, and the Stork Club became silly and old" (Blumenthal, 269). All of the most famous writers, actors, singers, athletes, journalists—one regular was the newswoman and TV game show panelist Dorothy Kilgallen (1913–1965)—politicians, and mobsters of the day were seen at the Stork Club, where "every other face was a famous one" (Simmons, 81). But "the snobbery" of such places included a

bare-faced racism: Billingsley, for example, "made no secret of the fact that he barred blacks and non-celebrity Jews" (Gavin, 33).

33. Edna Ferber's nickname for the Algonquin Round Table, not unlike Dorothy Parker's well-known name for the group, "the vicious circle." Ferber said of the Round Table crowd that they "were absolutely merciless if they disapproved. I have never encountered a more hard-bitten crew." As if to prove her point, clique member Alexander Woollcott once said, "I don't see why anyone should call a dog a bitch when there's Edna Ferber around"; she referred to him as "that New Jersey Nero who thinks his pinafore is a toga" (Teichmann, *Smart Aleck*, 247). Though the "spinster" disliked Woollcott, Algonquin "gossip had it" that she was in love with frequent collaborator George Kaufman (Bach, 143). Bennett Cerf, who knew many of the members of the Algonquin Group, said of Dorothy Parker that "she was something of a fraud all her life" and "a very dangerous woman" (34), though he found Benchley "a wonderful, wonderful man." Cerf added that, next to "a drunk" like Eugene O'Neill, Benchley was "a teetotaler" who "just played at [drinking]" (34).

34. Powell left *A Time to Be Born* out of this equation, though a bit later she described *Locusts* to Max Perkins as "a follow-up of *A Time to Be Born* (*Letters*, 135).

35. Wolcott Gibbs (1902–1958), drama critic, humorist, playwright, and short fiction writer for the *New Yorker*. A member of the Algonquin Group, he "famously parodied *Time Magazine* in 1936" ("Wolcott Gibbs," 1).

36. Arthur Kober (1900–1975). Humorist, playwright, and writer for the *New Yorker*, Kober worked in Hollywood films, including the Bette Davis vehicle *The Little Foxes* (Erickson), based on the Lillian Hellman play

37. The title comes from a line in Proverbs: "The locusts have no king, yet they go forth all of them by bands."

38. Powell found Algonquin members Wolcott Gibbs and James Thurber, for two, to be less than likeable. She tells uncomplimentary stories of both men, separately. For Gibbs, see especially *Diaries*, 364; for Thurber, *Diaries*, 212. But she did like Benchley, a man who "had the most winning smile on Broadway," and who was by all accounts I know of a very likeable fellow (Teichmann, *Smart Aleck*, 88).

39. Powell seems to have stopped working on this sequel after about 1945 (*Diaries*, 238). Then, in 1949, "in a nostalgic mood" following the death of her older sister, Mabel, she returned to it, "though with dwindling enthusiasm, for the rest of her years" (*Bio*, 220). Powell records that the disappointment of *My Home* had dampened her interest in the sequel, understandably (238). According to Page, eighty typewritten pages and "hundreds of pages of notes" still survive (*Bio*, 220). In a letter to Edmund Wilson's daughter Rosalind, Powell writes that even though Max Perkins

had been enthusiastic about the sequel and even though she had signed a contract with Scribner's to write it, she found the postwar period of *The Locusts Have No King* "too disturbing and exciting to bury myself again in [the] Ohio of thirty years ago" (*Letters,* 203).

40. John Philips Marquand (1893–1960), Delaware-born, Massachusetts-raised novelist known for his Mr. Moto series but "best remembered for his amusing, lightly satirical novels about well-to-do New Englanders struggling to maintain their aristocratic, Puritan standards in the 20th century" (Benét, 621).

41. Whether coincidentally or not, right beside Wilson's review is an advertisement placed by Scribner's for the novel. Once again the publisher's publicity department has misrepresented her work: here they say of *My Home Is Far Away* that it is "packed with . . . people you'll be glad to know" (95). It would have been much more to the point to have said it is "packed with people you'll be glad to get as far away from as possible." It is painful to imagine Powell's reaction to the double-whammy of the review and the ad positioned side by side.

42. Van Wyck Brooks (1886–1963), Pulitzer Prize–winning American critic and renowned biographer (Benét, 130).

43. William Hogarth (1697–1764), famed eighteenth-century English painter and engraver known for his satirical artwork. Powell's comparing her work to Hogarth's is especially apt, given that Hogarth's determination to portray the truth as he saw it barred him from a career as a more serious artist. As we have seen, Powell, too, always insisted on painting the truth as she saw it, despite what others said. Powell's friend Peggy Bacon was praised as "the only woman artist to successfully rival . . . Hogarth" (Tarbell, 34).

44. George Wettling (1907–1968) "played with virtually everyone in the Chicago jazz field, as well as [with] Benny Goodman, Billie Holiday, Sidney Bechet, and even Chico Marx" ("Drummerworld"). Two years before their meeting, Powell had learned of Wettling through her friendship with Misha Reznikoff, who told her that the drummer had taken up abstract painting, finding in the two art forms a close relationship. Wettling said that someone had taken him to the Modern Museum once, and he looked over all the paintings there and said, "I never knew there were that many drummers" (*Diaries,* 253).

Albert Edwin "Eddie" Condon (1905–1973) was a jazz musician, Town Hall broadcaster, and bandleader whose original New York club was located at West Third, where Powell first visited; the club then moved up to Fifty-Second Street at Sixth, and then to East Fifty-Sixth ("Eddie Condon").

45. Like Dodo, Dorothy Parker was known for her sexual prowess, which she herself often joked about. For example, about a party she once attended, she famously said, "One more drink and I'd have been under the host."

46. Delman shoes, made since 1919, were then as they are now some of the most expensive and stylish shoes made for women. Great stars such as Katharine Hepburn and Marlene Dietrich were known to have favored them (Delman, 1). Daché hats were made by Lily Daché, "the Michael Jordan of hat designers" (Hat Museum, 1). Favored by Hollywood stars, Daché hats are no longer made but are highly collectible; they are available in some upscale vintage shops and on some online auction sites.

47. Irony of ironies: The New School, which Powell ridiculed mercilessly in *The Locusts Have No King,* would offer in 2003 a course called "Dawn Powell's New York."

48. Glenway Wescott (1901–1982), another midwesterner moved to Manhattan, was best known for his popular novel *Apartment in Athens* (Page, "Biographical Notes," 499).

49. Orpha May Sherman Steinbrueck ("Auntie May") would live to be ninety. She died in September 1959. Powell was surprised to learn that her aunt had left her $1,000 (*Diaries,* 401).

50. London's W. H. Allen publishers would bring the book out in its first British edition, but not until 1954 (*Diaries,* 337). Powell attributed her renewed British success to "Bunny Wilson's praise" (*Diaries,* 317), though Edmund Wilson published no words on her work between 1944 and 1962. Presumably he had been in touch with the publisher on Powell's behalf.

51. According to Malcolm Cowley, the "older men at Scribner's" were often furious about "all the indecorous authors whom Perkins had been introducing." In fact, Cowley continues, many were stunned that the publishing house would bring out such a book as *The Great Gatsby* with the word "son-of-a-bitch" in it ("Unshaken" II, 33). In Powell's novel, the publishing family is equally guilty of silly (yet false) propriety.

CHAPTER 6: "EITHER THAT WALLPAPER GOES, OR I DO"

The quotation in the chapter title, reportedly the last words spoken by Oscar Wilde (1854–1900), seems an appropriate introduction to the last two novels by Dawn Powell. The two writers shared a similar sense of humor, and Powell's epigrams ("It's too nice a day to be outdoors" [*Golden Spur,* 37] and "Writers are not writers unless decently unpublished" 53], for example) are reminiscent of Wilde's. *The Wicked Pavilion,* too, "abounds in paradoxes" (Levin, 62). Readers may recall that, in another Wilde/Powell connection, a young Dawn had played Miss Prism in a college production of *The Importance of Being Earnest* (*Letters,* 15).

1. During these years Powell also produced *A Cage for Lovers,* published in 1957; considered by some a sort of better-than-average romance novel, it was so unlike her other works that she called it "a vacation from myself"

(*Diaries*, 382). Further, she said of it that "there is no wit or humor in this story, so it may be successful. Waugh, Huxley, Thurber—none were really able to make a decent living until they lost their sense of humor and practically their ability to feel" (*Diaries*, 357). Today James Wolcott considers *Cage* "a throbbing blouse" of a book (46), but in its day such discerning critics as J. B. Priestley and Edmund Wilson admired it, as did the *New York Times'* Lenard Kaufman, though its sales were disappointing. Writing it, Powell for the first and last time in her long career momentarily abandoned her satiric style to "pacify a public that seems to regard wit—especially if it sounds original or spontaneous—as immoral" (*Diaries*, 350). At this same time Powell reworked and abridged *Angels on Toast*, which was issued in 1956 as *A Man's Affair*.

2. Powell's proposed subtitle, "A Novel of Washington Square," appeared on not the front but the back cover of the book. The words are likely a tribute not only to the location of the Hotel Lafayette but also to one of her favorite authors, Henry James, whose 1880 novella, *Washington Square*, she certainly knew well. In fact, Powell says she is modeling *The Wicked Pavilion's* depiction of café society on that in another James novel, *The Ambassadors*, published in 1903 (*Diaries*, 318–19). Powell's book is divided into five parts; James's was divided into twelve, having first been serialized.

3. The book's foreword, taken directly from Mrs. Creevey's October 29, 1805, letter to her husband, reads, "Oh, this wicked Pavilion! We were kept there till half-past one this morning waiting for the Prince, and it has kept me in bed with the head-ache till twelve to-day" (Gore, 41).

4. The Right Honorable Member of Parliament John Macmahon (1754–1817); though I have located little information about him, his portrait, painted by English artist Thomas Lawrence (1769–1830), is available for viewing online.

5. The Prince of whom Mrs. Creevey speaks was the eldest son of King George III. George, Prince of Wales (1762–1830) would go on to become Regent in 1811 and King George IV in 1820. J. B. Priestley dubs him "the Prince of Pleasure" in his book of the same name, for the royal was boorish, loud, and extravagant in his spending—at the age of thirty-three he owed £630,000, "a stupendous sum for those days" (30) and even for ours. He and his brothers "did much . . . to bring contempt and ridicule to the monarchy" (15), including fathering several children, none of them legitimate.

6. Mrs. Fitzherbert (1756–1837), widowed twice, was born Maria Anne Smythe. "A full-bodied woman whose charms matched the Prince's opulent taste" (Priestley, 29), she and he "married," but the union was not considered legal in the eyes of English civil law. The two remained together from 1784

until 1811, their relationship lasting even through the Prince's unhappy but legal marriage to Caroline of Brunswick (26–31).

7. Before he was appointed Regent, the Prince spent much of his time in Brighton, "where he indulged his expensive passion for building and elaborate decoration until in the end he achieved his fantastic Pavilion." There he would throw parties every few days, though they were not at all as "wild" or even as "wicked" as has been supposed (Priestley, 32).

8. At least one person sought to preserve something of the Brevoort long before it was in danger of annihilation. It seems that the hotel's first owner, a Mr. Albert Clark of Boston, "was so devoted to undemocratic principles that when Lincoln was elected, he had a time capsule containing a Brevoort menu buried in a brick wall behind his office so that future generations would know that such refinement had once existed" (Batterberry, 227). The secret cache must have been discovered during the razing of the hotel.

9. A colloquialism meaning "detective."

10. Brendan Gill (1914–1997), novelist, critic, and journalist, wrote for the *New Yorker* for sixty years. Powell writes of having cocktails with him at the Algonquin (*Diaries*, 436), but not at the Lafayette, though in his review of *The Wicked Pavilion* Gill wrote movingly of the Lafayette and of having sometimes joined Powell there ("Rough," 157–58).

11. In these years Bendix was producing radios, phonographs, television sets, and washing machines. Powell likely means she never had a washing machine of her own, though beginning in 1938 coin-operated Bendix washing machines were being installed in New York City apartment houses ("Wash It Yourself," 1–2).

12. Much of this expansion occurred during Dwight D. Eisenhower's tenure as Columbia University president from 1948 to 1953.

13. One of Powell's and Wilson's favorite restaurants in the early 1960s, called after its address, 68 Fifth Avenue, is now a New School property (Wilson, *The Man in Letters*, 181).

14. Calvin Trillin refers to journalist and *New Yorker* columnist Joseph Mitchell (1908–1996), who had come to New York from North Carolina in 1929, as a "resident out of towner" (vii), a description reminiscent of Powell's own description of herself as a "permanent visitor." In a review of biographer-turned-literary-forger Lee Israel's 2008 confessional memoir, *Can You Ever Forgive Me*, in which a down-on-her-luck Israel admits having forged hundreds of letters, purportedly by the likes of Dorothy Parker, Edna Ferber, and Noel Coward, among others, Thomas Mallon calls Israel "the kind of Manhattan eccentric who might have caught the attention of Joe Mitchell" (15). Powell herself called Mitchell "one of our finest journalists, unique in his compassion and understanding for the haunted little lost men such as Joe

Gould. He transforms a forlorn, intolerably pathetic gentleman panhandler into an engaging, Dickensian orphan rogue" (jacket blurb, *Joe Gould's Secret*). Powell possessed the same sort of compassion for the world's lost souls as Mitchell did.

15. Powell's friend Edmund Wilson was likewise no fan of Robert Moses. See especially Wilson's *Apologies to the Iroquois* and a letter he wrote to his wife, Elena, in *Edmund Wilson: The Man in Letters* (Wilson, 177–78). According to a pair of recent *New York Times* articles, it seems that an effort is currently underway to reassess Moses's reputation as ruthless destroyer of city neighborhoods and to reevaluate him as a product of his time (Ouroussoff; Pogrebin, "Rehabilitating").

16. Readers may recall that it was Roger Angell who, along with Gore Vidal, had said "Dawn Powell" when editor Robert S. Fogarty asked him to name a forgotten author he would recommend to readers of the *Antioch Review*.

17. For photographs of some of the no-longer-extant locales Angell mentions and many he doesn't, see especially Berenice Abbott's stunning *New York in the Thirties*. Abbott (1898–1991), like Powell, was born in Ohio.

18. Seated with Edmund Wilson and John Dos Passos from time to time, of course, would be an ebullient Dawn Powell.

19. The Cedar Tavern will serve as the model for the saloon featured in Powell's last book, *The Golden Spur*. The original Cedar was torn down in the early 1960s; today's Cedar, at 82 University Place between Eleventh and Twelfth Streets, has for some time been one of several taverns visited on the weekly Greenwich Village Literary Pub Crawl (Lawliss, 85). Unfortunately, like so many other New York landmarks, it was torn down in the last decade to make room for apartment buildings.

20. In the 1940s and '50s, "still-semi-starving artists like Jackson Pollock, Willem de Kooning, Mark Rothko, Franz Kline" and Niles Spencer came to the Cedar "to hoist a few, get into fistfights, and hoist a few more." The original Cedar Tavern was located at 39 East Eighth Street, "amid the mid-century boho belt, close to the Brevoort Hotel, sometime home to Isadora Duncan, Edna St. Vincent Millay, and Theodore Dreiser. While de Kooning and his wife, Elaine, used the Cedar to play out their 50-year alcoholic co-dependent soap opera, Pollock was banned for ripping the men's-room door from its hinges. Beat writer Jack Kerouac was likewise tossed, supposedly for pissing in an ashtray" (B. Bennett, 1). Other writers, such as the poet Frank O'Hara (1926–1966), frequented the Cedar. According to Brad Gooch, the poet's biographer, O'Hara said that he and his writer friends would spend their time about equally at the Cedar Tavern, which the poet called "the artists' bar," and the San Remo, which he referred to as "the writers' bar" (Logan, 10). A son of photographer Genevieve Naylor (1915–1989) and artist Misha Reznikoff

(1905–1971), Peter Reznikoff remembers Eddie Condon's place on Third Avenue (until it moved uptown) as the "musicians' bar," a location he recalls Powell frequenting as well (telephone). The novelist mentions the San Remo in *The Golden Spur,* where, O'Hara said, "We argued and gossiped; in the Cedar we often wrote poems while listening to the painters argue and gossip. So far as I know, nobody painted in the San Remo while they listened to the writers argue" (Logan, 10). The San Remo, which was located at 189 Bleecker Street (near MacDougall), is said to have been "cool rather than politically and alcoholically inflamed" (PBS, "Inn Crowd," 2), as both the White Horse and Cedar were, though Dylan Thomas was a noted fan. The building, still standing today, was home for some years to Carpo's Café, still a writers' hangout, but then housed a Vietnamese restaurant called the Butterfly Grill.

21. Powell should have had few legal worries about her fictionalized portrait of Peggy Guggenheim (1898–1979), for in 1946 Guggenheim had herself published the first (and longest) part of her very unflattering three-part autobiography. In *Out of This Century: The Informal Memoirs of Peggy Guggenheim,* the author famously flaunts her promiscuous, hedonistic lifestyle. Still, Powell's publishers felt it necessary to include the by-now customary "None of the characters in this book are based on any living characters" caveat.

22. Alexander Brook (1898–1980) was married to Powell's friend, the artist Peggy Bacon, from 1920 to 1940.

23. Charles Houghton Howard (1899–1978), surrealist painter born in Montclair, New Jersey, according to a variety of online sources, or in New York City, according to Stacey Moss (95), was married from about 1933 to English painter Madge Knight (1895–1974); the marriage would last until her death (Moss, 97). Art historian Susan Ehrlich says that the couple, who worked in "abstract surrealism . . . created paintings and sculptures in which organic fantasy is wed to constructivist form" (79).

24. The ocean liner *Ile de France,* which made its first voyage in 1927, was "a floating Hollywood, a floating luxury resort in itself" known for its luxurious Art Deco interiors ("Ile de France").

25. Powell soon put some of these most descriptive letters to use in her novel *A Cage for Lovers.*

26. Houghton Mifflin would publish the collection of short stories, *Sunday, Monday and Always,* in 1952, a year after Powell wrote this letter to Ms. Wilson. The book received "extraordinar[ily] good reviews" (*Diaries,* 315), among them the one I cited earlier in which John Nerber compared Powell to Austen. The *New Yorker* briefly reviewed the collection as well, saying of Powell that "most of the time, she does her work with economy, wit, and warmth" (90). The reviewer went on rather proudly to point out that "four of the stories [in this book] originally appeared in this magazine" (90).

27. That week was October 17 through 23, 1954 (*Bio,* 245).

28. Novelist and essayist Mary McCarthy (1912–1989) was Edmund Wilson's third wife, he her second husband. Powell believed that McCarthy "hated [her] guts" for having "savagely" reviewed one of her books (*Letters,* 320); Page writes that Powell had "decidedly mixed emotions" about McCarthy ("Biographical Notes," 493) at least in part, it seems, because of McCarthy's stormy marriage to Wilson.

29. Powell was disappointed in Houghton Mifflin's advertising of *A Cage for Lovers,* writing in a letter to Wilson that "their catalog gives an extraordinarily obtuse picture of it" (245).

30. Cornelius G. Burke (1900–1971) was a poet, critic, and editor (Page, "Biographical Notes," 482).

31. Powell will dedicate *The Golden Spur* to Margaret de Silver, an act that will cheer the dying woman (*Letters,* 317).

32. It seemed a miracle to many when suddenly, in 1963, Phyllis recovered and was sent home from the hospital. As it happens, "she would live another 22 years" (*Bio,* 291).

33. The novel will open with a vivid account of the destruction of Wanamaker's, the famed department store.

34. In 1957, Powell's renewed fame in England, thanks at least in part to J. B. Priestley, reached even to Doncaster, in South Yorkshire, where a theater company had put on a show cheekily called *We've Got Nothing on Tonight,* a punny title that surely would have amused Powell. Although there is no evidence that she traveled to England in 1957—or to Doncaster ever—I have in my possession an autograph card signed and dated by the members of the theatrical company and by Dawn Powell herself, along with a "God Bless" and "Sincerely Yours" written in her hand. Tim Page confirms that the signature is hers. We have concluded that the actors must have mailed the card to Powell for her signature and that she then sent it back to them. This request for her autograph from across the ocean may have been a small bright spot in an otherwise largely grim year. The card is also signed by noted English comic actress Patricia Hayes (1909–1998), who, in another interesting Priestley connection, "spent 10 years in repertory theatre, making her name as Ruby the maid in J. B. Priestley's *When We Are Married*" (BBC News obituary).

35. Tim Page calls Sam Schwartz's one of several "popular speakeasies or restaurants of the 1920s" (*Bio,* 382n), but I locate no other definite record of it. I do find mention of a Schwartz's Restaurant, located far downtown on Broad Street (Simmons, 81), and of a "Sam Swartz's TNT," sans the "ch," in *McSorley's Wonderful Saloon* (Mitchell, 59). The description of the place that Mitchell provides, courtesy of Village "kook" Joe Gould, is close to Powell's.

36. Romany Marie's was a "basement tavern" in the Village where writers, architects, philosophers, and painters such as Buckminster Fuller, Edward Hopper, Eugene O'Neill, Stuart Davis, and Arshile Gorky "would gather in

the low-ceilinged room which was more a salon than a tavern. It was a place for the interchange and pollination of ideas" (J. Haskell, 1–4); it is where Edna St. Vincent Millay wrote what is now perhaps her most famous poem, "First Fig," originally published in 1920.

37. Three Steps Down was located at 19 West Eighth Street (Harris, 194). Floyd Dell's *Love in Greenwich Village* describes the former Village speakeasy, to enter which one walked down three steps; it was one of Dell's favorite haunts. Joseph Freeman, in *An American Testament*, recalls first meeting Dell, a man with "large eyes" and a "thin, translucent, sensitive face," there (243).

38. Familiar as the plotline might seem—some even say that "all western literature, from *The Odyssey* onward, is about the search for the father" (Dugan, 157)—Powell puts a satiric twist on hers. As Brigid Brophy writes, "A bastard's quest for a father would be a banal theme, but Miss Powell stands it on its head" (942).

39. Some sources even say that the fire had destroyed Wanamaker's (Hirsh, *Between*, 39); they seem to have been unaware of the much larger role the wrecking ball had played in the store's passing.

40. Powell never mentioned traveling by automobile (other than taxicab) until this period. Previously, she had always traveled by train or, in the city, by foot or bus.

41. As early as 1948 Wilson was complaining of a changing Greenwich Village (*Edmund*, 161), and in *The Fifties* the very proper Wilson found the Village "depressing" with all its "male and female beatniks in the streets, the girls in trousers" (636). It seems odd that Wilson should be complaining of trouser-wearing women in 1959; women had been wearing pants for nearly three decades by then, Katharine Hepburn's and Marlene Dietrich's trouser-wearing in the 1930s having created first a bit of an uproar and then a lasting fashion trend. Furthermore, such a stylish woman-about-New York as Beatrice (Mrs. George) Kaufman (1895–1945) had been wearing trousers even before "Marlene Dietrich ever dreamed of leaving the Fatherland" (Teichmann, *George*, 50). Pants for women had become even more popular during the World War II years, not only for "work [but for] play—Rosie the Riveter could jitterbug on her lunch break without ever leaving the floor" (Sheed, 1).

42. Ever adaptable, Powell had picked up and amended the language of the Beats: her "Endsville," like the more familiar synonymous term "Nowheresville," is evocative of '50s slang.

43. Powell had moved to Viking Press when Paul Brooks at Houghton Mifflin turned down *The Golden Spur (Diaries*, 385). She felt she had been "wrongly advised" and overly edited by senior editor Helen Taylor there (*Diaries*, 382), to the point that she joked that she ought to reduce her last name to "Pol," for "Powell," when combined with "Dawn," had "too many W's" in it (*Letters*, 299). Powell did not hold Rosalind Baker Wilson

accountable for any of her troubles at Houghton Mifflin, however, and the two remained close (*Letters,* 252n). Viking Press is the first of Powell's publishers in years who did not add the caveat that "none of the characters in this volume is based on any real persons."

44. Claire Van Orphen has a twin sister, Bea, who is quite unlike her sister. Bea is a widow (like Powell), while Claire has never married; Bea wears chic, up-to-date clothing while Claire dresses as a relic of a bygone era. Bea is more sociable, Claire more solitary. Perhaps these two women represent two different sides of Dawn Powell.

45. Though Rice remembers the Jumble Shop as being on Waverly Place, it was actually located at 28 West Eighth Street at MacDougal (postcard). Tim Page believes that the r staurant had moved to Waverly from West Eighth (telephone, October 28, 2007). During Prohibition it had been a tea room (Naureckas, "MacDougal," 1), but, growing into a larger restaurant, it "survived well into the 1960s" (Temple, 1), when Powell and Rice dropped in. The Jumble Shop makes an appearance in *The Golden Spur,* as one of a handful of bars in the Village that offers a "special brand of social security" (59–60).

46. There is some evidence that Powell had been sexually active in her younger years, and, as we have noted, that she had an affair with John Howard Lawson; she may have been romantically involved with Coburn Gilman as well. See Josephson's essay and Page's biography.

47. *Sweet Smell of Success,* a wildly popular film of those years (released in 1957), was adapted from Ernest Lehman's novella of the same title by the author, director Alexander Mackendrick, and playwright/screenwriter Clifford Odets (1906–1963), whom Powell had known from her days with the Group Theatre.

48. Astor's memoir, *Patchwork Child,* came out in 1962. *The Bluebird Is at Home,* published in 1965, the year of Powell's death, is subtitled *A Shrewd and Witty Novel about Love and Marriage among the Very Young and Very Rich in the 1930s.* Brooke Astor lived a long life; she passed away at the age of 105 on August 13, 2007. Since her death, her son and his lawyer have been embroiled in lawsuits alleging mismanaging her money and manipulating her into changing her will; in 2013, the men began serving prison terms.

49. Murdock Pemberton (1888–1982) was a playwright, a press agent, the first *New Yorker* art critic, and an Algonquin Round Table member (Fitzpatrick). Obituary, "Murdock Pemberton."

50. Strouse and Adams were responsible for the runaway hit *Bye Bye Birdie* and other critical and popular successes. In 1964, they would adapt Odets's *Golden Boy* for the Broadway musical stage. Another hugely popular play, it featured Sammy Davis Jr. in the leading role. Later, in 1970, the team would write the book for *Applause,* a reworking of the Hollywood film *All about Eve.* In 1989, Adams and Strouse would be inducted into the Songwriters Hall of

Fame, and in 2002, into the Theatre Hall of Fame. Incidentally, Adams, like Powell, is a transplanted Ohioan (Heisler, 6–17).

51. On February 14, 2007, I wrote a letter to Lee Adams telling him about my work on Powell and asking him for any information he might have on their aborted collaboration. To my delight, he called me back a short time later. He said that he remembered Powell as "lovely and demure—yet troubled," adding that she was "delightful and acerbic, but underneath there was always that darkness." He recalled that he and Strouse had finished two songs for the musical (Strouse recalls four) when the partnership was shelved because of the pressing demands of their work on *Golden Boy,* though in December 1964 the pair tried to interest her in the project again. At that time, Powell wrote, "I am so tired and blah and brainwashed these days that I really don't think I'm up to it" (*Letters,* 329). Later, in an e-mail Charles Strouse wrote to me, he called Powell "one of the best people I ever knew." When I subsequently spoke with him on the telephone, he said that the word "pincushion" forever comes to his mind when he thinks of Powell—that she was unusually warm and cozy, offering milk and cookies in her kitchen, and that she had "the most sharp, sophisticated small-townness about her." Sounding tearful, he then added, "I just liked her so much." Strouse said that he would include Powell in the memoir he was then at work on, titled for the time being *My Trip to Tomorrow.* He said that had I not reminded him about Dawn, he might not have remembered to include her. As it turns out, he did not. His book was published in 2008 under the title *Put on a Happy Face: A Broadway Memoir.*

CHAPTER 7: "TURN, MAGIC WHEEL"

1. It seems that Josephson is misremembering here. According to Frances Kiernan, the article that first called McCarthy "Lady with a Switchblade" appeared not in *Time* but in a 1963 *Life* magazine article, a review of McCarthy's novel *The Group* (519).

2. Powell had met Bennett Cerf years before; a photo circa 1943, included in this volume, shows her seated next to him at an event promoting the Council on Books in Wartime effort. According to *Books for Victory,* the CBW during World War II donated "millions of books to the troops. Everyday Americans contributed their old novels from home, while publishers and authors worked with the government to print and distribute free paperbacks for GIs and liberated civilians overseas" (Brozyna).

3. The lines continue: "These same social, sexual and career shenanigans can be observed in dozens of other hyper-prosperous urban settings where life has been transformed into a theatre of the self" (Howard, "Save Your Life").

4. The PEN Club (an international organization for "poets, playwrights, essayists, editors, and novelists") opened in New York in 1922. Its mission was to "dispel national, ethnic, and racial hatreds and to promote understanding

among all countries" (PEN, "About PEN," 1), though it seems at least in Powell's mind to have become something of a snobbish social club. Writer Francine Prose, a Powell fan, is a former president of PEN American Center; Powell sometimes referred to the exclusive organization as the "Penis Club" (Page, telephone, March 7, 2013).

WORKS CITED

PRIMARY SOURCES

New York Novels

Angels on Toast. 1940. South Royalton, VT: Steerforth Press, 1996.

The Golden Spur. 1962. Reprint, with an introduction by Gore Vidal, New York: Vintage Books, 1990.

The Happy Island. 1938. South Royalton, VT: Steerforth Press, 1998.

The Locusts Have No King. 1948. Reprint, with an introduction by John Guare, New York: Yarrow Press, 1990.

A Time to Be Born. 1942. South Royalton, VT: Steerforth Press, 1996.

Turn, Magic Wheel. 1936. South Royalton, VT: Steerforth Press, 1999.

Whither. Boston: Small, Maynard, and Co., 1925.

The Wicked Pavilion. 1954. South Royalton, VT: Steerforth Press, 1996.

Ohio Novels

The Bride's House. 1929. South Royalton, VT: Steerforth Press, 1998.

Dance Night. 1930. South Royalton, VT: Steerforth Press, 1999.

My Home Is Far Away. 1944. South Royalton, VT: Steerforth Press, 1999.

She Walks in Beauty. New York: Brentano's, 1928.

The Story of a Country Boy. 1934. South Royalton, VT: Steerforth Press, 2001.

The Tenth Moon. 1932. Reprinted as *Come Back to Sorrento,* Powell's original title, South Royalton, VT: Steerforth Press, 1997.

Other Novels

A Cage for Lovers. Boston: Houghton Mifflin, 1957.

A Man's Affair (abridged revision of *Angels on Toast*). New York: Fawcett, Gold Medal Books, 1956.

Novel Collections

Dawn Powell at Her Best. Edited by Tim Page. South Royalton, VT: Steerforth Press, 1994.

Dawn Powell: Novels, 1930–1942. Edited by Tim Page. New York: Library of America, 2001.

Dawn Powell: Novels, 1944–1962. Edited by Tim Page. New York: Library of America, 2001.

Three by Dawn Powell. Introduced by Gore Vidal. New York: Vintage Books for Quality Paperback Book Club, 1989.

Poem

"Dead Things." In *The Independent Poetry Anthology 1925,* edited by E. Ralph Cheyney, Harry Alan Potamkin, et al., 75. New York: Independent Poetry Anthologists, 1925.

Published Plays

Four Plays by Dawn Powell: Big Night, Women at Four O'Clock, Walking down Broadway, Jig Saw. Edited and introduction by Michael Sexton and Tim Page. South Royalton, VT: Steerforth Press, 1999.

Jig Saw. New York: Farrar and Rinehart, 1934.

Short Story Collections

Dawn Powell at Her Best. Edited with an introduction by Tim Page. South Royalton, VT: Steerforth Press, 1994.

Short Stories from the New Yorker: A Collection of Sixty-Eight Notable Stories. New York: Simon and Schuster, 1940.

Sunday, Monday and Always. Boston: Houghton Mifflin, 1952. Rev. ed., as *Sunday, Monday, and Always* with an introduction and further selection by Tim Page, South Royalton, VT: Steerforth Press, 1999.

Short Fiction

"And When She Was Bad—." *Breezy Stories* 12, no. 4 (August 1921): 350–56.

"Artist's Life." *New Yorker,* October 26, 1936. Reprinted in *Dawn Powell at Her Best,* edited by Tim Page. South Royalton, VT: Steerforth Press, 1994.

"Blue Hyacinths." *New Yorker,* July 15, 1933, 22, 24. Reprinted in *Sunday, Monday and Always.* Boston: Houghton Mifflin, 1952; also in rev. ed., edited by Tim Page, 173–78. South Royalton, VT: Steerforth Press, 1999.

"Bon Voyage." *New Yorker,* April 22, 1933, 17–18.

"The Daisy Chain." *New Yorker,* September 30, 1933, 19–20.

"Dinner on the Rocks." *Esquire,* April 1954, 57–58, 134–37. Reprinted in *Sunday, Monday, and Always,* rev. ed., edited further selection by Tim Page, 191–201. South Royalton, VT: Steerforth Press, 1999.

"Dynamite in the Office." *Coronet,* February 1938, 67–70.

"Elegy." *transition* 8 (November 1927): 55–59.

"The Elopers." *Saturday Evening Post,* August 24, 1963, 56+. Reprinted in *Sunday, Monday and Always,* rev. ed., edited by Tim Page, 211–18. South Royalton, VT: Steerforth Press, 1999.

"Enter Two Girls, Laughing." *Harper's Bazaar,* January 1939, 75–77, 92.

"I'm Glad She's Happy." *Redbook,* November 1939, 37, 94–96.

"The Little Green Model." *Munsey's Magazine,* February 1924, 135–45.

"The Nefarious Triangle." *Today's Woman,* November 1949, 46–47, 116–20.

"Not the Marrying Kind." No Source. Published after April 1926.

"Orchids for Rosanie." *Munsey's Magazine,* March 1928, 284–93.

"Precious." *Munsey's Magazine,* January 1928, 663–72.

"Such a Pretty Day." In *Short Stories from the New Yorker: A Collection of Sixty-Eight Notable Stories,* 303–12. New York: Simon and Schuster, 1940. Reprinted in *Sunday, Monday and Always,* 59–71. Boston: Houghton Mifflin, 1952; rev. ed., edited and further selection by Tim Page, 67–81. South Royalton, VT: Steerforth Press, 1999.

"You Should Have Brought Your Mink." *Story* [*Magazine*], January–February 1943, 98–103. Reprinted in *Sunday, Monday and Always,* 3–11. Boston: Houghton Mifflin, 1952; rev. ed., edited and further selection by Tim Page, 83–96. South Royalton, VT: Steerforth Press, 1999.

"Weekend in Town." *Saturday Evening Post,* July 25–August 1, 1964, 58–63.

Diary and Letter Compilations

The Diaries of Dawn Powell, 1931–1965. Edited by Tim Page. South Royalton, VT: Steerforth Press, 1995.

Selected Letters of Dawn Powell, 1913–1965. Edited by Tim Page. New York: Henry Holt, 1999.

Essays and Book Reviews

"Celebrating a Greenwich Village Christmas Idyll." *Chicago Tribune Magazine of Books,* December 1, 1963, Christmas Books, Section 9, 6.

"Dawn Powell" (autobiographical entry). In *Twentieth-Century Authors: A Biographical Dictionary of Modern Literature,* edited by Stanley Kunitz and Howard Haycraft, 1123. New York: H. Wilson, 1942.

"Dawn Powell" (autobiographical entry). *Story* 22, no. 9 (January–February 1943): 103.

"A Diamond to Cut New York." Selections from *The Diaries of Dawn Powell.* Selected by Tim Page. *New Yorker,* June 26 and July 3, 1995, 104–13.

Jacket blurb for *Bourgeois Anonymous,* by Morris Philipson. New York: Vanguard Press, 1965.

Jacket blurb for *Joe Gould's Secret,* by Joseph Mitchell (1965). New York: Vintage Books, 1999. Originally published as a review, *Washington Post,* 1965.

"Lovely Land of Never." Review of *The World in Vogue,* compiled by the Viking Press and Vogue Editors for Viking, etc. *New York Times,* November 3, 1963.

"Mary Petty Presents." Review of *This Pretty Pace,* by Mary Petty; preface by James Thurber. *Nation,* January 5, 1946, 20.

"Radio's Gift to Art." Review of *Fourteen Radio Plays,* by Arch Oboler. *Partisan Review,* May–June 1941, 251–53.

"Speaking of the Younger Generation." *Harper's Bazaar,* August 1949, 114, 179.

"Staten Island, I Love You." *Esquire,* October 1965, 120–25.

"Two Historical Novels." Review of *Young Bess,* by Margaret Irwin, and *The Violent Friends,* by Winston Clewes. *Tomorrow,* May 1945, 77–78.

"Vision of Don Juan." *Flair Magazine,* "All Male Issue," July 1950, 24–24, 99.

"What Are You Doing in My Dreams?" *Vogue Magazine,* October 1, 1963, 153, 212–13.

SECONDARY SOURCES

Aaron, Daniel. "Loaded Words." *New Republic,* April 8, 1996, 37+.

Abbott, Berenice. *New York in the Thirties.* Text by Elizabeth McCausland. Originally published 1939 as *Changing New York.* New York: Dover, 1973.

"About This Book." Publisher's synopsis of *Turn, Magic Wheel,* by Dawn Powell. May 15, 2005. http://www.steerforth.com/turn_magic_wheel.html.

Acocella, Joan. "Life and Letters: After the Laughs." *New Yorker,* August 16, 1993, 76+.

Adams, Lee. "Dawn Powell: Charm and Wit." Letters. *New York Times,* February 10, 2002, Arts, 2.

———. Telephone conversation, February 23, 2007.

Ahlstrom, Janice M., ed. "A Quote from 'Backward Glances' by Mary Casement Furlong." Addendum to "The Shore Club" by Percy Kendall Smith. *Historical Society Quarterly* (Lake County, Ohio) 9, no. 3 (August 1967): 167–68.

Alexiou, Alice Sparberg. *Jane Jacobs: Urban Visionary.* New Brunswick, NJ: Rutgers University Press, 2006.

"Algonquin Round Table." *American Masters.* PBS. September 9, 2003. http://www.pbs.org/wnet/americanmasters/algonquin_round_table.html.

Allen, Brooke. "Out of the Provinces, On the Town." *Wall Street Journal,* October 19, 1998, A24.

Altman, Billy. *Laughter's Gentle Soul: The Life of Robert Benchley.* New York: Norton, 1997.

Angell, Roger. Introduction to *Here Is New York,* by E. B. White. 1948. Reprint, New York: The Little Bookroom, 1999.

Atkinson, Brooks. "Customs of the Business" (full title truncated; illegible). Review of *Big Night,* by Dawn Powell. *New York Times,* January 18, 1933, n.p.

Bach, Steven. *Dazzler: The Life and Times of Moss Hart.* New York: Da Capo Press (Perseus Books), 2001.

Bailey, Blake. "Citizen of the City: A Biography of Joseph Mitchell." Review of *Man in Profile: Joseph Mitchell of* The New Yorker, by Thomas Kunkel. *New York Times,* May 15, 2015.

Baker, Carlos. *Ernest Hemingway: A Life Story.* New York: Scribner's, 1969.

Barnes, Clive. "Elegy for Tanny—Tanaquil LeClercq—Obituary." *Dance Magazine,* April 2001.

Barnes, Djuna. *Nightwood.* Introduction by T. S. Eliot. New York: New Directions, 1937.

Barnes, J. E. "A Hurricane in the Halls of Power." Review of *A Time to Be Born,* by Dawn Powell. Amazon.com, August 6, 2002. http://www.amazon.com/Time-Be-Born-Dawn-Powell/dp/.

Barnet, Andrea. *All Night Party: The Women of Bohemian Greenwich Village and Harlem, 1913–1930.* Chapel Hill, NC: Algonquin Books, 2004.

Barrett, Laura. "Material without Being Real: Photography and the End of Reality in *The Great Gatsby.*" *Studies in the Novel* 30, no. 4 (Winter 1988): 540–57.

Basten, Fred E. *Great American Billboards: 100 Years of History by the Side of the Road.* Berkeley, CA: Ten Speed Press, 2006.

Batterberry, Michael, and Ariane Batterberry. *On the Town in New York: A History of Eating, Drinking and Entertainments from 1776 to the Present.* New York: Scribner's, 1973.

Beach, Joseph Warren. *American Fiction, 1920–1940.* New York: Russell and Russell, 1940.

Beatty, Warren, director. *Reds.* Paramount Films, 1981.

Beebe, Lucius. *The Stork Club Bar Book.* New York: Rinehart, 1946.

———. *Snoot if You Must.* New York: D. Appleton-Century, 1943.

Beer, Tom. "Recommended Reading, Buckeye Baby." Review of *My Home is Far Away,* by Dawn Powell. *Newsday,* May 30, 2004, C44.

Begley, Adam. "Dawn Powell: From Forgotten to 'Classic.'" *Chicago Tribune,* January 7, 1996, 7.

Beha, Christopher R. "A Long Goodbye." Review of *The End of Your Life Book Club,* by Will Schwalbe. *New York Times Book Review,* January 6, 2013, 16.

Benchley, Robert. "Box Score." *New Yorker,* July 7, 1934, 28.

———. Review of *Big Night,* by Dawn Powell. *New Yorker,* January 28, 1933, 26.

Benét, William Rose. *Benét's Reader's Encyclopedia.* 3rd ed. Edited by Katherine Baker Siepmann. New York: Harper and Row, 1987.

Benfey, Christopher. "Sex and the City." Review of *Republic of Dreams,* by Ross Wetzsteon. *New Republic Online,* November 11, 2002. http://tnr.com/republicofdreams.html.

Bennett, Bruce. "New York Nightlife and Music—Cedar Tavern." *New York Magazine,* July 3, 2006. http://www.nymag.com/listings/bar/cedar_tavern/.

Bennett, Christopher. Personal letter, August 31, 2006.

———. Telephone interview, August 23, 2006.

Berg, A. Scott. *Max Perkins, Editor of Genius.* New York: Pocket Books, 1978.

Berne, Betsy. "What's Cool?" *Vogue,* July 1996, 114+.

Bernstein, Richard. "Midwestern Wholesomeness, Big-City Wit." Review of *Selected Letters of Dawn Powell, 1913–1965,* edited by Tim Page. *New York Times,* October 22, 1999, Arts, 34.

Between the Covers Rare Books. "*Turn, Magic Wheel,* by Powell, Dawn." AddAll Book Search listing, May 16, 2005. http://www.addall.com.

Bing, Jonathan, Maria Simson, and Jeff Zaleski. Review of *Dawn Powell: A Biography,* by Tim Page. *Publishers Weekly,* August 3, 1998, 61.

Birns, Nicholas. "Beautiful Lamptown: The Writings of Dawn Powell." *Hollins Critic,* December 2007, 2–16.

Black, Mary. *Old New York in Early Photographs, from the Collection of the New-York Historical Society.* New York: Dover, 1976.

Blumenthal, Ralph. *Stork Club: America's Most Famous Nightspot and the Lost World of Café Society.* New York: Little, Brown, 2000.

Booklist. Review of *Angels on Toast,* by Dawn Powell. December 15, 1940, 155.

Boorstin, Daniel J. *The Americans: The Democratic Experience.* New York: Vintage, 1974.

Boston Daily Globe. Review of *A Time to Be Born,* by Dawn Powell. September 24, 1942, 19.

Boston Evening Transcript. "Fiction of the Season from Various Hands." Review of *Turn, Magic Wheel,* by Dawn Powell. 1936. Book Section, 4.

Boston Globe. "Dawn Powell Has Arrived: Years after Her Death, a Wry Novelist Is Being Published to Critical Acclaim Because of the Efforts of a Few Dedicated Fans." January 16, 2000, A1.

———. "Dawn Powell's Durable Words." January 23, 2000. www.highbeamresearch.com.

Bouché, Louis. "Vignettes: Dawn Powell." Typewritten version of the artist's handwritten notes made by Bouché's daughter, Jane Strong. Unpublished, ca. 1950. Courtesy Katherine Degn, Kraushaar Galleries, New York, June 2008.

Boudreaux, Jonathan. "Seinfeld." November 24, 2004. http://www.tvdvdreviews.com/seinfeld1.html.

Bray, Robert. Introduction to *The Glass Menagerie,* by Tennessee Williams, vii–xv. 1945. Reprint, New York: New Directions, 1999.

Breit, Harvey. "In and Out of Books." *New York Times,* June 6, 1954, BR8.

Brickell, Herschell. "The Literary Landscape." Review of *Turn, Magic Wheel,* by Dawn Powell. *Review of Reviews* 93 (April 1936): 14–21.

Brontë, Charlotte. *Villette.* 1853. New York: Penguin, 1979.

Brophy, Brigid. "Solitaries." Review of *The Golden Spur,* by Dawn Powell. *New Statesman,* June 21, 1963, 942.

Brownrigg, Sylvia. Review of *Dawn Powell: A Biography,* by Tim Page. *Salon.com,* September 2, 2004. http://archive.salon.com/books/sneaks /1998/11/13sneaks.html.

Broyard, Anatole. *Kafka Was the Rage: A Greenwich Village Memoir.* New York: Vintage Books, 1993.

Brozyna, Andrew. *Books for Victory: The Council of Books on Wartime, 1941–46.* March 3, 2013. http://www.booksforvictory.com/2013/03/the-council-on -books-in-wartime-194146.html.

Buford, Bill. Jacket blurb for *The Diaries of Dawn Powell, 1931–1965,* by Dawn Powell, edited with an introduction by Tim Page. South Royalton, VT: Steerforth Press, 1998.

Bullock, Florence Haxton. "Grim Round of Pleasure." Review of *The Locusts Have No King,* by Dawn Powell. *New York Herald Tribune Weekly Book Review,* May 2, 1948, 6.

Burns, Ric. *New York: An Illustrated History.* New York: Alfred A. Knopf, 1999.

Burra, Peter. Fiction. Review of *Turn, Magic Wheel,* by Dawn Powell. *Spectator,* July 10, 1936, 72.

Bush, Stacy. "Books of a Lifetime." Review of *Dawn Powell: A Biography,* by Tim Page. *Austin Chronicle,* November 30, 1998. http://weeklywire.com /ww/11–398/austin_books_feature1.html.

Canby, Vincent. "Only on the Stage Does *Iceman* Truly Come Alive." *New York Times,* April 18, 1999, Theatre 1+.

Carlin, Margaret. "Enamored Author Stirs Dawn Powell Revival." Spotlight Review, *Rocky Mountain News,* March 3, 1996, 1+.

Carnes, Mark, ed. *Invisible Giants: Fifty Americans Who Shaped the Nation but Missed the History Books.* New York: Oxford University Press, 2002.

Carpenter, Teresa, ed. *New York Diaries, 1609–2009.* New York: Modern Library, 2012.

———. Personal e-mail, November 6, 2012.

Carr, Virginia Spencer. *Dos Passos: A Life.* Garden City, NY: Doubleday, 1984.

Castronovo, David, and Janet Groth, eds. *Edmund Wilson: The Man in Letters.* Athens: Ohio University Press, 2005.

Cather, Willa. "My First Novels (There Were Two)." In *Willa Cather on Writing as an Art.* 1920. Reprint, Lincoln: Bison Books, University of Nebraska Press, 1988.

Cerf, Bennett. *At Random: The Reminiscences of Bennett Cerf.* New York: Random House, 1977.

Chamberlain, John. Books of the Times. *New York Times,* December 12, 1935. https://www.nytimes.com/books/00/03/26/specials/mccarthy-marshall.html.

Chasteney, Robert W., Jr. *For Love of Ruth: A Celebration of English and American Literature.* Tucson: University of Arizona Press, 1997.

Chauncey, George. *Gay New York: Gender, Urban Culture, and the Making of the Gay Male World 1890–1940.* New York: Basic Books (Harper Collins), 1994.

Cheever, John. "The Peril in the Street." *New Yorker,* March 21, 1942, 17.

Churchill, Allen. *The Improper Bohemians: Greenwich Village in Its Heyday.* New York: Dutton, 1959.

Church of the Transfiguration. "A Brief History of the Little Church." November 13, 2005. http://www/littlechurch.org/history.html.

Clark, Barrett H. Playbill, *Big Night.* January 1933, 14.

Clark, Edwin. "Scott Fitzgerald Looks into Middle Age." Review of *The Great Gatsby,* by F. Scott Fitzgerald. *New York Times,* April 19, 1925, n.p.

Clurman, Harold. *The Fervent Years: The Story of the Group Theatre and the Thirties.* New York: Knopf, 1967.

Coates, Joseph. "Forgotten No More: Rediscovering the Shrewd Comic Vision of Novelist Dawn Powell." *Chicago Tribune,* April 22, 1990, 3+.

Coggin, John Dos Passos. Personal e-mail, December 3, 2013.

Cohen, Lisa. *All We Know: Three Lives.* New York: Farrar, Straus and Giroux, 2012.

Cohen, Randy. "We'll Map Manhattan." *New York Times Book Review,* May 1, 2005, 31.

———. "We Mapped Manhattan." *New York Times Book Review,* June 5, 2005, 23+.

Columbia, David Patrick, and Jeff Hirsh. *New York Social Diary* 2, no. 504 (June 9, 2003), 1–5. http://www.newyorksocialdiary.com/legacy/socialdiary/2003/socialdiary06_09_03.php.

The Columbia Electronic Encyclopedia. 6th ed. S.v. "Skywriting." New York: Columbia University Press, 2007.

Columbia University Libraries Special Collections. "Jewels in Her Crown: Treasures of Columbia University Libraries Special Collection, Literature, #221: Dawn Powell." September 16, 2005. http://www.columbia.edu/cu/lweb/eresources/exhibitions/treasures/html/long_topic11.html.

Conry, Kathleen. Personal e-mails, October 2 and October 23, 2006.

———. Telephone interview, July 29, 2006.

Contemporary Authors. "Dawn Powell 1896–1965." November 20, 2004. http://web5.infotrac.galegroup.com/itw/infomark/910/744/6919836.

Contento, William G. FictionMags Index. Updated November 1, 2013. http://www.philsp.com/homeville/fmi/ostart.htm.

Cowles, Fleur. "With *Flair* this Month: Dawn Powell." All Male issue, *Flair,* July 1950, 5.

Cowley, Malcolm. "The Last of the Lost Generation." *Esquire,* July 1963, 77–79.

———. "Profiles: Unshaken Friend, Part I." *New Yorker,* April 1, 1944, 32+.

———. "Profiles: Unshaken Friend, Part II." *New Yorker,* April 8, 1944, 30+.

Crichton, Kyle. *Total Recoil.* Garden City, NY: Doubleday, 1960.

Crowther, Bosley. "*Du Barry Was a Lady:* Mirthful Newcomer at the Capitol." *New York Times,* August 20, 1943. http://movies2.nytimes.com/dubarry/.

Cummings, Paul. "Interview with Peggy Bacon Conducted by Paul Cummings at the Artist's Home in Cape Porpoise, Maine." *Smithsonian Archives of American Art,* May 8, 1973, 1–36. http://www.aaa.si.edu /collections/oralhistories/transcripts/bacon73.htm.

Dabney, Lewis M. *Edmund Wilson: A Life in Literature.* New York: Farrar, Straus and Giroux, 2005.

———, ed. *Edmund Wilson: The Sixties: From Notebooks and Diaries of the Period,* by Edmund Wilson. New York: Farrar, Straus and Giroux, 1993.

"Dale Carnegie Training History." June 6, 2005. http://www.dalecarnegie.com /about_us/history.jsp.

Dana, Robert W. "Luchow's Marking 75th Anniversary." *Tips on Tables,* April 1957, 1+.

Davies, Paul. "Samuel Beckett." *The Literary Encyclopedia.* http://www .litencyc.com.

Davis, Hope Hale. *Great Day Coming: A Memoir of the 1930s.* South Royalton, VT: Steerforth Press, 1994.

Dawson, Barbara, et al. "A Finding Aid to the Esther McCoy Papers, Biographical Note." *Smithsonian Archives of American Art.* Updated February 22, 2005. www.aaa.si.edu/collections/findingaids/mccoesth.htm.

Dell, Floyd. *Love in Greenwich Village.* New York: Doran, 1926.

Delman Shoes. "About Us." December 12, 2006. http://www.delmanshoes .com/about_us/.

Delson, Susan B. *Dudley Murphy: Hollywood Wild Card.* Minneapolis: University of Minnesota Press, 2006.

Deubler, David. "Meet Artists, Writers, and Low-Lifes—and Guess Which Is Which." Review of *The Golden Spur,* by Dawn Powell. Amazon.com, October 24, 2005. http://www.amazon.com/Golden-Spur-Dawn-Powell /dp/1883642272/.

Dickstein, Morris. "Village People." Review of *Republic of Dreams: Greenwich Village, The American Bohemia, 1910–1960,* by Ross Wetzsteon. *New York Times Book Review,* July 21, 2002, 9.

Dirda, Michael. "Recommended: Best Novels of 1990." Review of *The Locusts Have No King,* by Dawn Powell. *Washington Post,* December 2, 1990, X18.

———. "*Satyricon* in Manhattan." Review of *The Locusts Have No King,* by Dawn Powell. *Washington Post,* March 18, 1990, X10+.

Dos Passos, John. "A Note on Fitzgerald." In *The Crack-Up,* by F. Scott Fitzgerald, edited by Edmund Wilson. New York: New Directions, 1945.

Douglas, Ann. *Terrible Honesty: Mongrel Manhattan in the 1920s.* New York: Noonday Press, 1996.

Drummerworld. "George Wettling." http://www.drummerworld.com /drummers/George_Wettling.html.

Dugan, Penelope. Review of *The Story of My Father: A Memoir,* by Sue Miller, and *Assembling My Father: A Daughter's Detective Story,* by Anna Cypra Oliver. *Fourth Genre: Explorations in Nonfiction* 8, no. 1 (Spring 2006): 157–59.

Dunlap, David W. *On Broadway: A Journey Uptown over Time.* New York: Rizzoli, 1990.

Dyer, Richard. "After Dawn: The Life and Art of Dawn Powell, Novelist and Woman About New York." *Boston Globe,* December 24, 1995, 37.

———. "Bio Continues the Revival of Dawn Powell." *Boston Globe,* September 23, 1998, C5+.

———. "Biography Rediscovers a Most Underrated Novelist." *Chicago Tribune,* October 1, 1996, 3.

———. "Dawn Powell's Sharp Pen Goes Right to the Heart." *Boston Globe,* July 26, 1995, 61.

Earle, David. "Dawn Powell, Flapper Stories, and the Pulps." *Boozehounds and Bookleggers* (blog), October 5, 2015. http://www.boozehoundsblog .com/dawnpowell/2015/10/5/dawn-powell-flapper-stories-and-the-pulps.

———. Personal e-mail, February 16, 2014.

Earnshaw, Doris. Review of *The Diaries of Dawn Powell, 1931–1965,* by Dawn Powell, edited by Tim Page. *World Literature Today* (Summer 1996): 705.

Edel, Leon. "The Deathbed Notes of Henry James." *Atlantic Monthly,* June 1968. http://www.theatlantic.com/past/docs/unbound/flashbks/james /jnote.htm.

Ehrlich, Susan. "Pacific Dreams: Currents of Surrealism and Fantasy in California Art." *PAJ: A Journal of Performance and Art* 52, no. 18.1 (January 1996): 72–80.

Evening World, Late Edition. "Wed to Vindicate Fannie Hurst, They Now Seek a Flat." January 3, 1921, 3.

"Exiles and Émigrés, Elisabeth Bergner." German 43, Information Resources Forum, Dartmouth College. May 3, 2005. http://www.dartmouth.edu /~germ43/resources/biographies/bergner-e.

Famous Texans. "Ann Miller." http://www.famoustexans.com/annmiller.htm.

Farnham, Eleanor. "Dawn Powell Gousha, '18, Speaker at Assembly." *Bulletin of Lake Erie College, Alumna Issue,* May 1940, 3.

Farnsworth, Marjorie. *The Ziegfeld Follies: A History in Text and Pictures.* Introduction by Billie Burke Ziegfeld. New York: Bonanza Books, 1956.

Feingold, Michael. "Dawn Powell's Acid Texts." *Village Voice Literary Supplement* 86 (June 1990): 12–14.

Feld, Rose. "Glitter Girl in the Spotlight." Review of *A Time to Be Born*, by Dawn Powell. *New York Herald Tribune Books*, September 6, 1942, 6.

———. "Novels of New York." Review of *Angels on Toast*, by Dawn Powell. *New York Herald Tribune Books*, October 6, 1940, 12.

———. Review of *The Wicked Pavilion*, by Dawn Powell. *New York Herald Tribune Book Review*, September 12, 1954, 12.

Ferguson, Otis. "Far from Main Street." Review of *Angels on Toast*, by Dawn Powell. *New Republic*, October 28, 1940, 599.

Finalborgo, Jane. "A Professor's Role in the New Dawn of a 'Real' Dorothy Parker: In and around Long Island University: Southampton." *Long Island University Magazine* 9, no. 1 (Winter/Spring 2001): 9.

Fischer, Carl, photographer. *Esquire* portrait. Telephone conversation, April 21, 2014.

Fiske, Dwight. *Without Music*. Foreword by Robert Benchley. New York: Chatham Press, 1933.

Fitzgerald, F. Scott. *The Crack-Up*. Edited by Edmund Wilson. New York: New Directions, 1945.

———. *The Great Gatsby*. 1925. Reprint, New York: Scribner's, Trade Paper ed., 2004.

Fitzpatrick, Kevin C. "Members of the Round Table." *The Algonquin Round Table: The Official Website of the Vicious Circle*. October 2005. www .algonquinroundtable.org/members.html.

Flaubert, Gustave. *A Sentimental Education: The Story of a Young Man*. Translated by Douglas Parmee. 1869. Reprint: New York: Oxford University Press, 2000.

Florey, Kitty Burns. *Sister Bernadette's Barking Dog: The Quirky History and Lost Art of Diagramming Sentences*. Hoboken, NJ: Melville House, 2006.

Fogarty, Robert S., ed. Editorial, *Antioch Review* 39, no. 4 (Fall 1981): 399–401.

Frank, Michael. "This Side of Heaven, Please, in the Village." *New York Times*, May 10, 2002, E31+.

Freeman, Joseph. *An American Testament: A Narrative of Rebels and Romantics*. New York: Farrar and Rinehart, 1936.

Friedman, Robin. "Mid-America Meets the Wicked City." Review of *The Happy Island*, by Dawn Powell. Amazon.com, December 26, 2002. http://www .amazon.com/The-Happy-Island-Dawn-Powell/product-reviews /1883642795/.

———. "A Rediscovered American Writer." Review of *The Golden Spur*, by Dawn Powell. Amazon.com, June 1, 2002. http://amazon.com/The -Golden-Spur-Dawn-Powell/dp/.

———. "A Tart New York Love Story." Review of *Turn, Magic Wheel*, by Dawn Powell. Amazon.com, December 2, 2002. http://amazon.com /Turn-Magic-Wheel-Dawn-Powell/product-reviews/1883642728.

Fuller, James C. "Fun with Foibles." Review of *The Locusts Have No King*, by Dawn Powell. *Saturday Review of Literature*, May 15, 1948, 19.

Gant, Michael S. Review of *Great American Billboards:100 Years of History by the Side of the Road*, by Fred E. Basten. *Metroactive*, January 10–16, 2007. www.metroactive.com.

Garner, Dwight. "Rhyming Name Dropper Returns." *New York Times*, December 15, 2008, Arts C1+.

Gates, Anita. "*Jig Saw:* Better a Cutting Word than a Dull Bushel of Babies." Review of *Jig Saw*, by Dawn Powell. *New York Times Late Edition*, March 31, 2001, B18.

Gates, Robert Allan. *The New York Vision: Interpretations of New York City in the American Novel*. Lanham, MD: University Press of America, 1987.

Gavin, James. *Intimate Nights: The Golden Age of New York Cabaret*. New York: Grove Weidenfeld, 1991.

Gelb, Arthur. *City Room*. New York: Penguin Putnam, 2003.

Geracimos, Ann. "Discovering Literary Wit of Dawn Powell." *Washington Times*, March 24, 1996, Arts, 1–2.

Gibbons, James. "The Novels of Dawn Powell." *Raritan* 20, no. 1 (Summer 2000): 142–59.

Gilbert, Morris. "In Search of a Father." Review of *The Golden Spur*, by Dawn Powell. *New York Times Book Review*, October 14, 1962, 40.

Gill, Brendan. Introduction to *The Portable Dorothy Parker*, xv–xxviii. 1944. Revised and enlarged ed., New York: Penguin, 1978.

———. "Rough and Smooth." Review of *The Wicked Pavilion*, by Dawn Powell. *New Yorker*, October 16, 1954, 155+.

Gilman, Coburn, trans. "She Had to Be Right: A Story." By Frederic Boutet. *Harper's Magazine*, December 1926, 99–101.

Gody, Lou, et al., eds. *The WPA Guide to New York City: The Federal Writer's Project Guide to 1930s New York*. 1939. New introduction by William H. Whyte. New York: Pantheon, 1984.

Goldstein, Malcolm. *George S. Kaufman: His Life, His Theater*. New York: Oxford University Press, 1979.

Gooch, Brad. *City Poet: The Life and Times of Frank O'Hara*. New York: Knopf, 1993.

Gopnik, Adam. "As Big as the Ritz: Scott and Zelda Go On Inspiring New Books." *New Yorker*, September 22, 2014, 103.

———. "Under One Roof: The Death and Life of the New York Department Store." New York Journal, *New Yorker*, September 22, 2003, 92+.

Gore, John, ed. *Creevey: Selections from* The Creevey Papers. 1903. Reprint, London: John Murray, 1948.

Gray, Christopher. "A Sixth Ave. Automat Sign, Wanamaker's Walkway." *New York Times,* June 1, 1997. http://www.nytimes.com/archives/wanamakers/html.

———. "Streetscapes: The Former Vanderbilt Hotel." *New York Times,* March 3, 2003, sec. 11, p. 7. Reprinted in *New York Architecture,* http://www.nyc-architecture.com/MID/MID026.htm.

———. "Streetscapes: The Half-Moon Hotel, a Symbol of Coney Island, Is about to Be Eclipsed." *New York Times,* May 7, 1989. http:www.nytimes.com/gst.fullpage.html.

———. "Streetscapes: The Old Gotham Hotel, Now the Peninsula New York; A History Shaped, in Part, by State Liquor Laws." *New York Times,* January 3, 1999. http:www.nytimes.com/gst.fullpage.html.

Green, Hannah. *The Dead of the House.* 1966. Reprint, New York: Turtle Points Press, 1996.

Green, Penelope. "Decorating a One-Bedroom for Comic and Rabbit." *New York Times,* July 20, 2003, 6.

The Greenwich Village Bookshop Door: A Portal to Bohemia, 1920–1925. "The Shop." Harry Ransom Center, University of Texas, Austin. http://norman.hrc.utexas.edu/bookshopdoor/theshop.cfm#1.

Grooms, Red. "When de Kooning was King." Review of *De Kooning: An American Master,* by Mark Stevens and Annalyn Swan. *New York Times Book Review,* December 12, 2004, 10+.

Gross, Margaret Geissman. *Dancing on the Table: A History of Lake Erie College.* Burnsville, NC: Celo Valley Books, 1993.

Guare, John. Introduction to *The Locusts Have No King,* by Dawn Powell, vii–xi. New York: Yarrow Press, 1990.

Guggenheim, Peggy. *Out of This Century: The Informal Memoirs of Peggy Guggenheim.* New York: Dial Press, 1946.

Hamill, Pete. *Downtown: My Manhattan.* New York: Little, Brown, 2004.

"The Hannah Green Papers." Stanford University Libraries. May 4, 2006. http://cgi.stanford.edu/dept/SUL/library/cgi-bin/sulair.

Hansen, Liane, with Tim Page. "Preview of Upcoming Segment on Author Dawn Powell." *NPR Weekend Edition,* January 8, 1995.

———. "Dawn Powell May Usurp Dorothy Parker as Queen of Wit." *NPR Weekend Edition,* January 8, 1995.

Harris, Luther S. *Around Washington Square: An Illustrated History of Greenwich Village.* Baltimore: Johns Hopkins University Press, 2003.

Hart, Moss. *Act One.* New York: Random House, 1959.

Harte, Barbara, and Carolyn Riley, eds. "Powell, Dawn, 1897–1965." *Contemporary Authors,* vols. 5–8: 915. Rev. ed. Detroit: Gale Research, 1969.

Haskell, Barbara, ed. *Swing Time: Reginald Marsh and Thirties New York.* New York: New-York Historical Society, 2012.

Haskell, John. "Buckminster Fuller and Isamu Noguchi." *KGB Bar Lit Magazine,* July 7, 2006. http://kgbbar.com/lit/columns/buckminster_fuller _and_isamu_noguchi.

Hassel, Holly Jean. "Wine, Women, and Song: Gender and Alcohol in Twentieth-Century American Fiction." PhD diss., University of Nebraska, 2002.

Hat Museum. "The Hat Museum." September 3, 2006. http://www .thehatmuseum.com.

Haun, Harry. "Old Vic/New Spacey." Playbill: *A Moon for the Misbegotten.* Brooks Atkinson Theatre. March 2007, 6+.

Hazlitt, William. "On the Aristocracy of Letters." In *Table-Talk: Essays on Men and Manners,* 199–207. 1821–22. Reprint, Whitefish, MT: Kessinger Publishing, 2004.

Heisler, Marcy. "Writers and Their Work: Lee Adams." *Dramatist* (November/December 2006): 6–17.

Hensher, Philip. "The Country and the City." *Atlantic Monthly,* September 1, 2001, 130–36.

———. "Groping for the Great American Novel." *Spectator,* July 6, 2002: 30+.

Hethmon, Robert H. "Days with the Group Theatre: An Interview with Clifford Odets." *Michigan Quarterly Review* 41, no. 2. (Spring 2002): 174–200.

———. "Memories of the Group Theatre: An Interview with Dawn Powell." *Tin House* 1, no. 3 (Winter 2000): 38–54.

Hirsh, Jeff. *Between the Rivers: Manhattan 1880–1920.* Charleston, SC: Arcadia, 1998.

———. *Manhattan Hotels 1880–1920.* Dover, NH: Arcadia, 1997.

History's Women. "Madame Récamier, Celebrated French Beauty 1777–1849." Accessed January 4, 2005. http://www.historyswomen.com /moregreatwomen/MadameRecamier.

Home Comfort Cook Book: Containing a Splendid Collection of Modern Recipes Chosen and Prepared by Experienced Writers on Culinary Art. St. Louis: Wrought Iron Range Company, 1918.

Horne, Gerald. *The Final Victim of the Blacklist: John Howard Lawson, Dean of the Hollywood Ten.* Berkeley: University of California Press, 2006.

Horwitz, Simi. "The Dawn Powell Festival: The Artist as 'Permanent Visitor.'" *Back Stage,* March 8–14, 2002, 45+.

Housing Works Used Book Café. "Soho's Best-Kept Secret." December 18, 2004. http://www.housingworks.org/usedbookcafe/.

Howard, Gerald. "The Dawn of Civilization." Review of *The Selected Letters of Dawn Powell,* by Dawn Powell, edited by Tim Page. *Hungry Mind Review* (Winter 1999–2000): 10.

————. "How Dawn Powell Can Save Your Life." *Salon,* September 30, 1999. http://salon.com/1999/09/30/powell/.

"Ile de France: The Great Ocean Liners." http://www.thegreatoceanliners .com/iledefrance.html.

Inge, M. Thomas, ed. *Ellen Glasgow: Centennial Essays.* Charlottesville: University Press of Virginia, 1976.

"Interchurch World Movement, January 1919–April 1921." Accessed November 31, 2015. http://library.columbia.edu/content/dam/libraryweb/locations /burke/fa/wab/ldpd_4492701.pdf.

Internet Broadway Database. *"The Lady Comes Across,* by Dawn Powell." Last revised November 26, 2005. http://www.ibdb.com/production.asp ?ID=1157.

Isherwood, Charles. "Let's Put On an Automat! Cue Cops and Cheesecake!" *New York Times,* March 31, 2007, B7+.

————. "A Long Wait for Another Shot at Broadway." Review of *Waiting for Godot,* 2009 Broadway production. April 26, 2009: Arts 6.

Jablonski, Edward. *Irving Berlin: American Troubadour.* New York: Henry Holt and Company, 1999.

James, Henry. *The New York Stories of Henry James.* Edited by Colm Tóibín. New York: New York Review of Books Classics, 2005.

Jefferson, Margo. "Characters 'Laboring to Maladjust.'" Review of *Dawn Powell at Her Best,* edited by Tim Page. *New York Times,* October 19, 1994, Arts 1+.

Jonathan Larson Performing Arts Foundation. "Ivy Meeropol." December 12, 2005. http:www.jlpaf.org/biographies.html.

Jong, Erica. "I've Got a Little List." *Nation* 267, no. 16 (1998): 32–35.

Joseph, John. "Dawn Powell—Portrait of an Often Overlooked Literary Great." Talk for the Greenwich Village Society for Historic Preservation, December 11, 2014. Published January 16, 2015. https://www.youtube .com/watch?v=efnLgvKNt7A.

Josephson, Matthew. "Dawn Powell: A Woman of Esprit." *Southern Review* 9, no. 1 (1973): 18–52.

Joslyn, Heather. "Bright Lights, Big City: Dawn Powell and the Glory of Revival." *Baltimore City Paper,* October 13, 1999. http://www2.citypaper .com/news/story.asp?id=6672.

————. "A Time to Be Reborn: How Dawn Powell Came Back." Imprints Literary Supplement, *Baltimore City Paper,* October 13, 1999. http://www .citypaper.com/special/printready.asp?id=6673.

Kantor, Michael. *Broadway: The American Musical.* Episodes 1–6. PBS Home Video. Educational Broadcasting Corporation and the Broadway Film Project, Inc., 2004.

Kasson, John F. *Amusing the Million: Coney Island at the Turn of the Century.* New York: Farrar, Straus and Giroux, 1978.

Kaufman, George S., and Edna Ferber. *Three Comedies: The Royal Family, Dinner at Eight, Stage Door.* New York: Applause Books, 1999.

Kaufman, Lenard. "Captive Cinderella." Review of *A Cage for Lovers,* by Dawn Powell. *Books: The New York Times on the Web,* November 10, 1957. http://www.nytimes.com/books/98/11/15/specials/powell-cage.html.

Keen, Suzanne. "A Writer's Long Lament: *The Diaries of Dawn Powell.*" Review of *The Diaries of Dawn Powell,* by Dawn Powell, edited by Tim Page. *Commonweal,* February 23, 1996, 24–25.

Keene, Anne T. "Dawn Powell." In *Invisible Giants: Fifty Americans Who Shaped the Nation but Missed the History Books,* edited by Mark Carnes, 230–34. New York: Oxford University Press, 2002.

Keyser, Catherine. *Playing Smart: New York Women Writers and Modern Magazine Culture.* New Brunswick, NJ: Rutgers University Press, 2012.

Kiernan, Frances. *Seeing Mary Plain: A Life of Mary McCarthy.* New York: Norton, 2000.

Kingwell, Mark. "Seventy-Five Years: New York's Lighthouse." *New York Times,* April 23, 2006, Section 14, 1+.

Kirkus Reviews. Review of *The Locusts Have No King,* by Dawn Powell. February 1, 1948, 64.

———. Review of *The Wicked Pavilion,* by Dawn Powell. July 1, 1954, 408.

Klein, Jef. *The History and Stories of the Best Bars of New York.* Nashville: Turner Publishing Co., 2006.

Lach, William, ed. *New York, New York: The City in Art and Literature.* Introduction by Brooke Astor. New York: The Metropolitan Museum of Art, 2000.

Lake Erie College (LEC) Student Bookstore online. July 12, 2006. http://www .lec.edu/campus/bookstore2/htm.

Landmarks Preservation Commission of New York. January 29, 2007. http:// www.nyc.gov/html/lpc.

Latimer, Margery. "The Agony of Growing." Review of *She Walks in Beauty,* by Dawn Powell. *New York Herald Tribune Books,* April 15, 1928, 38.

Lawliss, Chuck. *Retro New York: A Guide to Rediscovering Old New York.* Dallas: Taylor Trade Publishing, 2000.

Lawson, Jeffrey. Telephone conversations, August 25, 2012, and October 20, 2012.

Lehmann, Chris. "The Corporate Jungle." *Washington Post,* March 30, 2004, C.04.

Lehmann, Rosamond. "New Novels." Review of *Turn, Magic Wheel,* by Dawn Powell. *New Statesman and Nation,* July 18, 1936, 90.

Levin, Martin. "Bistro People." *Saturday Review,* October 2, 1954, 62.

Levy, Barbara. *Ladies Laughing: Wit as Control in Contemporary American Women Writers.* Amsterdam, The Netherlands: Gordon and Breach, OPA (Overseas Publishers Association), 1997.

Lewis, David Neal. On Shelby, Ohio. Dawn Powell Facebook page. https://www.facebook.com/pages/Dawn-Powell/109361745749723.

Lewis, Robert. *Slings and Arrows: Theater in My Life.* New York: Stein and Day, 1984.

Lewis, Sinclair. *Babbitt.* New York: Harcourt, 1922. http://www.bartleby.com/162/29.html.

Library Weekly. "Far-Off and Tomorrow: Dawn Powell." Review of *Dawn Powell: Novels 1930–1942,* by Dawn Powell. May 23, 2004. http://classiclit.about.com/library/weekly/aa090101a.htm.

Lingeman, Robert. "She Took a Village." *Nation,* November 16, 1998, 38–41.

Lloyd, James B, ed. "Stark Young." In *Lives of Mississippi Writers,* 484–88. Jackson: University Press of Mississippi, 1980.

Lockbridge, Richard. "The New Play: 'Big Night' an Angry Comedy by Dawn Powell, Opens at the Maxine Elliott." *New York Sun,* January 18, 1933, 16.

Logan, William. "Urban Poet." Review of *Selected Poems,* by Frank O'Hara, edited by Mark Ford. *New York Times Book Review,* June 29, 2008, 1+.

Lopate, Phillip. *Getting Personal: Selected Writings.* New York: Basic Books, 2003.

———, ed. *Writing New York: A Literary Anthology.* New York: Washington Square Press, 1998.

Loper, Carleen M. "Discovering Dawn Powell." Tart City, March 18, 2005. http://www.tartcity.com/DPowell.html.

Loschiavo, LindaAnn. "W. Ninth Turns 180: Highlights from a History of Socialites and Social Causes, Stars and the Bizarre." *Villager,* March 16–22, 2005, 1–5.

MacAfee, Helen. "The Library of the Quarter: Outstanding Novels." Review of *Turn, Magic Wheel,* by Dawn Powell. *Yale Review* 25 (Summer 1936): xii.

Mallon, Thomas. "Forging On: How a New York Writer Created and Sold Hundreds of Fake Letters." Review of *Can You Ever Forgive Me: Memoirs of a Literary Forger,* by Lee Israel. *New York Times Book Review,* August 3, 2008, 15.

Mandell, Jonathan. "More Than a Witty Novelist, She Wrote Plays, Too." *New York Times,* January 27, 2002, Arts: Theatre Section, 5+.

Mangione, Jerre. "The Almost Perfect Scream." Review of *Turn, Magic Wheel,* by Dawn Powell. *New Republic,* May 27, 1936, 80–81.

Mansfield, Howard, ed. *Where the Mountain Stands Alone: Stories of Place in the Moradnock Region.* Lebanon, NH: University Press of New England, 2006.

Marcus, James. Editorial Review of *The Selected Letters of Dawn Powell, 1913–1965,* edited by Tim Page. April 9, 1999. http://www.amazon.com/Select-Letters-Dawn-Powell/dp.

"Martin and Osa Johnson Safari Museum: The Johnson Story, The." Accessed August 19, 2005. http://www.safarimuseum.com/their_story.htm.

Maslon, Laurence. "Political Satire." *Broadway: The American Musical,* July 14, 2005. http://www.pbs.org/wnet/broadway/essays/political-satire/.

Matuz, Roger, and Cathy Falk, eds. "Dawn Powell 1897–1965." In *Contemporary Literary Criticism* 66:352–77. Detroit: Gale Research, 1991.

Maxine Elliott's Theatre: Dawn Powell Big Night. New York Theatre Program, January 1933. Playbill Vault. http://www.playbillvault.com/Show /Detail/8595/Big-Night.

McClatchy, J. D. Interview with Ned Rorem. "The Art of the Diary No. 1." *Paris Review* 150 (Spring 1999): n.p.

McGee, Micki, ed. *Yaddo: Making American Culture.* New York: Columbia University Press, 2008. Published on the occasion of the exhibition on Yaddo at New York Public Library, 2008–9.

McKay, Rick, director. *Broadway: The Golden Age.* Dada Films, 2004.

McNulty, Charles. "Sightlines: *Jig Saw* at the Bank Street Theatre." *Village Voice,* February 21–27, 2001. http://www.villagevoice.com/theatre /0112,mcnulty,23226,11.html.

Meyers, Jeffrey. *Edmund Wilson: A Biography.* New York: Houghton Mifflin, 1995.

Miller, Linda Patterson, ed. *Letters from the Lost Generation: Gerald and Sara Murphy and Friends.* Expanded ed. Gainesville: University Press of Florida, 2002.

Miller, Roger K. "Rediscovering Dawn Powell." BookPage, December 13, 2004. http://www.bookpage.com/0109bp/fiction/dawn_powell.html.

———. "Reintroducing Dawn Powell: Satirist Gets Overdue Respect." *Pittsburgh Post Gazette,* November 4, 2001, E8+.

Miller, Terry. *Greenwich Village and How It Got That Way.* New York: Crown Publishers, 1990.

Mitchell, Jan. "The Story of Luchow's." In *Luchow's German Cookbook,* 17–35. New York: Doubleday, 1952.

Mitchell, Joseph. *Joe Gould's Secret.* 1964. Reprint, New York: Vintage Books, 1999.

———. *McSorley's Wonderful Saloon.* 1943. Foreword by Calvin Trillin. Reprint, New York: Pantheon, 2001.

Moore, Lorrie. "I'll Cut My Throat Another Day." Review of *Selected Letters of Dawn Powell,* edited by Tim Page. *New York Times,* November 7, 1999. http://www.query.nytimes.com/gst/fullpage.html.

Morris, Alice. "Assorted Metropolitan Termites." *Books: The New York Times on the Web,* February 18, 2005. http://www.nytimes.com/books/98/11/15 /specials/powellcusts.html.

Morris, Sylvia Jukes. *Rage for Fame: The Ascent of Clare Boothe Luce.* New York: Random House, 1997.

Morrison, William. *Broadway Theatres: History and Architecture.* Mineola, NY: Dover, 1999.

Morton, Frederic. "And Where Went Love?" Review of *The Wicked Pavilion*, by Dawn Powell. *New York Times Book Review*, September 5, 1954, 5.

Mosle, Sara. "Paperbacks: Non-Fiction." Review of *A Time to Be Born*, by Dawn Powell. *Newsday*, September 15, 1991, 39.

Moss, Stacey. *The Howards: First Family of Bay Area Modernism.* Oakland, CA: Oakland Museum, 1988.

Mumford, Lewis. *The Culture of Cities.* 1938. Reprint, London: Secker & Warburg, 1940.

Muschamp, Herbert. "Greenwich Village as a Satirist's Milieu and Muse." *New York Times*, December 4, 1998, Arts, 1+.

Museum of the City of New York. "Berenice Abbott: Wanamaker's." 2006. http://www.mcny.org/wanamakers.

Naureckas, Jim. "11th Street, New York Songlines: Virtual Tours of Manhattan Streets." September 19, 2004. http://www.nysonglines.com/11st.htm.

———. "MacDougal Street, New York Songlines: Virtual Tours of Manhattan Streets." September 19, 2004. http://www.nysonglines.com/macdougal.htm#3st.

———. "Ninth Street, New York Songlines: Virtual Tours of Manhattan Streets." September 24, 2004. http://www.nysonglines.com/9st.htm.

Nemy, Enid. "Recalling Brendan Gill, Literary Man about Town." *New York Times*, April 16, 1998, Arts, 1+.

Nerber, John. "The Unguarded Moment." *New York Times*, June 29, 1952, 5.

The New School Catalogue of Course Listings. "Humanities: Special Topics: Dawn Powell's New York." Fall 2003, 44.

New York Department of Corrections. "Historical Résumé of Potter's Field, 1869–1967," 1–16.

New Yorker. Briefly Noted, Fiction: Review of *Angels on Toast*, by Dawn Powell. November 9, 1940, 95.

———. Briefly Noted, Fiction: Review of *A Cage for Lovers*, by Dawn Powell. November 2, 1957, 190.

———. Briefly Noted, Fiction: Review of *The Happy Island*, by Dawn Powell. September 10, 1938, 94.

———. Briefly Noted, Fiction: Review of *The Locusts Have No King*, by Dawn Powell. May 1, 1948, 101+.

———. Briefly Noted, Fiction: Review of *Sunday, Monday and Always*, by Dawn Powell. June 28, 1952, 90.

———. Briefly Noted, Fiction: Review of *A Time to Be Born*, by Dawn Powell. September 5, 1942, 59.

———. Briefly Noted: Review of *Selected Letters of Dawn Powell, 1913–1965*, edited by Tim Page. December 27, 1999, and January 3, 2000, 137.

———. Review of *The Diaries of Dawn Powell, 1931–1965*, edited by Tim Page. December 18, 1995, 120.

New York Herald Tribune. "There's Too Much Talk in the Country." Interview with Dawn Powell. July 3, 1964, n.p.

New York Magazine. "Cedar Tavern." Bar Guide, January 14, 2005. http://www.nymag/printthis.clickability.com.

New York Times. "Books and Authors." September 28, 1930, BR8.

———. "Farewell to Penn Station." Editorial. October 30, 1963, n.p.

———. "New York Adventures." Review of *Whither,* by Dawn Powell. March 15, 1925, 19.

———. Paid Notices: Deaths: Rice, Jacqueline Miller. January 18, 2004. *New York Times Archives.* http://www.nytimes.com/2004/01/18/classified/paid-notice-deaths-rice-jacqueline-miller.html.

Nichols, Elizabeth. Review of *The Locusts Have No King,* by Dawn Powell. *Library Journal,* April 15, 1948, 651.

Niel, Tim, director. *Peggy: The Other Guggenheim.* BBC. 2004.

Norman, Charles. "The Jazz Age Again." Review of *Whither,* by Dawn Powell. *New York Evening Post Literary Review,* April 11, 1925, 5.

———. *Poets and People.* New York: Bobbs-Merrill, 1972.

Obituary. "Carol Brandt." *New York Times,* October 27, 1984, 44.

Obituary. "Dawn Powell." *Village Voice,* November 18, 1965, 24.

Obituary. "Dawn Powell, 67: A Novelist and Satirist of New York Types." *New York Herald Tribune,* November 16, 1965, 33.

Obituary. "Dawn Powell, Novelist, Is Dead; Author of Witty, Satirical Books." *New York Times,* November 16, 1965, 47.

Obituary. "Fleur Cowles, 101, a Friend of the Elite and the Editor of a Magazine for Them." *New York Times,* June 8, 2009, A17.

Obituary. "Frances Keene, 83, Writer and Educator." *New York Times,* July 6, 1997, 41.

Obituary. "Helene Hanff." *Daily Telegraph,* April 11, 1997, 29.

Obituary. "John Mosher." *New Yorker,* September 12, 1942, 72.

Obituary. "Katherine Stearns." *Exeter Newsletter,* September 30, 2003. http://*www.seacoastonline.com/*katherinestearns.

Obituary. "Mary Orr, Actress, Writer." *Variety*.com, October 11, 2006. http://www.variety.com/index/orr.

Obituary. "Murdock Pemberton was First Art Critic for the *New Yorker.*" *New York Times,* August 21, 1982. http://www.nytimes.com/1982/08/21/obituaries/murdock-pemberton-was-first-art-critic-for-the-new-yorker.html.

Obituary. "Star Patricia Hayes Dies at 88." BBC News; BBC online network. September 20, 1998.

The Olive Thomas Collection. Hugh M. Hefner, executive producer. Timeline Films, 2005.

Otto, Whitney. *Eight Girls Taking Pictures: A Novel.* New York: Scribner, 2012.

———. Personal e-mail, April 6, 2013.

Ouroussoff, Nicolai. "Complex, Contradictory Robert Moses." *New York Times* Weekend Arts, February 2, 2007, E31+.

Page, Ruth. "Surrey Ride, Minus the Sentiment." Review of *My Home Is Far Away,* by Dawn Powell. *New York Times Book Review,* November 19, 1944, 4.

Page, Tim. "Biographical Notes." In *The Diaries of Dawn Powell, 1931–1965,* edited by Tim Page, 479–500. South Royalton, VT: Steerforth, 1995.

———. Chronology, Note on the Texts, and Notes. In *Dawn Powell: Novels, 1930–1942,* 1045–68. New York: Library of America, 2001.

———. *Dawn Powell: A Biography.* New York: Henry Holt, 1998.

———. "Dawn Powell at 100." In "The Centennial of Dawn Powell," 33–36. Western Reserve Studies Symposium, "Remarkable Happenings on the Western Reserve, or Whose Bicentennial Is It Anyway?" Kelvin Smith Library, Case Western Reserve University, October 18–19, 1996. Accessed October 28, 2015. http://www.case.edu/artsci/wrss/documents/Page.pdf.

———. Introduction to *Dawn Powell at Her Best,* by Dawn Powell, edited by Tim Page, ix–xxiii. South Royalton, VT: Steerforth Press, 1994.

———. Introduction to *The Diaries of Dawn Powell, 1931–1965,* edited by Tim Page, ix–xi. South Royalton, VT: Steerforth, 1995.

———. Introduction to *The Happy Island,* by Dawn Powell, vii–x. South Royalton, VT: Steerforth Press, 1998.

———. Introduction to *Selected Letters of Dawn Powell, 1913–1965,* edited by Tim Page, ix–xii. New York: Henry Holt, 1999.

———. Introduction to *Sunday, Monday, and Always,* by Dawn Powell. Rev. ed., edited by Tim Page, ix–xiii. South Royalton, VT: Steerforth, 1999.

———. "Letters by Dawn Powell to Edmund Wilson." *New Criterion* 18, no. 1 (1999): 10–20.

———. "The Muse of Rubberleg Square." *Timeline* 19, no. 4 (2002): 42–56.

———. Personal e-mails, November 26, 2005; September 26, 2006; November 16, 2006; April 7, 2007; April 13, 2007.

———. "The Resurrection of Dawn Powell." *Newsday,* October 28, 1991. http://pqasb.pqarchiver.com/newsday/access/102858367.html.

———. Telephone conversations, April 7, 2007; October 28, 2007; March 7, 2013.

Parish, James Robert. *The RKO Gals.* Edited by T. Allan Taylor. Carlstadt, NJ: Rainbow Books, 1974.

Parker, Dorothy. *Here Lies: The Collected Stories of Dorothy Parker.* New York: Viking Penguin, 1939.

———. *The Portable Dorothy Parker.* 1944. Rev. and enl. ed. Introduction by Brendan Gill. New York: Penguin, 1978.

Parks, Steve. "Forgotten Author Gets Revival at LIU." *Newsday,* November 12, 1997, B11.

Payne, Elizabeth Stancy. *Singing Waters.* Philadelphia: Penn Publishers, 1925.

Payne, Robert. "Parsifal in the Village." *Saturday Review,* January 12, 1963, 65.

PBS. "The Inn Crowd: Two Greenwich Village Bars That Mattered—The White Horse Tavern [and] The San Remo." *PBS Hollywood Presents: Collected Stories—On Writing—Greenwich Village,* 1–3. http://www.pbs.org /hollywoodpresents/collectedstories/writing/write_greenwich_1.html.

Pecadillo Theatre Company. "About Us." June 6, 2005. http://www .thepeccadillo.com/about.html.

Peden, William. "The City's Rural Lanes." Review of *Sunday, Monday and Always,* by Dawn Powell. *Saturday Review,* July 26, 1952, 10.

Pelham Parkway. "History of Pelham Parkway: Pelham Heath Inn." January 13, 2005. http://www.pelhamparkway.com.

PEN. "About PEN." Accessed February 4, 2007. http://www.pen.org/about.

Pen and Brush. "About Us." Pen and Brush: Dedicated to Women in the Arts since 1894. Accessed June 2, 2005. http://penandbrush.org/about.htm.

Peters, Ann M. "Travelers in Residence: Women Writing New York at Mid-Century—Dawn Powell, Edith Wharton, Mary McCarthy." PhD diss., CUNY, 2005.

Peterson, William. "Dawn Powell Returns to Lake Erie College." In "The Centennial of Dawn Powell," 37–42. Western Reserve Studies Symposium, "Remarkable Happenings on the Western Reserve, or Whose Bicentennial Is It Anyway?" Kelvin Smith Library, Case Western Reserve University, October 18–19, 1996. Accessed October 28, 2015. http://www .case.edu/artsci/wrss/documents/Peterson.pdf.

Petronius. *The Satyricon.* Originally published 1664. Translated by William Burnaby. New York: Random House Modern Library, 1929.

Pett, Judith. "Dawn Powell: Her Life and Her Fiction." PhD diss., University of Iowa, 1981.

Philipson, Morris. *Bourgeois Anonymous.* New York: Vanguard Press, 1965.

Pine, John C. "Powell, Dawn." Review of *The Golden Spur,* by Dawn Powell. *Library Journal,* September 15, 1962, 3069.

Pinsker, Sanford. "Satirist as Sisyphus." *New Criterion* 15, no. 2 (October 1996): 67–69.

Pogrebin, Robin. "Rehabilitating Robert Moses." *New York Times,* January 28, 2007, Art and Leisure, 1+.

———. "Sale Plans Hit Haven for Women in the Arts." *New York Times,* November 12, 2008, Arts, C1+.

Pool, Gail. "Living by Her Wit." Review of *Angels on Toast, The Wicked Pavilion, The Locusts Have No King, The Golden Spur,* by Dawn Powell. *Women's Review of Books* (July 1990): 20.

Poore, Charles. Books of the Times. Review of *The Golden Spur*, by Dawn Powell. *New York Times*, October 9, 1962, 39.

———. Books of the Times. Review of *Short Stories from The New Yorker*, by various authors. *New York Times*, December 13, 1940, 21.

———. "A Diversity of Novels: *Angels on Toast*." Review of *Angels on Toast*, by Dawn Powell. *New York Times*, November 8, 1940, 19.

———. "Greenwich Village Ghosts." Review of *The Wicked Pavilion*, by Dawn Powell. *New York Times*, September 9, 1954, 29.

———. "Walgrove Snood, a Poem." Fictional name. *New York Times*, December 4, 1932, 39.

———. "The Young and Unhappily Married." Review of *Bourgeois Anonymous*, by Morris Philipson. *New York Times*, May 1, 1965, 29.

Powers, Katherine A. "From the Wild West to the Wicked Genius of Dawn Powell." *Boston Globe*, October 25, 1998, N4.

Priestley, J. B. "Dawn Powell." Letter to *Village Voice*, December 9, 1965, 4.

———. *The Prince of Pleasure and His Regency, 1811–20*. New York: Harper and Row, 1969.

Publishers Weekly. Review of *Dawn Powell: A Biography*, by Tim Page. September 28, 1998.

Purdy, Christopher. "Christopher Purdy on Dawn Powell." *Ohioana Authors List*, February 2005. http://www.ohioana-authors.org/powell/purdy/php.

———, executive producer, WOSU Radio. "Dawn Powell." With Wayne Lawson, Executive Director, Ohio Arts Council, and Tim Page, John "Jack" Franklin Sherman, Rita Sherman. Performers Kassie Rose, Bruce Herman, Mandy Fox, Christina Ritter. *Ohio Arts Alive*, January 29, 2005. Ohio Arts Council, WOSU, Columbus, Ohio.

———. Personal e-mail, July 17, 2006.

Reed, Bill. "Queen Leer." *People vs. Dr. Chilledair*, Accessed March 26, 2005. http://people-vs-drchilledair.blogspot.com/2005/03/qu.html.

Rennison, Nick. *Reading the City: Old New York I. Bloomsbury.com Ezine*, Accessed June 14, 2006. http://www.bloomsburymagazine.com/ezine/Articles.

———. *Reading the City: Old New York II. Bloomsbury.com Ezine*, Accessed 14 June 2006. http://www.bloomsburymagazine.com/ezine/Articles.

Reznikoff, Peter. Personal-e-mail, August 17, 2013.

———. Telephone conversation, August 19, 2013.

Rice, Marcelle Smith. *Dawn Powell*. Twayne's United States Authors Series 715. New York: Twayne Publishers, 2000.

———. "'Split in Two at the Crossroads': The Novels of Dawn Powell." PhD diss. University of North Carolina, Greensboro, 1998.

Rich, Motoko. "Dorothy Parker Anthology Continues in Its Fresh Hell." *New York Times*, July 17, 2007, E2.

Rich, Nathaniel. "American Dreams: 'A Time to Be Born' by Dawn Powell." *Daily Beast,* May 25, 2012. http://www.thedailybeast.com/articles /2012/05/25/american-dreams-a-time-to-be-born-by-dawn-powell.html.

Riddle, Randy A. "Goatboy and the Music Machines—Forgotten Muses: Faerie Archives." Cool Cat Daddy. Accessed May 15, 2005. http://www .coolcatdaddy.com/gt-essay-farchives.htm.

Riegert, Ray. "New York Nostalgia: The Grand Old Hotels—The Best of the Best." GrandTimes. Accessed November 29, 2005. http://www.grandtimes .com/New_York_Nostalgia.html.

Roba, William H. "Floyd Dell in Iowa." *Books at Iowa* 44 (1986): 27–41.

"Robert Benchley and the Knights of the Algonquin, with Alexander Woollcott and Donald Ogden Stewart." *The Paramount Comedy Shorts 1928– 1942.* Kino Video, 2006.

Roberts, Rex. "Powell-ful: Dawn Powell." *Insight on the News,* October 1, 2001, 1–3.

Robinson, Ted. "Books for Girls Who Adore Being Thrilled." Review of *Whither,* by Dawn Powell. *Cleveland Plain Dealer,* June 20, 1925, 9.

Rogers, Michael. Review of *Angels on Toast, A Time to Be Born,* and *The Wicked Pavilion,* by Dawn Powell. *Library Journal,* September 15, 1996, 102.

———. Review of *Dawn Powell Novels, 1944–1962,* by Dawn Powell. *Library Journal,* January 1, 2002, 160.

———. Review of *The Golden Spur,* by Dawn Powell. *Library Journal,* December 2, 1997, 160.

Rosen, Charles. "The Lost Pleasure of Browsing." *New York Review of Books Blog,* October 13, 2009. www.blogs.nybooks.com/post/ . . . /the -lost-pleasure-of-browsing.

Ross, Lillian. *Portrait of Hemingway.* With a new afterword by the author. New York: Modern Library, 1997.

Ross, Mary. "A New York Literary Lion: To This Tale of Manhattan Dawn Powell Brings All Her Insight, Warmth and Wit." Review of *Turn, Magic Wheel,* by Dawn Powell. *New York Herald Tribune Book Review,* February 16, 1936, 8.

Rovit, Earl, and Arthur Waldhorn. *Hemingway and Faulkner in Their Time.* New York: Continuum, 2005.

Russo, Maria. "New York Finally Turns Out for Dawn Powell: Love Fest for the Novelist the Big Apple Once Spurned." *Salon,* January 27, 2000. http://archive.salon.com/books/log/2000/01/27powell/html.

———. "What to Read in October." Review of *Loving Graham Greene,* by Gloria Emerson. *Salon,* October 23, 2000. http://www.salon.com /2000/10/23/octoberfiction/.

Rust, Amy. "Philipson Leaves Publishing Legacy after 32-Year Career." *University of Chicago Chronicle,* July 15, 1999, 1–4.

Salter Reynolds, Susan. "Her Life as a Novelist and Playwright, In Her Own Words." Review of *The Diaries of Dawn Powell, 1931–1965*, edited by Tim Page. *Los Angeles Times,* November 16, 1995, 10.

Saturday Review of Literature. The New Books: Fiction. Review of *The Happy Island,* by Dawn Powell. September 18, 1938, 20.

———. The New Books: Fiction. Review of *She Walks in Beauty,* by Dawn Powell. May 12, 1928, 869.

———. The New Books: Fiction. Review of *Whither,* by Dawn Powell. April 18, 1925, 694.

Scanlon, Jennifer. *Inarticulate Longings:* The Ladies Home Journal, *Gender, and the Promises of Consumer Culture.* New York: Routledge, 1995.

Schickel, Richard. *Elia Kazan: A Biography.* New York: Harper Collins, 2005.

Scialabba, George. "Civic Virtues: Gore Vidal's Selected Essays." *Nation,* October 8, 2008. http://www.thenation.com/article/civic-virtues-gore-vidals -selected-essays/.

Schlesinger, Toni. "One-Bedroom Renovated Apartment." *New York Times,* June 14, 2001, Shelter, 1–2.

Schmich, Mary. "Summertime and Reading Is Bold, Breezy." Review of *A Time to Be Born,* by Dawn Powell. *Chicago Tribune,* June 9, 2002, Books, 4C1.

Schoenherr, Steven E. "The Evolution of the Department Store." Accessed February 11, 2006. http://history.sandiego.edu/gen/soc/shoppingcenter .html, 4.

Scott, A. O. "A Time to Be Reborn: After Decades of Neglect, Novelist Dawn Powell Again Burns as Brightly as the City She Loved." *Newsday,* November 1, 1998, B09+.

Scribner, Charles, III. Introduction to *Tender Is the Night,* by F. Scott Fitzgerald. 1934. Reprint, New York: Scribner, 2003.

Scura, Dorothy M., ed. *Ellen Glasgow: The Contemporary Reviews.* Cambridge: Cambridge University Press, 1992.

Sellar, Tom. "Powell to the People." *Village Voice,* February 6–12, 2002, Theatre, 1. http://www.villagevoice.com/arts/powell-to-the-people-7142547.

Selzer, Richard. "Keepsakes of a Satirist." Review of *The Diaries of Dawn Powell, 1931–1965,* by Dawn Powell, edited by Tim Page. *Wilson Quarterly* 20, no. 2 (1996): 77–78.

Sexton, Michael, and Tim Page, eds. and coauthors of introduction. *Four Plays by Dawn Powell: Big Night, Women at Four O'Clock, Walking down Broadway, Jig Saw.* South Royalton, VT: Steerforth Press, 1999.

Shafer, Jack. "The Joy of English." Review of *Alphabet Juice,* by Roy Blount, Jr. *New York Times Book Review,* November 16, 2008, 9.

Sheed, Wilfred. *The House That George Built: With a Little Help from Irving, Cole, and a Crew of About 50.* New York: Random House, 2007.

Sheehy, Catherine. "The Last Piece of the Puzzle." Review of *Four Plays by Dawn Powell. Theatre* 30, no. 3 (Fall 2000): 124–26.

Sherman, Beatrice. "The Great Amanda." Review of *A Time to Be Born,* by Dawn Powell. *New York Times Book Review,* September 6, 1942, 6.

Shubert Organization. "The Winter Garden Theatre." The Shubert Organization website. Accessed January 2, 2007. http://www.shubert.nyc /theatres/winter-garden.

Signs of the Times. "A Remarkable Example of Electrical Advertising." November 1914, 18.

Simmons, Matty, and Don Simmons. *On the House: History and Guide to Dining and Night Life in New York, Chicago, New Orleans, San Francisco, and Los Angeles.* New York: Coward-McCann, 1955.

Sinclair, May. *The Tree of Heaven.* New York: Macmillan, 1917.

S.L.R. "*Whither:* A Satire on the New York Army of Discontent." Review of *Whither,* by Dawn Powell. *Boston Evening Transcript,* March 14, 1925, 5.

Smalling, Allen. "A Time for Dawn Powell to Be Reborn." Review of *A Time to Be Born,* by Dawn Powell. Amazon.com, September 18, 2002. http:// www.amazon.com/Time-Be-Born-Dawn-Powell/dp/1883642418/.

Smith, Percy Kendall. "The Shore Club." *Historical Society Quarterly* (Lake County, Ohio) 9, no. 3 (August 1967): 165–67.

Smith, Wendy. *Real Life Drama: The Group Theatre and America, 1931–1940.* New York: Grove Weidenfeld, 1990.

Soloski, Alexis. "Bohemia on Toast: Dawn Powell's Village." *Village Voice,* May 14, 2002, S2+.

Soskin, William. "Laughing amid Café Society." Review of *The Happy Island,* by Dawn Powell. *New York Herald Tribune Books,* September 11, 1938, 3.

Soto, Gary. "*The Wicked Pavilion* by Dawn Powell." Review of *The Wicked Pavilion,* by Dawn Powell. *Los Angeles Times,* March 25, 1990, 10.

Springfield Daily Republican. "Literary Satire: New York Modes in Dawn Powell's Novel." Review of *Turn, Magic Wheel,* by Dawn Powell. February 23, 1936, 7E.

Springfield Sunday Union and Republican. "The World of Books: Dawn Powell's Story of Hard-Boiled Society." Review of *Angels on Toast,* by Dawn Powell. October 27, 1940, 7E.

Stage Door. Screenplay by Morrie Ryskind and Anthony Veiller. Adapted from the play by George S. Kaufman and Edna Ferber. RKO films. 1937.

Sticha, Denise S. Review of *Dawn Powell: Novels, 1930–1942,* by Dawn Powell, edited by Tim Page. *Library Journal,* September 15, 2001, 80.

Stonehill, Judith. *Greenwich Village: A Guide to America's Legendary Left Bank.* New York: Universe Publishing (Rizzoli Books), 2002.

Strausbaugh, John. *The Village: 400 Years of Beats and Bohemians, Radicals and Rogues: A History of Greenwich Village.* New York: Harper Collins, 2013.

Streitfeld, David. "Book Report." (On Gore Vidal and Dawn Powell.) *Washington Post,* September 10, 1989, X15.

Strouse, Charles. Personal e-mail, February 26, 2007.

———. Personal interview, April 6, 2007.

———. Telephone interview, March 6, 2007.

Sullivan, Frank. "Greetings, Friends!" *New Yorker,* December 24, 1960, 27.

Tanenhaus, Sam. "Mr. Wizard." *New York Times Book Review,* October 26, 2008, 1+.

Tarbell, Roberta K. "Peggy Bacon's Pastel and Charcoal Caricature Portraits." *Woman's Art Journal* 9, no. 2 (Fall 1988–Winter 1999): 32–37.

Taylor, Alan. Introduction to *The Assassin's Cloak: An Anthology of the World's Greatest Diarists,* edited by Irene Taylor and Alan Taylor, vii–xix. Edinburgh: Canongate Books, 2000.

Taylor, Irene, and Alan Taylor, eds. *The Assassin's Cloak: An Anthology of the World's Greatest Diarists.* Edinburgh: Canongate Books, 2000.

Teachout, Terry. "About Last Night." *Arts Journal,* September 10, 2004. http://www.artsjournal.com/aboutklastnight/archives20040905.shtml.

———. "Far from Ohio." In *A Terry Teachout Reader,* 3–6. New Haven: Yale University Press, 2004.

———. Introduction to *The Dud Avocado,* by Elaine Dundy, vii–x. 1958. Reprint, New York: New York Review Books Classic, 2007.

———. "Laugh and You Laugh Alone." *National Review,* December 23, 1996, 54–55.

_____. "Little Miss Wolfsbane: About Last Night." *Arts Journal,* October 13, 2015. http://www.artsjournal.com/aboutlastnight/2015/10/little-miss-wolfsbane.html. Np.

Teichmann, Howard. *George S. Kaufman: An Intimate Portrait.* New York: Atheneum, 1972.

———. *Smart Aleck: The Wit, World, and Life of Alexander Woollcott.* New York: William Morrow, 1976.

Temple, Sandra. "The Tea Rooms: The Night Owl." *Greenwich Village Gazette,* December 31, 2006, n.p.

Terrell, Dorothy à Beckett. *Last Year's Nest.* New York: D. Appleton, 1925.

Terwilliger, Lewis. "Probing the Mazes of Manhattan." Review of *The Golden Spur,* by Dawn Powell. *New York Herald Tribune Books,* November 4, 1962, 13.

Time. Books. Review of *The Happy Island,* by Dawn Powell. September 19, 1938, 69–70. http://content.time.com/time/magazine/article/0,9171,931767,00.html.

———. "The Election: The New House." November 13, 1944. http://www.time.com/time/magazine/article/0,9171,801531,00.html.

———. "Feast of Peanut Brittle." Review of *A Time to Be Born,* by Dawn Powell. September 7, 1942, 115+.

————. "The New Pictures." Film review of *The Killers,* from the short story by Ernest Hemingway. September 9, 1946, 88.

————. "Southern Impudence." Review of *Southern Charm,* by Isa Glenn. January 9, 1928. http://www.time.com/time/magazine/printout /0,8816,881759,00.html.

————. "Wash It Yourself." *Time Archive,* December 29, 1947. http://www .time.com/time/magazine/article/0,9171,804450,00.html.

Tobin, Jacqueline L., and Raymond G. Dobard. *Hidden in Plain View.* New York: Anchor Books, 2000.

Tóibín, Colm. Introduction to *The New York Stories of Henry James,* vii–xvi. New York: New York Review of Books Classics, 2005.

Tomkins, Calvin. "Living Well Is the Best Revenge." *New Yorker,* July 28, 1962, 31+.

transition 8 (November 1927). Edited by Eugene Jolas and Elliot Paul. Book description from antiqbook.com. Accessed March 31, 2013. www .antiqbook.com.

Trillin, Calvin. Foreword to *McSorley's Wonderful Saloon,* by Joseph Mitchell, vii–xi. 1943. Reprint, New York: Pantheon, 2001.

Trilling, Diana. *The Beginning of the Journey.* New York: Harcourt, 1993.

————. "Fiction in Review." Review of *The Locusts Have No King,* by Dawn Powell. *Nation,* May 29, 1948, 611–12.

————. "Four Recent Novels." Review of *A Time to Be Born,* by Dawn Powell. *Nation,* September 19, 1942, 243–44.

————. "Powell's People." Letter to the Editor in Response to "Dawn Powell, the American Writer," by Gore Vidal. *New York Review of Books,* April 14, 1988. http://www.nybooks.com/articles/4466.

Trilling, Lionel. *The Middle of the Journey.* 1947. Reprint, New York: Scribner's, 1975.

Tufel, Alice L. "Going Sane: Dawn Powell's Vision." *New England Review* 23, no. 3 (2002): 155–65.

Turkel, Stanley. "An Infamous Challenge." From *The Great Hoteliers: Pioneers of the Hotel Industry.* Bloomington, IN: AuthorHouse, 2009.

Twentieth-Century Authors: A Biographical Dictionary of Modern Literature. Edited by Stanley Kunitz and Vineta Colby. New York: H. Wilson, 1942.

Updike, John. "The Glittering City: New York Reflected in American Writing after 1920." Lecture given December 5, 1995, one of a series of talks titled "Art Creates a City," Metropolitan Museum of Art, New York. Reprinted in *More Matter: Essays and Criticism,* 79–96. New York: Knopf, 1999.

————. "An Ohio Runaway." *New Yorker,* February 20, 1995, 262+.

Vaill, Amanda. *Everybody Was So Young: Gerald and Sara Murphy, A Lost Generation Love Story.* New York: Houghton Mifflin, 1998.

————. "Laughing on the Outside." *Washington Post,* November 15, 1998, X06.

Van Gelder, Lawrence. "William Slater Brown, 100, Writer of the Lost Generation." Obituary. *New York Times,* June 28, 1997. http://query.nytimes.com/gst/fullpage.html?res.

Van Gelder, Robert. "Business in Bars." Review of *Angels on Toast,* by Dawn Powell. *New York Times,* October 20, 1940, 6.

———. "Some Difficulties Confronting the Satirist." *New York Times,* November 3, 1940, 102. Reprinted in *Writers and Writing,* 132–34. New York: Scribner's, 1946.

Van Tassel, David D., and John J. Grabowski, eds. *The Encyclopedia of Cleveland History.* Bloomington: Indiana University Press, 1987.

Vidal, Gore. "Dawn Powell, the American Writer." *New York Review of Books,* November 5, 1987. http://www.nybooks.com/articles/4622.

———. "Dawn Powell: Queen of the Golden Age." In *The Last Empire: Essays 1992–2000,* 16–29. New York: Vintage, 2002. Reprinted from *New York Review of Books,* March 21, 1996.

———. *The Golden Age: A Novel.* New York: Vintage Books, 2000.

———. Introduction to *The Golden Spur,* by Dawn Powell. New York: Vintage Books, 1990.

———. Letter. Reply to Diana Trilling's Response to "Dawn Powell, the American Writer." *New York Review of Books,* April 14, 1988. http://www.nybooks.com/articles/4466.

———. "True Gore: Gore Vidal Picks Five Favorite Post-War Novels." Salon.com, May 10, 1999. http//archive.salon.com/books/bag/1999/05/10/vidal.html.

———. "The Woman behind *The Women:* Why Did They All Hate Clare Boothe Luce?" *New Yorker,* May 26, 1997, 70+.

Village Voice. "Our 25 Favorite Books of 1995." Review of *The Diaries of Dawn Powell 1931–1965,* by Dawn Powell, edited by Tim Page. December 5, 1995, SS23.

"Vincent Sheean." *Traces,* April 3, 2006. http://www.traces.org/vincentsheean.html.

Virginia Quarterly Review. "Notes on Current Books." Review of *The Golden Spur,* by Dawn Powell. 39 (Spring 1963): xlix.

Voiles, Jane. "This World: The New Fiction." Review of *The Locusts Have No King,* by Dawn Powell. *San Francisco Chronicle,* June 13, 1948, 19.

Walbridge, Earle F. "Powell, Dawn." Review of *The Wicked Pavilion,* by Dawn Powell. *Library Journal,* September 1, 1954, 1504.

Wald, Alan. "The Urban Landscape of Marxist Noir: An Interview with Alan Wald." *Crime Time,* no. 27 (2002): 81–89. Accessed September 8, 2006, at http://www.crimetime.co.uk/features/marxistnoir.html.

Waldau, Roy S. *Vintage Years of the Theatre Guild 1928–1939.* Cleveland: Case Western Reserve University Press, 1972.

Walker, Stanley. *The Night Club Era*. New York: Stokes Co., 1933.

Wallen, James. *Cleveland's Golden Story: A Chronicle of Hearts That Hoped, Minds That Planned and Hands That Toiled, to Make a City "Great and Glorious."* Cleveland: William Taylor Son and Co., 1920.

Walton, Edith. "Café Society." Review of *The Happy Island*, by Dawn Powell. *New York Times Book Review*, September 4, 1938, 7.

———. "An Ironic Comedy of Lit'ry Manhattanites." Review of *Turn, Magic Wheel*, by Dawn Powell. *New York Times Book Review*, February 23, 1936, BR7.

Ware, Caroline F. *Greenwich Village, 1920–1930*. Berkeley: University of California Press, 1994.

Warfel, Harry R. *American Novelists of Today*. New York: American Book Co., 1951.

Warstler, Debra. "Dawn Powell's Journal of 1915: A Prelude to Her Ohio Novels." MA thesis, Northeastern University, 1996.

———. Personal e-mail, October 3, 2006.

Waters, John. "John Waters' Top 10." *Artforum International* 37, no. 2 (October 1998). https://www.questia.com/magazine/1G1-21230368/john-waters-top-ten.

Watson, Roderick, ed. *The Poetry of Scotland*. Edinburgh: Edinburgh University Press, 2002.

WBFO. "NPR's Selected Shorts on WBFO: A Celebration of the Short Story." WBFO 88.7, June 2006. http://www.wbfo.org/programming/shorts.php3.

Weiner, Lauren. "Dawn Powell: The Fruits of Revival." *New Criterion* 17, no. 10 (1999): 23–28.

———. "Metropolitan Life: The Novels of Dawn Powell." *New Criterion* 11, no. 6 (1993): 33–41.

Wetzsteon, Ross. *Republic of Dreams—Greenwich Village: The American Bohemia, 1910–1960*. New York: Simon and Schuster, 2002.

White, E. B. *Here Is New York*. New York: Harpers, 1949.

"William Peden Short Story Collection: Personal Stories." March 31, 2007. http://library.missouri.edu/specialcollections/bookcol/peden/pedenjournals/.

Williams, Ellen, and Steve Radlauer. *The Historic Shops and Restaurants of New York: A Guide To Century-Old Establishments in the City*. New York: Little Bookroom, 2002.

Williams, John. "Columbia Acquires Dawn Powell Archives." *New York Times*, March 13, 2013. http://artsbeat.blogs.nytimes.com/2013/03/13/columbia-acquires-dawn-powell-archives/?_r=0.

Williams, William Carlos. *The Collected Poems of William Carlos Williams. Vol. 1: 1909–1939*. New York: New Directions Books, 1986.

Wilson, Edmund. *Apologies to the Iroquois, with a Study of The Mohawks in High Steel by Joseph Mitchell.* New York: Farrar, Straus and Cudahy, 1960.

———, ed. *The Crack-Up.* By F. Scott Fitzgerald. New York: New Directions, 1945.

———. "Dawn Powell: Greenwich Village in the Fifties." *New Yorker,* November 17, 1962, 233–37. Reprinted in *The Bit between My Teeth: A Literary Chronicle of 1950–1965,* 526–33. New York: Farrar, Strauss and Giroux, 1965.

———. *Edmund Wilson: The Man in Letters.* Edited and introduction by David Castronovo and Janet Groth. Athens: Ohio University Press, 2005.

———. *The Fifties: From Notebooks and Diaries of the Period.* Edited and introduction by Leon Edel. New York: Farrar, Straus and Giroux, 1986.

———. *The Forties: From Notebooks and Diaries of the Period.* Edited and introduction by Leon Edel. New York: Farrar, Straus and Giroux, 1983.

———. *Letters on Literature and Politics, 1912–1972.* Selected and edited by Elena Wilson. New York: Farrar, Straus and Giroux, 1974.

———. "A Novel by Dawn Powell." Review of *My Home Is Far Away,* by Dawn Powell. *New Yorker,* November 11, 1944, 93–94.

———. *The Sixties: From Notebooks and Diaries of the Period.* Edited and introduction by Lewis M. Dabney. New York: Farrar, Straus and Giroux, 1993.

———. *The Thirties: From Notebooks and Diaries of the Period.* Edited and introduction by Leon Edel. New York: Farrar, Straus and Giroux, 1980.

———. "Upstate Diary 1960–1970." Selections from *The Sixties. New Yorker,* June 12, 1971, 43+.

Winter, Jessica. "Out of the Past: *Tape* by Stephen Belber, *Jig Saw* by Dawn Powell." *Village Voice,* January 30–February 5, 2002, Theatre section, 1.

WNYC. "Women with Attitude." Selected Shorts. New York Public Radio, April 10, 2005. http://www.wnyc.org/shows/shorts/episodes/2005/04/10.

Wolcott, James. "Dawn Patrol." *Vanity Fair,* February 1990, 42+.

Woolf, Virginia. *Mrs. Dalloway.* 1925. New York: Harcourt Brace, 1964.

———. *A Room of One's Own.* New York: Harcourt Brace, 1929.

———. *A Writer's Diary, Being Extracts from the Diary of Virginia Woolf.* 1954. Edited by Leonard Woolf. New York: Harcourt Brace, 1973.

Wyndham, Francis. "Finding Truth at Two Extremes." *Spectator* 284, no. 8958 (2000): 39–40.

Zeidner, Lisa. "Angel on Toast." Review of *Dawn Powell: A Biography,* by Tim Page. *New York Times Book Review,* November 15, 1998, 10+.

Zeitz, Joshua. *Flapper.* New York: Three Rivers Press, 2006.

INDEX